VN

The Life and Art of Vladimir Nabokov

by ANDREW FIELD

Macdonald
Queen Anne Press

A *Queen Anne Press* BOOK

© 1986, 1987 by Andrew Field

First published in the United States in 1986 by Crown Publishers, Inc.,
225 Park Avenue South, New York, New York 10003

First published in Great Britain in 1987 by
Queen Anne Press, a division of
Macdonald & Co (Publishers) Ltd
3rd Floor
Greater London House
Hampstead Road
London NW1 7QX

A BPCC plc Company

Jacket photographs — Front: Philippe Halsman; © 1968 by Jane
                            Halsman Bello
                      Back: Michael Manni

British Library Cataloguing in Publication Data
Field, Andrew
    VN: the life and art of Vladimir Nabokov.
    1. Nabokov, Vladimir — Biography
    2. Novelists, American — 20th century —
    Biography
    I. Title
    813'.54   PS3527.A15Z/

ISBN 0-356-14234-5

Parts of this book have previously been published in *Nabokov: His Life in
Art,* © 1977 by Andrew Field, and *Nabokov: His Life in Part,* © 1966 by
Andrew Field

Printed and bound in Great Britain by
Hazell Watson & Viney Limited
Member of the BPCC Group
Aylesbury, Bucks

To Meg,
again and again

Reality would be only adulterated if I now started to narrate what you know, what I know, what nobody else knows, what shall never, never be ferreted out by a matter-of-fact, father of muck, mucking biographitist.

VLADIMIR NABOKOV
Look at the Harlequins!

Introduction

ONE MUST BEGIN (AND END) WITH RUSSIA. FOR, ALTHOUGH
Vladimir Nabokov spoke three and a half languages—Russian,
English, French, and a little more German than he ever found it
convenient to admit—and lived for protracted periods in six
countries—Russia, Germany, England, France, America, and
Switzerland, Russian culture was, both consciously and uncon-
sciously, always his guiding star. He lived a quiet life in interesting times and yet was a wild Russian in spirit as well as a great
writer.

Nabokov was born as the old Russian empire entered its final
period. It was a contradictory time: There was the grayness of
end-of-the-century Russia as captured by Chekhov, but there was
also the high stylishness of the *World of Art* movement immediately afterward, and the boisterous and innovative Russia of the
Futurists such as Mayakovsky and Khlebnikov and the modernists such as Stravinsky. The beginnings and ends of empires
are always exciting times. Under Alexander II (1868–81), in
whose government Nabokov's grandfather held high office, Russia freed its serfs and set in action a tremendous thrust of industrial growth. The growth continued after the assassination of
Alexander II, but all vestiges of liberalism were swept away in
the reactionary rule of Alexander III, from which Nabokov's
grandfather was finally dismissed. Count Witte, the most liberal
minister in prerevolutionary czarist cabinets, fought hard to contain Russia's inclination to become a heavily overarmed nation,

but even Witte would spit at mention of the weak parliamentary Duma, which he helped found in 1904. Nabokov's father was a prominent member of that Duma and a member of the highly educated and powerful St. Petersburg intelligentsia, which, when the crunch came, could not hold power and lost Russia to the Bolsheviks in 1917. Czar Nicholas II was a weak and foolish man, but he was a Russian, too, and shared many characteristics with those who opposed him, principally a propensity toward absolutism and a disinclination toward rationalism. Nicholas presided over the ruin of an empire, while Nabokov created his own artistic empire, but Nabokov and Nicholas, who may have shared common blood, were not so very different. They both came from cosmopolitan St. Petersburg, which played at politics and culture and took a Fabergé-service picnic to the edge of a volcano. In a very real sense Nabokov the English novelist was the last strange blossom of that great and fated culture.

VN is how he frequently signed himself and saw himself after fame came. His family often called him that. It was a faintly Napoleonic form of address. He cut a figure that was truly grand, and yet vulnerable in some ways and fraught with irony.

Nabokov's was a unique voice in literature, and by almost all testimony, he was an exceptional individual, and it is already clear beyond doubt that interest in him is growing rapidly and will continue to do so. But there still are mysteries about the man and his work. The terms of Nabokov's will withhold publication of his private papers until fifty years after the death of both his wife and his son. Moreover, one of the few personal publications relating to Nabokov in the near-decade since his death has been the correspondence (in Russian) between him and one of his sisters, and it is notable less for what it tells us than for the number of ellipses inserted in the text. Thus, the "real" life of Nabokov might not have been known until after the death of every reader of the original edition of this book, and even then it cannot be certain whether a full life would have been revealed. There are grounds to suppose that Nabokov never intended that the details of his life be known. It is the purpose of this book to describe that secret life.

VN is written for the near-century of readers who might otherwise have had to settle for a somewhat lacquered life of Nabokov. The two books (not to mention the bibliography) I have written about Nabokov before, a critical study, *Nabokov: His Life in Art* (1967), and a partial biography, *Nabokov: His Life in Part* (1977), only lead to this one.

There are advantages that come with time. At last Nabokov has ceased to be quite such an exotic. Much more has been discovered and the broad outline of his life is widely known to the common reader. It is no longer necessary when discussing his work to trot out detailed plot summaries of obscure works. One can now look back on Nabokov and his work simply to talk about them. It is time for all the important sealed doors to be opened.

I spent comparatively little time with Nabokov in Boswellian terms—a week at the end of January 1969, then four days in November of the same year, and finally a marathon month, all of January 1971—but it was more time than anyone else with a "biographitist" intent ever spent with the man, and I worked hard. I came to him with a prior knowledge of his texts and contexts and came away with, not the full story, but the foundation stones on which that full life could be constructed. There is occasional scaffolding where one would prefer a finished room, but I suspect that that will always be the case with Nabokov's life. The point is that the basic structure is there, the contours are clear.

It is important to stress that Nabokov himself was, above all, a biographer. There is, in fact, a German academic book about him called *Fictitious Biographies,* and it puts that case very well. Like Virginia Woolf and W. H. Auden, Nabokov was both repelled and fascinated by biography, which he called psychoplagiarism. He greatly feared it (more, really, than he feared Freudianism and hated communism), but in his work he has shown, perhaps more than any other modern writer, that biography is a genre like any other and has more unexplored potential than most.

VN counts upon (some) readers who are able to enjoy life and art intermingling like a two-part invention in music without confusing the two separate parts.

NABOKOV BROODED OVER THE LOSS OF HIS RUSSIA WITH A greater intensity than any other writer of his generation, the first "homeless million" of our century of exiles. Yet while there is an intense sense of Russia in much of his writing, nowhere will you find enameled descriptions of peasants in a generalized country-side. His Russia was very much a private Russia, which may properly be termed the Kingdom of Nabokov. There are explanations in this Kingdom of Nabokov not only for his personality, but also for all his themes including those of *Lolita*. There are shadows in the Nabokov family tree from which masterpieces were made.

In chapter 3 of *Speak, Memory* Nabokov lingers over the figure of his great-grandmother, who in 1859 was in the papers as a result of a fiery dispute with a Parisian dressmaker who had made the neckline too revealing in the dresses her daughters were supposed to wear to a costume ball. The fiancé of one of her daughters caused a bit of a scandal when he attempted to throw someone out a window. That fiancé was Nabokov's future grandfather, Dmitri Nabokov.

Nabokov remarks in his autobiography that his great-grandmother had a passionate nature and was not as virtuous as her concern over her daughters' necklines might lead one to believe. This maternal great-grandmother was named Nina. She was a Shishkov and came from the province of Samara. Nina brought more than twenty-six thousand hectares of land to her marriage with Baron Ferdinand Korf, who was from a German but russified family.

The mature writer Nabokov dwelt upon the name Shishkov. He uses it in one of his most autobiographical stories, "Goosefoot" (1932), about a schoolboy named Putya Shishkov, who has a fight at school when he is teased about a duel being fought by his father. Nabokov also published some poems under the pseudonym Shishkov in the thirties.

Nabokov's passionate great-grandmother had a lover, who, it happens, was her future son-in-law, Dmitri Nabokov. The precise details of their strange alliance will probably never be known. They could have come together in St. Petersburg or in Finland, where Dmitri Nabokov was stationed during the Crimean War in 1854.

Nina had been one of the great beauties of the Russian court. The marriage of her daughter Maria to Dmitri Nabokov was arranged, perhaps even ordered by Czar Alexander II, the great reformer who was to free the Russian slaves a year before Abraham Lincoln freed the American ones. But the character of Alexander's court was quite the same as all those since Catherine the Great's: it was morally very casual. The long romance of Nina von Korf and Dmitri Nabokov had, however, a quiet and plangent conclusion. Nina came to regret what she had done, and she removed herself to a distant estate where she died cut off from all family and friends.

Maria von Korf had just turned seventeen, and Dmitri Nabokov was sixteen years older than she. He was much taken up with, besides his mother-in-law, an intensely active administrative career at court, which eventually culminated in his appointment as minister of justice in May 1878. Maria tried in vain to resist the arranged marriage to her mother's lover. She was "almost forcibly" married to him.

Nabokov's cousin, the composer Nicolai Nabokov, was the only one in the family to write openly about this awkward circumstance. He caused embarrassment in several quarters of the family who have chosen to scoff at his tale, but it was confirmed twice by other Nabokovs. Nicolai Nabokov wrote:

"Her husband was her mother's lover. As sometimes happened in the prudish nineteenth century, it was convenient

for lovers to have an official link. It gave them easy and free
access to each other and made things look *convenable* . . .
    "I was their chaperone," she said, "but, believe me, I did
not like my role at all." . . .
    She never grew to love her mother's lover, and this is why
the fatherhood of her five other children was never quite certain . . .
    Like so many eccentrics of the nineteenth century [she]
talked freely about everything. When I once asked her what
was hidden in the golden medallion she wore on her neck, she
opened it, showed it to me and said wickedly: "It is hair . . .
but not from your grandfather and not from anybody's head.
You see how curled it is?"

She also claimed that, when she was a young beauty, she and
some friends had stripped naked in their box at the new Paris
Opera, so that, before they were removed, all the binoculars were
trained on them rather than the stage.
    The liaison between the great-grandmother and the grandfa-
ther of Vladimir Nabokov is one of the great secrets of the
Nabokov family. It is, of course, nothing but a neat reversal of the
story of *Lolita:* the man marries the daughter in order to be able
to continue more easily to be her mother's lover. That is one of
the reasons the theme of incest figures fleetingly but powerfully
in Nabokov's fiction starting in the thirties, and also why incest
and family history become such major themes in *Ada.* In Nabokov's last novel written in Russian, *Solus Rex,* he mocks Freudianism by employing an Italian psychiatrist who believes that a
person's psychic problems derive not from one's parents but from
the problems of one's ancestors. Nabokov knew these stories well
and was obsessed with them as themes. His grandmother Maria
had many lovers, and it was rumored that she had children by
Alexander II. At the very least they must have been fleeting
lovers, because Maria told her granddaughter Elena that the czar
had nearly chosen her as his mistress over Katya Dolgoruky. All
carriages in Petersburg pulled to the side of the road to salute the
czar's carriage as he passed. The czar himself on several occasions
pulled to the side when he saw Maria Nabokov's carriage. She
called him "my czar."
    Maria gave birth sixteen times. Of her nine living children,
three were rumored in both court and family circles to be bas-

tards of Czar Alexander II, and of these Nabokov's father, who
was born in 1869, was most frequently mentioned. Nabokov
scoffed at all this, and at the same time allowed that he could feel
Peter the Great's blood in his veins. The matter was not helped
by a very Romanov countenance in the faces of two of the boys,
one of them Nabokov's father. A family member prepared a table
showing the "total incredibility of the Alexandrite myth." This
table is based upon the letters and historical accounts of
Alexander II's life in which it can be demonstrated that at least
two of these alleged czarly fatherings would have had to occur
when Alexander was deeply involved with Katya Dolgoruky in
one of the major affairs of his life. The historical juxtaposition of
the circumstances of the czar's life in this period seems convincing. Nabokov's father was *not* the bastard son of Alexander II.

But the story does not end there. Dmitri Nabokov's career was
closely tied with that of the Grand Duke Konstantin, the czar's
brother, from about 1850, when he began to serve in the Marine
Ministry. In 1861, on his return from Paris, Nabokov's grandfather was reattached to the Marine Ministry as director under
Grand-Admiral Grand Duke Konstantin. When his brother appointed Konstantin as vice regent of Poland in 1862, the grand
duke took Dimitri Nabokov with him as his personal aide. Nabokov worked intimately for nearly twenty years with the grand
duke, who was godfather to one of his children. Most historical
sources agree that it was Grand Duke Konstantin rather than the
czar himself who was the motivating force behind the emancipation of the serfs in 1861. The French *chargé d'affaires* in St. Petersburg at that time described Konstantin's influence on the czar
in the following manner:

> The Grand Duke Konstantin, who for all his feverish activity
> could not evoke any support in any class in Russia, had at this
> moment a stronger influence than ever before on the excellent
> but disturbed and perplexed mind of his brother.

Konstantin was called the Red Duke by reactionary circles in the
court. What is certain is that his salon was the only one in Russian royal society of the time where intellectuals and intelligent
conversationalists were welcome. In most they were actually forbidden.

The band of state servants—most of them lawyers—around the

grand duke gradually passed over to the circle of the czar himself. Konstantin ended a rather sad and isolated figure. After the assassination of Alexander II, it was left to Dmitri Nabokov to attempt to salvage as best he could the reforms instituted by the grand duke, in the manner of a ship's captain during a storm who must jettison much of his cargo in order to save something of it. The reign of Alexander III, the son of Alexander II, was extremely dark. Everything foreign was bad. Jews and non-Orthodox Christians were "plotting to destroy Russia." Education had to be kept in strict control, the power of the censor increased.

When archreactionary circles moved (in the end, successfully) to have Nabokov's grandfather dismissed from the ministry, one of the charges they used against him was his heavy indebtedness as a result of his wife's grand style. It was true. Real wealth would not come into that branch of the Nabokov family until Dmitri Nabokov's children made wealthy matches.

All excesses at the czar's court were relative. Maria was wildly extravagant and got her husband into serious debt. But she was modest compared with the Grand Duke Konstantin himself, who once paid the unheard-of price of twenty thousand gold francs for a hundred cases of Chateau d'Yquem. Maria, who was very beautiful, unhappily married, passionate, high-living, and in close proximity to the grand duke for more than a decade, was probably his lover, and he may have been the father of some of her children. Few Nabokovs are sketched as caustically in *Speak, Memory* as Vladimir's grandmother Maria with her ever-present ivory fan, almond milk, and little mole showing through her makeup like a currant. Most family members who believe in the possibility of bastardy in the family, such as Nabokov's sister Elena or his cousin Nicolai Nabokov, the composer, who discusses the matter in his own memoirs, tend—mistakenly, I think—to lean to the czar theory. In speaking to me of "the blood of Peter the Great" Nabokov may have been taking a more pedantically careful and accurate position on the rumor. The rumors were real and strong during the childhood of Vladimir Nabokov, and the theme of the "bend sinister" came to furnish many of his novels and stories.

Dmitri Nabokov had remarkable commitment to his career, and in this he was merely the most outstanding in a line of a century and a half of state servants. The links were there, and there was no difficulty at all in finding a position after his graduation from law school in 1845. His father had been a schoolmate and close friend of Count Lütke, who was one of the tutors to Grand Duke Konstantin. It was his father who had gone with Lütke on the expedition to Novaia Zemlia, the place that figures so prominently in *Pale Fire*.

It takes some effort to see Dmitri Nabokov as a "liberal" from the perspective of our time because he was above all a faithful servant and organization man in a difficult period. But rather than step back when the new direction of Alexander III became clear, as so many did, Nabokov's grandfather extended the application of new law reforms to Russia's Baltic possessions, took steps to improve both the judiciary and the jury system, and set up a commission to improve civil and criminal law. He was one of very few Russians in a position of power in this decade of pogroms to raise the issue of the legal rights of Jews.

Russia did have thirteen years of peace during the reign of Alexander III from 1881 to 1894. And the first years of the reign of Nicholas II had an unprecedented spurt of economic growth. Railway lines webbed their way up and down Russia. The difficulty was that behind all this peaceful growth was the very real intent to make Russia an aggressive power in both Europe and the Orient. But Czar Nicholas was a very stupid czar and didn't understand his own place in society, much less the way in which new forces were exerting themselves in Russia, while the most necessary elements, the educated and professional classes, were being pushed to the side. If you read copies of the better Russian newspapers in the period at the end of the reign of Nicholas, you are reading papers reflecting a very sophisticated national life but one characterized by constant inanities and frustrations.

Vladimir Nabokov's father, V. D. Nabokov, followed in his father's footsteps and went farther in the views he held publicly, though, owing to history, of course, not as far in his career. V. D. Nabokov was a leader of the center-right Kadet Party, a member of the first Duma, who was supposed to be on the verge of appointment to a ministry by Nicholas II (Nicholas had brought Dmitri Nabokov back from the political shade), and in the emigration he was briefly minister of justice for the first phase of the provisional government in the Crimea and founded *The Rudder*, the main émigré newspaper for two decades in Berlin.

For most people, Nabokov's grandfather and father by themselves would provide as much of a family tree as anyone needed.

But the failure of czarist Russia to live up to them, and to survive, soured everything. It seems as though Nabokov could not forgive old Russia its death, and throughout his life he spoke of the Romanov dynasty and much of the old way of life and culture in Russia with contempt. One member of the Nabokov family thought that the breaking point was undoubtedly the assassination by mistake of Nabokov's father in Berlin in 1922 by right-wing Russian Fascists, who proclaimed that they were defending the czar: "His death 'for his friends' at the hand of an extreme rightist ignited an unextinguishable *blind* hatred in Volodya's soul towards everything connected with old, right-wing czarist Russia."

Whether that judgment is justified or not, Nabokov began to lay heavy stress on his family history as if it would have to be his history of Russia. He went to absurd lengths, which only served in the end to highlight the centuries-long marginal position of the Nabokovs as untitled nobility. At first, in his memoirs, Nabokov claimed that he was descended from a minor prince Nabok in the retinue of Genghis Khan. Later, in an interview, he broadened the claim slightly and declared that he was descended directly from Genghis Khan. Both of these claims are highly unlikely. Last names were not used in the horde in the thirteenth century, and what records there are give no indication of any prince or officer who might be such a sought-after ancestor.

The first attested mention of the Nabokovs in Russian history is from a seventeenth-century copy of a fifteenth-century register of a land dispute in which Filatka, Avdokima, and Vlasska Nabokov, sons of Luka, are accused of having improperly taken possession of part of a neighbor's land, which was in the province of Vladimir, north of Moscow. Their names point to the probability that these Nabokovs came from the less cosmopolitan portion of the new landowning class, because their Christian names are derived from local saints.

The Nabokovs probably came into Russia through the province of Ryazan, which functioned as a buffer state between Rus and the Tartars, first siding with one, then with the other. The first Nabokovs in Russia were likely Turkestan, Caucasian, or even Egyptian functionaries of the Tartars who came in the thirteenth or fourteenth centuries. Dmitri Nabokov was called "the Chinaman" behind his back. In any event, in the considerable social revolution that was engineered by Peter the Great, the number of Tartar princes was dramatically increased in order to lessen the value of nobility to such an extent that it became an offense in law to accuse someone of being "a Tartar prince."

The Nabokov clan were military people, vice governors, academics, owners of moderate-size estates, and in one case, commandant of the Peter and Paul Fortress during the time Dostoevsky was imprisoned there. Several good marriages in the latter half of the nineteenth century made the family quite wealthy.

By any standard the Nabokov family is both interesting and distinguished. Nabokov's obsession with his family may also be explained in several other ways: the curiosity of the natural scientist, the instinct of the ironist, and the danger of rootlessness as a consequence of his family's emigration.

In the opinion of Prince Alexandre Galitzine, a member of one of the handful of most noble families in Russian history and a cousin to the Romanovs: "We have many Nabokovs in the family. They were rich. I should think rather a catch. We had a famous name—very—but money is nice, too. One wasn't snobbish. Certainly they were untitled nobility and certainly *de bonne famille*. But minor!"

Such plainspoken judgment from above was not countenanced in Nabokov's world view. In one of his English poems, "An Evening of Russian Poetry" (1945), Nabokov wrote: "Beyond the seas where I have lost a scepter," and he meant it. After all, hadn't the Nabokov family held the scepter? It was Dmitri Nabokov who carried the scepter at the coronation of Nicholas II in 1894. The lost scepter became a colossal metaphor for the great poet, king in exile. Ironically, the greatness of Nabokov as a writer came from the wry and mocking self-knowledge of Narcissus as he leaned over to embellish the reflection in the pool, knowing full well the absurdity of the effort. This knowledge is the real tragedy of Humbert in *Lolita* and Charles Kinbote in *Pale Fire*, while the belief that your own reality can stand forever triumphant while the reality of everyone else is curtly dismissed is the sad delusion of the character Vadim Vadimovich and the man Vladimir Vladimirovich Nabokov in *Look at the Harlequins.*

To see Vladimir Nabokov as Narcissus is not to reduce him. Rather, the intensity of his narcissistic passion, translated into many works of great art, makes Nabokov a towering archetype in the history of literature.

THERE IS AN INTERESTING THEORY THAT ONE OF THE MAIN
reasons for the disintegration of the Romanov dynasty was not
simply the weakness and lack of intelligence of Nicholas himself.
It was also caused, this theory suggests, by the failure of the Russian nobility over several generations to stay in the provinces and
administer the empire properly. It wasn't for want of trying: at
one stage heavy fines were levied against the provincial nobility
who settled in St. Petersburg without permission. They paid the
fines and came anyway. There can be no reproach leveled against
the Nabokovs in this regard. Over many generations, in various
regiments, deputations, and appointments, they showed that they
were ready to go anywhere, do anything. Dmitri Nabokov's father served as a representative of the crown in Pskov and Samara,
and his father before him was decorated by Catherine the Great
for his successful participation in battles against the Turks and
the Crimean khan, who was a vassal of the Turkish sultan. He
was eventually made major-general in charge of the garrison of
Novgorod by Catherine's son.

Dmitri Nabokov's father and two of his uncles were the first
Nabokovs to be attached to the court in St. Petersburg at the beginning of the nineteenth century, and they all made good marriages. The mother of Nabokov's grandfather was a Nazimov,
which means that he has links with one of the most prominent
families in the doomed aristocratic uprising in 1825 against Czar
Nicholas I in Pushkin's time. The failed Decembrist uprising was
Russia's last opportunity to catch up with Western Europe.

Nabokov's grandfather represented the second generation of Nabokovs at court, and this almost certainly helped him evade the stain of failure which blotted the career of Grand Duke Konstantin for his unsuccessful regency of Poland. The grand duke had an arrogant and supercilious air, and he was, unfairly, made to assume much of the blame for the Polish uprising against the Russians in 1863. Nabokov's grandfather was well known for his seriousness and the long hours he devoted to administrative procedures, first in the Russian navy and then in Poland. Nina and Maria were both frequently at court, and it is known that the grand duke himself lobbied hard with the czar for the early elevation of Nabokov to the ministry. Numerous memoirs of the period when Dmitri Nabokov was minister of justice show that he continually worked himself to near-exhaustion. Few events had such a fatidic effect on Russian history as the assassination of Alexander II, the czar-liberator. The emancipation of the serfs, it must be said, was in large part motivated by fear of a peasant uprising. The assassination converted many of the socially sensitive nobility (who are portrayed in Tolstoy's writing of this period) into instant reactionaries. Dmitri Nabokov's career would certainly have been vastly different had Alexander survived.

He dashed from his country home by horseback. The memoirs of the French ambassador to St. Petersburg of the time declare that the dying czar was attempting to bring in a new constitution. Nabokov family tradition has it that Alexander sent a one-line note to Dmitri asking him to bring the new laws to him the evening before he died. They supposedly were signed but vanished when in a few days the reactionary Prime Minister Pobedonostsev took control of Russia through Alexander III. Dmitri Nabokov was at the deathbed, quietly sobbing as he stood behind the royal family. One thing that the czar had done for Nabokov in the year before he died was to offer him the title of baron or an ancient abbey in the south of Russian Poland. More than half a century later Vladimir Nabokov would regret (ironically, of course) that his grandfather had chosen the property over the title, but the czar had probably been well informed that his minister needed the money to pay his debts, for he made the gift not only in a delicate manner, but also as entailed property that was to pass to Nabokov's eldest son so that it would be income-producing

and not subject to sale to finance further whims of Maria Nabokov.

The new Czar Alexander III would, in the beginning of his
reign, scarcely have dismissed any of his father's ministers. Nabokov carried on, under attack both in the court and in the press,
for four more years. But it had to come. The czar wrote to him:

Greetings, Dmitri Nikolaevich,

*Better than anyone you know my desires concerning
the judiciary and how very incorrect and undesirable
has been the direction followed by so many areas of our
legal structure. Since to date I have seen little improve-
ment in the Ministry of Justice, it seems to me doubtful
that I shall see my desires realized in the present circumstances, and that is why, although it is with great
regret, I have resolved to ask you to leave the Ministry
of Justice. This is all the more regrettable to me because
you were named to your post by my dear Father. While
I give you full credit for your efforts to improve the administration with which you were entrusted and for
your good management, especially of late, this is nonetheless insufficient, because I desire much more ...*

Pobedonostsev was most likely the secret author of that letter.
Dmitri Nabokov as minister of justice had been the first person to
attempt to put brakes on the absolute power of the monarch.

In 1938 Nabokov published a play, *The Waltz Invention*, in
which the farcical posturing and pushing of government ministers, and the constant danger in the play that everything will be
destroyed, reflect the tragic farce that was czarist politics. That
play is simply an artistic rendering of family stories that Nabokov
heard from the time he was a young boy about the minister of
justice trying to contend with the deluded autocracy of
Alexander III. (It should be said, though, that *The Waltz Invention* is also a play about mistaken intention, political and sexual.
The entire play is a fantasy. It has much in common with
Twelfth Night, and the element of literary parody, always present in Nabokov, is considerable.)

We do have one fleeting glimpse of the nature of Dmitri Nabokov's personal life through a passing comment in the memoirs of a legal colleague. It was remarked that Dmitri Nabokov was capable of showing mercy in the performance of his professional life because he himself knew how heavy the burden of life can be. There was one task where he could not exercise mercy, however, for he had to supervise the trial and execution of the killers of Alexander II. One of the assassins was pregnant. She was executed immediately after she had given birth.

Dmitri Nabokov lived in a St. Petersburg townhouse on Glinka Street, one of the fine streets of St. Petersburg. It was a very large three-story house that Nabokov had separated into many vast apartments. He and Maria lived on the first floor but in separate apartments. Between the two apartments were great salons for parties and receptions, and also a huge study, where Nabokov often worked until late into the night. On the floor below his five daughters lived with a corps of lady companions, governesses, and ladies' maids. There was also a schoolroom there, and the eldest daughter, who was named Maria, had qualified as a teacher in order to assist the tutors in their instruction of her younger brothers, all of whom lived in a wing of their own. Their country home at Batovo, where Dmitri sometimes would live in virtual permanent residence in the years before and after he was minister of justice, had fifty rooms.

Because it was thought that fresh milk was essential for a beautiful complexion and it was feared that freshness might be lost in transport from the barn, a cow was installed in one of the far rooms and was tended and lived there happily for many years. A much smaller house at Batovo, on a rise over the River Oredezh with lovely woods and much wildlife, was built by Maria who often went there alone. It was eventually sold separately.

The elderly Dmitri Nabokov was restored to favor by the new czar, Nicholas, and awarded a cluster of medals and decorations, including the Order of Alexander Nevsky, with diamonds. But even during the time of Alexander III, Nabokov's two youngest daughters, Elisaveta and Nadezhda, were made ladies-in-waiting. There are pictures of them in formal gowns that show us they were both genuine beauties. Nadezhda's photograph is in a dress of considerable splendor made for a ball in 1903. It is an Old-Russian-style gown designed especially for her by Serge Diaghilev in the *World of Art* manner, which was then at its height, with edgings and patterns of precious stones on the broad collar and high cloth peak by Fabergé. Vladimir Nabokov's disdain for the supposed vulgarity of Fabergé is well-known. Perhaps this was because Fabergé became a symbol of the wild excesses of the detested Romanovs. All the Nabokov houses of the period had some Fabergé, together with the new telephones imported from Sweden, and Pears' Transparent Soap from England.

There was one black sheep among Dmitri Nabokov's nine children, Vsevolod, who, according to some, followed a prostitute to Siberia and was the model for the hero of Tolstoy's novel *Resurrection*, in which the same thing happens. But such events were not unknown in that idealistic phase of the Russian nobility, and there are other candidates for that prototype as well. Leo Tolstoy and Dmitri Nabokov did, however, have one close friend in common, the legal expert A. F. Koni. However that may be, Vsevolod vanished without a trace. All of the other children made, in terms of wealth at least, brilliant matches. In view of the scale on which the family was living and the large number of children, they had to. There were a fair number of divorces and remarriages among Vladimir's uncles and aunts, and they were as often as not good matches, too.

The eldest daughter, Nina, first married Baron Rausch von Traubenberg. The marriage took place in the Winter Palace. Their son Yury was Vladimir Nabokov's closest friend in childhood, perhaps the closest friend he had in life. Nina's second husband was Vice Admiral Kolomeitsev, who was one of Russia's few heroes of its disastrous 1905 war with Japan, because he saved the life of the commander-in-chief of the fleet during the battle of Tsou-Shima. At the time that Nina met him, he was the captain of the imperial yacht *Diamond*.

The next sister, Natalya, another beauty, had her own coming-out ball at the Ministry of Justice with Alexander II in attendance. Her hand was much sought after, but she married for love and, it appears, lived happily ever after. Her husband de Peterson was a diplomat who served as consul general for Russia in Rumania, Belgium, and finally the Netherlands, where he stayed for twenty years. Their son, Peter de Peterson, attended Cambridge after Vladimir Nabokov. The third daughter, Vera, married a man who was a major landowner in four provinces.

Nabokov's eldest son, also named Dmitri, made the most spectacular marriage of all, to Lydia Falz-Fein, whose family owned Askania-Nova, one of the great properties of Russia. Its cattle were supposed to be without number, though it was known that the property had more than one hundred thousand cattle dogs. The property also had many exotic animals and was turned into a nature preserve under the Soviets. The marriage didn't last, although Vladimir Nabokov did come to know the Falz-Feins in Southern Russia in 1919 and in the Berlin emigration, where he once received a small writer's subsidy from them. But Nabokov did not get on with the Falz-Feins and, in fact, intensely disliked them. The next son, Sergei, was awarded the Gold Medal at the Imperial School of Law and eventually served as governor of two provinces. He married a Tuchkov, a member of another old Russian family. A Tuchkov had been Ivan the Terrible's czarina. The youngest son, Konstantin Nabokov, never married, or, as Nabokov put it, he was "indifferent to women." (Konstantin was not the only one of Nabokov's paternal uncles who was homosexual. Nicolai Nabokov was told by his grandmother that she had to reproach one of her older sons for taking too great an interest in one of his younger brothers. "What are the servants here for?" she mischievously instructed him.)

Konstantin Nabokov had a very successful diplomatic career and was posted to Washington for several years, where he represented Russia at the Portsmouth, New Hampshire, peace conference presided over by Theodore Roosevelt that led to the treaty with Japan. Konstantin Nabokov adored America and knew the country from one end to the other. He also had postings to India, about which he wrote a book, and to England, where he was left as the minister plenipotentiary after the death of the ambassador there while the 1917 revolution was in progress, and where he decided to spend the last years of his life.

The youngest sisters of Nabokov's father were Elisaveta and Nadezhda. Elisaveta married (the first time) Prince Heinrich Sayn-Wittgenstein, who belonged to the czar's Hussars and was a Gentleman of the Imperial Court. He had a fine house not too far from the "Nabokov compound" and extensive landholdings in two provinces. This prince was the grandson of one of the generals who fought Napoleon. Nadezhda married Dmitri Wonlar-Larsky, from a half-Polish, half-Russian family probably second in wealth in this listing only to the Falz-Feins.

Nabokov's father, also Vladimir Nabokov, was deeply in love with a girl named Katya Ignat'ev, but she was in love with the Grand Duke Mikhail and so refused him. But she didn't marry the grand duke and went to serve as a nurse in the Russo-Japanese war. After this courtship, Nabokov proposed to and married the girl next door to the Batovo estate, Elena Ruka-vishnikov, whose family was enormously wealthy. They owned Siberian gold mines. But in terms of their position in Russian society, the Rukavishnikovs were far more marginal than the Nabokovs. Though it was strenuously denied by some members of the family, including Vladimir, these Rukavishnikovs were related to the well-known merchant family. Some of the aunts used to gossip spitefully in the parlor that a Rukavish-nikov had once been the manager of a Nabokov estate. One of the insults that Nabokov's father had to endure, according to another family member, was a satirical drawing in the journal *Capital and Estate* by Konstantin Korovin, the leading Russian Impressionist painter, showing the politician Nabokov dressed like a merchant's wife.

There was no easy way in Russia for wealthy merchants to climb out of their class. The best-known instances of such a rise in class were the Stroganovs, who became Siberian multimillion-aires of such power that they could not be ignored. But when the Stroganovs were finally ennobled, the family was listed as "noto-rious people" by origin in the official chronicle of the nobility. Elena Rukavishnikov's branch of the family, which claimed de-scent from a member of the Pugachov Rebellion, had crossed the line from this sort of merchant and industrial wealth into noble society only in the 1890s.

Nabokov's father and mother had a loving marriage. All the same, it should be quite clear from the register of marriages just given that wealth always figured in the marriages of Dmitri Na-bokov's children. To put it another way, the newspaper article that supposedly caused Vladimir Nabokov *père* to call its editor out to a duel in 1908 by stating that he had married for money was essentially incorrect, and yet, it was too close to a raw nerve in the family. The Nabokovs all married not just for money but, without any doubt, with money in mind as well. Nabokov gives a fleeting glimpse in *Speak, Memory* of his maternal grandfather as a rather rough and uncivilized man. Certainly the fact that the young couple began to live, in the Russian expression, "in full stride" must have done something to provoke the cartoon attack, though the real basis of the slur was the fact that Nabokov's father had crossed the line politically from his egalitarian but essentially conservative father and was standing in the vanguard of a new, more radical political thrust. *The New Times*, the paper in which the attack was said to have been made, was very reactionary.

Whatever the political distance between them, and whether or not Dmitri Nabokov was, in fact, his biological father, his son had the same extraordinary capacity for sustained work as the minister of justice and exceeded him in that he was also a most effective orator. It was V. D. Nabokov, with the wealth of the Rukavishnikovs behind him, who paid Dmitri Nabokov's debts.

There were close ties of affection between most of Vladimir Nabokov's uncles and aunts, and in *Speak, Memory* Nabokov says that he used to play with all of his many cousins and was at one time or another secretly or openly in love with all the girls. But Maria and Dmitri somehow stood apart not only from each other, but also from the entire sprawling family group of their children and grandchildren. It is another glimpse at high speed, but I wonder whether the portrait of a bitter and senile Dmitri Nabokov denouncing his own children which Nabokov gives us in *Speak, Memory* does not have as its only possible explanation the fact that some of them were not, in fact, his children. That is speculation, but it is entirely in character with Nabokov's compulsion to tell the truth and yet conceal entirely at one and the same time.

V. D. Nabokov functioned as a legal expert—rather than a lawyer earning his living—with a special interest in criminal law. He didn't have to "earn a living." He read papers at various legal conferences in Russia and abroad, and in 1904 he published a collection of them. He was a deeply convinced advocate for abolishing the death penalty. Still another speciality concerned the law pertaining to homosexuality, for which he coined his own Russian word, which translates roughly as "same-sexedness." He wasn't quite as good at coping with "same-sexedness" on a nontheoretical basis, however, because two brothers and his brother-in-law were homosexuals, and his second son Sergei showed very clear early signs of a tendency toward it. Nabokov's father was very judgmental about it. The family was sensitive enough about the occurrence of homosexuality, I was told by one Nabokov family member, that Vladimir *père's* children were carefully watched for any signs of it, and sexual uncertainty and homosexuality became a major motif in Nabokov's writing.

Nabokov's father had graduated from the University of St. Petersburg in 1891 and then done further study in Germany. He was appointed a Gentleman of the Chamber at Court in 1895 and had great success, primarily because he was a very polished dancer. But that aside, his intelligence and his lack of sufficient means did not make him the eligible young man he might otherwise have been at court. He became an adjunct instructor in criminal law at the Imperial School of Law. An old émigré told me that two law professors had been overheard discussing Nabokov's future father on the steps of the law faculty: "He is talented and could play a great role in Russia's future. But he has no money. First we must find him a rich wife."

Those who admired him and had vaulting hopes for his future became fearful, after his marriage to Elena Rukavishnikov, that he would be spoiled by the luxury. After he was elected to the First Duma a political colleague wrote of him:

> He glided along the floor of the Tavrichesky Palace with the small dancing walk he had used at balls in the past in which he had on more than one occasion artfully led a cotillion. But he had early outgrown all these gleaming inconsequential things in the extraordinary life that he led. He had too energetic a mind to be satisfied for too long with success at balls. A political conscience burned in him as it did in many enlightened people of the time . . . If there was a degree of condescension in his smile it was purely of an intellectual nature and not at all rooted in class. Even the representatives of the working class could not but agree with the political thoughts of this talented deputy, but all the same Nabokov's personality gave rise to class hostility among certain of them, a feeling of unfriendliness which he did not at all experience towards them.

It was said that Nabokov's father was on the czar's list for a ministerial position but was dropped as a result of a speech he made in the Duma in which he condemned firing upon the work-

ers who had come to petition the czar peacefully in front of the
Winter Palace in January 1905, the famous "Bloody Sunday" that
began the slow apocalypse of revolution ending in the Bolshevik
coup of 1917. Nabokov had made the speech without prior notifi-
cation to the czar. When the czar dismissed the Duma, Nabokov's
father crossed the border into Finland with some political colleagues and issued a protest proclamation to the nation. Its only
effect was a three-month prison sentence for Nabokov and a pro-
hibition against his taking part in subsequent Dumas. He served
the term with his elegant portable rubber bathtub in a private cell
where he read and studied Italian. He wrote letters to his wife on
toilet paper and bribed a guard to smuggle them out to her. After
that Nabokov worked as an unelected leader of the Constitutional
Democrat Party (the Kadet Party) and on the publications
Speech and *Law*. These publications often sailed very close to the
wind in advocating reforms opposed to the czar's policies. The
Kadets were the intellectual party of St. Petersburg and had, besides Nabokov himself, many outstanding members such as
Prince Obolensky. It was sad that the Kadets were effectively removed from the political process, and it was sad that Nicholas
and Russia were deprived of the only people who might have
been able to avert the deluge.

Czar Nicholas, encouraged by his wife and certain rabid ad-
visers and ministers, would not relinquish an iota of his power.
There were massive strikes. First thirteen workers were killed,
then nearly thirty. In August 1915, about twenty-seven thousand
workers went on strike in the capital. The czar arrested strikers
and closed the Duma. Sixty-four thousand workers from thirty-
four factories struck in response. All in all there were nearly a
thousand strikes in the capital alone in 1915, and 1916 was worse.
While all of this was happening the Constitutional Democrats,
who did not oppose the czar or czardom, engaged in eloquent but
futile editorial debates about the future of Russia. Even at the
point when all was lost, V. D. Nabokov complained that, if only
Prince Michael had had the courage to accept the throne, everything could have been averted. It is the most valid cliché of the
Russian Revolution that "they did not get their white gloves off
in time to fight," and no one wore finer gloves than V. D. Nabokov. Delay was the hallmark of the Kadets and, eventually, of the
entire provisional government. The Duma didn't do the wrong

thing—it did nothing, and that was the worst thing of all. The Russian Revolution wasn't won by the Bolsheviks—it was lost by the czar and the Social and Constitutional Democrats.

Perhaps given the situation of Russia and the foolishness of the czar, the Russian Revolution really was inevitable. Russian political life under Nicholas was quite as mad as that shown in the *Waltz Invention.* The czarina gave the mad Rasputin's comb to Nicholas so that some of his strength would flow to the czar at ministerial meetings. The liberal opposition parties fought among themselves, though they never adequately focused on what precisely the factional differences between them were, in part because their members, including V. D. Nabokov, were almost all committed Freemasons and so had a strong common bond as well as sharp differences. The liberals made an effort to influence and guide the czar, while at the same time promoting consultations with and making secret financial donations to the Bolsheviks on the grounds that all the political forces of Russia "must learn to talk with one another." There is a case to be made for considering *The Waltz Invention* not a fantasy play at all but a plainspoken commentary about the critical moments in modern Russian history.

The two great political acts of Nabokov's father were his speeches protesting Bloody Sunday in 1905 and the speech against the Kishinev Jewish pogrom in 1903. They were brave and ringing speeches but made in a social and political context unused to free speech, and so they came to nothing. The Kadets let slip the opportunity to press the czar for further reforms in 1905. The Kishinev pogrom was, like the Beilis trial for the supposed "ritual murder" of a Christian child in 1913 (V. D. Nabokov also wrote about it), a self-evident horror, but what was required in all these instances was not a speech but some form of effective political action, and of this the Kadets were simply incapable.

In spite of all his talent and bravery, Nabokov's father wasn't the right man at the right time, and neither was he a leader of men. In addition to the sense of his own superiority that he could not hold back (after all, like his son, he really was in very many ways superior), there may have been a certain inconsistency between what he said and what he did, a sense of different standards for himself. That must be said because V. D. Nabokov published two long articles on dueling in his journal *Law* in 1908 (subsequently republished as a separate monograph) in which he condemns the practice without any reservation:

> Moreover, I would ask you not to think that the thoughts and
> conclusions I reach here have been drawn from this special incident. On the contrary, I consider that in regard to the question of dueling, as in many other matters, it would be
> exceedingly dangerous to introduce individual cases, and on
> the basis of these special circumstances, perhaps unusual, perhaps embarrassing or foolish, as the case may be, to construct
> some sort of theoretical base.

Nabokov condemns the air of romance with which dueling is surrounded and concludes:

> Let the false mantle of eloquence be ripped from this repulsive habit, and the halo of supposedly high motives also be
> taken from it. And when it stands before us in its true light,
> in its dreadful nakedness, then everyone in whom a feeling of
> ethics lives and who listens to the voice of reason will draw
> back from it. At that moment we shall be done with dueling!

Nabokov, in *Speak, Memory*, says clearly that his father was to fight in a duel. There may have been some confusion on the part of the young Vladimir, who was, after all, only seven or eight when these events took place. Certainly V. D. Nabokov had been caricatured in a cartoon that implied he had married for money. But the duel may have been unconnected with that or with him. The articles that V. D. Nabokov cites as commentary on his own involvement in a duel in the 1908 monograph he wrote have now all been found. They concern an important Duma duel, but V. D. Nabokov was not even a second and is nowhere mentioned in the many press accounts of the affair. Nabokov's involvement must have been political and peripheral. An eight-year-old boy could easily have muddled the circumstances of a duel his father would have been very much concerned with but not actually involved in. Matters relating to challenges and duels were reported very attentively in the Russian press, and so it is rather unlikely that even a challenge involving someone as well-known as V. D. Nabokov would have gone unreported.

There is the other possibility: should it happen that Nabokov's father was involved in a duel after having written what he did against the practice, it would partly explain the source of the paradoxical character of his son, who wrote a "pure" novel about a nymphet, collected butterflies but expressed disdain for their beauty, was a fervent American who lived in Switzerland, held spartan views on translation but altered and augmented the translations of his own novels freely, held biography in contempt and yet used it as one of his major themes in his fiction, and so on. The behavior of Nabokov, father and son, is not really hypocrisy but rather a highly developed sense of private standards and a cultivated horror of appearing obvious and ordinary in any way.

In the years prior to 1917 the aristocracy of St. Petersburg, the Venice of the North, was infected by what we now call radical chic. It was centered in the Nabokov house at 47 Morskaya. Morskaya was one of the finest streets of St. Petersburg. Elegant sleighs with tall-hatted drivers and fur blankets across the laps of the passengers drove up to the imposing house (after the revolution it became the Danish embassy) for political and legal meetings, parties, and small concerts given by world-famous musicians such as Koussevitzky. The house saw a succession of princes and Jewish intellectuals, bankers and poets. As they were ushered into the house, Nabokov's father would conduct his guests around for mutual introductions with each of the servants with whom they would solemnly shake hands. Works of the finest Russian and European painters were hanging on the walls. No one lived better in icy and magical St. Petersburg.

Vladimir Vladimirovich Nabokov was born April 10 (Old Style), 1899, in the Nabokovs' pink granite townhouse. Nabokov preferred the New Style birthdate of April 23, because it is also Shakespeare's birthday. His birth took place in the second-floor east-corner room.

One of the colleagues of Nabokov's father in the period when he was an editor of the liberal St. Petersburg newspaper *Speech* has left us in his memoirs the first recorded recollection of the future writer Vladimir Nabokov as a baby:

> In Nabokov's study there was a large photograph. Over the baby carriage in which the future writer Nabokov lay in magnificent costume with costly lace, the father, mother, and Uncle Rukavishnikov were bending over the baby and looking

at him with expressions of ecstasy. I had the impression that
this would be an extremely abnormal upbringing in fatally
over-abundant circumstances.

Vladimir was first given to a wetnurse and then to a nurse before
graduating to a governess. But Nabokov was not, if the term is
carefully understood and applied, a spoiled child. His father was
strict with him and gave him stern instruction of the old school.
When he was being taught to skate he felt his first erection and
asked his father about it: "It's just something like a blush. Think
of something else!" Vladimir called him "sir" until his death. He
was given rigorous training in languages, sport, and art by tutors
who sometimes were of unquestionably high standard. His art
teacher, for example, was Mstislav Dobuzhinsky, a recognized
artist of the *World of Art* period, who did finely evocative city-
scapes of St. Petersburg and won acclaim for his stage decorations
for the Moscow Art Theater. It was originally intended by his
mother that Volodya would be an artist. Dobuzhinsky's use of
open stylization, using bare artifice to underscore and stress reality, should probably be taken into account as a possible formative
influence upon Nabokov. Dobuzhinsky and Nabokov kept in
touch in the years of emigration and exchanged a few letters.
His parents openly worshiped their child and put an enormous
amount of energy into his cultivation. True, his father and
mother were wealthy "Russian Edwardians" whose children
were looked after by tutors and servants and who saw them only
at dinnertime, but the relationship of the parents toward the child
was clear and intense. In succeeding years they had four more
children, but, Vladimir's sister Elena always insisted, their relationship with him was the special one. One of Vladimir's earliest
recollections is of sobbing together with his mother as they both
sat at the foot of a staircase, and another is of his mother intensely
instructing him to *remember*. And remembering, needless to say,
was one of the passions of the mature Nabokov.
Years later, in the emigration, Nabokov's mother would become physically ill if she had not had a letter from Vladimir for
a week. Sergei, who was born the following year, was somehow
the unloved one. His sister Elena thought that perhaps he had
come too soon after the birth of Vladimir. Sergei stuttered terribly, and from the age of five it was noticed in the family that he

always seemed to have a crush on some other little boy. This distanced him from his father emotionally. V. D. Nabokov was vexed to have the "problem" appear yet again in his own son. He didn't express open disapproval of Sergei as he did of the behavior of his brother-in-law Ruka. He simply turned away from the boy. It was very easy, living in town and country houses with many rooms and wings, for a child to withdraw slightly if it chose and living both in the family but also in its own splendid isolation. The last children, Elena and Kirill, were the babies of the family while Vladimir was becoming a young man. They, too, both worshiped their oldest brother. Vladimir gave Elena instruction in poetry and drawing, and he had a special tie to Kirill because he carried him to the font and was his godfather.

The other child who was somehow distanced from the family group like Sergei, according to her younger sister, was Olga. She was born in 1903. Nabokov was clearly afraid of having a biographer meet this sister:

> You will never meet my sister Olga as long as I'm alive. No, darling. Here I put my foot down. No, darling. As I say, you will never meet her, because she's not a person to whom . . . Because it's a waste. It's, it's a *terrible* waste of time. She's a very strange woman. In many ways she's quite infantile. She's absolutely concentrated on herself, not only on herself but on today's minute. She was a very beautiful girl, an extremely gifted person in music. She had a beautiful voice. Her love of music redeems many of her other characterstics.

A very similar sort of judgment may be made about her brother: Nabokov as Narcissus. If this identification is correct then Nabokov was doubly right in his rejection of Freudianism. Right firstly, because narcissism, which is usually separated clinically into primary and secondary phases, is the name for a stage of the personality before such things as sexual urges manifest themselves. And right secondly, because the main thing Narcissus must not do (as the prophet Tiresias told his mother the water nymph Leiriope) is recognize himself.

Freudianism, or any systematic theoretical key to the roots of the personality, aims to achieve recognition of the self, or to put it another way, to solve the problem of personality. Whether the system of psychoanalysis is hokum or provides a true scientific mirror is not as important as that basic fact. One way that Narcissus may protect himself (and I mean that quite literally: protect his self as a wholly self-sufficient and autonomous universe) is artfully to choose pools that will provide false reflections. The art of Nabokov is furnished with mirrors, reflecting windows, and characters who choose the wrong doubles, read the wrong meanings in texts, declare the impossibility of ever seeing someone or themselves whole, and obdurately fail to recognize a true reflection when it presents itself. This is the personality of Narcissus, who does not by any means always and immediately fall into the pool, as well as the character of the art of Nabokov. Narcissus falls in love with his reflection in the perfect pool in Thespia into which not even a leaf has ever fallen, but he does understand that he has fallen in love with his reflection just in time to prevent himself from falling in. He suffers, but at the same time he takes pleasure in his torment of love that cannot be requited, because he is Narcissus and must admire himself in any state. The most faithful of his many discarded loves, Echo, grieves with him at a distance.

Did Nabokov know about narcissism as a personality trait? Most certainly he did, because the first psychiatrist who took up and employed the Greek myth was Havelock Ellis, at the end of the nineteenth century. Ellis was the sole psychologist whose work Nabokov accepted. Nabokov had read his Havelock Ellis thoroughly: it was in his father's library in St. Petersburg (there was also Krafft-Ebing in a circular bookcase in the corner with an illustration that he said had etched itself in his memory forever), and later, when he was confined to bed with neuralgia for a time in Berlin, he sent a friend to get Ellis and other psychological case studies for him from the Berlin University library. Nabokov said that he had always had a deep interest in strange psychological states. In the world of Ellis the individuality of each case is respected and catalogued in the same way that butterflies are carefully classified. Freud did use the concept of narcissism, but not until 1910–11. He took the notion from a psychiatrist named Sadger, who in 1908 proposed it as an umbrella term for the personality of those who choose same-sex partners. Freud himself, though he did write important articles that popularized the term in 1914, 1921, and 1923, appears to have had a rather vague notion of narcissism. At first he saw it as a perversion and only a passing phase in the human personality, but then he decided it was a phenomenon arising from the lustful libido and thus gave it an important place in the development of one's sexuality. That is a misuse of the ancient and profound myth and Ellis's careful reading of it.

Primary narcissism is the understanding of the world after the love of one's mother has been internalized by the child who cannot yet have knowledge that a world exists outside of itself. Vladimir Nabokov was a bright and talented child who grew up in hothouse conditions with a surfeit of parental love. It was never withdrawn, and so the young Vladimir matured with an invincible aura of confidence not only in himself but in his ability to recreate reality at will. Because he was such a narcissist, his art was fired with confidence for half a century. It was only necessary that he never mistake his reflection for his true face. Aesthetic bliss at all times and by all means. Meaning, never.

It is usually held that narcissism can never occur in its pure form. It's a question of degree then, with primary narcissism inevitably shading into secondary narcissism, which can successfully navigate in the real world, and finally, of course, common egotism must figure in the equation as well. But the powerful moment of blissful narcissism, when it does happen to occur, must forever be the underlying psychic signature of the person. Lucky Narcissus can love himself with the same unconditional passion that his mother loved him. Death exists, if at all, only for others. There is nothing weak or foolish or even greedy about this. It simply is. One cannot choose to be Narcissus as one can choose to be egotistical. There is, however, a price to be paid for the blissful state. Narcissus is lonely (Nabokov's own definition of himself), and, of course, he must live with a certain paranoia, ever in danger from spies and secret agents. He must develop ways to escape when he is placed in traps and prisons.

If one delves into the scientific literature on the subject, many of the outstanding features of Nabokov's writing are identified as characteristic of narcissism. B. Grunberger, for instance, one of the leading psychiatric theoreticians of narcissism, points out that the narcissist is constantly menaced by the world of *things*. That is only natural, since there is only one self and everything else is thing. This theme begins to play strongly in Nabokov's second novel, *King, Queen, Knave* (1926) and is much more than a stylistic innovation that links him with the object-orientation of the French *nouveau roman* several decades later. For the narcissist, repetitions are absolutely necessary. They are a quest for the pattern of the past, and their very rhythm lulls disquiet. The narcissist may suffer referential madness, the theme of Nabokov's 1946 short story, "Signs and Symbols," in which everything in creation becomes a reference to oneself, which also explains *audition colorée* where language becomes privatized with unique colors in which letters and words are seen in the mind as they are said or read. Nabokov's mother experienced *audition colorée*, and she also was the extravagantly favored child in her own youth. It is less evident because the form and stylistic brilliance of his books vary so much from one another in comparison with most other writers, but Vladimir Nabokov really does have one tale to tell: the shadow that pursues or is being pursued by someone. That is the only story Narcissus knows.

Everyone requires a narcissism factor—love of self—in order to be capable of other forms of love, and all love must contain some narcissism. However Narcissus appears rarely. True narcissism may be surprisingly free of petty egoism, and it is certainly true of Nabokov's novels that, although they are self-referential through and through, they only rarely demonstrate a clear connection with the life we know Nabokov led. Yet it is always there. Nabokov acknowledged in a letter to his mother after she had read *The Defense* that the novel was brimming over with private family recollections.

The younger Nabokov children were brought up by tutors and governesses. Elena told me that her mother never held her on her lap and never played with her as a child. It would appear, from *Speak, Memory* and the testimony of his sister, that Nabokov had considerably more attention from his parents than that. Elena told me, "My mother adored him. Of all the five children. This was really an adoration."

Nabokov/Narcissus sidestepped death through a belief in spiritualism. Nabokov has written about how his father very casually told him that he didn't have to go to church if he didn't want to, but Nabokov did not speak of the deep belief that remained with him all his life. For Nabokov believed that you can communicate beyond death, and he stocked many of his novels and stories with incidents and occurrences in which this happens. An American professor has written an entire small book on the moments of se-ance and near-communion from the beyond in Nabokov. That is the mystical Nabokov who "knows more than I can say in words." You either believe that or you don't.

Nabokov's spiritualism derived primarily from his mother, who believed very deeply in these things. There were supposedly paranormal phenomena surrounding young Kirill until her husband finally put his foot down: "No more seances! That's enough!" Nabokov spoke about the possibility that electrical forces are souls of the dead, a motif in *Pale Fire:* "I've gone very thoroughly into all this. People are held back because of their ter-ror of the unknown which is innate in man. Space, time, electric-ity. We know *nothing* of these things!" But it is probable that one important side legacy of this tradition of family spiritualism was the concept of the book-as-universe, with the Creator (Nabokov) out there in control and from time to time communicating with a character through a rebus or a dog or a puddle. Nabokov only very rarely had to do with mediums and adopted an ironical tone in talking about this sort of thing. But he did believe in other worlds. He didn't actually do it, but he originally intended the hero of *Bend Sinister* (1947) to meet his maker at the end. Cin-cinnatus in *Invitation to a Beheading* (1935) walks away from the puny figures who have been torturing him toward much larger creatures of his own dimension on the horizon. Nabokov's last two novels, *Transparent Things* and *Look at the Harle-quins!*, are teeming with the supernatural. In this as in many other things Nabokov is very Russian. Vladimir Nabokov and Andrei Bely, the twentieth-century novelist whom Nabokov praised most highly, are the two great modern Russian writers who play with spirits in their writing.

3

THE TORRENT OF ENGLISH/RUSSIAN/FRENCH THAT BURST upon the readers of *Ada* was the way that the Nabokov family actually spoke. Nabokov said that he had the perfectly normal childhood of any trilingual child, but, in fact, this macaronic discourse was his unique "family" language. When he was a student he used to annoy his teachers by salting his essays with English words, and he has made a strong claim that he did not write in Russian but created his own special Russian. Similarly, he did not "write in English" but created his own unique English.

His attitude toward his languages underwent many changes until the time at the end of his life when all came together and he began to write openly for a polyglot audience willing or able to understand him speaking in his natural voices all at once. For them, there was still a maze of literary references and puzzles to be penetrated, and if they made it through to the other side of the maze, they would be confronted with the dark cave of personal meaning into which light could never, never penetrate. George Steiner has put forward the view that Nabokov's multilingualism is the determining fact of both his life and his art. It is a very important fact, to be sure, but I don't think Steiner's case can be sustained as anything but opinion, because Nabokov said and believed firmly that he didn't think in any language but in images, and that a phrase in Russian or English would only form after the fact, like the ocean foam of his brainwaves. One of his denigrations of Freudianism was that there is a great deal more to an ocean than the breaking of its waves.

English, Russian, and French were all his "maternal languages," and he could hardly be unfaithful to any of them, although the feeling of struggle between them in his mind was very real and constant. That no other writer had ever undergone his sort of linguistic struggle, as Nabokov claimed (Joseph Conrad was always brought in here by Nabokov in interviews about his multilingualism as a favorite straw man), is simply not so. In the Russian emigration alone there were nearly a dozen writers who wrote or did auto-translations in another language. As regards major writers who have written in two languages, there is Nabokov's compatriot Elsa Triolet, Eugene Ionesco (the West is only just becoming aware of how much writing he did in Rumanian before passing over into French), and, of course, Samuel Beckett. The feeling of pain and undecided loyalty that Nabokov projected for himself was another matter. It was undeniably deep and intense.

Nabokov gave his first love a Russian nickname, but, typically, it derived from a French name. He called his first love Lusya, but her real name was Valentina. Lusya is a Russian diminutive of Lucille, the name of the sister with whom Chateaubriand was in love, and the name eventually became Lucette in *Ada*. The importance of Chateaubriand, romantic exile and author of melancholy imaginary travels, whose style is credited with enriching the French language, is only now being realized in regard to understanding Nabokov's work, particularly *Ada*. Chateaubriand was well represented in the rich old-fashioned library of Nabokov's father, and he was a set author at school.

The first writing Nabokov ever did was not his Russian poetry but an attempt to translate Mayne Reid into French when he was ten. (He used the year of this first attempt at authorship to explain to someone in Berlin that his muse was only twelve years old!) Nabokov also loved Washington Irving's "The Legend of Sleepy Hollow." In addition to Nabokov's obvious early languages, we should also not forget the taxonomic Latin and the butterfly descriptions from distant parts of Russia that could be found in the Nabokov library. Nabokov had three mother tongues, but perhaps he was already an exotic émigré of the mind in his childish imagination.

Though he went abroad several times during his childhood, Nabokov remembers very little of these trips in *Speak, Memory*. He accompanied his parents on holiday trips to Biarritz in 1901 (he remembered a shining wet roof), 1907, and 1909. They took him to the Riviera in 1903 and 1904. It is the magic of the trains that he remembers and evokes so well in his memoirs. The center of his emotional life was Vyra, the summer house near Batovo that the Rukavishnikovs had given to their daughter as a wedding present. A photograph of Vyra—it was either burnt down or dismantled after the revolution—has now come to light, revealing it to be, surprisingly in view of the sun-filled evocation of it in *Speak, Memory,* a rather ordinary very large old house. It was a wooden house, painted gray with a low wrap-around ground-floor veranda in brick. The interior main staircase was iron. Nabokov's mother liked the old-fashioned air about the house and had not had electricity installed. It was the sort of late-Victorian period house that one sees a lot of in seaside towns in America. Vyra was the place where he saw the most of his parents, and it was also the place for the solitary and intense pleasure of butterfly collecting. The area, it is generally agreed, has the most attractive countryside in the environs of the (then) capital.

The paths and gardens, which were kept to an English standard, the patios and drives, the ponds and marshes, the grounds and fields, the roads, the Oredezh River and the wooden bridge over which he used to bicycle with his father after the servant Osip brought his father's cycle out to the veranda, everything in the Siversky region—the colors, the sounds, the smells—became intimately familiar to the young Nabokov. He spent from four to five hours every good summer morning chasing butterflies. Nabokov's love of this particular place was so strong that many of the poems set in the area, which he wrote well into the twenties, still glow with sentimentality.

The calendar and a large family supplied whatever Nabokov's own sensitivity and a happy childhood did not attend to. Though Nabokov's birthday fell in the city season, his saint's nameday, and his father's, too, of course, fell on July 15. In the Russian tradition the nameday celebration is a more important one than the actual birthday. Nabokov's mother and his sister Elena had their nameday on May 21, which was approximately the beginning of the Vyra season. Sergei's nameday was June 5. Olga's was July 11. A summer then contained no less than six major family fêtes, which were usually celebrated with an elaborate festive picnic very like those depicted in *Ada.*

What is clear beyond any doubt from Nabokov's published and extremely extensive unpublished poetry of his youth is that the Russia of his childhood summers is everything to him—in one poem he speaks of Russia as being in the murmur of his blood and the riot of his dreams. Russia is, he claims, both the end or goal and the beginning of his life, something that is always before him. He said that the loss of Russia was the most terrible stress in his life.

Nabokov once confessed that as a youth he had a weakness for the unimportant parlor poet Apukhtin, and much of his early poetry is written in the manner of Apukhtin with a touch of the scenic ecstasy of Fet thrown in. Apart from intermittent flashes of success in his youthful poetry, Nabokov remained a not very impressive poet until he began to utilize his gifts of irony and narrative in his later Russian and English verse. But if his early Russian poetry does little to increase Nabokov's artistic stature, it does much to tell us where he comes from and who he really is. Churlish though he is about fate, Nabokov himself acknowledged the importance of his given moment in history to me in the strongest possible terms: "If I had been born four years later, I wouldn't have written all those books." What he meant quite simply was that his presence as a young man in the twilight of Russian literature and culture was the critical factor in his formation as a writer.

St. Petersburg was less attractive than Vyra because it meant school, a stricter regimen, and the piercing cold winter. But there were the pale violet mists and light fogs of St. Petersburg, the smart trotting horses, the gray-blue of officers' greatcoats on promenade. One saw beautiful ladies of fashion, urchins and beggars, red-cheeked doormen, and a somber policeman on a bridge. The cupolas of cathedrals sparkled in the sky, and everywhere there were wooden shop signs with painted illustrations: crossed rolls of crimson cloth, blacked boots, a horn of plenty half effaced with time. The capital roared and clattered, the creak of the barges could be heard as they pressed up against one another on the Neva.

Nabokov's St. Petersburg romance with Valentina Shulgina lasted almost exactly one year, from the end of the summer of 1915 to the end of the following summer, when he was seventeen. Nabokov met her just after he had recovered from a serious case of typhus, just as it was for Ganin in *Mary*. She was one year younger than Nabokov. She had a brother and two sisters, one a beauty very like her but slightly older and taller and slimmer. Her father was an estate manager. In the Russian version of his memoirs Nabokov said rather sneeringly that her father had a patronymic out of the nineteenth-century playwright Ostrovsky, that is, a rather comic mercantile name. In 1915 their mother rented a summer dacha for the family in the region. He first encountered her when he rode out with his tutor to extend permission to her brother to have a soccer match on one of the Nabokov meadows. Valentina looked down on him from high up in an apple tree where she was perched. Decades later Lucette would be placed in that tree at that first meeting in *Ada*. Another likely marker of that first love is the short poem given to the poet Fyodor Godunov-Cherdyntsev in *The Gift*. It is a perfectly undistinguished little poem, an exhortation to remember between young lovers, which Nabokov has cited as his favorite among all his Russian poems, and it appears to be set on the wooden bridge over the Oredezh.

Nabokov's father eventually became concerned about the romance, probably because one of the servants had been spying on the couple and had informed on Vladimir. In *Speak, Memory* Nabokov relates that his mother showed disdain for the denouncer and took to leaving a glass of milk out for Vladimir's late returns in the evening. His father gave him a short lecture on the duty and means by which a gentleman avoided getting women into trouble and was disturbed to learn, on questioning, that they had already had intercourse (in a hidden away corner of one of the meadows) without taking any precautions. "What? You filled that girl?!" Nabokov told me his father exclaimed.

That autumn and winter Nabokov would meet her in the Tavrichesky Gardens, a park at the end of Sergievskaya Street where her family had an apartment. Nabokov never went to the apartment with her, and she never went to 47 Morskaya with him. Their romance was conducted largely in corners of parks, obscure rooms of museums, and cinemas. In retrospect Nabokov felt that there had been a scarcely perceptible decline in the romance when the summer ended, and they went from Vyra to St. Petersburg. However that may be, during 1915 he was often absent from school.

Nabokov wrote many poems about her and was preparing a substantial book of his poetry just before he left Russia. The book, which was to have been titled *Open Windows*, never appeared, though some of its contents went into the two books of poems that Nabokov published in 1923 in Berlin. *Open Windows* had, however, gone as far as preparation for the printer, and in a note to himself the young poet made a listing of the categories of the 227 poems. Thirty-one of them are listed as concerning V.SH. In recalling this project Nabokov winced at his choice of title.

In that same year of his romance with Lusya, 1915, the young Nabokov became a multimillionaire, after his maternal Uncle Vasily, always called Ruka by his foreign friends, died and left Vladimir his estate. Vasily or Ruka had in several respects a Proustian personality; he suffered from asthma and was always in perilous health. Ruka had mentioned casually to his nephew that he intended to nominate him as his heir. Nabokov later regretted that he had not visited his uncle more often, and also that fate had snatched his inheritance away from him almost as soon as he got it. Nabokov's awkward, bespectacled younger brother Sergei doted on his uncle, who scarcely noticed him. The plaintive French song composed by Ruka that Nabokov strains to remember in *Speak, Memory* was, in fact, memorized and written down by Sergei.

Ruka lived even more grandly than the Nabokovs, and he traveled as far afield as America. The *romance* that Nabokov heard his uncle sing was at his castle in Pau near the Pyrenees. Ruka's only "job" in life was as *attaché* (in what specific capacity it was never made clear) of the Russian Imperial Embassy in Rome. While there he had rented the famous and very beautiful palazzo Villa Torlonia, which, in later decades, was Mussolini's residence.

The house that Vladimir inherited was truly grand. It was designed by Rastrelli, who also designed the Winter Palace. The house, still standing, has well-proportioned eighteenth-century columns. It originally belonged to Czarevich Alexei Mikhailovich and has, among other things, a secret staircase for assignations or escapes. It was a far grander house than Vyra. Its disadvantage was that it was located in a rather wet area. The one product from the estate was peat. Today it serves as a museum of the region and is the only place in the Soviet Union where a tiny portion of the work of Vladimir Nabokov is freely available, for some of Nabokov's early poems about the local countryside and the Oredezh are on display there.

Like his nephew Sergei, Ruka stuttered badly. He had extremely dark eye sockets, an exaggerated mincing walk, a swooping mustache, and he carried a silver-knobbed cane. He looked rather like a pantomime artist of the Chaplin school. He was very fond of his handsome nephew, but he embarrassed Volodya and made him feel terribly awkward. Uncle Ruka has been well described in *Speak, Memory*, but the whole story has not been told: Uncle Ruka was in love with his nephew Vladimir and used to cause awkwardness in the family by trying to fondle him too much in public when he was a little boy. The peasants on Ruka's estate had their own nickname for him, a plainspoken word meaning "the-bottom-feeler."

Nabokov himself has described some of Uncle Ruka's mannerisms as Proustian; for example, colors could jar his nerves badly. There is to my eye something about Ruka that almost qualifies him to be a character out of Vladimir Nabokov. The character that comes specifically to mind is *Pale Fire*'s Charles Kinbote, for whom John Shade's poem is a giant code of lost Zembla. Uncle Ruka loved codes. In *Speak, Memory* Nabokov cites the way in which his uncle turned Hamlet's most famous line into ciphers. Nabokov liked secret meanings and numbers, too. In one of his unpublished youthful manuscripts the title page bears the numbers 5 6 14 19 31 43. The other epigraph to the same manuscript collection was a haiku, in Japanese. Nabokov had no Japanese friends at Cambridge, but Crown Prince Hirohito visited Cambridge while Nabokov was there and Hirohito's special interest was ichthyology, which Nabokov was then studying, so it is very likely that Hirohito had something to do with composing the haiku for Nabokov, since there were no Japanese students at Trinity or studying ichthyology then. In a letter to his mother Nabokov described meeting Hirohito, whom he thought looked like a monkey. The haiku is not very elegant:

> *I want the youthful curiosity*
> *To chase butterflies*
> *Forever!*

Strangeness and strange games are certainly shared by Uncle Ruka and Charles Kinbote. Vasily Ivanovich Rukavishnikov is not the model for Kinbote, of course. But the feeling that Ruka provided the secret staircase to the creation of the comic and pathetic Kinbote has a compelling logic. Homosexuality was always a presence and a problem in the Nabokov family, and that is sufficient explanation for the remarkable gallery of homosexual characters one meets in Nabokov.

Nabokov's future knowledge of this and other subjects was doubtless initiated in the massive library of the house on Morskaya. There one may find Havelock Ellis's *The Sexual Instinct and Its Morbid Manifestations* and a good collection of psychological case histories. The library had about ten thousand volumes, its own catalogue—first printed in 1909 and then a supplement was issued—and a librarian. V. D. Nabokov, according to his son, was a lover of old-fashioned literature (which is confirmed by the catalogue, which has very few of the contemporary Russian modernists) and in the main came into contact with writers only through his administrative function as president of the Literary Fund. His personal friends consisted of journalists and politicians.

Nabokov had one of his own poems privately printed in a lilac folder with an epigraph from *Romeo and Juliet* in 1914. In 1916 he had his first book of poems published in five hundred copies, also at his own expense. Joseph Hessen, a close friend of Nabokov's father, protested that this was very unseemly in a seventeen-year-old boy. Nabokov's father agreed but said there was nothing he could do about it because the boy now had his own money. (Nabokov's father had been very much against his son's inheriting Ruka's estate at such an early age.)

Nabokov's nominal entry into real prerevolutionary Russian literature began in the library when the librarian typed out one of his poems, which was printed by the monthly *The Historical Courier* in July 1916. Its editor was an admirer of one of his aunts. (He published once more, before the blade fell on old Russian culture—a poem that appeared in another prestigious and stolid journal, *Russian Thought*, in March 1917.) Nabokov kept the purple carbon of that first poetic manuscript sheet for a real literary journal with him for years in emigration as either a lucky talisman or a remembrance of the promising past that ended so abruptly.

THE NABOKOVS HAD HAD TWO CARS, ONE OF THEM A BENZ, but by the time Vladimir Nabokov was enrolled at the Tenishev School they owned a long black Rolls-Royce limousine. Cars were very rare in St. Petersburg then, and, a former Tenishev student told me, children playing in the Summer Garden would run toward the street calling out *"Avtomobil! Avtomobil!"* whenever one chanced to drive along the Neva Quay. Nabokov's reputation at the school was that of a snob, and the long black Rolls was an important factor in this characterization. In his memoirs Nabokov sneers at the recollection of a teacher who requested that he have the chauffeur at least drop him off a block away, in deference to the school's commitment to democratic sentiments. His sister remembers quite firmly that she asked the chauffeur to do exactly that before they arrived at her school.

The Tenishev School, which had been founded only at the turn of the century, was a product of liberal St. Petersburg. Its auditorium was the place where a large number of intellectual and artistic meetings in the city took place, including those of the Literary Fund of which Nabokov's father was president while his son was a student at Tenishev. While the numbers of students were not large—no single class ever contained more than thirty boys—the academic standards were extremely high, in spite of the fact that the school practiced a degree of "progressive permissiveness," to the extent that any formal examinations and grading only occurred once, at the end of the term. Even though it was just a secondary school, young lecturers from St. Petersburg University were hired to give extra lessons in advanced subjects such as criminal law and political economy. Not only the most advanced but also the most expensive school in Russia in its time, the Tenishev School had in its less than twenty years of existence an outstanding record of achievement by its graduates.

Prince Tenishev had founded the school with a gift of slightly over a million rubles, an unheard of sum for the time. The school's commitment to democracy was evident from the beginning in the way that it incorporated itself as a commercial or business school in order to be able to evade the "Jewish norm" restriction of 5 percent, which was being vigorously applied by the minister for education to all academic schools. Information on the graduates of the school makes it clear that a very high percentage of the student body was, in fact, Jewish. Nabokov's own year, for example, was half Jewish, though it is really impossible to tabulate these things precisely since every class always also had at least a few students from baptized Jewish families. The famous poet Osip Mandelstam was one of these. He graduated from the Tenishev School some years before the young Nabokov.

During most of its existence, the excellence of the Tenishev School derived mainly from its headmaster, Alexander Ostrogorsky. He not only gave the school its norms of progressive excellence, but also successfully steered it through the turbulent straits of 1905, when it might have foundered. There was deep republican sentiment in St. Petersburg after 1905's Bloody Sunday. There were demands for a democratic constitution, and Czar Nicholas responded to them with further repression. Then came a general strike during which there was no water except what had been stored in bathtubs and no electricity, so that kerosene lamps, which were not that far in Petersburg's past, suddenly reappeared everywhere. The university went on strike, and the strike spread to numerous secondary schools. As it happens, the Tenishev School was situated on Mokhovaya, or Moss, Street, next to another school, the Third Classical State School. A delegation of students arrived from this school with the request that the *Tenishevtsy* join in the strike with them. All the students gathered in the auditorium, and the headmaster announced that he and all the other teachers would leave so as not to prejudice their deliberations. Fiery speeches were made by the boys in which it was declared that the Tenishev School must close its doors until Russia became a republic with a free press, the right freely to hold public meetings and to have unions and religious liberty for all.

The school had been founded upon the principle of inculcating such strength and independence in its pupils. The headmaster always shook hands with a boy when he spoke with him. All the teachers adopted an informal, adult air with them, and students were frequently invited to their homes for tea. There was a student reading room with all the leading journals and newspapers, and the older boys were even allowed to smoke there. Nabokov, who had the habit from his mother, could smoke up to sixty short Russian cigarettes a day. Corporal punishment wasn't allowed. The worst that might happen was that a student might be asked to leave the school for the day. The difficulty was that, had the resolution been carried forward, the government would almost certainly have seized the opportunity to close down the school. The headmaster appeared and informed the boys with sadness that, since the meeting had extended beyond the closing time of school, he could not accept their resolution. The teachers had a motion of their own that declared a strike unnecessary inasmuch as the current political situation made study quite impossible anyway.

Osip Mandelstam, who was far more sympathetic to the school than was Nabokov, caught the precious and unique Tenishev atmosphere in an autobiographical essay:

> And all the same there were good boys at Tenishev. They were made out of the stuff of the children in Serov's paintings. They were little ascetics, monks in their own puerile monastery where in their notebooks, instruments, lovely glass flasks, and German books there was more spiritual sustenance and internal order than in the lives of the grown-ups outside.

Mandelstam looked back on the boys playing soccer, and it seemed to him as though the students had been taken to England and reclothed there to give an imitation of Cambridge students. He looked back to the auditorium meetings and saw a steady procession of esteemed lords who came to address a parliament of boys. Ostrogorsky had died shortly before Nabokov became a

Tenishev student, but the strong social atmosphere he had created didn't change. The students had their own mildly ironic song, which went:

> *We know a little bit about a lot of things*
> *And can weigh it all with judgment cool*
> *'Cause we are the pupils of the Tenishev School,*
> *Yes, pupils of the Tenishev School*

But Nabokov was, simply, too much of a super-individualist to fit in even in this school dedicated to individualism.

There were two school magazines, *The Tenishevian* and *Veranda*. They had originally been single-copy handwritten journals that were passed around in the classroom, then turned into mimeographed journals, and then, because one of the editors had an uncle who was one of the major publishers of St. Petersburg, they appeared in elegant printed form during the last years when Nabokov was a student. No copy of these magazines has as yet come to light, but it is known that Nabokov contributed to *Veranda*. One old boy told me that to the best of his recollection these magazines consisted largely of essays on the value of friendship.

Nabokov had two quite close friends in his class. Samuil Rozov was always academically at the top of the class. He was also the smallest boy and ferociously brave. In soccer games he would throw himself upon their most feared classmate, Popov, who had been left back five or six times, and who terrorized all the boys and some of the teachers, too. Nabokov claimed that Popov was the only person in his life he was afraid of, and that years later he would sometimes wake up from nightmares about him. Once Rozov prepped Nabokov a few minutes prior to an oral examination for which he had not prepared, and as luck would have it the examination consisted precisely of the things Rozov had been telling him about. The teachers had all they could do to get Nabokov to shut up. The other close friend was Savely Kyandzhuntsev, the good-natured joker of the class. Nabokov met him years later in Paris. The Kyandzhuntsev family was offended when they read Nabokov's description of Savely as "fat, indolent, and charming" because the Kyandzhuntsev family, they said, had given Nabokov money during some of his lean émigré years.

The study of literature at the Tenishev School was on a university level. (For that matter, all studies were advanced—the chemistry course, for example, was planned by an assistant of the world-famous Mendeleev.) But the course was extremely old-fashioned in many ways and didn't include any of the Russian modernists except Alexander Blok. The headmaster Ostrogorsky had compiled anthologies called *The Living Word* which consisted of poems and extracts of classical Russian prose. Beginning with the medieval "Song of Igor's Campaign" Nabokov studied the lives and chief works of all the old Russian classical writers such as Derzhavin, Fonvizin, Zhukovsky, and Griboedov, before moving into a quite thorough study of Pushkin, his ties with sentimentalism, and his relations with his poetic contemporaries, particularly Venevetinov and the pessimistic philosopher Chaadaev. Every major work of Pushkin was studied closely. After Pushkin, Gogol and Lermontov were read in much the same way. Turgenev was paid less attention, and Tolstoy and Dostoevsky were missing from the syllabus. It is true that Nabokov coasted academically in his last two years, and during one of those years he was often absent. But what he studied at the Tenishev School is important because, apart from the passion he later developed for the work and theories of the great Symbolist writer Andrei Bely, this study fixed most if not all of his scholarly critical taste for the rest of his life.

All who have commented on Tenishev, with the exception of Nabokov, are agreed that the outstanding teacher by far was the red-haired Vladimir Gippius. Gippius, a published poet on the fringe of the reigning Symbolist and Acmeist movements of the time, was a difficult personality, who was known to have strong likes and dislikes of students. There was unquestionably a personality conflict between them. Nabokov has written about what a hard time Gippius gave him by reading poems from his 1916 collection aloud to the class. What Nabokov did not say was that Gippius's manner was particularly devastating because he had an extremely dry and deadpan humor. He would often invite student groups to his house, and it is said that there, in the company of his red-haired wife and son, he would change character and become an extremely relaxed and jovial person. Gippius and a history teacher, V. R. Sommer, who married the headmaster's widow, had the greatest influence among the students not only because of their special knowledge, but also because they most genuinely treated the students as adults.

It could be argued that Vladimir Gippius was the most important teacher that Vladimir Nabokov ever had. It was from Gippius, surely, that he mastered the fine art of strong and vicious opinion. Once again, it is from Mandelstam's great *Noise of Time* that we may take a defining sketch of Gippius behind which we can glimpse the future Nabokov:

> V. V. Gippius [was] a teacher of literature who taught the children a much more interesting science than literature—literary malice . . . Beginning with Radishchev and Novikov, Vladimir Vasilevich established even that far back a personal relationship with Russian writers, a malicious lover's acquaintanceship full of exalted envy and jealousy, light disrespect, and the consanguine disrespect which one is accustomed to find in families . . .

Once Nabokov was sent home by Gippius for having fibbed about a prank during which he fell in the school's fishpond. His most serious collision with Gippius, however, was over the disinterested and rather supercilious essay he wrote about the events of February 1916, when the provisional government of Alexander Kerensky overthrew the czarist regime after a series of mutinies against the old order in St. Petersburg and the provinces. The infuriated teacher turned on Nabokov and, using a familiar form of address that showed great contempt, told him: *"Ty ne Tenishevets!"* ("You're not a Tenishev boy!") The events, stresses, and changes in Russia proceeded at such a tempo after 1905 that nearly all young people felt involved in the political future of Russia. Nabokov didn't at all. The world of politics he left entirely to his father.

As it happened, however, Nabokov's favorite teacher, George Veber, was an historian, though in later years he couldn't remember his name: "I am one of those memoirists who begin their recollections with the phrase, 'I do not remember.' So I do not remember his first name. I think it was Nikolai. He was quite a famous historian. He was the best teacher of history that I have ever met in any college or university in the world. He was a small man with a pointed beard and a rather dry way of talking, always

fingering his beard and wearing an old-fashioned pince-nez."
Veber was famous for his panoramic lectures, which always
spanned all of Russian and world history in an hour.

The thing that saved Nabokov's reputation at the school was
his ability as a goalkeeper. Nabokov was a first-class soccer
player, and he and his brother Sergei, along with another boy
named Cherepennikov, were always sure to be selected for the
soccer team to play in interschool competitions. Sergei, however,
only lasted "two disastrous years" (Nabokov's words) at Tenishev because of his romances. He was more of a dandy than his
brother and always wore spats and dressed in the Germanic *stil
moderne* that was popular with Russian fops.

Many poets came to read at Tenishev, including Mandelstam,
Gumilyov (who was shot by a Bolshevik firing squad), and Khodasevich, who became the principal poet of the emigration and
one of Nabokov's best critics. These lunchtime hallway readings
were one of the activities organized by the students themselves.
The use of the hallways rather than the more formal "Commedia" theater was not as disrespectful as it might sound. Everything at the Tenishev School was done on a grand scale. The halls
were elegant, wide, and well lit. Some of them had elaborate wall
displays of plants under glass. During recreation period Nabokov
would frequently be seen leaning against a hallway wall rather
than taking any part in the games in the yard. Nabokov was disdainful of the hallway readings, because, he said, he thought his
own poems were better. The only living poet for whom he had
respect was the greatest of the Russian Symbolists, Alexander
Blok. He never met Blok, but once he and his father were in a box
at the showgrounds where the Wright brothers were demonstrating their plane, and Blok was in the box next to them, and once
Nabokov remembers passing him on the street. After 1917 Nabokov long continued to have respect for Blok, in spite of the fact
that he passed over to the Bolsheviks. That was very rare for Nabokov, but then Blok died very soon after the revolution.

Nabokov teamed with Andrei Balashov to publish his second
book of poems. Some copies of this book only reached him by
post in the Crimea shortly before he left Russia. In his youthful
idealization of the poet/hussar in the tradition of Lermontov, Balashov was rather like Nabokov's friend and cousin, Yury Rausch
von Traubenberg. Balashov was the one who, years before, had

brought to school the cartoon showing Nabokov's father as having married for money. Thus, in *Speak, Memory*, Balashov is described as his best friend who betrayed him but then showed
perfect honor in concealing how he broke his ankle in the fight
that followed with Nabokov. He was an extremely taciturn person and, though he knew several people who knew his old friend
Volodya, he never spoke of him, nor did he go to hear him read
when Nabokov came to Brussels in the thirties.

Many years later in emigration Samuil Rozov and Nabokov
exchanged long letters about their schooldays. Rozov recalled the
taste of their constant cabbage and meat pies. Nabokov remembered other lunchtime details such as the classmate who had a
passion for salt, and the yogurt desserts that they ate with alumi-
num spoons. Nabokov also recalled their first laboratory experiments—the sprouting pea, grape sugar, the wonder of litmus
paper, and then, in later years, the teacher whose demonstrations
never worked and so would cheat to obtain the desired results.
Nabokov confessed to Rozov that he was a little jealous of the
way in which everyone seemed to love him at the school and how
casually he responded to this affection, almost as if he didn't notice. Nabokov could be quite condescending not only with his
schoolmates, but also to his teachers. Once a geography teacher
whom he didn't like misspelled the River Nile as "Nil" in Roman
letters on the blackboard. When he left the room for something,
Nabokov went to the board and made the correction in a very
conspicuous way. His classmates reprimanded him: "What did
you do? You've humiliated him!" It is true. Nabokov was not by
nature a true Tenishev student or member of any other group
throughout his life.

The best thing about the school, as far as Nabokov was concerned, was the soccer. Only when goaltending could he be solitary and yet a member of the team. His recollection of soccer
games by the massive arches of the Tenishev courtyard—the feel
of the ground underfoot, the sting of the ball, a particular player
positioning the ball to score with slender but very powerful legs,
the ball receding into the sky after Popov's explosive kick—all
later went into his novels, and he regretted it, because he felt that
using these scenes in his fiction had deprived his memories of
their life. Nabokov's 1937 letter to Rozov is unique for both its
length and its warmth. Decades later, in the seventies, his wife

remarked: "He has grown more reserved. He would never write a letter like that now." Nabokov's depiction of the school in *Speak, Memory* is by contrast with the glowing letter quite dour. In different ways they are both true records and certainly confirm that Nabokov was never indifferent to the liberal and progressive school on Moss Street.

Every year the upper classes of the Tenishev School went on a major excursion in early May. For most of the boys it was the highlight of the year and was looked forward to intensely. Because of World War I and the revolution, Nabokov went on only one, to Finland. He hated it.

The trips were always painstakingly organized. The Finnish trip lasted exactly four days. It began with the group proceeding by train from St. Petersburg to Imatra. Even though the beginning of May is a bad time for butterflies in Finland, Nabokov took his butterfly net, which caused him difficulties with his escorting teacher, who happened to be a naturalist. "He should have been rather pleased to have a young boy who knew everything about butterflies," Nabokov told me. "He didn't like it . . . It would have been all right if I had been a group collecting butterflies. But one boy who was totally immersed in collecting butterflies—that was abnormal." Nabokov also complained about the hygiene conditions: "It was a horrible trip, horrible trip. Horrible. I remember it was the first time in my more or less conscious life when I spent one day without a bath. It was terrible. I felt filthy. Nobody else seemed to mind."

But there is now an entirely different account of the Finnish expedition. An older alumnus named Vladimir Sozonoff, who is currently writing his own autobiography in French, read my 1977 account of the Tenishev School in *Nabokov: His Life in Part* and agreed broadly with everything in it except Nabokov's account of the Finnish expedition. According to Sozonoff the four days were spent in a hotel and on a steamship. He remembers that there were showers and adds: "Really here Nabokov reminds me of the little princess of the Andersen tale." It seems likely to Sozonoff that Nabokov must have received a bad report on this trip and thus felt rather ashamed of the outing.

Nabokov did have another, much more mature outing to Finland in the winter of 1916. He went to Imatra on a short vacation with his mother, and while there he became the lover of Eva, a woman six years older than himself. He wrote thirty-nine poems about her. Nabokov was upset, however, when he discovered that at the same time she was seeing a short fat man with gold buttons. Three years later he met Eva again in England, and they took up their affair once more. There was a comic but difficult situation on this 1916 holiday because Ivan, the old valet of Nabokov's Uncle Ruka, who had come with them, got into trouble while being massaged by an elderly Finnish woman in a steambath. "It was unlike him," Nabokov said. "He lost his head."

While Nabokov and his mother were in Finland in 1916, his father went to England as part of a literary delegation that included Nemirovich-Danchenko and the novelist Aleksei Tolstoy, as well as the influential critic Kornei Chukovsky (later to become famous as a children's poet). The young Nabokov had visited Chukovsky with his father and inscribed a poem in the famous *Chukokkola*, which featured poems and drawings by Blok, Pasternak, Mayakovsky, Sologub, and virtually every other modern Russian writer. Nabokov's father gave Chukovsky a copy of the boy's book of poems, which Chukovsky treated harshly: he wrote a polite letter of praise but enclosed, as if by mistake, a rough draft of the letter, which expressed a sharper opinion.

The group including Nabokov's father met Wells, Conan Doyle, Robert Ross, and Edmund Gosse while they were in London, and they were invited to Buckingham Palace, though the meeting with the king wasn't a very long one. When the Nabokovs returned from Finland and London it was to the long-awaited republican Russia, which would, however, have less than a year to live.

By 1916 Nabokov was a full-fledged provincial dandy, preparing to take a year off for a butterfly expedition to Siberia before entering Cambridge. Both things happened, though in quite different ways. The butterfly safari with the eminent entomologist Grum-Grzhimaylo eventually came to pass as an imaginary trip in Nabokov's most mature Russian novel, *The Gift*. And when he went to Cambridge it was from Berlin, not St. Petersburg.

Unlike other St. Petersburg schools, the Tenishev School required no uniform. In his last year Nabokov began to dress in the English manner, so that he did indeed give the impression of visiting royalty as he got out of the Rolls-Royce every morning at the impressive carriage gate of the school. It was the forgivable affectation of a very individualistic seventeen-year-old. The sister of one of his classmates gave him her poems to read, and he returned the manuscript to her with a schoolteacherly comment scrawled on it: it was first of all necessary, he told her, for an important poet to have mastered grammar. When the Bolshevik coup began in September 1917, Nabokov ostentatiously sat and played chess with his friend Shmurlo while gunfire could be heard on Liteiny, not far from the boy's house. Nabokov's mother telephoned him in distraction and told him either to stay there or come home. Then one of the older servants, Alexei, put a plate of cold meat on the table and went away. Russia, the Russia of old, had ceased to exist except as a well of painful longing and a golden source of inspiration and memory.

St. Petersburg had been renamed Petrograd, and the streets had filled with the rootless and the impatient, longing for what they thought would be populist Bolshevik power. Nabokov's aunt had come upon a crowd in a city square. They were listening to a speaker who could just be seen above the crowd. It was Lenin. "What's he saying?" she asked the man next to her. "What does it matter?" was the reply. "He's one of ours." Nabokov's father regarded Lenin as an annoyance who would soon tire himself out and go away. Volodya wrote a high-spirited schoolboy poem about his own emerging poetic greatness. He was in bed recovering from appendicitis at the time and sent it as a letter to his Tenishev friend Saba Kyandjuntsev. It contained some contemptuous remarks about the revolutionaries on the streets of the city. He called them little gray people who had crawled out of mouseholes. They had permanent marks of slavery on their blackened hands, and they wanted, he said, a freedom that would put an end to passion, dreams, and beauty. Of course, the poem was simply the pose of a young man trying to sound like a Russian Wilde. He wrote jokingly to a friend that it had reached the point where cab drivers were offering a hundred rubles for his autograph.

Kerensky's provisional government fell. Nabokov's father had been its passive recording secretary. Alexander Kerensky had wanted the Nabokov limousine to flee abroad in, but V. D. Nabokov had warned him that the car was not in sufficiently good shape for such an historic journey. (There were fewer than a dozen Rolls-Royces in prerevolutionary Russia, and so their maintenance was more than a problem—interestingly, it has been revealed that another of them was owned by the family of Alexander Solzhenitsyn.) In the final days V. D. Nabokov gave refuge in his townhouse to some English officers and an American woman with two small children. Sergei and Vladimir had had to be sent south at the beginning of November, or else they would have been conscripted into the Bolshevik army. The train trip took four to five days. The whole family, which went south in various groups, was extremely lucky in getting out safely. Elena had reached the Crimea with the three youngest children and two governesses, one English and the other an older nurse who had been passed to the Nabokovs from a friendly family that was distantly related to them. The older woman, Evgeniya Hofeld, remained with Nabokov's mother and became her best friend during their years of mutual poverty in Prague. The English gov-

erness, Miss Greenwood, had been remonstrating with Nabokov's father for several years that he owed it to his family, given
the conditions in Russia, to deposit at least some money abroad,
but he felt strongly that that would be an unpatriotic thing to do.
Nabokov's father let things go too long and was lucky to get a
ticket (first class as it turned out) to be able to leave Petrograd at
all. In the end they were able to carry away only some necklaces,
rings, and bracelets. There was a lovely and valuable double
string of pearls, and this little cache of jewelry helped considerably when the family reached Berlin. But when they were in Yalta
they were—in Nabokov's words—at first desperately poor. Sergei and Vladimir had traveled in a private compartment that they
kept locked all the way, which provoked some curiosity and led
some soldiers at a stop to clamber up on the roof of the wagon and
urinate on the boys through the fan vent.

Once in Yalta the Nabokovs encountered the daughter of a
very close political ally in the Kadet Party. She had married
Count Panin, who owned a beautiful villa there. It had courtly
gardens like those one saw on the Riviera, but these gardens, Nabokov recalls, were even more lush and green. There were a large
number of cypresses and many imported trees. They were given
a house on the estate. It had long corridors and many small rooms
and had served as the headquarters of the southern branch of the
czar's Okhrana or secret police. Nabokov's father was appointed
minister of justice, or minister of minimal justice, as he joked
(because he had so little effective power) in the Crimean government, and so their family situation assumed a deceptive nor-
malcy. They were in the Crimea for sixteen months.

For Vladimir it was an exciting place for butterfly collecting.
He made six short expeditions into central and northern areas of
the Crimea. One of the places he visited was the legendary Bakh-
chisarai, famous for Pushkin's mellifluous poem about it. There
were excellent collecting grounds on the rocky slopes of the
mountain Ai Petri and also on the hilly pastures on the northerly
side of the mountain. Once Nabokov was taken for a spy in the
guise of a naturalist by a Soviet patrol, and his life was at risk. He
incorporated various of his Crimean adventures in *Glory*, which
is, he told me, one of his three most autobiographical Russian
novels (the other two are *Mary* and *The Gift*). There is also a
matter-of-fact chronicle of some of those Crimean days, because

the seventy-seven species of butterfly and more than a hundred species of moth that he captured were the basis for his first published scientific paper. It appeared in the English journal *The Entomologist* in 1923. The mounted butterflies themselves were left with the librarian of the Panin estate, and years later Nabokov used to wonder whether they had by chance survived and were part of some permanent collection. He imagined that, had he been caught in Bolshevik Russia, he would have tried to live an obscure life as an entomologist.

The Crimea fell under Bolshevik control from time to time, but then the Whites would regain control. As a result, the men often had to guard the house at night. On one occasion their house was searched by Bolsheviks, and fate played a trick worthy of Vladimir Nabokov, because one of the searchers was named Nabokov, and Nabokov's father had chosen the elegant pseudonym of Dr. Nabokov, pretending to be a physician. They got out of that scrape because the Nabokovs' chauffeur, who had turned up in the Crimea and briefly joined the family, knew how to talk to the searchers.

After that the Germans, who were one of several interventionist nations in the Russian Revolution, came, as a result of which the Crimea passed again to White control. Life was surprisingly full. There was theater, newspapers, café life. Owing to Nabokov's father's position in the government, the family moved to Livadia, which had been the czar's estate in the Crimea. Nabokov's first literary success came when he was in the Crimea. He translated a German song for a concert singer who was the wife of a friend of his father's, and the rendition was very well received. V. D. Nabokov's friend, the musician Vladimir Pohl, said that Nabokov's father had asked him to exert a guiding influence on Volodya's development. He had said to him: "You know, it's simply a tragedy what's happening with Volodka! He's capable, writes good poetry, but does nothing but chase and catch butterflies. Couldn't you, Vladimir Ivanovich, have some influence on him and get him to tear himself away from butterflies for a little while to occupy himself with poetry?" Nabokov dedicated his series of religious cameo poems, *Angels*, to Pohl. His influence may have been considerable, because Pohl was a mystic: "I tried to direct the thoughts of the young Nabokov in the direction that interested me, mysticism. Volodya asked me to give him books on these questions, and since the library at Livadia was huge, I piled him up with material on the subject."

Nabokov published at least three short poems in the émigré newspaper *Voice of Yalta* in September and October 1918. He was doing translations from French and English poetry in this period. In his autobiography Nabokov has spoken of how he first felt the pangs of exile in the Arabian-nights atmosphere of southern Russia. In his notebook poems of this period there is an air of calmness and rich color. In his long poem, "The Crimea," written in London in 1921, the region is spoken of as a rose that has been presented to him by God and a place where Pushkin stood at his side and smiled at him. There is no sense at all of the war that raged around and finally throughout the area. The Whites were in a hopeless position against the Red tide from the north. They stayed as long as they did only because the disorganization of the revolution demanded Red units on more important fronts.

While he was in Yalta, Nabokov acted in *Liebelei* by Arthur Schnitzler. In the period prior to the revolution Schnitzler enjoyed enormous popularity in Russia, and there were some who held him to be virtually an honorary Russian writer. Nabokov remembers the occasion as a professional production: "I may have been paid. I was certainly paid." He has written in *Speak, Memory* of how, offstage, he continued his romance with Valentina by post—he even had plans to return to Petrograd and rescue her— while at the same time he betrayed her in the festival-like atmosphere in which he found himself living.

At the time of the Russian Revolution, Russian literature, before that essentially a literature of two cities, benefited from an influx of vitality and warmth from the south in writers such as Yury Olesha and Isaac Babel. While in Yalta Nabokov became quite friendly with the poet Maximilian Voloshin, who had been born in the area and had returned there to live. Voloshin was the most important of the poets then resident in the Crimea. He had become very well-known a decade earlier on the periphery of the Symbolist movement (and not only for his poetry: he had fought a duel with Nikolai Gumilyov) and was the first to translate Henri de Regnier and Barbey d'Aurevilly into Russian. In the period after 1917, which was when he wrote some of his most important poetry, Voloshin advocated acceptance of the revolution in a spirit of quasi-mystical quietude and wrote about the brotherhood of all Russians in spite of the passions of the civil war. There were some who counted him a great poet.

Nabokov met Voloshin through his father, who had been on friendly terms with him through his work on the Literary Fund in the capital. The nine-year-old Volodya once came to have his hair tousled by Leo Tolstoy, who had come to St. Petersburg to see *The Power of Darkness,* while his father stopped to chat with Tolstoy on the street. It was from a Literary Fund meeting that Nabokov's father brought back to his son the opinion of Zinaida Gippius, another distinguished poet and the cousin of Nabokov's Tenishev teacher, that his son, whose self-published book had just appeared, would never be a poet. Apart from Voloshin, Nabokov's father was particularly friendly with Nikolai Minsky, Russia's first important Jewish poet.

Voloshin was famous for his bonhomie and cordiality, and he took a great deal of interest in the young Nabokov. Nabokov years later regretted that he could recall so little of his many meetings with Voloshin. They used to meet in a Yalta Tartar café, where they sipped wine and discussed poetry. Nabokov remembers Voloshin once declaiming in this café at night while the sea boomed only a few yards away. Nabokov also went to Voloshin's Crimean house, a large but unpretentious sprawling seaside cottage. From the window of his study, Mount Karadag, rising by the sea, looked very like a profile of Voloshin's own head, for he had the head of a friendly fury, masses of gray and red hair blowing in all directions in the stiff Crimean breezes, and a beard that seemed to grow right up to his gray eyes. Though he was a massive man, he moved with great lightness and grace. Voloshin did not elect to leave with the other Russians in 1919, instead accepting with quiet courage the harshness and finally the horror of life in the Soviet Union. When he learned of Voloshin's death in 1932, Nabokov recalled, in a letter to his mother, that it was Voloshin who had taught him how to write poetry.

It was through Voloshin that Nabokov first became acquainted with the metrical theories of Andrei Bely, which are very important in Nabokov's intellectual biography. Voloshin talked to Nabokov about Bely's theories at great length, and then Nabokov found a copy of Bely's book in the library at Livadia. Bely was one of the most important members of the "younger generation" of the Russian Symbolists, a wild and perhaps deliberately imma-

ture but always brilliant artist. He was the son of a prominent
mathematics professor, and his articles on versification are frequently illustrated with highly abstruse diagrams. This was the
period when Nabokov was giving his sister Elena drawing lessons, and he also taught her how to chart poems according to the
Bely system. To make the geometric figures more impressive
they were sometimes drawn in colored pencil. In a few cases Nabokov would make the secret geometric figure a part of the poem
itself—in an early poem called "The Great Bear," for instance,
the charted half-stresses form a picture of that constellation. In
his "Notes on Prosody," which are an appendix to his two-vol-
ume study of Pushkin's *Eugene Onegin*, Nabokov acknowledges
the influence of Bely. It is the only "influence" that Nabokov was
ever to admit in print. There are strong parallels in personality
between Bely and Nabokov, not only the tendency of both writers to be radically different in form at all costs and to join fact and
fancy in their writing, but also the weakness, already mentioned,
of both men for paranormal phenomena and the occult.

It had almost come to seem that life in the Crimea might go on
as it had been indefinitely. Even a severe toothache in May
1918—the beginning of a lifetime of dental trouble—became the
pretext for a poem. No one on either side knew what was happening or what was going to happen. Reality came with the death
of Nabokov's close friend and cousin, Yury.

Yury and Volodya had shared a cult of the romance of danger.
With Nabokov it was a superficial attraction, but for his cousin,
whose family had a long and deep military history, it was in the
marrow of his being. Yury, whose parents divorced, had been
sent to live at Vyra during the summer of 1916. The two cousins
had shot at each other with airguns on the little wooden bridge
and played a game in which one lay with his head on the ground
while the other passed over it at high speed and with minimal
clearance standing on a swing. Yury von Traubenberg wanted to
ride back into St. Petersburg on his charger. He received his
commission just before he came to the Crimea, where his regiment was fighting in the north. In one encounter a Red machine-
gun nest was decimating the regiment's cavalry. The young
baron requested permission to attack, galloped ahead, and his
forehead was cleaved by a line of bullets. That senseless death
derived too directly from the Mayne Reid stories that he and Vo-

lodya had loved to enact, but in Yury's own terms it was perfect. The death was a shock to the aristocracy and especially to the aristocratic youth of the province in peril, at a time when mere death and catastrophe had become mundane, essentially private matters. Nabokov told me that the Crimea was permeated with narcotics during the despair of the Russian exodus at the end.

Vladimir was a pallbearer at Yury's funeral. A large and very solemn funeral procession came from the church to the Yalta quay, where a line of British soldiers stood at attention, which Nabokov remembered as a nice touch. There was also a first-class military band. Only a few weeks before, a phalanx of Nabokov cousins, Yury among them, who had come together for the first time in such numbers, had strolled briskly along that same broad quay arm in arm in the breeze.

Nabokov had contemplated joining the White army. He said he remembered trying on the boots, but the government was about to fall and his father decided the family should leave. Nabokov wrote two poems about Yury, one in January 1919, the other in August. The first poem (both were printed in *The Empyrean Path*) speaks about the things they shared: a love of danger and indifference to what the future might hold. We shall meet, the poet tells his friend, one day in an aerial kingdom. The second poem, "In Memory of a Friend," speaks of the death as having occurred in the same spirit as the games they used to play together as lads when berries substituted for blood. There was an awkwardness here that perhaps lasted for a lifetime. In the first version of his memoirs, *Conclusive Evidence*, Nabokov is extremely eager to enter the White army, even though it is not for banal patriotic reasons but simply to be able to go back and rescue Valentina. In the Russian and two later English versions this passage is smoothed down. In *Glory* Martin is ready to perform great exploits, but his neurotic mother tries to interfere and hold him back from danger. In *The Gift* Fyodor sets out to glorify his father, who has somehow been accused of cowardice for not having gone to war. Cowardice was something Nabokov must have thought about. He was nineteen and in perfect health. Certainly in the Berlin émigré community in the twenties there was a question hanging over the head of a young man who had not gone to fight, and the first émigré book to be published about Nabokov, by Princess Zinaida Schakovskoi in 1979, raised exactly this point. There was an idealized commitment to bravery in much of the early Nabokov poetry as well as *Glory,* and there were also tormented, "lower" characters such as Smurov, the hero of *The Eye,* who has not fought and who even lies about his supposed war exploits. Many of Nabokov's polarized characters dramatize this very private interior struggle.

The entire Crimean cabinet was booked on a single ship, the *Trapezund,* and the Nabokov family was on this ship, too, but everyone was taken off at the very last minute because representatives of the French government, which was coordinating the departures, suspected, wrongly, that one of the ministers was taking government funds with him. To their credit the ministers of the provisional Crimean government were the last to board the ships. The evacuation consisted of a hundred and twenty-six vessels, which brought 145,603 people to Constantinople. The Crimea did see a fair bit of corruption and bribe-taking in its final days, but this particular money in question had already been used to evacuate personnel and minor officials on the first ships. It was very close in the end. Though Nabokov portrays the chess game he was playing with his father on deck as he sailed away from Russia forever, the captain of their ship had been barely able to leave the wharf in time. Some shrapnel was actually hitting the ship at its mooring, and the captain, though he didn't yet have permission to leave, finally said, "Enough!" and got under way. The Nabokovs' ship was a small vessel called *Hope.* The ship went through the Black Sea to Constantinople, where it had a stopover of four days, but the refugees were confined on board. There weren't enough bunks, and the food came either in meager rations or sudden unexpected profusion. The ships were dirty, the seas rough. Nabokov in later years gave his wife's recollection of her own departure from Russia by this same route to Martin in *Glory,* using just a pinch of his own memories. A fuller recollection of the *Hope* came from his sister Elena. There were lice, she had to sleep on an unhinged door, and the food was dog biscuits. Nabokov winced at what he regarded as such obvious émigré clichés, but he did grant that it was, in fact, something like that. Yet it is important to understand that, if Narcissus could not be expected to participate in a war, neither would he notice mundane refugee hardship. On the aptly chosen *Hope* Nabokov wrote poems about dark cypresses, singing prayers in Latin, the silky surface of the water, and the crystal moon that might or might not be as clear in Russia. In a poem addressed to his native land he tells Russia that it is all the same to him whether Russia is now called slave or whore, because for him Russia is the recollection of his happiness, the place where he was a child in love and a god. The Nabokovs disembarked in Athens and spent the following few weeks in a modest hotel in the port city of Piraeus. Years later Nabokov was amazed to find that he had spent so little time there, for it seemed to him to have been a much longer stay. He had three romances there, one of which had begun on board ship.

Greece made little impression on Nabokov. One long poem, "Dream at the Acropolis," is an account of a sudden and intense recollection of Russia while inattentively listening to a guide extolling the Doric columns of the Parthenon. He returned there that night and strolled among the columns with some friends, holding the hand of one of his young ladies. Her name was Novotorshkaya, and we know nothing about her, just as, by contrast, we know everything about Nabokov's affair with the older poetess "Alla" (*Glory*) but do not know her name. Another love affair that Nabokov told me about was with a girl named Nadezhda Gorodkovskaya, and that may have been the third romance in Greece, because he called it "an unbroken thread," which would seem to indicate a dalliance that was continued in England, but he didn't specify from where or when that particular thread stretched. That evening on the Acropolis was spent in the company of the two sisters of the (future) famous literary historian, Prince D. S. Mirsky, the Communist prince about whom Edmund Wilson has written. Mirsky was one of the émigrés who decided to return and subsequently perished in a Soviet concentration camp. Nabokov and Mirsky didn't get on well together. In Nabokov's recollection Mirsky was an amusingly almost perfect physical double for Lenin. Nabokov said that if history had worked out differently the Mirsky family rather than the Romanovs might have ruled Russia, because they were descended from Catherine the Great's favorite lover, to whom she was said to have considered giving the throne so that it would not pass to her son, whom she did not like.

Greece was just a stopping place for the majority of the emigrants, though there was a substantial Russian community there with its own church, school, and hospital. Nabokov's uncle Sergei was in charge of the Red Cross rescue mission in Greece.

The Nabokovs went to Berlin through France. They passed

through Paris, but once again Nabokov scarcely noticed it. It was just a place for a poem about his youth.

The Nabokovs had left Russia on April 15 (New Style) and arrived at Constantinople two days later. They were in Greece from April 21 until May 18, when they boarded the New York bound Cunard liner *Panonia*, which took them to Marseilles on May 23. Had he remained on board the *Panonia*, foxtrotting his way across the Atlantic, Nabokov would have hastened his fate by twenty-one years, and he was fond of saying that it would have been a good thing. On May 23 the family went to Paris by train, where they stayed only briefly before crossing to London on May 28.

There was still sporadic military action in the Russian empire, but neither Sergei nor Vladimir wanted to join the so-called Gallipolician Movement, which aimed to mount a counterinvasion through southern Russia and topple the Bolsheviks. The movement lasted for a number of years, and Nabokov contributed a poem to *The Gallipoli Messenger*, which appeared in Sofia in 1923. The first husbands of both of his sisters became officers in the movement. It was decided that Sergei and Vladimir would go to university in England, and even after graduation Vladimir was to have no inclination to join. In *Glory*, Nabokov's Cambridge novel, Darwin questions his friend Martin about his decision to undertake a mission into the Soviet Union: "This is absurd," reflected Darwin, "absurd and rather peculiar. Stayed quietly in Cambridge while they had their civil war, and now craves a bullet in the head for spying." Nabokov felt that there were people in the movement who were sometimes not gentlemen.

IN 1919 THE FAMILY STOPPED FOR A FEW MONTHS IN LONDON during the summer at 6 Elm Park Gardens while university arrangements were being made for the two boys. Because of the chance occurrence that Nabokov's Imatra lover also lived at Elm Park Gardens (there were many émigrés in the area), he resumed his affair with Eva once more. He also remembered that he was friendly with the young Elizabeth Lutyens at Elm Park Gardens. He saw Rozov in London and read his new poems to him. Rozov laughed at them, and Nabokov played billiards with him. As it happened, Rozov, who was entering London University, was able to help his friend at school one more time. Nabokov had not taken any Tenishev documentation into emigration with him, and so, he had been told, he would have "to endure the terror of an examination" to get into Cambridge. Rozov lent him his transcripts, and Nabokov was granted exemption from the examination. Nabokov said that he did explain that his transcripts were almost exactly like Rozov's but that the admissions officers may have thought that the meaningless Russian documents were his own. He certainly stretched one point slightly to ease his way into Trinity: on his application he described his father as Senator Nabokov.

Sergei went to Oxford, but there was some difficulty there, and he quickly transferred to Cambridge, too. Vladimir entered Trinity College in 1919 and graduated with first-class honors in French and Russian in 1922, and a second in Part 2 of the Tripos (literature and history). He was unhappy at Cambridge, because it was there he felt the full trauma of all that he had lost. By contrast, his brother Sergei was ecstatically happy there. He opened his suitcase, a cloud of perfumed talc arose, and he enjoyed the happiest years of his life. For the first time in their lives the two brothers saw a bit of each other, chiefly through playing tennis together.

At Trinity Nabokov was an ordinary entrant, that is, a "pensioner" rather than a scholar. In other words, he had no university scholarship, though he did have an émigré scholarship from a Berlin organization in which his father played a prominent role. He began university as an ichthyology student, but he soon dropped that because he felt that the study of fish was interfering with the Russian verse he was spending most of his time writing. Ichthyology may have been chosen as a result of a first-term acquaintanceship with Paul Leiris, a brilliant student who subsequently became a well-known painter and an ichthyologist at Wood's Hole in the United States. Nabokov and Leiris boxed together and once, when Leiris was preparing for a match against Oxford, Leiris knocked Nabokov out. Nabokov remembered him as "an Indian prince," neither of which he was. Leiris was Sinhalese.

In *Speak, Memory* Nabokov describes his years at Cambridge as an attempt to make himself a Russian writer; in *Other Shores* this becomes simply an attempt to retain Russia. In a sense the two things really were the same for Nabokov. He felt that he had insufficiently appreciated Russia while he was there. England, he said, was a love affair that happened too soon.

Just how unhappy Nabokov was in England is shown by a remarkable little article that he published in October 1921 in the émigré newspaper his father had founded in Berlin. Titled "Cambridge," the article is the sole instance in which Nabokov placed his contemporary impressions in print in nonfiction form before his memoirs. It is the purple prose of an emotional young Russian. He saw England as too orderly and artificial, English faces as being too much like shaving-cream advertisements. The English, he felt, were foreign to the whirlwind of inspiration and the malevolence and tenderness that can transport the Russian. It is a Dostoevskian cry from the heart in which he even talked about "the Russian soul." For Nabokov there was a permanent glass wall between the Englishman and the Russian, and, even drunk, the Englishman could not be deeply enough stirred to bare his chest or hurl his cap against the earth. This was indeed the most Russian time in the life of Vladimir Nabokov, the legacy of his mother who used to kneel and kiss the soil every summer when the family returned to Vyra from the city. The belief in the "glass wall" between the Russian and the Englishman was given to Martin in *Glory*.

In *Speak, Memory* Nabokov tells of using an article of his father's in speaking for the White cause at a Union debate in Cambridge in 1920. The event was actually held on November 28, 1919, at a visitors' debate of the Cambridge Magpie & Stump Society. The minutes of the M&S record that Mr. V. Nabokoff, speaking third, saw Bolshevism as a loathsome disease and described Russia as a piano, the pieces of which were in the process of being distributed among several claimants. Nabokov advocated cessation of financial aid from England, support for the White General Denikin, and a complete Western boycott of the Bolsheviks. The mood of the meeting was overwhelmingly for sympathy with revolution, though there were feelings expressed, too, that Bolshevism should definitely not be allowed in Cambridge.

An undated letter from his father, which was probably written in late 1920 or early 1921, urged him to take heart and get the degree. He did that, but he makes it quite clear in *Speak, Memory* that he did very little work for his degree. He didn't have to do any work once he had switched from fish to French and Russian: the languages he had learned from childhood and the basic literary education he had had at the Tenishev School were more than sufficient for a First. In his memoirs Nabokov has a sense of hallowed halls and staircases trodden by great poets in Cambridge. In his 1921 Russian article the towers of Cambridge fall before his imagination like stage sets, unreal against eight centuries of turbulent Russian history. In *Speak, Memory* his Trinity Lane room is shown to us by a transparent piece of newspaper at the moment of conflagration in his fireplace and by the tinkling sound of a thin sheet of ice in the washbasin being broken by a toothbrush. In the Russian article the room is described in a more plainspoken manner: a dirty red divan, a gloomy fireplace, and ridiculous little vases on ridiculous little shelves. Once again, the apparently conflicting views of Nabokov can be brought into focus fairly easily if one understands that both views have equal validity, and all depends upon the context and the audience he is addressing.

Nabokov boasted of not once having gone to the library while he was at Cambridge, though he said that he attended lectures regularly and took verbatim notes, which carried him through the exams. Though he stoutly denied it, it seems clear that his Cambridge lecturer in Slavonic, Alexander Goudy, was the prototype for Moon, the Cambridge lecturer in *Glory*. Goudy was an Irishman who had taught at Cambridge from 1905. Nabokov said that he was invited to Goudy's for tea once, and that he hadn't been a hit. He saw much more of his tutor, Ernest Harrison, who is mentioned by name in *Speak, Memory*. He was frequently summoned to Harrison's room because of various misdemeanors. Nabokov had turned to his tutor for assistance in obtaining scholarship aid early in 1920, but he received none. In a letter to his mother written in early 1920 he called Harrison a vile man. In discussing him with me he called him an extraordinarily stupid man. Harrison was a distinguished classicist and one of the foremost teachers at Trinity in his day. He possessed an old-fashioned reserve, though he was a dedicated teacher known for always keeping his tutorial pupils past the hour. There could have been in Nabokov's reaction to him the sort of grudge that sometimes follows the receipt of a favor in life, for Nabokov was actually expelled from Trinity as the result of a prank. (We don't know what it was.) The classmate who did the illustrations for his Russian translation of *Alice in Wonderland* betrayed him under interrogation. Harrison got the expulsion order lifted for Nabokov.

He remained a little bit to the side throughout his Cambridge years. He was not, which is not entirely clear in *Speak, Memory*, Trinity's goalkeeper, so he must have played on either the second or third team. Nabokov told me indignantly that he was made much of at Cambridge, but Trinity recollections of him are few. A survey of surviving Trinity men for the years Nabokov was a student yielded almost no recollection of him there. Trinity had nearly a thousand students. Nabokov's friends were in the handful of Russians among them.

In first term Nabokov was the roommate of a student named Kalashnikoff. (He, too, dressed himself up a little for the English, calling himself de Kalashnikoff.) Nabokov claimed that Kalash-nikoff was subject to fits of dark Slavic moodiness, particularly as the year wore on and he had to face the prospect of being sent down. In fact, he was not sent down, and, when Nabokov left the Great Court of Trinity, where they had shared rooms on the R staircase, it was together with Kalashnikoff. They continued to room together at 2 (now 38) Trinity Lane in rooms above what is now a sporting goods store. In *Speak, Memory* Nabokov muddled the length of time he roomed with Kalashnikoff and forgot that he transferred to Trinity Lane with him. Sometimes, according to Nabokov, Kalashnikoff could scarcely abide the sight of someone reading and would make attempts to throw Nabokov's books and poems into the fire. The roommate, he claimed, was politically re-actionary and an anti-Semite, who continually tried to press the Protocols of Zion upon him, but, with that said, Nabokov allowed that he could be charming at times. In any event, Nabokov claimed that he chose the English spelling "-ov" for the final syl-lable of his name in order to differentiate himself from his room-mate. (He also wanted to avoid the English propensity to pun and turn him into Nabokoffee.)

Kalashnikoff and Nabokov, together with another friend, Prince Nikita Romanov, on occasion formed a secret band of three responsible for numerous sophomoric nighttime pranks. When they were caught, it was always necessary to undergo an explanation of the affair with Mr. Harrison, and Nabokov re-membered that there were periods when he saw Mr. Harrison as often about disciplinary as tutorial matters. Once a surprise counterattack was staged upon the Russians' rooms by some other students. Another time a small fine had to be paid for some pastries thrown through a window. One day his housekeeper came to him in a state of excitement: "A terrible thing has hap-pened, sir. A terrible thing. I really don't know how to tell you." For a moment, Nabokov wrote to his mother, he thought the po-lice had come for him. But it was merely that his soccer boots, left to dry by the fire, had caught fire.

On several occasions Kalashnikoff and Nabokov were romantic rivals. Through Kalashnikoff Nabokov met Svetlana Zivert', to whom he became engaged and almost married in 1923. As for Kalashnikoff, Nabokov met him once more, by chance on Fifth Avenue in New York in the 1950s. He was a stockbroker and wearing a green metallic suit, which made him look, Nabokov thought, like the gangster he always knew he was.

Because he was not much burdened with study, Nabokov's social life at Cambridge was quite full. He visited country seats, went on long cycling expeditions, trips to London (for each of which he needed Mr. Harrison's permission, and he went often), dress balls, and occasional visits to "the lower class." He had a protracted romance with a particularly attractive waitress. Nabokov told me that from the time he inherited his Uncle Ruka's estate and had gold coins in his pocket for expensive St. Petersburg restaurants he grew accustomed to conducting three and even four romances simultaneously. He lived and loved in much the same way at Cambridge on no gold coins at all. All Nabokovs, Nabokov said, fall in love easily. He had social friendships, too. He used to go roller skating regularly in London with a girl named Nina Chevchivadze, whom he would meet decades later in America because she was Edmund Wilson's neighbor on Cape Cod.

Nabokov had three major simultaneous love affairs at Cambridge, two of which were with older women. One he identified to me only as Margaret Fancyname. She was a Danish war widow. Looking back on their affair, he decided that she was a very unpleasant person, which he somehow hadn't seen at the time. Inasmuch as he also tried to maintain some "lower-class dalliances" at the same time, there were inevitable difficulties: "One forgets—one would call Katy Mary or Margaret."

His other two Cambridge love affairs both went back to prerevolutionary times. Nabokov admired a young lady selling balloons at a ball in London. His roommate said, "Oh, that's Marinka," and introduced them. She turned out to be Marianna Shreiber, a girl with whom Nabokov had played and been wildly in love with in St. Petersburg when he was nine. In fact, she had been his first girlfriend, and his attachment to her had continued through his love affair with Valentina. She was now a ballet dancer in London. Vladimir and Marianna became lovers. He would go to London, and she made many trips to Cambridge to be with him, but she dropped him abruptly when she chanced to learn of his other simultaneous love affairs. Before that he had proposed to her, but she had declined. It was Marianna Shreiber who told Nabokov that she wanted to marry someone who "would leave something substantial behind, like a bridge!" And the third serious love affair was the continuation of his romance begun in Finland in 1916. He proposed to Eva as well, and she, too, turned him down, though their love affair went on for several years. Eva was a Polish Jew. Nabokov was friendly with her brother, a student at Peterhouse and a brilliant linguist, while he was an undergraduate.

Nabokov identifies five of the classmates with whom he spent most time by initials in *Speak, Memory*. They are Peter Mrosovsky, Bobby de Calry, Nikita Romanov, Kalashnikoff, and a J.C. There is, however, one English acquaintance who looms rather larger in the memoirs. He stands for the Englishman's inability to comprehend Russia or the Russians and particularly his tendency to view Lenin in a rosy light. Nabokov calls him "Nesbit" and admits openly that he is doing his best to disguise his true identity because he has become "not unknown among his peers." Nabokov goes to great lengths to try to explain to "Nesbit" that Russia before the revolution was a place that did have considerable free speech, and that Russian émigrés are much more diverse in character than the phrase "czarist elements" suggests. "Nesbit," Nabokov told me, was Rab Butler, for many years leader of the Conservative Party, deputy prime minister, and Britain's most famous "near prime minister." Eventually he became the head of Trinity College after his retirement from politics. Nabokov claims that Butler pestered him with questions and arguments about Russia for nearly two years. Another illustrious Englishman whom Nabokov knew, though less well than Butler, was Lord Mountbatten.

Though Nabokov was disdainful of England while he was there, it should be noted that in this period he adopted what fellow émigré intellectuals in Berlin for years afterward saw as his reserved English manner. Even before he graduated, he had begun to export English poets—Byron, Keats, and Brooke, about whom he wrote a long impressionistic article—to émigré Berlin through translations. He wrote poetry in English, and two of these poems appeared in undergraduate journals. Though the very strong influence of Russian poetry is more evident, Nabokov has written that his Russian poems of this period have English poetry running over them like mice. In addition to *Alice in Wonderland*, Nabokov also put in a lot of time translating Rolland's

Colas Breugnon into Russian for the publisher The Word. (It appeared in 1922.) There is an unquestionable marriage of the English and Russian literary traditions in the short poetic dramas that he wrote between 1922 and 1924. The form is an imitation of Pushkin's "little tragedies" such as *Mozart and Salieri*. But in three of the four plays the subject matter is taken from English life and literature, and one of them, *The Wanderers*, purported to be a translation from the English of Vivian Calmbrood, an anagram of Vladimir Nabokov. Though both plays involve two brothers and have a similar plot, Nabokov disclaimed any knowledge of Richard Cumberland's play, *The Brothers*, which was written in 1768, the date Nabokov gave to his mock play.

In addition to Vivian Calmbrood, Nabokov also masqueraded as "Cantab" in some of the Russian poems which he published in his father's newspaper. When he visited Berlin and later settled there for nearly two decades, it is recorded that he frequently wore his Trinity blazer. It is wholly characteristic of the way he behaved all his life that while in England he should adopt a double-dyed Russian air and then, in Berlin among the Russians, bear the characteristics of an English sportsman. Nabokov had a fairly good English wardrobe. He nearly got into trouble over it in 1925 when he wrote a letter to the editor from Berlin to an English newspaper on *audition colorée*, as a result of which he heard shortly afterward from his tailor, whom he had neglected to pay before leaving Cambridge.

7

Nabokov didn't exactly go to Germany after graduation in 1922: it would be much more precise to say that he went to
the large and thriving émigré colony in Berlin. He said that he
had never wanted to set foot in Germany. It wasn't an active dislike as much as complete indifference. The émigrés went to every
corner of the planet, but the main settlements were determined
by two factors, proximity to Russia and the availability of working permits. England wasn't as attractive for most Russians as
Germany and France. The next most popular places to settle
were Czechoslovakia and Yugoslavia. The Russians who were
warmly received in England were the eminent princely families
such as the Obolenskis and the Trubetskois. Berlin and Paris
were the natural first preferences of most émigré families, particularly professional and intellectual families. Vladimir went to
Berlin and lived by giving lessons. His brother went to Paris and
lived by the same means.

It was expected that the Bolshevik regime would fall very soon.
Berlin was a short and direct train trip to St. Petersburg. It was
close, too, to Finland and the Baltic states, through which families
were still being smuggled out of Russia. Also, though there were
basic differences between the German and Russian characters,
there was a strong interest in Russia and things Russian in Germany, and many German business interests willingly catered to
Russian needs. This was particularly true of publishing, because
the price of paper and printing were both very low in Weimar

Germany, and Berlin was at that time the largest publishing center in Europe. For a time there were hopes that Russian books published in Germany would be permitted to be exported to the Soviet Union. There were actually more Russian-language books being printed in Berlin than in either Petrograd or Moscow. The total Russian population of Berlin was only a little under two hundred thousand, but they tended to cluster in a few neighborhoods on one side of the city, the southwestern suburbs of Charlottenburg, Schoneberg, and Wilmersdorf, and many Germans complained that nothing was spoken on certain streets of the city except Russian. Owing to the roaring inflation of the time, another attraction of the city was that reasonable accommodation could be had rather cheaply, especially if one had access to foreign currency. Refugee relief organizations—Nabokov's father was briefly an official of the largest of these—received and gave their funds in hard currency. As a tutor in languages (mainly English) and sport (mainly tennis) Nabokov worked for the wealthier émigré families and was usually paid in hard currency, so that, while he was never well-off, and was occasionally quite poor, he stood to the side in the inflationary flood. Nabokov almost always lived in the flats of German military men, because they had lost the most through inflation and had the most rooms to rent. Because so many of them lived in such roominghouse situations, the Berlin Russian émigrés had, ironically, a rather communal life-style. Their living quarters were heated and they ate regularly for the most part, but they were living in much the same conditions as many of their fellow Russians in Petrograd, with one important exception: freedom. The permanently temporary *pension* life of Russian émigrés in Berlin—shabby but carefully tended furniture, politely distant landladies, lithographs that tended to repeat themselves throughout the city, creaking elevators—has been chronicled by several émigré writers and by Nabokov in *Mary*, *The Gift*, and *The Eye*. Berlin was, for some at least, a provincial but cosmopolitan Russian city. Berliners themselves were in a somewhat preoccupied if not stunned state as a result of their recent past and the present inflationary stresses, and, whether it was for these or other reasons, they showed no condescension to the Russians in their midst. There were some difficulties. The openness and loudness of some Russian family disputes were incomprehensible to some German landlords, and matters sometimes became very difficult indeed when, as happened often enough, Russian tenants married the German war widows who were their landladies. Joseph Hessen recalled in his memoirs how he chanced to be in the same pension as Andrei Bely, who was then in the process of separating from his wife with night-long conversations alternating with periods of silence, which reduced the landlady to a state of frenzy. But the mood of most of the Russians there was rather more Chekhovian.

When Nabokov and his brother Sergei came to live in Berlin after Cambridge, it was arranged for them both to have jobs in a bank. Nabokov said that Sergei worked there five days before he quit and went to Paris, while he lasted three hours. The only thing that Nabokov could recall about that incident in his life was that he wore an English sweater, which didn't suit a German bank. An émigré memoirist claims he worked there for two weeks.

The Nabokov family gives a reasonably good idea of how the émigrés occupied themselves, not only in Berlin. Nabokov's Uncle Dmitri obtained a job as a magistrate in a small town in Pilsudski's still-free Poland. Another uncle, Sergei, after having served in General Wrangel's army and with the Red Cross in Greece, became a car dealer in Bucarest. His Aunt Vera went to Paris with her husband, and the vice admiral obtained a position in the aircraft industry. Two aunts, Natalya and Nadezhda, opened tea rooms, and a third, who was now the Princess de Sayn-Wittgenstein, after several years of poverty and hardship, made her way to Rumania where she enjoyed the favor of Queen Marie. A cousin went into advertising. Another struggled to earn her living as a seamstress. Nabokov's cousin Peter de Peterson remembers visiting Vladimir in Berlin in those years and urging him to do something practical or at least to switch to writing in a language in which there might be a future for him. But in those years, his cousin said, he was determined to remain a Russian writer.

The largest Russian-language publisher in Berlin was The Word (Slovo), which was backed by the largest German publisher, Ullstein, and managed by Joseph Hessen, the colleague and close friend of Nabokov's father. The newspaper, *The Rudder* (*Rul'*), which was first edited by Nabokov's father and then by Hessen, was also backed by Ullstein. The arrangement had

come about because Hessen and Nabokov's publishing activity in
St. Petersburg was well known to Ullstein, who was a firm anticommunist and whose expansive inflationary empire wanted a
stake in the new Russia that would arise after the fall of the Bolsheviks. The arrangement had been made by a cunning lower-
level employee of the old *Law* who conducted the negotiations
himself and then handed the virtually ready-made arrangement to
Hessen and Nabokov when they arrived. The Ullstein empire
was housed in a massive building covering a full city block. It had
leather-appointed offices, a huge reference library, and editors
and researchers everywhere. Business worth billions of inflationary marks was conducted there in an atmosphere of subdued gentility. The offices of The Word and *The Rudder* were not in this
building and were much more spartan, but The Word's working
capital allowed them to publish about twenty titles a year, and
the circulation of *The Rudder*, which was about forty thousand,
was sufficient to employ a staff of twenty-two, though most were
only part time. *The Rudder* paid the equivalent of about four or
five dollars for a poem and twenty-five to thirty dollars for a short
story. Nabokov said that, if he remembered correctly, the basic
rate was a dollar for four lines of poetry or three hundred words
of prose. Young Nabokov's poetry appeared in *The Rudder* virtually every week for months at a time in the period starting in
1921, while he was still at Cambridge, until 1925. Nabokov's
early poetry is weak (by his own mature estimate as well, though
now there is a tendency to exaggerate the value of everything he
wrote on the part of some ardent Nabokovians), but it gradually
grew stronger. The paper was an ideal place for a young writer to
practice his craft. Nabokov's poems were also sprinkled through
other almanacs and journals of the time such as *Northern Lights*,
The Spindle, Facets, The Future of Russia, and *The Fire Bird*.
The Fire Bird, in particular, was set in elegant type on glossy
paper with brilliantly colored illustrations. There were few Russian émigrés who could afford the furs and the expensive cars advertised in its pages, but the very existence of such lavishness on
the old scale bears witness to the energy and hopes of Russian
culture in Berlin in those years.

The very first Russian poem that Nabokov published in the
emigration was signed V. V. Nabokov, but even while he was
still at Cambridge Nabokov switched to the pseudonym Vladimir

Sirin (pronounced SEE-reen), which he kept through 1939. The obvious reason was not to be confused with his illustrious father or be seen to be riding on his coattails. Sirin had also been the colophon of the most sophisticated publishing house in St. Petersburg. In Slavic mythology the *sirin* derives from the siren (Nabokov was, mistakenly, convinced that there was no connection between the two) and thus was a particularly good choice for a writer such as he became because the creature is connected with the idea of metamorphosis. At any rate, it was widely known from the start in Berlin émigré society that Vl. Sirin (the signature he first used) was the young Vladimir Nabokov. He felt that the constant presence of his poetry in the paper aided him considerably in obtaining the children of wealthy, cultured families as students.

The pseudonym became unnecessary less than two years after Nabokov began to use it, when his father was mistakenly assassinated in the Berlin Philharmonic Hall on March 28, 1922. Nineteen-twenty-two was one of the most important years in the life of Vladimir Nabokov. It profoundly changed his life.

The murder of Nabokov's father was an absurd mistake, quite like the murder of John Shade in *Pale Fire*. Like Shade, Nabokov's father died as he was writing a literary essay about opera. He'd broken off his last installment in a mood of confident pause. Shortly before V. D. Nabokov's death, he had handed in a new chapter in his memoirs of a lifetime's passionate observance of opera and theater in St. Petersburg. The concluding sentence in the last part published in the émigré journal *Theater and Life* was: "But about this—and how Wagner took our opera scene by storm—another time."

Pavel Miliukov, who had been an important minister in Kerensky's government, was delivering a speech at the Philharmonic Hall on the theme Russia and America, and some thought that the speech might be politically significant. Miliukov was introduced by Nabokov's father. He had told the family that he regarded the speech as a bit of a bore but that he had to be there in his capacity as editor of *The Rudder*. In the previous day's issue Nabokov had called Miliukov one of the finest statesmen of modern times, a gesture of fine courtesy to his former political and editorial colleague who had now turned political opponent. It was clear to Nabokov that there would not be a meaningful rapprochement between Miliukov's left and the moderate Kadets. For Miliukov was flirting with the Bolsheviks, evidently counting on Bolshevism's mellowing to such a degree that the emigration's more radical left could eventually join forces with it. This was Miliukov's New Tactic, which he initiated in 1921. It involved the renunciation of personal property and a declaration that a democratic Russia could get along very well without the monarchy. This last statement was the spark that ignited the reactionary monarchist assassins.

The hall was filled to overflowing, but the other Nabokovs had all stayed home. Just before he left, one of his daughters had sewn a button on for him. Miliukov had reached the conclusion of the first part of his speech—he always talked on and on—when a young man got up from his seat in the second row and ran toward the platform, gun in hand. Five or six shots rang out. Nabokov had turned to his *Rudder* colleague Avgust Kaminka and asked him why he wasn't applauding just before the shooting began. A second gunman was also running forward. Without hesitating, Nabokov's father threw himself toward the gunman who was firing. He might have been trying to shield Miliukov but was more likely attempting to disarm the gunman, who was firing not only at the platform but also once or twice into the audience. One woman was shot in the knee. Hundreds of people screamed and dived under their chairs, Miliukov among them. Nabokov succeeded in deflecting the hand of the man who was firing. They both fell to the ground. When V. D. Nabokov was pulled off the assailant, it was found that he had been shot twice, once slightly below the heart. He had probably died instantly.

The second assassin remained free for some minutes. He leaped onto the stage and began to wave his pistol about and shout melodramatically: "We have avenged the murder of the czar!" He then managed to fire a third shot into the prostrate body of Nabokov before he was tackled, and it was never satisfactorily determined which of the three bullets had killed him. Both of the gunmen were then set upon and badly beaten and bloodied before they were tied up on chairs and the police and ambulances arrived.

The first killer was named Shabelsky, the second Taboritsky. The investigation revealed that the two men had been roommates in a shabby Munich boardinghouse. Shabelsky suffered from a serious nervous disorder. He had been shell-shocked in the civil war, and his fiancée had been killed by the Bolsheviks. He gave the appearance of being distracted and yet could do things like multiply large numbers in his head and recite Cicero by heart. Taboritsky, it appears, was the brother of a Baltic army officer well known for his theories of vigilante justice. Both men had got themselves half-drunk before the meeting.

The event so shook the twenty-three-year-old Vladimir that he is said to have been not entirely in possession of himself for some time. He spoke openly of challenging both the killers to duels. But they were in jail. (Under Hitler, Shabelsky was, of course, released. He went to Brazil and lived peacefully until his death in 1950. He published a hate-filled book in which he proudly related his version of the killing.) The man who was probably behind the plot was the editor of the journal for which Taboritsky worked, *Ray of Light*, but there was insufficient evidence to charge him. *Ray of Light*, a conspicuously black journal, also gloated over the killing, cast doubts on Nabokov's heroism, and taunted Miliukov because he returned directly to Paris instead of attending the funeral. The last at least was true. A convention of Russian Fascists was meeting in Berlin at the time, and there were good grounds to fear that further attempts on the life of Miliukov might be made. Nabokov subscribed to the views of those who knew Miliukov that, whatever his other failings (Nabokov never had a very high opinion of him intellectually), he was an absolutely fearless man. Miliukov's action cast considerable doubt on that view.

The funeral was held at the Russian Embassy Church on the Unter den Linden. In 1922 the Russian embassy had not yet passed over to Soviet control. One man, the well-known satirical poet Sasha Chyorny, whose poetry had influenced the young Mayakovsky and who was a particularly close friend of Nabokov's father, could not restrain himself and fell into a fit of hysterics. Ivan Bunin, who knew V. D. Nabokov only slightly, wrote a memorial article in which he said: "God grant all good things to the future, 'new' Russia. But when will she again have her Nabokovs? In the former, old Russia there were such people. She can be proud of them. For now, alas, Russia must be in mourning . . . There are no two opinions about the deceased—and is this not in itself a stunning commentary in our time especially?"

V. D. Nabokov was buried in the Greek Orthodox cemetery in

Tegel, only a few yards from where the great composer Glinka
was then buried. In his later years Nabokov paid a small sum to
have the grave tended, though he never went back to visit it because he determined never to go to Germany again after the rise
of nazism, and he mistakenly placed the grave in East Berlin—it
is in the Western sector.

Nabokov's *Rudder* colleague Avgust Kaminka organized
things and managed the family's affairs immediately after the
killing. The widow was eligible to receive a small widow's pension from the Czech government. Prague was, after Berlin and
Paris, the third major center for Russian émigrés, and Czechoslovakia was more sympathetic to the problems and needs of the
Russian émigrés than any other country in the world. Nabokov
went to Prague for a month to help settle the family, after which
he went back to Cambridge because he still had six months left to
finish his degree.

Nabokov's mother had been relatively untouched by the 1917
revolution, because she was indifferent to material possessions.
This was a characteristic of a large segment of the emigration
which has not been understood by the West, and this has irked
many Russians considerably, not least Nabokov himself. The
memoirs of Joseph Hessen record how Hessen noticed for the
first time with amused surprise the contents of his Berlin apartment when they were being prepared for auction after the death
of his wife. Almost all the Russians lived in the past and spent
much of their present talking about Russia. However, Nabokov's
mother, even with her lifelong companion, Evgeniya Hofeld,
could never adjust to a life where everything was not done for
one. Beds were always unmade, dirty ashtrays were everywhere.
Elena never recovered from the death of her husband. Hessen had
telephoned the apartment after the killing and spoken with Vladimir. He didn't say anything except that they had to come at
once. Nabokov understood but returned to finish reading a Blok
poem that he had begun with his mother. Hessen relates the
shock he felt when he observed her on arrival. She wouldn't cry,
she had the face of a statue, and her entire personality changed
forever. Elena Nabokov lived for seventeen very difficult years
raising her children but remained thoroughly immersed in memories of her past until she died in Prague in 1939.

Her son was no less deeply affected, but the effect on his personality was more complicated, less straightforward. Nabokov could not accept the death of his father—in a letter to his mother and in one of his longer Russian poems, which ends, "You haven't changed much since your death," the expectation of re-union with him is very explicit. One sign of the effect the killing had on him was that he resolutely refused to talk about it until the end of his own life. Unfortunately, I didn't learn about this until after I had tried to talk about the death and the poems he wrote about his father with him: "Ah yes! Well, there was also this side, this kind of, how should I put it? Ah, well I wouldn't call it, well, the one that I wrote two or three days after my father's death. Yes, at Easter. I remember that very clearly. Ah, I don't know. I think those were my *worst* clichés."

Nabokov had proposed to Svetlana Zivert' and been accepted shortly before. He had known her for three years (she was only thirteen when he first met her) but not very well. Their engagement was to have been announced on March 29, the day after the murder. Life was made to continue "normally." Nabokov took his degree and came back to Berlin. The engagement was announced. The energetic and confident way in which Nabokov met the world was, if anything, doubled. He dressed smartly, went to balls, had a few feminine friendships on the side as before, fully participated in the best of Berlin émigré life. But certain fundamental things had changed forever.

IT IS A SIMPLE BUT STRIKING MATTER. AFTER THE DEATH OF
Nabokov's father all mention of God vanishes from his poetry.
The exception to this is his long "University Poem," which is
written in Pushkinian stanza form (stood on its head!), and it is
quite possible that the reason for this is that the poem was written
before the death of his father and merely published in 1927. Nabokov claimed that his religious poems were only a youthful literary affectation. Now, after his death, it should be said that they
were surely much more than that.

His two early books of poetry, *The Empyrean Path* and *The
Cluster*, were both published in 1923. They were dedicated to the
memory of his father, and, in fact, the poems had been selected
and arranged by his father in concert with Sasha Chyorny, while
Vladimir was at Cambridge. Not only did Nabokov's father and
mother like Chyorny very much personally, but the young and
the older poet found each other's verse sympathetic. Nabokov
spoke about him to me with great warmth:

> He was an extraordinary person. A very lovable man. I
> think he was a first-rate poet. Actually, most of his output
> was light verse, the kind of light verse that Russians favored
> so much, with a political satirical slant.
> I remember him as a very small person, luminous eyes, a
> very pleasant sort of accent. And then in Berlin he started to
> write serious verse. He was very successful. He had some ex-
> cellent poems in *The Fire Bird*. I think he was the literary

editor of *The Fire Bird*. He helped me a good deal in—I
wouldn't say praising my verse—but in sort of suggesting
that you might send your poems here or there.

Nabokov called Chyorny his first literary patron, though not in
terms of cash, of course. Just a few years later, on a visit to see his
son in France, Chyorny helped fight a housefire, which he
shouldn't have done because he had a weak heart, and collapsed
and died.

There were 127 poems in *The Empyrean Path*, 36 in *The
Cluster*. *The Empyrean Path*, in particular, was taken severely to
task in nearly all the reviews of it which appeared. Typical of
these was a notice in the short-lived but excellent journal *The
New Russian Book:*

> Sirin has everything one needs to be a poet: he has truly po-
> etic perceptions, his poems are musical and integral units,
> and, in spite of all this, the collection *Empyrean Path*, with
> the exception of several poems which are really good, is a bor-
> ing book. This is not because the author wants talent, but be-
> cause one cannot pass over all the achievements and gains of
> contemporary art, reject all currents and schools, and employ
> images which have long since faded and ceased to be symbols.

The review was signed with a pseudonym but was actually written by one of Nabokov's good friends, Yury Ofrosimov, who
would some years later commission and produce Nabokov's play,
The Man from the USSR. The comments of Ofrosimov are exact
and fair. Yuly Aikhenval'd said much the same thing reviewing
the book in *The Rudder:* "In general, the poems of Sirin do not
give as much as they promise." A large number of the poems are
graceful (or, sometimes, forced) paraphrases of the nineteenth-
century classics, especially Tiutchev and Fet. But part of the
problem of the poems' antiquarian air is also the casual prominence given to the deity.

No one else was publishing Russian poetry like that in the
1920s. It's not merely the specific mentions of God. The poems
enact a ritual of prayer, grace, purity, radiance, and the unity of
the poet's soul with all creation and the Creator. There is a short
poem about Dostoevsky in which the writer's wail throws God
into perplexity—could His creation be so bad? In another poem

each new day is like a "dewdrop of paradise." Yet another shows the cross that can be seen in the sky at the moment that Mary gives birth. Two poems come close to an identification of the poet with God. One speaks of the things that "God and I" know. It is not likely that such poetry can be merely a pose.

Stylistically, certainly, Ofrosimov spotted the almost total lack of any connection with contemporary poetry. We have already seen how the young Volodya was too haughty to go and hear some of the greatest Russian poets of his time read, and the old-fashioned air of the verse he wrote five and six years later came logically from that. The notebooks in which he wrote most of the poems were expensive cloth-bound books that he brought with him from St. Petersburg. The covers had the miniaturized patterns of old-fashioned upholstery and perfectly matched the tone of the poems inside. But such poetry was also the poetry that his father and mother loved and knew by heart. Although each tended to keep religious faith at a little distance from institutionalized religion, both his father and his mother were devout. It is hard to see any reason their son would not have joined with them in their faith, since, when all the pains and awkwardness of youth are put aside, his childhood was a reasonable approximation of paradise.

He was the first surviving son after a stillborn boy, so the attention lavished on him would not be hard to understand even if his parents had not been so wealthy. He had everything. Though both his parents adored him, they also adored each other. He was in paradise but not quite the center of the universe. Why should he not address the world in joyful and occasionally downright biblical tones?

It is true that Nabokov in maturity considered the loss of Russia to be the greatest ordeal of his life. Yet he did have his passionate memory of it and, like most Russian émigrés until the 1930s, the real hope of returning to it one day. But on March 28, 1922, creation was called into question. Two things happened at once. First, the actual world became quite spectral, even for an émigré. (And the émigrés, not only Nabokov, tended to regard their new circumstances and countries as not quite real.) And secondly, eternity continued to exist—the certainty that he would one day see not only Vyra and his own childhood but also his father again—but there was a difference now: God was no longer necessary or even welcome to the young Nabokov. Narcissus could in a very real sense create reflected worlds at least as diabolically intricate as God's. The worlds he created would be entirely his and would do what he wanted them to, sometimes in a spirit of lightness and affirmation, sometimes in a spirit of hideous cruelty and coldness. Such, at any rate, is an explanation for the emergence of the writer who, more than anyone else in the history of literature, accepted the calling of "creator" with intense, almost literal seriousness.

Nabokov wrote several poems on his father's death. The one titled "Easter" was an affirmation of religious faith, a call to resurrection by the power of poetic song. It appeared in *The Rudder*. The most interesting poem remained unpublished but was copied out by a friend of the family, perhaps from the album of Nabokov's mother, and so has survived in a literary archive. In this poem, "In Memory of V. D. Nabokov," there is nothing figurative about life after death. In one line Nabokov says: "I feel it: you are walking so close to me." And in the conclusion of the poem, the "shade" (*veter tvoi*) of his father bends over him at night to hear him vaguely murmuring one name, "more sonorous than sobbing, sweeter than any earthly songs, and more profound than any prayer." That name is his father's. The poem is by far the most open and "human" thing ever written by Nabokov.

In the two years after 1922 the theme of death becomes important in Sirin's writing. Death is particularly evident in his dramas. *The Wanderers* concerns a near-patricide. The strange hero of the play describes himself as "a goblet of rays of light and pus,/ a mixture of toad and swan." In the end the swan wins: the father isn't slain. *Death* is a two-act play set at Cambridge in 1806 (Byron appears briefly in it) about a tutor who suspects that his young wife has deceived him with a friend and disciple. The tutor sends a false message to his disciple saying that his wife has just died. The disciple is given a potion, which may or may not be poison. The disciple awakes to find himself talking to his tutor, who declares that he is only an echo of his former thoughts. But here, too, it is by no means certain that death has actually occurred. In the end the tutor tells his disciple that it was all a hoax, but the disciple has gone mad and thinks he is in a parodic afterlife which is proceeding as though it were real. *Death* is one of Nabokov's most interesting early works.

A third, *The Pole*, is about Scott's fatal expedition to the South

Pole in 1912. It is a more prosaic play. The specific inspiration for the drama was a visit to the British Museum, where Nabokov saw Scott's journals under glass. *The Grandfather* is set in France in 1816 and concerns a nobleman who escaped death in 1792. He confronts his executioner, who's now a senile old man, by chance. When they are alone the aged former executioner brings an ax, hopping gaily from foot to foot. It would seem that the intended victim has dispatched the executioner.

The longest work in this series of plays is *The Tragedy of Mister Morn*, written in 1924. Here death does occur. In fact, in the end everyone in this play is faced with death, each accepting it in his own way. "Mister Morn" is a king who has temporarily lost his kingdom and had to pass in disguise as a commoner. He is a magnificent coward who will accept the idea of his own death only on the condition that it occurs in view of the whole world. He wants to leave with an immortal exclamation. This play is about an individual caught in history's net and trying to extricate himself with dignity. For Morn anyone beside himself is nothing but a part of a thousand-eyed observer who watches him suspiciously from mirrors. He is the first of Nabokov's Narcissus figures, near perfect and yet pathetic. He compares his impending death with falling toward his own reflection in a well, a metaphor that will occur to most of the protagonists of Nabokov's novels.

These first dramas by Nabokov are not strong. They have far too much of the closet drama about them. Yet in them we see the themes of the unreality of death, blessed madness through artistic transformation of the terms of one's life, the confrontation between the vulgar or cunning executioner and his unexpectedly triumphant would-be victim, cowardice and total bravery, and the mirror as a doorway connected to paranoia.

There is one other poetic scenario of this period that is most intriguing and, in view of Nabokov's subsequent statements about his aversion to music, not a little surprising. This is a poetic accompaniment entitled *Agaspher* written for a staged pantomime accompanied by music. This collaborative undertaking was performed once in Berlin. The Agaspher is a wandering lover tormented by dreams of earthly beauty and is historically an erotic variant on the theme of the Wandering Jew. He claims that he would sell the heavens in order to sin with the object of his love, which appears differently to him in every century. In the past he has been Marat and Byron. He vows to chase his inexpressible dream from age to age. It is clear then that by 1924 we have variants on all the themes that were to be fully developed in *The Defense, Invitation to a Beheading, The Waltz Invention, Pale Fire,* and *Lolita.*

While these themes from the unsuccessful early dramas were the seedbeds out of which his greatest work would grow, there was also another broad field of activity in 1923–24 that had an entirely different character. For Nabokov then wrote and published (throughout 1924 and in the first months of 1925) a torrent of short stories, twelve in all. Considering that all his stories were done in several drafts, and that he wrote the closet dramas during this same period and published thirty-six poems, it is fair to call 1923–24 the watershed period in Nabokov's artistic career. Even if the actual income was very small, he was now a full-time professional writer who gave various lessons during the day before he began to write in earnest during the night, often until well past midnight. Even this list of his published work gives an inadequate picture of how much he wrote then. There is a cluster of stillborn stories and poetic works as well, which I have read in manuscript: "The Venetian Woman," "Russian Is Spoken Here," "Youth," "Man and Things," and "Sounds." These, as well as the first two of the 1924 stories, "Wingstroke" and "The Gods," are of no artistic interest. The stories tend to be highly overwritten poetic prose. He published many of these stories in the Baltic émigré newspaper *Today* and the Berlin weekly *Russian Echo,* which he spoke of as his "wastebaskets." But two of these stories, "Vengeance" and "A Chance Occurrence," are remarkably strong and fully worthy of republication, as, for its historical interest, is the newly discovered 1923 story, "The Word."

Nabokov's third story in print (it may have been the first story he ever wrote) appeared in *The Rudder* in April 1924. "Well-Being" is a monologue addressed to an absent lover with whom the narrator has quarreled. It's a very awkward story because there is so much information included only for the benefit of the reader, since they are things the narrator and his lover should not need to recall or be told. The lovers have arranged, after their quarrel, to meet at the Brandenburg Gate, but she hasn't come. The story is basically an overly fervent description of the people who wander by the gate and of the landscape. The happiness that

could not be found in her is seen to be floating and breathing
everywhere around him. This story and another one, "Letter to
Russia," were to have been part of Nabokov's first novel, *Happiness*, much of which was abandoned but which essentially grew
into his first novel, *Mashen'ka* (*Mary*), in 1926. The important
thing to observe is the early strength of Nabokov's almost du-
biously ferocious optimism in the face of all the tragic losses in his
personal, family, and national life. He would always maintain this
defiant optimism. *The Gift* (*Dar*) was to have been titled *Yes*
(*Da*), and the motif of happiness is still present in *Ada*, which is,
of course, *Ah, yes*. Many of Nabokov's mad heroes such as
Smurov in *The Eye* and Hermann in *Despair* are aware that the
world doesn't believe in their happiness, but they turn their backs
on the "real" world. Nabokov's émigré contemporaries were in
the main writing in a mood of extreme sadness and despondency.

A 1925 story, "A Guidebook to Berlin," is another instance of
early Nabokovian prose poetry. The little story is divided into
sketches of mundane bits of Berlin life. A book of similar sketches
has supposedly been written by Martin's friend Darwin in *Glory*.
The present does not really exist except as a storehouse for the
future, and we are told that it is the task of the writer to show ordinary life in the way that the somewhat flattering mirrors of the
future will depict it. No one would see more clearly or better
project as a statement of overall human existence the peculiar in-
substantiality of émigré life.

"Eden," the most interesting section in "A Guidebook to Berlin," is a description of the Berlin zoo. (The émigré quarters of
the city abutted the zoo.) The narrator tells us that the zoo is as
close to a model of paradise as man is capable of creating. We
should recall here Nabokov's description of the genesis of *Lolita*
many years later. It came to him, he said, when he read about a
chimpanzee who had been taught to draw and whose first drawing was of the bars of his cage. It is clear that Nabokov understood the cage in much the same way that the poet Blok
understood it—as the dual metaphor of artistic form and tragic
human fate.

Another 1925 story, "The Fight," is about an imagined incident that the narrator works up in his mind using the German
man who habitually sunbathes beside him every day. But we
only learn that the incident is imagined at the end of the story.

Nabokov uses exactly the same mechanism in *The Gift* where Fyodor Godunov-Cherdyntsev, the poet/hero, imagines that the man on a park bench near him is a German poet, whereupon the imaginary German poet takes out an émigré newspaper to read. In the 1924 story "Port" a pathetically aimless Russian confuses dream and reality once again. After sitting in an émigré restaurant, where, of course, there is no other reality on the other side of the door, he sees a prostitute who, he is convinced, is a girl he has known in the past. He obdurately tries to speak Russian with her, while she tries out little phrases in the various bartering languages she knows. Or might it be that she really was that girl hiding her true identity? The Russian, who has no clear past, present, or future, ends up sitting on a wharf and looking up at the sky through which a shooting star is passing. The shooting star figures frequently in Nabokov's early poetry.

Yet another early story, "A Catastrophe," which Nabokov published in the Riga newspaper in 1924, sets a Russian narrator against a German hero, and simple reality against a foggy world of imagined possibilities. The Russian sees a slightly tipsy German fall off a tram. As the doctor bends over him lying on the pavement and about to die, the German stands outside of himself and becomes another narrator wondering why the girlfriend he was going to meet isn't there. This story and the play *Death* and *The Tragedy of Mister Morn* are Nabokov's earliest major uses of the theme of the double. In his mature work it is hard to find a single novel without it. The double is usually identified in literary history as the peculiar theme of E. T. A. Hoffmann in the nineteenth century. One of Nabokov's early students in Berlin was a young academic specialist in Hoffmann. Thus, it is quite possible that the theme could have partially derived from this association. But, of course, Hoffmann's influence upon Nikolai Gogol was quite significant, and Gogol wrote a short story called "The Double." One unpublished poem that Nabokov wrote shortly after his arrival in the Crimea contains his first mention of the theme. This poem, also called "The Double," appears in the manuscript collection *Open Windows*. Nabokov's "The Double" speaks of "my pale double, my companion" in much the same vein as the narrator of *A Guidebook to Berlin* refers to his "constant drinking companion." Whatever its source, the insistent image of the double had a history in Nabokov long before Hermann killed Felix or Humbert killed Quilty. I suppose that the double may be understood as simply one mirror, the basic vision of the narcissistic personality. It is also the self gone into emigration. Once, in 1971, Nabokov and I stood waiting for the elevator at the Montreux Palace Hotel and discussing the émigré years. As the door slid open for us, Nabokov stopped short in his conversation and said quite simply about himself, "The past is my double, Andrew." That feeling is certainly very strong by 1924.

The main thing about the early stories is that, even where, as it frequently is, the theme is madness, there is a solid fundament of émigré real experience and feeling. The 1924 *Rudder* story "Bakhman" concerns a demented pianist. It's a tale told to the narrator by his former manager who, in turn, relates it to us. Bachman is so queer that he can enter a party being given in his honor and sit down and read a newspaper. He meets a lame woman in whom he has no interest whatsoever, but she becomes fascinated by him and forges a tie with him by going to every one of his concerts and sitting in the front row. In the end she becomes more important to the pianist than his art. The woman is married, but her husband, though quite aware of her strange passion, doesn't interfere and lives his own life. The woman and the mad musician sleep together only once, just before her death, and we are told that during this night they discover "words of which the greatest poets in the world have not dreamt."

Two of the 1925 stories, "Christmas" and "The Return of Chorb," are about bereavement. In "Christmas" a father rummages in the papers and things that belonged to his son, who has recently died. The father is sure that soon he, too, will die, but he is suddenly startled by a rustling sound. The son had been a lepidopterist, and the sudden presence of heat in the cold room had caused one of his cocoons to hatch. It is, as in Nabokov's poems on his father's death, the sign of symbolic resurrection. (One oddity of this story is that it takes place slightly outside of St. Petersburg, and thus it seems clear that the story is set in prerevolutionary Russia. Many émigré writers steadfastly avoided describing the emigration. Nabokov, on the contrary, went back to old Russia in subject matter very rarely. His use of details from his prerevolutionary past transposed into émigré stories is a constant in his writing.) "The Return of Chorb" is about an émigré's grief for his bride who has been accidentally killed on their honeymoon. Chorb roams a strange town to find a prostitute. He doesn't want to have sex with her. He merely wants her to sleep in the same bed with him. He awakens, sees what he thinks is his wife lying beside him, and screams. At that moment his dead wife's parents, concerned about the long silence from their daughter, are led to the hotel room where a confrontation of terrible silence takes place. But the story isn't about this bizarre circumstance. It is about intense grief. "The Return of Chorb" was termed a masterpiece by one critic (the first time that Nabokov received praise of that order in print), and he made it the title story for a 1930 collection of poems and stories.

Clearly the early stories focus relentlessly upon the grief and loneliness of émigré life, even though the characters are eccentrics and there is often an inexplicable chord of optimism. The subject matter reflects accurately the lived experience of the entire emigration in its first half decade. Not only Nabokov but every member of the emigration had lost friends, lovers, and family during the volcanic upheaval of 1917. Everyone suffered a kind of queer suspension in time and space, hope and despair at the same time. Madness and suicide were common. Nabokov and Nabokov alone caught and fixed this atmosphere—gay, free, and tragic—of Russia's first lost generation. In this sense the early émigré intelligentsia belongs to Nabokov (there were other writers such as Teffi who described the life of the uneducated) in the same way that the gray generation of the 1890s belongs to Chekhov. At this period in his life Nabokov was writing very much in the manner of Ivan Bunin, who was then the foremost émigré artist, with attention to minute detail and with great surges of lyricism. It is curious that Bunin himself paid so little attention to the emigration in his art. Nabokov's writing, and especially his short stories, consistently shows a realistic inclination at the very same time, beginning from 1928, that a more mannered and artificial form of storytelling also comes to the fore. So one should not really speak of a movement "from-to" in his prose. It is a question, rather, of following the development of a major and a minor line, and many of his best achievements in the "minor" (or realistic) line, such as *The Gift* and "Spring in Fialta" and *Pnin*, are not minor works at all.

As it happens, the greatest short story Nabokov was ever to write was written in his very first year of prose publication, 1924.

It appeared in one of the "wastebaskets," *Russian Echo*. The story, "The Potato Elf," stands on a par with Bunin's "The Gentleman from San Francisco" and the best stories of Chekhov, Babel, and Olesha. Part of the reason for its success lies in its use of emotional realism within the context of an outwardly grotesque canvas. That combination would remain characteristic of all Nabokov's best works. The story is tightly compressed and springs out with extraordinary force at the end. The dwarf, assistant to a stage magician, who once takes his wife Nora as his lover, becomes a hermit, which is the calling of many Nabokov heroes. They are either hermits or they are in flight. Fred the dwarf ends in flight, too, and death, when he learns that he had had a son by Nora. He dies of intense joy running after Nora, who took pity on him and could not bring herself to tell him that their son has died. The "potato elf" is chased by all the laughing, screaming little boys of the small town, but in his joy he is like the pied piper of Hamlin, deceived instead of deceiving, and he imagines that all the little boys are his. The mixture of themes in "The Potato Elf" is essentially like that of most of the other 1924–25 short stories. The difference is the near-perfect proportion in which the themes are blended and the slowly building and then madly racing pulse of the tale, a model of the short-story form. With a mighty somersault of the imagination grief becomes joy, reality becomes the aesthetic bliss of a sinister and gay fairy tale.

THE DEATH OF NABOKOV'S FATHER IN 1922 WAS FOLLOWED less than a year later by the loss of his fiancée. We shall probably never know the exact cause of the broken engagement, but we have documented evidence of what happened in broad outline through an extraordinary letter that Nabokov wrote to Svetlana Zivert' after he left her and Berlin, intending at first never to return. The letter, which cannot be printed in our century, significantly shortens the distance between Nabokov and his art. It offers an unparalleled intimate picture of Nabokov, and it is a startling picture.

In the one published photograph that we have of Svetlana Zivert' together with her sister, Nabokov, and her cousin (and Nabokov's roommate) Kalashnikoff, it appears that she is about twenty. In fact, when this photo was taken, probably in the weeks before the murder of Nabokov's father, she was about to turn seventeen. She was, all evidence agrees, one of the beauties of Russian Berlin. Nabokov had been discreetly friendly with her since she was fifteen and was waiting until she was old enough, seventeen, for her family, a widowed father and a guardian aunt, to allow her to accept a proposal. She was a tall, almond-eyed girl with an ebullient, sunny personality. Her nickname was Svetik. Nabokov's own name for her was often Sunshine ("Svet"). The Zivert's were a Russian family of Baltic origin, very old-fashioned and strict. Something happened. One friend of Svetlana's in later life said that Vladimir had made an only slightly immodest suggestion to her, for a "strange kind of kiss." Svetlana naïvely told her aunt about it, whereupon Nabokov was immediately declared a perverted man and the engagement was broken. The aunt was reactionary and regarded the Nabokovs as dangerously leftish, so she might have been merely seizing upon an excuse. On the other hand, in the only discussion that Nabokov had with me about his first engagement, he said that the affair had had its tragic side, but he wouldn't say more than that. He did say, however, that he intended to write a novel about it one day.

Svetlana's father had been a prominent engineer in St. Petersburg. Besides her sister Tanya, she had a younger brother named Kirill. The Zivert's had had a very large apartment on fashionable Millionnaya Street. The apartment had its own ballroom, and it was there by chance that the last ball of Petrograd was held in 1916 before the deluge. It was a ball for youth, and a Tenishev pupil remembers being taken home from the ball in his father's car through the near-empty streets of the city and suddenly seeing a surging throng of workers and soldiers slapping up Bolshevik proclamations about the abolition of capitalists and landowners on all the walls. Even as a very young girl, this pupil remembers of Svetlana, *"vse napereboi za nei ukhazhivali:* everyone madly courted her."

Svetlana was very much at the center of all the Berlin balls and social affairs, which is probably why her rejected fiancé decided to leave the city altogether. In 1924 Nabokov traveled through Dresden, Strasbourg, and Dijon to Nice, where he did farm labor with Italian migrant workers. The letter that he wrote to Svetlana from Nice supplies one of the few clear glimpses into the inner life of Vladimir Nabokov. He complains that it is difficult for him to become indifferent to their time together because it was the greatest happiness he had had or, for that matter, would ever have. He cannot understand why they had to be parted in the way that they were, and he tells her that he still loves her. Before he left Berlin he was having hallucinations in which he saw her standing by his armchair or in a corner. Nabokov assures Svetlana that she's in no way to blame for what happened and tells her that from now on his writing is going to be the only thing that is important in his life. He says that he is considering migrating to Africa. (Many Russians went there, and it represented a kind of Foreign Legion escape for them.)

The letter reveals a rather surprising hidden self-portrait in a minor novella that Nabokov published eight years later in 1930. The novella is *The Eye*, and its hero Smurov is one of the last characters in Nabokov's fiction with whom I would have thought to connect him directly. Yet the resonance between the farewell letter and the defiantly detached "observer" is undeniable. The letter that Nabokov wrote to Svetlana Zivert' could be seamlessly inserted into the great rhetorical flourish at the end of the tale.

The Eye is a novel about the artistic process. The Smurov who speaks to us in the first person is the "easy" portrayal of the narrator. A different Smurov emerges from each other character. Smurov seeks to fuse them together into one true portrait, and the reader must try, too. It is quite impossible. Only in a casual remark toward the end do we learn that Smurov is a poet. It is a question very much open to debate as to whether *The Eye* is a study of a writer who cannot separate himself from his creativity and so fails as an artist, or whether it is a diabolically cunning illusion performed by a first-rate artist: success in the guise of failure. It is not even certain whether Smurov is alive or a fictional ghost, since the story proceeds after he has supposedly committed suicide. Another character enters the room, and it is himself, distanced. Smurov tells us that he lives by a kind of psychic momentum, the same device that Nabokov uses in his drama *Death*. We are following a false path when we search for the real Smurov in *The Eye*, and particularly so if we try to align Nabokov and his character. But that does not mean that, among the many mirrored reflections that comprise the story of the failed romance of Smurov, there aren't fiendishly concealed true facets of the real romantic failure of Nabokov in 1922. The Nice letter is emotional and very Russian. It was written in the same year and in the same sort of tone as his article about Cambridge. It is a matter not of self-analysis but of control. Smurov, like Nabokov himself, has a morbid awareness of all the possible falsely or correctly perceived reflections of himself, and he must have total control over the army of ghost reflections. If the connection that I make between Nabokov and Smurov is correct, it goes a long way to explaining the previously somewhat puzzling declaration by Nabokov in the foreword to the 1965 English translation of *The Eye* that the book contains the favorite characters of his literary youth.

Svetlana Zivert' married a handsome and heroic young officer who had lost a leg in the civil war. When, many years later, she was widowed, Svetlana drew very close to Russian Orthodoxy and lived for many years in Connecticut beside a church where she painted icons. She is still alive but does not wish to say anything about this distant incident in her life. The Schakowskoi book on Nabokov in Russian, which was the first to name Svetlana, correctly speculated on how different Nabokov's artistic voice might have been had he, in fact, married someone so strongly tied to old-fashioned Russian ways.

In Nice Nabokov had arranged to get a job on the farm of Solomon Krym, who had headed the short-lived Crimean government and had also been a friend of Nabokov's father. Krym was a comanager of the enterprise, which was owned by very wealthy Russians. He had come to France without knowing any French, studied at a boys' school, and ended up an expert vintner. Krym was himself a poet and a wit, and a man who was at the same time an extremely cultured Russian and someone who was full of fascinating Oriental lore. They became very good friends, and Nabokov remembers that, although Krym was not himself a lepidopterist, he very well understood Nabokov's need to drop his work sometimes and go in search of his butterflies. Once, when Nabokov was in the fields doing his farmwork, an elderly Englishman came by on horseback, dismounted, and asked him to hold his horse. The old man, who then pursued a two-tailed pasha around a fig tree, was startled when the bronzed young peasant inquired in taxonomically perfect Latin about which species he had been able to find in the region.

There were groves of cork trees on the plantation, and the orchards consisted of peach, apricot, and cherry trees. Nabokov was very fond of the peaches and apricots, to the point where the songbirds and sunsets on the estate came to have a peach-apricot flavor in his mind. Nabokov worked the rows of the vegetable fields, plucking asparagus, sweet peas, and corn. He was also a cherry picker, though at first with more enthusiasm than professionalism:

> Picking cherries is quite an art, quite an art. The first time I
> worked quite fast and took the ripest cherries and put them
> inside this basket which was lined with so-called American
> cloth, oilcloth. I hung it on a branch. It tumbled down and all
> the cherries were spoiled. I had to start all over again.

He would get up at six, work through the morning, drink wine, go swimming and sunbathe in the nude at about one, then return to work.

The journey to the south of France was used in *Glory*. Decades later the summer itself was used in *Ada*. The seminal scene of the burning barn—it is not actually shown in the novel—is remarkably like an incident that took place a few days after Nabokov's arrival at Beaulieu. Nabokov awakened in his attic room in the warm night to cries of what he gradually realized was *Feu! Feu!* being shouted everywhere. He was left alone in the house as everyone ran to fight the fire in the barn. They were all dipping and passing buckets from a nearby pool. When Nabokov came out to help, there was pandemonium all around him. Because he was unfamiliar with the grounds, Nabokov stepped into the water by mistake and suddenly found himself swimming. Nabokov, of course, denied that there was any connection between that scene in his life (recorded in a letter that he wrote to his mother) and the scene in *Ada*.

Nabokov had written to Svetlana that he was going to go to some corner of the earth where even her shadow couldn't reach him. But he recovered quickly enough from this mood. If chapter 46 of *Glory* bears any relation to reality, he may have seen Svetlana once more. During the summer he wrote one postcard to a girl named Vera Slonim whom he had met shortly before leaving. Nabokov and his future wife first saw each other when he came to the office of her father's short-lived publishing firm, where she was working, to negotiate a translation of Dostoevsky into English. They met shortly after that at a charity ball and began to see a lot of each other after Nabokov graduated from Cambridge and came to Berlin to live, because Nabokov often came to their apartment to play chess with her father. Vera Evseevna remembers meeting Svetlana once. At this point Nabokov was still seeing his usual three or four young women, somehow, between his lessons and his frenetic nighttime writing, which he would do scrunched up on his *pension* sofa with his writing pad held against his knees. Nabokov's recollection of himself as a young man as being a multitude of different people has considerable basis in historical fact.

10

VERA EVSEEVNA SLONIM WAS BORN IN ST. PETERSBURG ON January 5, 1902. She was one of three sisters. Her father had studied law but never practiced. During the early 1900s, Jews were entering into Russian life in a way that they had never been allowed to before, but it was at the same time the period of the "percentage norm" and many other restrictions. One of these was that a practicing lawyer had to be a Christian. Conversion was allowed and, indeed, was very simple. Evsei Slonim would not convert on principle, however, and instead taught himself forestry and became involved in financial management. His sensitivity to the issue of anti-Semitism was great. This attitude was carried on by his daughter and has been remarked upon by almost everyone who has known her. It was not a matter of religion but of family pride stretched to the extreme. Nabokov and his wife were perfectly matched in this way.

Vera was an exceptionally intelligent child and had finished six classes of the Obolensky Gymnasium in 1916 when she was only fourteen. Her early school entry had required a special permit from the Ministry of Education. The Slonims went to Odessa in the spring of 1916, and she finished her seventh term in a local school there. Even at the Obolensky she had sometimes not been a regular student but had simply sat for the end-of-year exams. It had been her intention to study physics at technical college in St. Petersburg. The Slonim family was more radical politically than the Nabokov family, but that changed quickly after the Bolsheviks seized power. In the St. Petersburg days Evsei Slonim had made wise forestry investments, and he had a partnership in a business that supplied the wooden support beams used in mining shafts. He had built a small feeder-line railway especially to bring timber from one estate to the banks of the Western Dvina River, where it was bound into enormous rafts and navigated to Riga by specially skilled peasants. A few years before the revolution Slonim was wealthy enough to purchase the greater part of an entire town in southern Russia, which he had planned to turn into a model city with a canal system.

Slonim was lucky in that his partner in timber was a friend of Hugo Stinnes, a Dutchman who was then one of the wealthiest men in the world. Through this connection it was possible for Slonim between 1920 and 1922 to arrange the speculative sale at a very low price of his own and other people's properties in Russia (after all, everyone knew that the "return" wasn't more than a few years away), and this enabled Slonim to set up successful and promising businesses in Berlin. Vera worked for her father in his import/export business (tractors were one of the major items) in 1922, and then in 1923 she went to work in his new publishing business, Orbis. She used her salary for things like horseback riding in the Tiergarten. In the very first years of the Berlin emigration there really were smart balls for charity organized by society ladies, car races, boxing matches (Nabokov wrote a poem about one in 1924), variety and pantomime shows. Both Vladimir and Vera attended all of these.

There began to be difficulties in 1923, and then, of course, the mad inflation started. Evsei Slonim was ruined once again. But both Vladimir and Vera had very smart clothes, she from the few years of her father's prosperity in the emigration, he from his years at Cambridge where one had had to have a certain amount of good clothing. Speaking of the years just before and throughout the European period of their marriage until the late 1930s, Vera has been at pains to stress that they were never poor in any clichéd way, and that, in any case, they were living in a milieu where money was never even thought of, much less talked about. If one cared about some more money, there were always additional jobs to be had. One could afford everything except a car, which no one wanted anyway, and the most expensive restaurants, where one was frequently invited by well-heeled friends.

That stylish exile is the emigration that the Nabokovs take

pride in, and if the evidence sometimes casts a shadow on this
version of reality, there can be no doubt that they themselves
never doubted it. Nabokov's cousin Nicolai wrote of Vladimir
and Vera in their Berlin years: "Nor did they ever complain or
lose their innate cheerfulness. They appeared gay and delight-
fully amusing when I visited them in Berlin." Certainly the Berlin that they lived in, the fashionably casual city with its famous
baggy clothing and homburgs of the twenties, was a comfortable
city for this sort of émigré intellectual life. The already famous
Albert Einstein once turned up for a full-dress Russian charity
ball, where there were Germans as well as Russians, wearing a
crumpled old smoking jacket, one is tempted to say, like a
Nabokov character. Of all the cities that Nabokov resided in,
Berlin happens to be the one that tourists from the future can
visit most easily because of the vogue for documentary film in
Berlin in the twenties. Walter Ruttmann's famous *Berlin, Sym-
phony of a City* places artificial stress on the tempo and theme of
a city at work—in this it was catering to the values of its audience—and has too many cheap effects such as the juxtaposition of
hungry children in the street with the food in a fine restaurant,
but for all that it does show the casual anarchy of Berlin in 1923,
certain aspects of which do indeed have the air of a Russian city.

In a letter to his mother in August 1924, Nabokov remarked almost parenthetically that it was time for him to marry and settle
down. No one expected that the girl he would marry would be
Vera Slonim. One of my sources for this period says that the
news of the marriage caused a sensation in émigré Berlin. Intense
personal privacy would be the constant throughout the life of Vera
and Vladimir. He had fits of garrulousness of which she did not
approve. She maintains that his life really consisted of his creative
work, and, when I had to interview her about her own life, she
could see no reason why she should be present in her husband's
biography. With laughter and tears Nabokov tried to help me:
"You can't help being represented! We're too far gone! It's too
late!" The marriage is and probably always will be a largely
closed book. The world will have to content itself with hints
about the relationship in the portrayal of Zina and Fyodor in *The
Gift*. Zina is shown as a guiding force who has absolute confidence that one day Fyodor will create work that will make Russia
gasp and mourn what it has lost. That much at least is certain

about Vera. She went to Sirin's poetry readings before she knew him, and she was and is not only his most devoted fan, but also very probably the first one, apart from his mother, who had total faith in his unique genius.

They had to have two witnesses when they were married in the Berlin town hall on April 15, 1925. They purposely chose two of their most casual acquaintances. In later years they disagreed about whether his mother even knew about the marriage. As they were coming out of the hall, one of their witnesses, who was German, told Nabokov that the doorman had congratulated him. "I said, 'How nice!' " Nabokov told me. "We just walked out. I didn't have, you see, a *penny* in my pocket! We had to pay a certain sum. We had paid. That was all we had."

Nabokov told Vera about the sort of romantic life he had led. She wasn't angry, more puzzled, because she had been brought up in an entirely different way. As she grew up, she became irritated by the constant attendance of her governess and had asked her mother when she could be free of her. When you are married, she was told.

There is some information about four women with whom Vladimir was having affairs in the years up to and during the time when he was getting to know Vera. They were, to say the least, a mixed lot. Olga Gzovskaya was one of the most prominent Russian film stars in Berlin. Nabokov probably met her through the Hessen family, with whom she was friendly. Joseph Hessen gave many parties for members of the émigré intelligentsia. Gzovskaya also frequented the Berlin salons of Nabokov's father. She has been described as an extremely talented comic actress who wished to play more serious roles, and also as a strongly driven careerist who tried to keep a finger in every film or theater grouping of all political tendencies. That affair was over by 1922, Nabokov said. Another girlfriend was an attractive Jewish blonde named Roma Klyachkina. After her death years later in Paris, a mutual friend named Raissa Tarr sent the letters he had written to Roma as a young man back to Nabokov in Switzerland. They may have been destroyed. The third love affair was with Beata Inaya, a girl with an olive complexion and extremely deepset dark eyes which gave her an Indian air. I very nearly missed this affair, because "Inaya" means "other" in Russian. The conversation with Nabokov and his wife went like this:

"Then you had a cousin of . . ."
"Yes, my darling. I had lots of girl pupils."
"And Inaya, was she a student?"
"No, she was not. *Don't* bring up those names! He is
going to *pounce* upon those, on all those names!"

The fourth affair was with a fat woman in a family to whom he
gave lessons. The basic incident is related in *The Eye.* This affair
is known because Nabokov told a subsequent lover about it.

In 1924 and 1925, Nabokov was probing his way toward constructing the novel *Happiness,* which ended as *Mashenka* in
1926. In doing this he was also exorcising the memory of Valentina Shulgina. Nabokov did not take his characters entirely from
life. There was always some radical splicing, inversion, or other
imaginative change. Except, that is, for the depiction of "Mary"
in the first novel:

> Honestly, I do not think that my works contain people that
> have been formed out of the disjointed members of a real
> sweetheart and so on. A phrase here. A gaze there. A phase in
> a third place. Except for the Mashen'ka girl, who was a real
> girl. About that I'm quite frank. There's hardly any inven-
> tion.

We are justified then in taking chapters 6, 8, and 9 of *Mary* as a
vibrant and very real supplement to the portrait of "Tamara" in
Speak, Memory. Tamara and Mary taken together do equal Valentina. The strength of her characterization is amplified considerably when the two sections of the two books are placed together
and accorded the status of true record. For Nabokov himself,
however, the effect was reversed. By placing it all on paper—
rowing with her on the Oredezh (there is also a poem about this
in *The Empyrean Path*), biting her neck as they kissed passionately, their long telephone conversations in which she would
sometimes place the phone over her breast, and he would pretend
that he could hear her heart beating—Nabokov neutralized and
deadened it for himself. He always claimed that "using" something or someone in his fiction effectively made it fictional in his
memory. If that account is accepted as a nearly true record, Vladimir was obsessed with Valentina. He wanted to marry her, and

when she scoffed at that possibility out of sturdy realism about their differing social status, he dreamed of setting her up in rooms as his mistress.

The plot of *Mary*—young émigré goes to railway station to meet his former lover who is arriving from Leningrad—derived from a simple incident. One of the Nabokov family maids was arriving by train from Estonia and bringing with her the dachshund from Russia that Nabokov described so wonderfully years later in *Speak, Memory* as a furious émigré dog in an ill-fitting coat. Nabokov went to the station to meet them. The maid's name was Adele. Her route—and this is the way it always was when the Nabokovs related any incident to me—was less certain:

> "This was the maid who was with us in the Crimea. She went to London with us and then came to Berlin and afterwards returned to Russia or to Estonia, and after a certain time she again came to Germany, and I went to meet her. She was the sort who just didn't know where to live, here or there. Many Russians called their dogs Boks, and so she came to us in Berlin with this Boksusha, from Petersburg or Estonia. This dog hadn't seen us for at least, say, six, seven years."

> "First, you've got it mixed up. She had been the housemaid in Petersburg, and then, when you went to the Crimea, she went home to Estonia."

> "No, no, she came with us."

> "And then from the Crimea she went to Estonia."

> "That's like our girl. That's right. They all do. From the Crimea, having completed a perfect circle, she joined us in Berlin and brought the dog. The dog was whining in an ill-tempered way and suddenly something flashed through her mind, and she began to rush all over the room. It was a large apartment in Berlin. Dashing all over the room in a fit of terrific excite-

ment, and five minutes later she made a growling noise and was exactly the same dog she had always been. This was the descendant of Chekhov's dog. Adorable."

"If he decided to sit on your leg, he *would* sit there."

Ganin decides at the last moment not to meet the train, because he suddenly understands that the affair is over and that Mary doesn't exist except as his image. Smurov makes the same decision in *The Eye*, that Vanya doesn't exist except in his imagination. This is axiomatic in Nabokov. Past and present loves are more intense as images and ideals than they could possibly be in their own right. This quixoticism of memory and love can be followed throughout Nabokov, which is not to say, of course, that he didn't strive all his life to feel Boksusha's shiver of excitement at a past that was suddenly totally restored, even if it was only for the most fleeting moment and even if the restoration was more apparent than real. But he lacked the innocence to believe. The magician can never be fooled by his own tricks, and so a spirit of coldness and cynicism began to infiltrate his art.

Apart from the feeling that they had been expelled from their Eden of the North, the cultured émigrés in Berlin were not badly situated. There were blocks where more Russian than German was heard on the streets, journals and publishing houses abounded, there was always a Russian play on the boards. Though it was to be only for a brief time, the cultural energy of Russian Berlin was at first greater than that of either Petrograd or Moscow in the years just prior to 1917.

The minor Symbolist poet and close friend of V. D. Nabokov, Nikolai Minsky, ran a coffee house at the Nollendorfplatz on the western side of Berlin. On Fridays there would be literary evenings, and émigré and traveling Soviet writers and intellectuals mingled freely. Describing this time of flux, Nicolai Nabokov wrote in his memoirs:

> In retrospect, it seems difficult to imagine that once upon a time ... so many diverse, famous, and at times antagonistic personalities could have met peacefully and fruitfully and have enjoyed their time together. Such a confluence could

never have been produced within the borders of the Russian motherland before or after the Revolution, and less than five years later it would have been impossible abroad.

Minsky's House of Arts lasted from about 1920 to 1925.

Nabokov and his wife lived in various rooms in larger flats in the Russian quarter of Berlin, chief among them Luipoldstrasse. They lived extremely busy lives. Nabokov told me that he objected terribly to the drudgery of the lessons he had to give in Berlin and far preferred the period starting in the middle thirties when fees that various organizations arranged for readings of his works in large auditoriums would sometimes supply enough money to live for up to three months. Describing the routine of the lessons he said:

> It used to tire me out terribly because it was necessary to go from one corner of town to another. I always got up tired. I would write all night. Then it was necessary to drag myself from place to place for lessons. In the rain. They would give me dinner in the houses. This was very pleasant. They would give me really astounding meals in one house. And with such enjoyment, so charmingly did they feed me. This has fixed in my memory. But then there was another type who would say, after an hour's lesson, excuse me, but I must go back to the office, to the office, and then he would accompany me back to the western part of the city attempting to make me continue the lesson all the way.

He estimated that he must have had something on the order of forty regular pupils during the decade. The lessons were for the most part in French and English and tennis, but he also gave boxing lessons and lessons in prosody. Once Joseph Hessen arranged a boxing demonstration at one of his salons in order to generate some lessons for Volodya. His sparring partner was Hessen's son George, who couldn't see too clearly without his glasses. The match presented a rather comical sight: two Russians in shorts with boxing gloves under bright lights in a Berlin living room. George unexpectedly landed a blow that gave Volodya a gushing nosebleed. As he explained apologetically afterward: "Suddenly the fog cleared for a moment, and I could see him." It was to have been a mock fight that Nabokov won, and so perhaps

Nabokov wasn't being watchful. He told me that he thought the problem might have been that he had had too much fun at Hessen's expense during the rehearsal.

Many of the details of these lesson-giving years appear in *The Gift*. His pupils were mainly young people, but there were businessmen, too. One of his pupils turned out to be a Soviet agent. Another was the son of the well-known Siberian counterrevolutionary Kozhevnikov. Nabokov told me some admiring anecdotes about this Kozhevnikov, who had been a hero in the civil war against the Bolsheviks in the Far East but eventually perished there. Once, he said, Kozhevnikov was being pursued, and there was no way to escape. So he climbed a telegraph pole and pretended he was repairing it. His widow, who had considerable money though she lost a lot of it through bad investments, wanted her son to have the best possible education. Nabokov taught him English and tennis, though there was actually very little age difference between them. These were particularly good lessons because he could always be sure of being paid in dollars. "That was the whole trick," said Nabokov.

On a few occasions Nabokov was engaged as a tutor of the sort he himself had had in St. Petersburg and at Vyra. Once, shortly after he was married, he was paid to take a boy to a Baltic resort while his parents were away. When they arrived they were informed that there was no place for them at the hotel. Just then a flushed man coming from the bar with a full glass in his hand indicated to Vera that he could provide a bed for her, however. Nabokov spun on his heel and hit the man on the jaw, dousing them both in sticky liquid. That resort and that incident were given to Nabokov's second novel, *King, Queen, Knave*.

By far his most important steady pupil was a boy named Shura Zak, whose parents were extremely wealthy. Beginning in 1927 and for a period lasting nearly two years, Nabokov gave him daily lessons in tennis, boxing, and English. This amounted to a full-time job in terms of both time and salary. These were the first years of relative comfort and security for Nabokov in the emigration, and it was in this period that he produced his second novel. When Ullstein brought out both his novels in German translations, Nabokov at once dropped his lessons and "blew" the money. He and Vera went on a vacation in the Pyrenees by first-class sleeper compartment.

For the ordinary run of lessons Nabokov would sleep very late in the morning, usually until eleven, and then go to give his lessons in the afternoon. But during the time he was working with young Shura he kept regular hours. He would go to the boy's house every day at six in the morning for breakfast. After breakfast he would lead his pupil in a session of gymnastics, and then the morning would be spent in sports and language lessons. In effect, Nabokov was a one-man finishing school for the boy, but his real job was to be a companion to him. Nabokov described him to me as a very attractive and intelligent lad but pathologically shy. After lunch and lessons they would frequently go for long walks. He would return home at about three in the afternoon.

The only student whom Nabokov obtained for prosody lessons was Mikhail Gorlin, who published one book of poetry in 1936 and very shortly afterward perished in a Nazi concentration camp together with his wife, the poet Raissa Blokh. To his subsequent regret Nabokov savaged her poetry in a *Rudder* review. Nabokov gave Gorlin English lessons, too, and they studied Milton together. They met from two to four times a week for many months. Gorlin, Nabokov recalls, was working with Professor André Mazon in Paris on the medieval Igor tale. Mazon was the first serious challenger of its authenticity. Nabokov himself was tempted by the theory, though Vera pointed out that he didn't carry the temptation any farther. "No, I can't make up my mind," he replied: "I can't. There is no proof. But there are such *strange* coincidences. Whoever wrote the Slovo and whoever wrote the Zadonshchina shared the same source. Like Taylor and Mallot."

Gorlin was a tiny fellow with curly hair who passionately loved poetry. It was said that not only could he not do things like swim or ride a bicycle, but also he didn't even know how to run. Yet, though he was very young, his name was well known to émigré academics, and Roman Jakobson is supposed to have said of Gorlin: "We await him with impatience and put much hope in him." He was certainly Nabokov's outstanding student in the European years.

It's difficult to explain what prompted Nabokov to write the attack on Blokh's 1928 volume, *My City*, when he was teaching Misha Gorlin. Nabokov thought that he was still too imbued with the spirit of harsh criticism associated with the poet Gumilyov. He regretted the review but did not change his opinion that Blokh was a bad poet. Decades later the shadow of the concentration camp fell across the memory of these two gentle young poets he had known. Nabokov said that, thinking of Blokh and Gorlin, he had wanted to make a statement about the Nazi camps in *Pnin* but that somehow or other he only touched upon them and that subject. He spoke with great feeling: "Oooloo, ooo!!! There is a sense of responsibility about this theme which I think I will tackle one day. I will go to those German camps and *look* at those places and write a *terrible* indictment . . ."

In spring and summer the relative importance of tennis lessons grew. In April 1926, Nabokov was given free membership in a "good" Berlin tennis club solely on the basis of his game. He would get three dollars for a tennis lesson, and a sunny Saturday might hold ten lessons: "I never had it, but it was a kind of possible dream." During this decade of his life Nabokov was extremely wiry. In a snapshot of him on a picnic with Vera and one of his German landlords, Herr von Dalwitz and his wife, he doesn't look as though he could weigh a hundred and forty pounds. But his weight didn't deter him from playing soccer throughout his residence in Berlin. He played with an émigré team called Unitas that competed with German clubs in Berlin. Nabokov laughed as he recalled the name of the club: "That is a word which now is used everywhere in the Soviet Union for the water-closet. Oh, yes, they put a z there—Unitaz." His last soccer game was played in 1935. Unitas was playing a team of rough factory workers and did not do too well that day. Their goalkeeper was knocked unconscious with the ball in his grip and had to be carried from the field. His head was rather brutally stomped on, he had two broken ribs, and, he said, "there were other parts of my anatomy ill-treated that day, too." Nabokov remembered that when he came to, the first thing he was aware of was a teammate impatiently trying to pry the ball, frozen in his grip, out of his arms.

One of Nabokov's teammates on Unitas was the young émigré writer Alexander Drozdov. Nabokov remembered him as a first-rate soccer player. "He looked a little bit like Bill Buckley. That type. Pink complexion and blue eyes." Drozdov edited one of the better early émigré journals, *Northern Lights*, in which Nabokov published one poem. In addition to his short stories, Drozdov published many patriotic articles, which Nabokov considered rather brilliant. But the patriotism turned to superpatriotism and then to attacks upon émigrés. One of his articles caused Nabokov, he said, to challenge him to a duel, but the challenge wasn't accepted. Drozdov began to do most of his writing for *On the Eve*, a newspaper that was the primary political bridge between the Bolsheviks and the émigrés, and then he was gone, back to Russia.

There was an enormous sense of intrigue, uncertainty, and flux in the émigré colony. The emigration, however great its other losses, possessed the lion's share of Russia's contemporary artistic and intellectual achievement, and many who were sympathetic to the revolution—Gorky, Pasternak, Ehrenburg—were perched in Berlin trying to make up their minds. Nabokov remembered seeing Bely in cafés, but he never had anything to do with him. The true emigration, he insisted, kept absolutely away from these pro-Bolshevik and fellow-traveler elements. Of course Nabokov was the whitest of the White. A fellow émigré poet recalled that Nabokov used to follow Soviet literature and engage in disputes about it:

> At that time, in the twenties, when names like Bulgakov, Akhmatova, Pasternak, Babel, Zoshchenko were glittering, Nabokov was one of the first to guess that soon there would be an end to Russian literature, and that authority was getting ready to step on its throat. People argued with him: There was nothing new about censorship in our literature, Russian writers had long ago learned to express themselves between the lines. But it was Nabokov who turned out to be right. Perhaps he argued less convincingly, but his intuition was truer.

Bunin was the writer the Soviets most wanted to lure back. "But he didn't go," Nabokov said. "They were ready to accept him with open arms. But at the last moment he didn't go. I think it was quite difficult for him not to go. It was a great temptation, a great temptation. But he didn't."

The one great loss to the emigration, as far as Nabokov was concerned, was the return of Andrei Bely, and that furnished a tragic and exemplary tale: "What we know of Bely's later writings, everything that we know, has appeared in the light of the

Soviet regime. It has been doctored and pruned, and there are a lot of things which he wrote which have never and will probably never come to light. He was *treemehndously* unhappy in Russia." As for writers like Ehrenburg, they were beneath consideration as far as Nabokov was concerned: "As a writer he doesn't exist, Ehrenburg. He is a journalist. He was always corrupt."

The émigrés who considered going back were called "change of landmark people." Aleksei Tolstoy, with whom Nabokov's father had been quite friendly, returned to Russia and wrote a novel in which he made cutting remarks about Nabokov's diplomat-uncle Konstantin. Nabokov considered him "completely tainted." Another of them, whom Nabokov knew slightly, wrote the first book about the emigration to appear in the Soviet Union in decades in 1963. Nabokov wasn't even mentioned in this book, but in 1966 he was discussed in another Soviet book, *Mirages and Reality: The Notes of an Émigré* by Dmitri Eisner, where he is described as a lean and slightly decadent young man, educated at Oxford, and an artist with no theme.

An effort was made to get "Sirin" to go back. There was a reasonably well known but unimportant writer named Tarasov-Rodionov, who was widely considered to be a Soviet agent in Berlin. His best-known work was a novel called *Chocolate*. He left a note for Nabokov at a bookstore he frequented. Nabokov told me that he never once bought a book in Berlin, but that he would read whole books little by little in the bookshops. Tarasov-Rodionov spread a panorama of the splendid things he would return to see and write about. Years later Nabokov made a comic scene of this meeting in *Bend Sinister*. He had simply gone to the meeting out of curiosity: "Just for the *heck* of it, I decided to do it." They were in a Russian-German café, and it happened that a man who was selling shoelaces—in fact, a former White officer— said something to them in Russian. "Oh, so that's what you're doing to me," said Tarasov-Rodionov, and that put an end to the recruitment. When Nabokov asserted that no Russian artist of any stature would return, Tarasov-Rodionov replied: "Well, you are wrong. I've just talked to Prokofiev, and he is returning." Other major figures besides Prokofiev and Bely included Sergei Esenin, Marina Tsvetaeva, Prince Mirsky, Viktor Shklovsky, and Pasternak. A few like Shklovsky and Pasternak survived, but the others ended tragically.

On November 18, 1927, on the tenth anniversary of the 1917 revolution, Nabokov wrote a stirring émigré *profession de foi* for *The Rudder*. The article is Nabokov's sole piece of political rhetoric in his European period. He had spoken at the Cambridge debate, but his speech was mostly one of his father's articles that he had memorized. In the 1927 article Nabokov speaks stirringly of "ten years of contempt, ten years of fidelity, ten years of freedom." Bolshevism is simply "Philistine boredom," whereas the emigration is a wave of Russia that has left her shores and is enjoying a spiritual freedom such as no other people have perhaps ever enjoyed. Nabokov ends his article by proclaiming: "Let us not curse exile. Let us repeat in these days the words of that ancient warrior about whom Plutarch wrote: 'During the night, in desolate fields far from Rome, I would pitch my tent, and my tent was Rome to me.' " Amusingly, the moving citation from Plutarch was Nabokov's own invention. "An Anniversary" is Nabokov's public face in its best profile. It is a document that has a place in the intellectual history of Russia in the twentieth century.

Until about 1927 Nabokov maintained high hopes of a return after the fall of the Soviets. "Not later. Not later. But until then it was an optimistic mist. A mist of optimism. I think that by the middle thirties we had just given up the idea of going back. And it didn't matter much, because Russia was with us. *We* were Russia. We represented Russia. The thirties were pretty hopeless. The thirties were romantic and hopeless. It was romantic despair."

Both of Vera's parents died in 1928. Her father's death came after a protracted and expensive illness. She began to do interpreting in the city, chiefly for American tourists. Her German was excellent, though she chose not to socialize with Germans. She took a stenography course in 1930 and then worked for about eight months for a legal firm that acted for the commercial section of the French embassy. Sometimes she worked on contracts and letters at home as well as in the office, and she worked at the French Embassy. At the same time, she also was giving English lessons. But her main source of income was from French stenography. She came to be called on particularly for conventions. Her last work of this sort, which was already in Hitler's time, was a wool convention at which four of Hitler's deputies appeared. She was apparently put forward because they couldn't find another suitable simultaneous translator. She told the man who'd suggested her that she wouldn't be taken, because she was Jewish. She contacted the chancellery of the appropriate ministry anyway and forewarned them that she was Jewish. She was told: "Oh, but it doesn't make *any* difference to us. We pay no attention to such things. Who told you we did?" That was in 1935, and it was frequently cited by Vera Nabokov as her favorite story about Nazi Germany. The story shows Vera Nabokov acting with steely cool and fearlessness as the menace of fascism gathered.

It is, however, difficult to understand how anyone could have survived in Berlin in 1936–37 by stressing her Jewishness. Vera Nabokov had blond hair and spoke good German, and could easily have been taken for German or Scandinavian. The Nabokovs lingered, almost until the last possible minute, in Hitler's Germany. Certainly, steely bravery was a part of Vera's self-image. She said proudly that once, before she met her husband, she was to have taken part in an assassination attempt upon Trotsky, but Trotsky's trip to Berlin was, unfortunately, canceled at the last minute.

The Nabokovs agreed that, whatever its drawbacks, from their particular perspective life in Berlin was in many respects far more interesting than the second stage of emigration in Paris. Émigré culture was flourishing, there was still hope, Sirin was recognized, there was intrigue and color. It was the most intense period of his literary life. In terms of his writing, this seventeen-year span would have no equal until the years at Cornell.

11

THERE WERE TWO MAJOR LITERARY SALONS IN THE EARLY years of émigré Berlin. One was for young writers and the other for older, established writers. Sirin visited the one as an old master and the other as the most promising of the young Berlin émigrés, "our new Turgenev."

The older circle was that of Raissa Tatarinov (in later years, when she was living in France, she shortened it to Tarr), the wife of one of the editors of *The Rudder*. She had an exceptionally gracious nature and the ability to bring together people of sharply differing views in a harmonious way, though there were no German writers at her salon and very few "change-of-landmark" émigrés either.

Madame Tatarinov's literary circle met once a week, usually in large apartments and houses, though as usual there were difficulties in establishing the venue in my conversations with the Nabokovs years later:

> "It was not a sitting room, it was our bedroom, dar-
> ling. Because it was the room where the beds were in
> one corner."

> "You had another little room."

> "We didn't have our guests in the living room. It was

much too small. It was in the big room, where there was plenty of room. There was a big table where we would have tea and cakes and everything. It was not on Passauerstrasse but on . . ."

"NO, NO, NO! It was there, because I remember we were living at the von Dalwitz house in Passauerstrasse, and it was at the latest 'twenty-eight."

However that may have been, the Tatarinov gatherings always proceeded in the same very precise way. Someone would read. Someone would recite or perform. Afterward tea was served. After that anyone who wanted to could make comments or ask questions. "And then we went home. That was it."

Nabokov made a practice of reading his stories or extracts from his novels in progress at the Tatarinov circle, his poetry in the younger group, which was called the Poets' Circle. It is recorded that on one occasion in the early period of the Tatarinov salon Nabokov's sister Olga, who was by then a striking beauty, recited some of his poetry. There were times when Nabokov read critical pieces, too. One was called "The Triumph of the Do-Gooder" and was about Soviet literature. Another, more fleeting literary club that Nabokov belonged to was called Arzamas. It was named after a group to which Pushkin had belonged. And in addition to that, there was a Russian restaurant, the Green Parrot, on Passauerstrasse where the poets who appeared in *The Rudder* used to gather regularly. The literary life of Russian Berlin was expressed in spoken form as much as in print.

At one of the Tatarinov gatherings in the beginning of 1926 Nabokov had a far more resounding success than the one his translated lyrics won him in the Crimea. It was a "booklaunch" in the decades-later sense of the term for a talented writer who was also the son of V. D. Nabokov. Nabokov read *Mary* in its entirety in a three-hour sitting with one intermission. The company included the distinguished philosopher Grigory Landau and *The Rudder*'s regular literary critic Yuly Aikhenval'd, a key figure in Madame Tatarinov's circle. The novel was warmly received. It was Aikhenval'd that evening who spoke of Sirin as our "new Turgenev." Nabokov told me that Aikhenval'd had been very kind to his first novel in that he scarcely mentioned it in his *Rud-*

der review, which isn't really a fair description of the review. The review, if it was slightly more restrained than the exalted verbal opinion, was all the same warm and laudatory. There were nine other printed reviews, two of them by well-known writer Mikhail Osorgin and the literary historian Konstantin Mochulsky, only one of which was more positive than Aikhenval'd's. That review was a second notice in *The Rudder*, two weeks after Aikhenval'd's (which says much about the paper's commitment to the fortunes of the young Nabokov), which said: "This is a page not only in the biography of a young author, but also in the history of Russian literature, and not merely its émigré branch. *Mashen'ka* has something about it of the national self-awareness of the Russian intelligentsia." Unfortunately, the critic then goes on to compare Sirin not only with Turgenev, but with Chernyshevsky. Could this absurd comparison have been the seed of the parodic attack on Chernyshevsky in *The Gift*? Such insignificant incidents that blossom into major themes may be seen throughout Nabokov's career. However that may be, all ten of the reviews were respectful. *Mary* had a clear *succès d'estime* in émigré Berlin and Paris. During that evening in January 1926, Landau's wife, in the time set aside for commentary, said that the problem with the novel was that its style was overly polished, which was a more plainspoken variant of Aikhenval'd's Turgenev compliment, which may have had a certain amount of concealed reserve in it. (Actually, the true influence in the rich, evocative style was that of Bunin, but then Aikhenval'd was right in that Bunin himself belongs in the Turgenev line of literary descent.) Nabokov may have listened to the criticism, since his next novel was a radical departure from the first, and the evocative throb, though it was always present in his prose, was kept strictly subordinate until about 1935 when he was a fully acknowledged master of Russian modernism. Then he allowed it to come back again in short stories such as "Spring in Fialta" and in his longest and last Russian novel, *The Gift*. The carefully controlled vibrato of *Mary* sounded most fully, of course, in certain of his English works, most notably in *Speak, Memory* and, to a lesser extent, *Pnin.*

Mary is built on the simple and time-honored principle of the Grand Hotel grouping: a number of people living in a single hotel, rooming house, dormitory, or ship and the—always—complex web of relationships that develops among them. *Mary* is, however, deceptively simple and terse. We don't learn, for example, that the opening scene with Mary's husband takes place in a stalled elevator until later, by which time all the inhabitants of the *pension* have been introduced and several secondary plots set in motion. The novel's hero is having an affair with a girl toward whom he feels a mounting sense of revulsion. One evening he goes to the movies with both her and another girl who is hopelessly in love with him, and it chances to be a film in which he has been a prominent extra. That incident in the novel is based on an actual occurrence, when Nabokov went to the movies with a friend, the writer Ivan Lukash, and just this did happen, for, like many young Russians in Berlin Nabokov had frequently worked as a movie extra. Lukash refused to believe that it was really his friend who had flashed across the screen. There is another scene in *Mary* that interests me very much indeed: the hero searching in Mary's husband's room for any photographs. For this scene is very much like the spying Smurov does in his rooming house in *The Eye*. Could such an incident have taken place in the young Nabokov's life?

Although the progression of the action in *Mary* is rather rapid, the tale at the same time has a certain stillness and conveys the impression of being a series of hundreds of very carefully chiseled cameos or bas-relief scenes. Some of these cameos have a Chekhovian ring:

> "Do you, well, do you love Russia?"
> "Very much."
> "That's precisely it. One must love Russia. Without our émigré love there's nothing left for Russia. No one there loves her."

This novel's reputation has doubtless not been helped by Nabokov's affectionate but very condescending introduction to its English translation, published forty-five years after its first appearance in Russian. But the novel cannot be squashed. It has some of the evocative power of *Speak, Memory*. Like Hemingway's first novel *The Sun Also Rises*—which was also published in 1926—the novel occupies a special and, in my view, notable place.

Yuly Aikhenval'd was the leading émigré literary critic. In the years just prior to the revolution he and Kornei Chukovsky were the most influential nonacademic literary critics. His three-volume collection of impressionistic essays, *Silhouettes of Russian Writers*, went through many editions. The son of a rabbi from the south of Russia, he became a Christian not in rebellion or for social convenience but, some said, through a sincere belief that acceptance of the Orthodox faith might somehow bring him closer to Russian culture, which was the main love of his life. He was a very small man, and his expression was permanently crinkled by near-sightedness that his glasses did little to correct.

Aikhenval'd was an extremely strict judge. Although Joseph Hessen was editor of both the publishing house The Word and *The Rudder*, he could not budge Aikhenval'd to write a word of praise about The Word's novels by the popular émigré writer Mark Aldanov, which Aikhenval'd did not like. Doubtless there was some element of hesitation, too, in his opinion of *Mary*, which caused Hessen to have to bring in a second reviewer. Yet he was unquestionably the first important critic to grant recognition to Nabokov. Although he had not much liked Nabokov's early poetry, he had spotted his talent even before *Mary* and had clipped out and collected all the Sirin pieces that appeared in newspapers and journals. Looking back on Aikhenval'd as a critic, Nabokov said:

> He adopted a strange method of writing an article on this or that author in the style of that author. That produced a stylistically pretentious effect. At the same time he had been responsible for demolishing two *frauds*, two puffed-up writers, Briusov and Gorky. I think he was a first-rate critic. The only thing I disliked about his style was this somewhat precious way he had of using the words and phrases of his author. His style was too sweet perhaps. But very honest. Extremely honest.

Aikhenval'd was a true Russian, or, more precisely, he showed the Russian character at its finest. Everyone seems to have liked him. He always used to tell the story against himself of how he had been snubbed by Tolstoy.

It is noticeable that Jews, if one includes both the nonpracticing and baptized for the moment in a loose categorization, played a key role in émigré culture. This role may sometimes be overlooked for the simple fact that this influence was most frequently exercised in the manner of Aikhenval'd, that is, without any special cause or barrow to push. Fondaminsky's support of *Contemporary Annals* in Paris for twenty years, Marc Slonim's key role in encouraging Russian literature in Prague, Hessen's editorship of *The Rudder* and The Word, another publishing house, Petropolis, which was run by Raissa Blokh's elder brother, Mark Aldanov's editorship of *The New Review*, Roman Grynberg's of *Aerial Ways*, there are many examples. Nabokov has been accused in the emigration of having deserted Russian Orthodoxy (in the history of Russian literature, even in the Soviet period, very few major writers have done this), whereas in marrying Vera Slonim Nabokov participated in an important and fruitful cultural intermingling.

King, Queen, Knave appeared in 1928. Aikhenval'd praised this novel in much stronger terms than the previous one, and this time there were many other positive reviews as well. The Nabokovs gave a small party just after the book was published. There were about eight people there, and it lasted until about one in the morning, which was unusual. The guests spent much of the evening talking animatedly about Russia and reciting poetry while gathered around the stove in the corner of the room. Aikhenval'd was soon to depart on a short lecture trip among the émigré community in Estonia, and he was in an especially good mood because he had just received word from his family in the Soviet Union (he had been expelled in 1922 along with many other intellectuals) that he had become a grandfather. The evening was extraordinarily successful. As Nabokov was seeing his guests out, Aikhenval'd somehow caught the cuff of his overcoat on an ornamental projection on the stairway, and the young novelist had to, literally, get his critic off the hook. On his way home Aikhenval'd crossed the Kurfurstendamm and saw too late a tram clattering its way through the Berlin night, a death exactly like the one Nabokov had depicted four years earlier in "A Catastrophe." After his death the Tatarinov circle was formally named the Aikhenval'd Circle in his honor.

As its title suggests, *King, Queen, Knave* is a stark triangle. The source of the novel's title is a posthumously published Hans Christian Andersen tale of the same title. Andersen's fable was written in 1868, but certain of his friends thought it too revolutionary and persuaded him not to publish it. Nabokov denied that the Andersen tale had anything to do with the genesis of his novel, but a Russian translation of that fable had appeared in *The Rudder* in February 1927. Nabokov began to write his novel in July of that same year and finished it in June 1928. Nabokov's attention was obviously caught by the manner in which the tale is told: all of its characters are paper figures living in a house of cards, and the novel is effected in just this two-dimensional fashion. But what Nabokov was really about in this novel can be understood if it is placed against a background of, in the Russian tradition, the consciously highly artificial theatricality of Meyerhold or, more immediately, the German Expressionism that was all around him.

Nabokov claimed to know almost no German and to be indifferent to the Germans and German art. In the English introduction to *King, Queen, Knave*, Nabokov says: "I spoke no German, had no German friends, had not read a single German novel either in the original or in translation." In *The Gift* Fyodor thinks to himself that *even* the Berliners around him must have poets among them, puny perhaps, but poets all the same.

Only one interview with Nabokov was published during his entire European émigré period. It appeared in the Estonian paper *Today* in November 1932. Nabokov railed against what he said were the commonplaces and inaccuracies of this interview, but I think it more likely that the older writer was simply trying to erase the more plainspoken answers that he then gave in regard to influences, a subject on which he always was prickly. When the interviewer asked Sirin about the charge that his work simply imitated foreign models, he said:

> That's amusing! Yes, they have slated me for being under the
> influence of German writers whom I do not know. I speak
> and read German poorly, by the way. One might more prop-
> erly speak about a French influence: I love Flaubert and
> Proust. It is curious that I felt my closeness to Western cul-
> ture while I was still in Russia, but here, in the West, I have
> not consciously followed any Western writer. Here one espe-
> cially feels the charms of Gogol and—closer to us in time—
> Chekhov.

It provides a useful formula: themes of Western literature for his Russian readers, the time-honored stylistic tricks of Russian literature for his English readers. That does not mean at all that Nabokov is derivative. It is simply that his writing manner has a

much-stamped passport, and the reader who is not comfortable in
French and Russian literature and German film and Expressionist
art must lose not the text but a certain vital context.

It is useful, too, to have the simple declaration that Nabokov
did read and speak German, however poorly, for later he would
deny that he knew any German at all. One of the most valuable
scholarly finds in recent years concerning the sources of Nabokov's early work began with a passing derisive mention of a best-
selling German novel, by Leonhard Frank, in a 1932 Nabokov
short story, "The Reunion." Frank's novel is *The Brothers*. It is
about incest, and thus, "philistine tripe" though it may be, it has
to be counted as one of the background sources of *Ada*. But that
mention in the story led the investigating scholar to compare
Frank's work with Nabokov's writing of the period, and a remarkably close passage was found in Nabokov's chess novel, *The
Defense*, which he was writing at the time (1929) that *The
Brothers* appeared. Frank wrote:

> All the shop windows were now illuminated . . . and a life-
> sized wax figure, a man with two heads, one face cheerful and
> one bitterly aggrieved, constantly drew aside the lapels of his
> coat, showing first a pique waistcoat stained with ink, and
> then—beaming—the other side, snow-white, because the
> fountain pen in the pocket was of a non-leaking sort.

And now Nabokov in *The Defense*, which appeared in Fondaminsky's *Contemporary Annals* about six months after the appearance of Frank's novel:

> He stopped stock-still in front of a stationery store where the
> wax dummy of a man with two faces, one sad and the other
> joyful, was throwing open his jacket alternately to left and
> right: the fountain pen clipped into the left pocket of his
> white waistcoat had sprinkled the whiteness with ink, while
> on the right was the pen that never ran.

Were it not for the chance mention of Leonhard Frank in the
short story, there would have been every reason to assume that
the two Berlin novelists were merely looking at the same shop
window. Frank, who was a far more complicated and interesting
writer than Nabokov allows, stood on the periphery of German
Expressionism. Many of his stories are intensely sexual and are

told in a rapidly shifting manner clearly taken from contemporary German cinema. This essentially was where Nabokov also stood, on the periphery of German Expressionism but incorporating many of its innovations into his novels. There can be no doubt that during his bookshop visits Nabokov paid attention to a good deal more than Russian literature. It is not too much to say that Nabokov is, among other things, the sole Russian Expressionist writer.

One further illustration will suffice. *The Gift* is Nabokov's most sustained treatment of his life in Berlin in the twenties. In 1934 Nabokov received an important gift. A friend who was an historian and the son-in-law of one of the editors of *The Rudder* provided him with a list of the names of aristocratic Russian families which had died out. Nabokov, who was just beginning to write *The Gift,* used one of them, Godunov-Cherdyntsev, for his hero, and the list essentially furnished the names of Nabokov's major characters for the next five years. But what of the name of the heroine of *The Gift,* Zina Merz? Zina isn't an Orthodox Christian name. Merz is a perfectly plausible russified German Jewish name. The real significance of the name, however, lies elsewhere, in a rather mischievous hidden coding. Two of the main leaders of the Berlin Dada movement were Kurt Schwitters and Richard Hulsenbeck. They represented antagonistic tendencies within the boisterous movement. In an essay on the history of Dadaism and in his *Dada Almanach* Hulsenbeck held that ". . . Dada is carrying on a kind of propaganda against culture . . . All in all art should get a good thrashing." Schwitters was strongly opposed to the cultural nihilism and political activism of Hulsenbeck and advocated a Dadaism committed to pure art. He called his movement Merz: "Hulsendadaism is oriented toward politics and against art and culture. I am tolerant and allow every man his own opinions, but I am compelled to state that such an outlook is alien to Merz. As a matter of principle Merz strives only toward art, because no man can serve two masters." The explanation of Zina that suggests itself after one knows this is, I fear, rather awkward, for Zina is the easy anagram of Nazi. If so, it is another instance of the sort of mad secret doodle that Nabokov would, as we shall see, leave to posterity in the name of his greatest heroine, Lolita, thereby plunging himself into the whirlpool of psychological speculation that all the world knows he despised so much.

12

NABOKOV NEEDN'T HAVE KNOWN MUCH GERMAN AT ALL IN order to be greatly influenced by German art in Berlin. He was from the first not only a working extra but a film buff and Berlin was, of course, the Hollywood of its time. The most important Berlin filmmaker for Nabokov was in all probability Fritz Lang. Lang's *Scarlet Street* has to be taken into account, decades later, in the stylistic conceptualization of *Lolita*. The hard metallic edge of *King, Queen, Knave* probably owes something to Lang's famous *Metropolis*. It's reasonable to assume that *King, Queen, Knave* was written with a clear eye on the possibility that it might be made into a film. That would certainly provide the most logical explanation for the sudden shift into German characters. Nabokov complained in a letter to his mother that the characters in the novel he was writing were boring him to distraction. But he saw it through, and he later wrote another novel, *Camera Obscura* (subsequently retitled *Laughter in the Dark*), without Russian characters.

When the characters of *King, Queen, Knave* aren't thinking of each other as objects, they make objects of themselves. Feet go out of control, a head is at risk of sailing around the room, a wife becomes a clothes mannequin, a husband a corpse with glasses. In this cardboard stylization only the husband, Dreyer, seems at times to have a secret, real life. When their train stops at a station Dreyer strolls on the platform and toys with the idea of running away to circle the world. He doesn't, but he is one of the early

Nabokovian characters who dream of finding a way out of their constricting world. In the 1930 short story, "The Aurelian," the hero is swept away by this urge.

The knave of the novel has just a suggestion of a real life in the past when he was a boy in his native village. Dreyer once had a genuine love affair, but—a very Nabokovian theme—he regrets it when he chances to meet his old love because this "Erika number two" spoils his memories of the original Erika he knew. If we judge Nabokov's philosophy by the consistent behavior of his most sympathetic characters, then we are bound to draw the conclusion that he chooses to see the world in an antiplatonic way. That is, the illusion or the memory, the shadows on the wall, always have preference over the reality.

The novel is clearly not "about" Berlin or Berliners. It is a skeletal, eternal story, and, when its movement has once been traced, any other set of characters could be led over Nabokov's carefully placed chalk marks. Different as they are, Marta Dreyer (who almost drowns her husband) and Charlotte Haze (who is almost drowned *by* her husband) join hands across borders and decades. If there is a Russian influence upon *King, Queen, Knave*, it is that of Andrei Bely, specifically, Bely's innovative use of distance and the geometric figures formed by various relationships as a means of conveying the emotional value and reality of those relationships. Nabokov's figures are placed "in an unseen geometric figure, and they were two points moving along it, and the relation between these two points could be felt and calculated at any given moment—and although it seemed that they moved freely, they were, however, strictly bound by the unseen, merciless lines of that figure." This statement applies equally to Bely's prose.

Mannequins are important in *King, Queen, Knave*. This, at least, was a realistic feature of the novel, because it was the period of the first robots, and the large shops and department stores along Berlin's Friedrichstrasse were full of them.

In early 1928 Nabokov had mounted a forced march to complete *King, Queen, Knave*, which he had begun the previous year. He went to a doctor, a lung specialist, and paid a fee to find out how to kill his heroine: " 'I have to kill her,' I said to him. "He looked at me in stony silence." As he worked on the novel he had the urge to put it aside and occupy himself with butterflies again, but he resisted. Butterflies were one of the passions Nabokov sacrificed throughout most of the twenties. In 1925, while on the way to his pupil Shura Zak early in the morning, he saw an extremely rare large moth on the trunk of a linden tree near the Charlottenburg railway station. He captured it with his hat and took it alive straight to the astounded owner of a nearby butterfly shop to whom he sold it. In 1926 he had visited the Entomological Institute at Dahlem on the outskirts of Berlin with a Russian friend. While there he became acquainted with the noted entomologist Moltrecht, a corpulent and red-cheeked scholar with a politician's extinguished cigar clamped between his teeth, who gruffly but delicately handled the butterflies and spoke of them so eloquently and with so much feeling that Nabokov was deeply moved. The novel was finally completed in May, when his mother came to visit them from Prague, and he read the entire work to her in five or six successive evenings.

Nabokov was a good performer, and in those years there were many literary evenings, though they usually did not pay or paid very little. In the main he read poetry. The following dates for public readings have been gleaned from public newspaper announcements and accounts: a reading on March 25, 1924, at the Flugerverband (Schoneberger Ufer 40); on April 18, 1924 (Fasanenstrasse, 78, am Kurfurstendamm); a reading at an unspecified place (of a poem about Pushkin which appeared four days later in *The Rudder*) on June 10, 1925; a reading on April 1, 1926, in the apartment of Joseph Hessen; another reading at an unspecified place on April 9, 1926; a literary evening in October 1926, where he was summoned from the audience and did an impromptu recital with great success; on November 24, 1926; a reading of a poem about Joan of Arc on November 18, 1927 (Fasanenstrasse, 23); on November 24, 1927, at an assembly marking the tenth anniversary of the Volunteer White Army; on November 28, 1927, at the Café Leon with Ofrosimov and another friend; at an Easter Festival on April 24, 1928; and at an evening celebrating the centenary of Tolstoy's birth on September 12, 1928. Somewhat later, on March 3, 1930, Nabokov read *The Eye* in its entirety to a large auditorium.

That chance list might, of course, be only a part of the total number of literary evenings where Nabokov read. He was a popular reader, and in those readings that I have discovered through press accounts the success of Sirin is almost invariably singled out. On November 24, 1926, for example, during an evening dedicated to the theme of St. Petersburg, Nabokov read a series of sonnets on the city, and a newspaper account of the evening reported: "For a long time the audience held him on the podium with its applause." As we discussed these readings Nabokov said rather matter-of-factly: "I always had a friendly audience, being a man of *tremendous* charm when I was young. I had, I . . . Really, darling, really!!" His wife was smiling quizzically as he spoke. "And should I say yes, or should I say no, or what?" "I dunno . . . And humor. Charm and humor." There was laughter, led by Nabokov.

The vaguely cinematic atmosphere of *King, Queen, Knave* obviously proceeded naturally from Nabokov's work as a film extra in the same way that the text-cum-footnotes form of *Pale Fire* has roots in his American academic experience. He did most of his film work in 1923–24, and Vera did some, too, before she knew him. The payment for such walk-ons amounted to about two days' rent, never significant enough to matter but always welcome. In July 1924, a minor film star whom he was seeing (it was after his affair with Gzovskaya, but Nabokov could not remember her name) took him to meet her director. She told him that Nabokov was an actor who had had a great deal of experience in southern Russia, which would have been a reference to the part he played in the Schnitzler play in the Crimea. Nabokov was walked around and looked over approvingly for two hours and then offered the lead in a new film, but like so many plans in feverish Berlin nothing came of it.

The film industry was at its height in Berlin between 1925 and 1930. And Russian companies were very active. The three main Russian companies were Viking-film, Nivo-film, and Kharitonov-film. Gzovskaya acted for Kharitonov. In addition, several Russian directors such as Bukhovetsky and Protazanov worked for the large German organizations UFA and EFA. Nabokov remembered one film in which he was prominently seen because he happened to be the only person there wearing evening dress (his old London dinner jacket), and so the camera focused on him during a scene showing an audience at the theater: "I remember I was standing in a simulated theater in a box and clapping, and something was going on on an imaginary stage . . . I don't think *that* film will ever be found. I got that little job through somebody who'd go there, and I went instead. You know, that kind of thing." The film would seem from the description of that scene to have been *The Dying Torch*, which was produced by Dewesti and starred Mozzhukhin, the prerevolutionary film star who is mentioned in *Speak, Memory*, but the search for a copy of the film has been going on for many years now, and it may indeed no longer exist. Only a handful of archival copies of Russian films made in Berlin survived the bombings of World War II.

Nabokov worked with his friend Ivan Lukash, another aspiring young writer, to produce film scenarios. Lukash and Nabokov saw each other frequently for several years. Lukash was also from St. Petersburg, and since he published poetry under the pseudonym Ivan Oredezh, we may assume that he had even more in common with Nabokov. An accepted script in those years might earn the equivalent of about five thousand dollars in today's terms. They never made it, but at one point they had requests from three different directors to submit scripts. Nabokov grasped that the genre had its own demands, and he gave himself over to the task of scriptwriting with his usual determination. He had a filmic sense and may be considered one of the earliest novelists to have demonstrated this talent. His best scenario, *The Love of a Dwarf*, became "The Potato Elf." That did indeed come close to being made into a film when the Hollywood producer Lewis Milestone, who had received an Oscar for *All Quiet on the Western Front*, read a manuscript translation of the story that was done by an émigré who was working in Hollywood. Milestone not only wanted to turn "The Potato Elf" into a film, but he also wanted to bring Nabokov to Hollywood to develop other story lines as well. The producer's agent met Nabokov in Berlin in January 1932 and wrote in his diary afterward: "He grew very excited at this. He told me that he literally adores the cinema and watches motion pictures with great keenness." Unfortunately, this meeting took place only a few months before the Great Depression put the brakes on Hollywood budgets.

Nabokov and Lukash also invested a lot of time in the early years in the popular Blue Bird Theater on Holzstrasse, a cabaret loosely modeled after a famous theatrical café (Nabokov had gone there) in literary St. Petersburg. The Blue Bird was run by the talented director Yuzhny and featured dramatic skits. Both Lukash and Sirin had acknowledged authorship of sketches in the programs. The skits were not casual affairs. A great deal of care and skill went into the costumes and scenery. In a letter to his mother in 1925 Nabokov describes how he had spent the previous day: He got up at seven and went to the outskirts of the city for a film take from which he didn't return until five. The next day his eyebrows were still blackened from the makeup that wouldn't come off, and he was still seeing bright spots in front of his eyes from the blinding lights. Between five and eight he had given lessons, and after eight he attended a rehearsal for a new show at the Blue Bird. Blue Bird shows began at eight thirty, and there were ten to twelve skits, each lasting about ten minutes. There were ten new shows each year. Nabokov didn't say in his letter to his mother, but doubtless it was also true that still later that night he worked for many hours on his writing. He was for most of his life an insomniac and slept only a few hours a night. He had told the interviewer for the Estonian paper: "Sometimes I write for twelve hours nonstop. I grow ill when I do this and feel very badly. And sometimes one has to copy out what one has done innumerable times—there are short stories on which I have worked for two months. Sometimes it's necessary to rewrite and change every word."

Unfortunately the Blue Bird paid only sporadically, and in the end Nabokov threatened them with legal action. "They still owe me money!" he told me with undiminished indignation half a century later. Another unprofitable venture on which Nabokov worked with Lukash and a composer named Yakobson from Riga was the staged ballet/symphony called *Agaspher* about which Nabokov exclaimed: "Horrible! If I have it, if I see it, I will destroy it!" Nabokov wrote other pieces for Russian cabarets and theaters together with Lukash. The other writer from the Blue Bird with whom Nabokov was friendly was Yury Ofrosimov, the one who later, as a director, commissioned Nabokov to write *The Man from the USSR*, a play about a double agent.

Lukash had also begun to write just before the revolution. He was perhaps Nabokov's most promising rival of his generation in Berlin. At one time Lukash was associated with the slightly pretentious Ego-Futurist movement and published poetry in the style of Walt Whitman. (Whitman had been popularized in Russia by Kornei Chukovsky.) He served as a White officer during the civil war and was married to an Armenian girl in Berlin. They had a child. Nabokov recalled that the baby would be deposited on a window sill while Lukash paced up and down imagining a routine on which they were working. Lukash was an even more prolific writer than Nabokov in the early years of the emigration. In 1923, when Nabokov published his two books of poems, Lukash published three books of prose. He published numerous short stories and sketches in the same journals that Nabokov published in, and, in all, eight books. They are old-fashioned historical novels, which are sometimes quite good and enjoyed a certain popularity in the émigré community.

Lukash's two best books were *The Flames of Moscow* and *The Snowstorm*, a novel about the life of Moussorgsky in St. Petersburg. *The Flames of Moscow* concerns the various intrigues and movements in Russia in the period after Catherine the Great. It has much in it to explain the age-old problems of Russia, and much to place the Silver Age of Russian literature and the emigration that was its concluding phase in perspective, as when, for example, a character meditates on St. Petersburg and the rest of Russia. The passage is worth quoting because it perfectly frames the subject of this book historically:

> But the masses that thronged somewhere down below, under the portals of the Empire, the primitive, ignorant, uncultured people with bushy beards right up to their eyes, with a revolting habit of bowing right to the ground, merchants waddling like fat blue geese, priests with long greasy hair who looked like bearded women, the sour smells and stuffiness of the poor houses, the dusty deserts of the provinces—this unendurably dull and depressing Russia, gaudy and absurd, heavy and violent—roused in him feelings of hostility, fear, and disgust. He ardently desired her freedom, culture, civic rights—he hardly knew himself what he wished—that she might grow light, tall, and graceful like the colonnades beyond the Neva, like the beautiful glittering goddess on that lofty dome.

One remembers the young Nabokov's haughty schoolboy poetry. He could see those columns and that statue a very short stroll from his father's St. Petersburg townhouse.

Nabokov described Lukash as an exceptionally talented man with marvelous Russian but at something of a disadvantage in the emigration because he was so absolutely Russian and thoroughly divorced from any contact with Western culture. He said of his novels: "They are beautifully written. The style is superb. But they lack something, they lack some kind of compositional fire which he never had." Nabokov uses Lukash as the character Bubnov in *Glory*. It is made clear there that there was a certain edginess in the friendship of Nabokov and Lukash. Like Lukash, Bubnov wears a bow tie and has an open face with a high forehead. Nabokov said that Lukash was such a purely Russian type and that either he or his father—he couldn't remember which—had been used as a model by Repin. He had a Tolstoyan nose. Eventually Lukash left Berlin. He went to Riga and then to Paris with his family to ghost the autobiography of a popular singer named Nadezhda Plevitskaya. Later, after the kidnapping of General Miller in Paris, it was revealed that Plevitskaya and her husband had been active Soviet agents in Berlin. It was then assumed among Berlin émigrés that the guileless and talkative Lukash must have told Plevitskaya at least as much as he heard from her, for Lukash knew every Russian in literary Berlin, and the Soviets were interested not only in wooing émigré writers, but also in keeping track of their activities.

Nabokov told the story of Plevitskaya in one of his English stories, "The Assistant Producer," in 1943. The circumstances of the story more or less echo what did happen in 1938. The story's La Slavska has sung both for the czar and for Comrade Lunacharsky. Her husband is a former White general who was a secret Soviet agent. Nabokov had known Plevitskaya reasonably well. He used to meet her and her husband at parties. "I actually visited her where she lived in Berlin. Then I met her in Paris. Plevitskaya had a fine voice. I think she had some talent, but she was rather trite. She was a corny singer." I asked Nabokov why he had written a story that followed such a well-known incident (to Russians, that is) so closely. Once again he didn't answer. "Ah, why. Oh, why. I don't know. Perhaps yes. Yes, it's closer to a general reality than I ever approach. Perhaps yes." "The Assistant Producer" is one of those Nabokov stories that is presented like a movie scenario, in this case a cheap movie scenario that is quite improbable.

Shappy émigré Berlin was charged with intrigue. The émigré cabdriver who indignantly ordered visiting Soviets from his taxi might turn out to be a Soviet agent himself. *The Rudder*, which was virtually a large family unit of Russian liberals most of whom had known and worked with each other for more than a decade, was nearly penetrated by the NKVD. A secretary at the paper who was burdened with a seriously ill mother and had no means to have her cared for adequately, was approached by a young writer with a proposal to make paid reports on what was happening in the office twice a week. *The Rudder* was at that time printing many smuggled-out reports from within Russia. When the writer was revealed to be an agent, he vanished from Berlin. Nabokov had given him lessons. It is said that this writer, Ivan Konoplin, became a major in the Soviet army but was caught up in the purges and died in a concentration camp. There was probably something of this, too, in the eloquent articles praising the emigration by Nabokov's fellow poet and soccer player Alexander Drozdov (he was the only one before Nabokov to do this) just two years before his own return to the USSR.

One intermittent long-term job that Nabokov had was to translate news articles for an English paper. The stories were written by the nephew of the Korostovetz who had signed Russia's surrender with Nabokov's Uncle Konstantin in 1905. There were difficulties about whether Nabokov and his wife worked on the articles together or separately, and also whose daughter the wife of Korostovetz was:

> "Well, anyway, I remember her very clearly. A very attractive woman. And I remember the first time that I went to his hotel. He lived in a small but rather good hotel in the Freidrichstrasse. I went to see him to talk about those translations we were doing, Vera and I, of his terrible, *terrible* articles."
>
> "You."
>
> "No, no, really. We were married then. That was 'twenty-five. Yes, we knew each other quite well. He paid me—what?—about five pounds."
>
> "You."
>
> "You helped me, darling, enormously."
>
> "I only remember that I helped you on one night

> when it was about two o'clock in the morning, and he
> was still dictating his article."

This particular insignificant recollection becomes important because of two matters that emerged in the course of it. As Nabokov
described this first meeting with Korostovetz:

> I came to him about eleven o'clock in the morning. Very
> early for me. I generally got up at one o'clock or two o'clock.
> And I came into his small hotel room. It was the first and the
> last time in my life that I saw a man getting out of a bed
> completely dressed. Completely. He even had a hat on. It's
> true. It's true. He had his shoes on, even. It was cold in the
> room, so he didn't bother to take his shoes off. This was *very*
> Russian in a way.

This odd observation of 1925 survived in Nabokov's descriptive
warehouse and was used exactly twenty-five years later in his
memoirs to describe the strangeness of his tutor "Lensky," who is
described as coming "seemingly straight out of bed but already
shod and trousered." As regards the business of polishing the articles, Vera Nabokov said very simply, "Your English then was a
little shaky," which provoked a great explosion of protest from
her husband: "No! No, no, no, no! It was as good as ever. It was
my first language, let's not forget that. My *first* language. When I
was two, three, four my mother used to translate Russian words
for me."

Another workmanlike job of those years was on a dictionary,
Russian/French and Russian/German, but Vera was very insistent that Vladimir had had nothing to do with that. In any event,
they wouldn't identify the dictionary.

By 1928 Nabokov had written two novels, twenty-two short
stories, and nearly a thousand poems. If one wishes to think in
broad categories, the novels were artifice, the poems very revery
and sentimental recollection, and the stories were reflections of
émigré life. In time his stories, like his poetry, would become artifice, too. Nabokov regarded the short-story form seriously. He
would compare short stories to smaller forms of butterflies to be
found above the timberline.

Nineteen twenty-eight and nineteen twenty-nine were good
years. Ullstein had purchased the translation rights to his first

novel, but it hadn't appeared for the longest time, and he had begun to doubt that it ever would. It finally appeared in 1928, and Ullstein bought the rights to the second novel as well. A collection of his best short stories, *The Return of Chorb*, was being prepared for publication in Russian, and Ilya Fondaminsky made a trip from Paris to Berlin one of the main purposes of which was to recruit Sirin's work for the journal. Prior to that time only some poems by Nabokov had appeared in *Contemporary Annals.* A long and generally happy association with the journal began with the appearance of his first major novel, *The Defense*, in 1929, followed by *The Eye* in 1930. The real stroke of good fortune was that, in addition to the two Ullstein contracts, both novels were serialized, in 1928 and 1929 respectively, in a German newspaper. He received in all the equivalent of about eight thousand dollars in today's terms. "We blew it on butterflies in the Eastern Pyrenees. We went there in February, stayed till June of 1930, came back penniless. How we managed that . . ." His wife interrupted him: "We were not penniless." "Well, as you remember, there were other reasons why the money became scarce very soon. But anyway. And after that we started to earn money again little by little."

The months in the windswept Pyrenees were a return to his passionate pursuit after slightly more than a decade in which he had been able to do little more than some collecting in the woods around Berlin. The highlight of the trip was when he captured a butterfly of the genus he used to capture at Vyra in his boyhood. The seriousness with which he collected was reflected in the scientific article he published on the trip the next year: "Notes on the Lepidoptera of the Pyrenees Orientales and the Ariege." It appeared in the same journal, *The Entomologist*, in which he had published his first article on Crimean butterflies.

Looking at the group of Nabokov's stories written prior to 1930 we see certain patterns emerging. There is the hero who wanders, literally or in his mind. And there is the *chudak* or eccentric who is fixed upon some point or game. There is also a marked polarization—some stories are insistently positive, while others, such as "Terror," are about madness and despair. In "Terror" the narrator cannot see any connection with the reflection he sees in the mirror, and he has a double. Four of Nabokov's novels, *The Defense*, *The Eye*, *Glory*, and *Despair*, are enlargements of these basic themes.

In 1925 and 1926 the young Nabokov took part in two mock literary trials that enter into his artistic development with surprising weight. Mock trials of characters, authors, or books have a strong tradition in Russian culture. (When *Lolita* appeared émigrés held a mock trial of it in France.) Perhaps the mock trial is an innocent outgrowth and reflection of the very real pressures of censorship and suppression that have always plagued Russian literature. However that may be, in July 1926 Nabokov had a prominent part in such a mock trial staged over Tolstoy's *The Kreutzer Sonata*. Nabokov played the part of the murderer in Tolstoy's story speaking in his own defense. According to the report of the trial in *The Rudder* (July 18, 1926) he was quite good at it. He wrote a short story called "Music" in 1932 which plays upon *The Kreutzer Sonata* as a theme, but much more important than that, the form of the murderer's confession was used by Nabokov in *Despair* and in *Lolita*.

The other trial in which Sirin participated, in 1925, has only recently come to light. It is of even greater importance in tracing the history of Nabokovian ideas. In 1925 Nikolai Evreinov's play *The Main Thing* was playing across Europe (in competition with Pirandello), and a trial of the play was held together with staged excerpts from it at the Ball of the Union of Russian Journalists in Germany. Sirin, who was made up to look like Evreinov, argued the case of the magician hero who wishes to make reality over into a transcendent illusion. (This is a central idea that we can follow in Nabokov from *The Eye* and *Glory* through *Pale Fire* and *Look at the Harlequins*.) Nabokov, when questioned about Evreinov, was, it now appears, evasive, saying only that he had met him once, which was true enough. The subtitle of Evreinov's play is *A Comedy of Happiness*, which may have something to do with the proposed title *Happiness* that Nabokov planned first for *Mary* and then for *Glory*. On the basis of the Evreinov trial it is fair to place Evreinov behind Nabokov as a major Russian influence, in some respects perhaps even as important as Gogol.

Luzhin, in *The Defense*, is the first of Nabokov's great strange heroes. Another Luzhin appeared in the 1924 short story "A Chance Occurrence." This story was essentially an early version of *Mary*: an émigré train waiter finds himself on the same train with his wife whom he believes to be still in the Soviet Union, only he doesn't realize it. Nabokov had formed the name Luzhin (incorrectly, his wife would maintain) from Luga, which was located just south of Vyra. If the first fictional Luzhin was cut off from everything he had had in life, Luzhin the chess grandmaster is incapable of having any ties in life. His real life was knotted in the memory of having been taught chess by his father's mistress.

Nabokov had the ability, and the propensity, to project himself imaginatively into the lives of freaks. One of his Crimean poems in 1919 had been about dreaming that he was a dwarf. It has been suggested and may be so that Nabokov's eccentrics and freaks are a defensive distortion so that he could write about himself with no possibility of an autobiographical bridge being thrown down by the critic or biographer. *The Defense* is Nabokov's first major work because it successfully blends the realistic and emotional harmonies of *Mary* with the cold and formal abstractness of *King, Queen, Knave.* Chess is a particularly valued skill among the members of the Russian intelligentsia, of course, and Nabokov succeeds beautifully in rendering the totally irrelevant seediness of the players and the settings in which they play. But it wasn't an easy atmosphere for Nabokov to create even though he was a good amateur player. "I suddenly realized," he said, "that I knew nothing about championship matches." To remedy this he spent three days at a championship match on his first trip to give a reading in Paris in early 1929. He watched Nemtsovich and Alekhine play, and he observed the odd Alekhine, who could relate only to very old women. It was at this exhibition that Nabokov said he was about to beat Nemtsovich in one of those exhibition shows where the grandmaster plays against a roomful of competitors simultaneously. "He had lost the game, when over my shoulder a hand appeared and moved a pawn." That was the account Nabokov gave of the loss.

Nabokov's own chess skill was even more specialized than the position of goalkeeper in soccer. He composed chess problems, some of which were printed in *The Rudder* and *The Latest News,* particularly in the early 1930s, though he was not, as has been assumed, a regular composer of such problems: the total number that he published during his first European period would appear to be less than a dozen. (He also made up some crossword puzzles and took great pride in having coined the Russian word for them, *krestoslovitsa.*) The chess problem is a game totally controlled by the person who sets it. The chess game, in contrast, is strict anarchy in that it proceeds according to rules but has tens of thousands of possible paths to follow.

Luzhin is usually identified with two great players of the period, Tartarkover and Rubenstein, who suffered from a split personality and had an intense fear of mirrors. Nabokov first acknowledged that there was something of Rubenstein in Luzhin, but later he withdrew that and said: "He was so like Luzhin that it was difficult to explain that I didn't know Rubinstein."

Given that its subject is chess, *The Defense* is all the same one of the simplest of Nabokov's patterned novels. There are no fantastically complex moves to fool the reader, and we do not have to play chess ourselves while reading it. There is a continuing use of windows, tiles, and squares, but this is nothing more than a thematic motif and the tendency of the demented grandmaster to turn everything into a chessboard in his mind. There is a swift move in which sixteen years pass in the course of a single paragraph, and the shift of both focus and time between chapters 4 and 6 is also intricate. Luzhin marries in what can be called a chess move, and his death, of course, is easily identifiable as a suicide mate.

Luzhin's defenselessness is shown in comic scenes (this is one of the first times that Nabokov showed his hand as a humorist) in which he either misunderstands or understands too precisely. When asked politely how long he has played chess, he at first says nothing and then suddenly replies: "Eighteen years, three months, and four days." His courtship is a parody of the proper order of things—his future fiancée runs after him to return the filthy handkerchief he has dropped. And the scene in which the dazed Luzhin becomes involved with a group of tipsy Berliners is pure Keystone comedy. In the end Luzhin understands chess so well that he can scarcely resolve the, for him, more difficult problem of how to leave a room. Chess is very much a surrogate for life. *The Defense* is one of Nabokov's most clearly antiplatonic tales: shadows of people and objects do in fact give rise to chess combinations in Luzhin's mind. Luzhin's awkward balance between two opposing realities is shown in his fear of heights—the third dimension that takes him beyond the chessboard. In the concluding scene Luzhin barricades himself in a room and hurls himself downward, imagining at that moment that eternity is a chessboard toward which he is falling: " 'Alexander Ivanovich,

Alexander Ivanovich!' screamed several voices. But there was no Alexander Ivanovich." In one sense there never was an Alexander Ivanovich, because this is the first time that the reader learns his name. Before this he was always just Luzhin. It is interesting that for Nabokov the end of the novel was not necessarily death at all. Nabokov explained to me: "As I approached the conclusion of the novel I suddenly realized that the book doesn't end." That means then that *The Defense* has a conclusion rather like *Invitation to a Beheading* where the hero stands up and leaves his own execution to walk toward creatures like himself. There are in all at least nine Nabokov novels in which the heroes seek or find an exit into another dimension. Nabokov also told me that he had intended to impart a sexual aspect to Luzhin, who would see a black beard on his wife, but that he abandoned that element of the novel.

When *The Defense* first appeared it was immediately recognized as a major achievement. Khodasevich praised it highly. Zamyatin, author of the antiutopian novel *We*, who had just been allowed to emigrate after a personal appeal to Stalin, said that it was the most important émigré novel he had read. There was a slight disappointment when Ullstein failed to take the third Sirin novel for translation into German, but that after all was only money. Nabokov was now a recognized writer with a regular reading public. The circulation figures for one lending library that were published in an émigré journal show that Sirin books were borrowed nearly three hundred times that year.

He had admirers, and, which always comes with fame, he now had enemies, too. An important coterie in émigré literature formed around the Parisian almanac *Numbers*, which began to appear in 1930. The critic Georgy Adamovich and the poet Georgy Ivanov, who had a certain reputation prior to the revolution, were its two leading contributors. There were numerous talented younger writers and poets in the *Numbers* group, chief among them Gaito Gazdanov, Boris Poplavsky, and Anatoly Shteiger. Younger writers in the emigration had frequently complained that established writers made no effort to encourage emerging talents or to cultivate a climate in which literature could grow and move forward. *Numbers* filled this need to some extent and was a fine journal, but one inescapable feature of the journal (it published eight thick almanac-style issues over four years) was the total absence of the work of most of the acknowledged masters of Russian literature living abroad: Ivan Bunin, Vladislav Khodasevich, Alexander Kuprin, Mark Aldanov, and Mikhail Osorgin. Part of that might have been due to the personalities of Adamovich, Ivanov, and also Zinaida Gippius—wherever they congregated there was bound to be controversy and animosity—but it is possible that these absences were prompted by an unwillingness to contribute to the journal after the attack on Sirin by Georgy Ivanov in the first issue of *Numbers*. Oddly, there was a brief contribution by Sirin in that first number, a reply to a questionnaire on the influence of Proust. Nabokov replied drily that one cannot possibly calculate such things as literary influence.

The Ivanov article was a survey of the first three Sirin novels plus the collection of short stories and poems, *The Return of Chorb*, which had just appeared. The article was a strong personal statement unsullied by any specifics—two sentences by Nabokov are quoted as examples of his bad writing, but the article fails to refer to a single incident or character in any of the novels, nor does it name, much less discuss, any of the short stories in the *Chorb* collection. Ivanov does allow the talent and glitter in Sirin's writing. He exempts *King, Queen, Knave* and *The Defense* from discussion beyond repeating Adamovich's formulation that they are clever imitations of French and German models. His attack is concentrated upon *Mary* and the short stories. The stories are "vulgarity not without virtuosity," whereas the poems are "simply vulgar." Sirin's art, if it is stripped of its imitation of foreign models, is "an in-no-way complicated counterfeit" of the tradition to which he aspires to belong. Sirin is "an imposter, a cook's son, a black sheep, a low scoundrel." Ivanov names some of the most insignificant Russian poets and adds that, since Sirin is a person of capability, he may yet surpass these teachers.

Ivanov was counterattacking to defend his wife, the writer Irina Odoevtseva, whose novel *Isolde* had appeared the year before and been reviewed unfavorably by Nabokov in *The Rudder*. Odoevtseva herself had sent him a copy inscribed in a coyly friendly fashion.

Nabokov struck back at Ivanov and Adamovich. Some months later, in July 1931, the imaginary English writer Vivian Calmbrood made his second appearance in Russian, this time in a pretended translation of the long poem "The Night Journey." The poem was an *ad hominem* attack on a critic with an "Adamic head" who bestowed his "delicate favors" in an "effeminate style" and on a decadent poet, overconcerned with death, who tries to play the part of a new Petronius and who is advised, sitting in his bathtub with a rose and a razor and about to commit suicide, "to take some soap/and wash for a change." The supposed narrator of the poem, Chenston (a partial anagram of *honorable* in Russian) tells Vivian Calmbrood how "sinister gentlemen" follow his muse. The remarks of Chenston about his own art and on literary back-scratching are of interest. Chenston confesses that "there is a bloodthirsty streak/in my gentle muse," and he has contempt for those who bustle after immortality in the dull world of journals. Chenston complains:

> There is no air in such a narrow world.
> I shall take my muse away.

But even that wasn't the end of it. In December 1931, Nabokov wrote a story called "Lips to Lips." It was about an émigré widower who writes an unspeakably wretched novel called "Lips to Lips" and is maneuvered into financing an almanac called *Arion*, which promises to print it. The man's naïveté about literature is both hilarious and touching. He chooses the name of a well-known poet for a pseudonym and knows Pushkin by Tchaikovsky's opera. His style is pure popular romance: "Take me, my chastity, my suffering . . ." The old man chances to overhear a conversation about himself and understands that he is being printed only because he is supporting the almanac financially. He dashes away, but as the story ends: "He knew that he must forgive everything, otherwise the 'to be continued' would never materialize."

Nabokov's story was submitted to *The Latest News*, which was the Paris equivalent of *The Rudder*, edited by Pavel Miliukov, and the paper for which Adamovich was the regular literary critic. The story was reluctantly accepted, but at the last minute *The Latest News* probably heard legal rumblings and grew frightened. The story is a very transparent and rather vicious satire on Adamovich, Ivanov, and Gippius and the way they had courted and milked a certain Alexander Burov, whose dreadful novel *There Was a Land* did appear in *Numbers*, initially in just

The cloth and leather-covered poetic notebooks that the young Nabokov took with
him into exile. (*Field collection*)

Nabokov's paternal grandmother, Maria. (*Nabokov—His Life in Part*)

Nabokov's paternal grandfather, Dmitri Nabokov, government minister under Czars Alexander II, III, and Nicholas II. (*Nabokov—His Life in Part*)

The fleeting moment of Russian parliamentary democracy: Nicholas II poses with the Duma. (*Illustrirovannaya Rossiya, Paris, 1930*)

Nabokov's father, V. D. Nabokov, poses with novelist Aleksei Tolstoy (*center*) and Vladimir Nemirovich-Danchenko (*right*), one of the founders of the Moscow Art Theatre, on their trip as a cultural delegation to England in 1916. (*Chukovsky collection*)

Nabokov's mother, Elena, circa 1900. (*Field collection*)

The barn, last remaining vestige of the Nabokov country estate, Vyra, near St. Petersburg. (*Courtesy of a Soviet admirer of Nabokov*)

Rozhestveno, the estate near Vyra belonging to Nabokov's Uncle Ruka, which he inherited just before the revolution. (*Courtesy of a Soviet admirer of Nabokov*)

Nabokov (*standing*) and his brother Sergei. St. Petersburg, 1916.
(*Nabokov—His Life in Part*)

Nabokov in his final term at the Tenishev
School. St. Petersburg, 1916. (*Nabokov—
His Life in Part*)

Nabokov's closest friend, his cousin Baron
Yury Rausch von Traubenberg. Crimea,
1919. (*Field collection*)

V. D. Nabokov, passport photo. Berlin, 1919.
(*Nabokov—His Life in Part*)

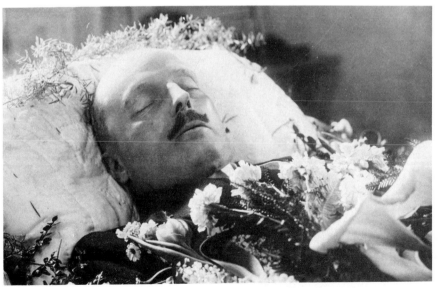

V. D. Nabokov before burial. Berlin, 1923.
(*Anonymous member of the Nabokov family*)

Joseph Hessen (*holding portrait of V. D. Nabokov*) and the staff of *The Rudder.* (*Berlin, 1930*)

Nabokov at 30. Berlin. (*Nov', Estonia*)

such a three-page fragment and subsequently in its entirety. The paper had the plates destroyed, and twenty-five years elapsed before the story was finally printed. That started what Nabokov called his "lively feud" with Miliukov's paper and Adamovich. That feud extended through the Vasily Shishkov incident into Nabokov's American period, in which he throws a few darts at Adamovich (whom he calls Uranski) and Ivanov in *Pnin*—long after one would have thought it mattered, and for an audience that could have no notion of the feud. When I questioned Nabokov about this, he relented: "He's a difficult person. Still, I think I was wrong. I would not go out of my way to attack him nowadays, but I certainly do not regret the fun I had in exposing the frailty of his critical pronouncements thirty years ago." Then, in 1973, he reverted and used an old favorite joke of his about Adamovich in an introduction: that he had two passions in life—Russian poetry and French sailors. In one of his early émigré reviews Nabokov had confessed that he liked a good fight, providing that his opponent was honorable.

There was one further incident in Nabokov's quarrel with *Numbers,* but its roots have not been satisfactorily determined. In 1930, in what would be its last issue, *Numbers* published a work later titled *Novel with Cocaine.* The author was given as "M. Ageyev." All are agreed that Ageyev is a pseudonym. One scholar has argued forcefully that the novel, and a short story published under the same name four years later, were by Nabokov. If that were so, *Novel with Cocaine* would be another stage in the Shishkov mystification of Adamovich and his group. But the attribution has been denied by the Nabokov family.

The short novel is full of Nabokovian phrases, but that in itself is no proof of authorship. Nabokov's style, after all, is very distinctive, and to execute a superficial imitation of it in the manner of a *New Statesman* competition would not have been beyond the powers of many of the writers who contributed to *Numbers.* Nabokov himself, after all, joked in a letter to his sister that he, too, could write a letter "in the Sirin style." Many in the emigration did.

A more serious complication, however, is that the novel and the story provide certain thematic material for *Glory* and *Invitation to a Beheading,* works written several years *after* the appearance of *Novel with Cocaine.* There is an explanation: *Novel with Co-*

caine could have been a counterattack by Georgy Ivanov (whose own style had been savagely parodied by Nabokov) in order to show how "easy" the Sirin style really was. Nabokov might well then have taken up the several "Ageyev" themes as his own form of exquisite revenge.

It has been suggested that Nabokov "had the pleasure of seeing Adamovich hail, and *Numbers* publish, an *imitation* Nabokov novel." The fact is that *Novel with Cocaine* had no impact whatsoever, so, if it was a pastiche meant to belittle Sirin, whoever in the *Numbers* camp was responsible for it had nothing to gloat about and every reason to remain silent. It's inconceivable that Nabokov himself would have remained silent forever about such a trick in view of the pleasure he had in retelling the Shishkov joke. The only logical reason Nabokov had to remain completely silent about "M. Ageyev" is if he rose to the challenge and took several motifs from the not terribly impressive little novel and showed how they could be deployed in art of a high order. The connection between the name of the Ageyev character Sinat and Nabokov's Cincinnatus is scarcely open to question. The only thing that can be said with absolute certainty is that there is *some* link between the work of Ageyev and Sirin. But there are many stylistic points indicating that Georgy Ivanov would be a more plausible author than Nabokov. A Moscow émigré from Turkey named Levi has also been nominated, unconvincingly.

In any event, by 1930–31 it was quite clear that Nabokov had become effectively isolated and estranged from most of the other important Russian writers abroad. On the one hand, he was a dashing and attractive young artist of considerable achievement, but on the other, he stood clearly aside from any group in much the same way that he had once disdainfully leaned against the walls in the Tenishev School watching the other children at play—or so he told me. He had a fortress marriage in much the same way that he had had the Kingdom of Nabokov in prerevolutionary Russia. And the very first signs of Nabokov-the-master could be seen in his visits to the Poets' Circle.

The Poets' Circle had been formed by Misha Gorlin before he was twenty. He recruited his members from the young people attending another circle. In the end there was a membership of about twenty-five. Gorlin remained the organizing force behind the group until its dissolution in 1933 at the time of the Reichstag fire. A fair number of the members made their mark as minor poets. Besides Gorlin and Raissa Blokh, there were Sophia Pregel', Eugene Rabinowitch (the physicist-poet better known as the founder of *The Bulletin of Atomic Scientists*), and Victor Frank. One visitor to the circle was one of the original members of the Resistance in France and was shot by the Nazis when they took Paris. Nabokov and the poet Vladimir Korvin-Piotrovsky were the acknowledged leaders of the circle. The circle met once a week, sometimes in a café, sometimes in someone's apartment. Nabokov did not always come, and, when he did (this was also true of his attendance at the Aikhenval'd Circle), he was late, usually with the explanation: "I got lost in my writing and didn't realize how the time had flown." He would always have a distracted air, obviously still lost in some story or poem.

Someone would read a poem, and then the "unhypocritical" discussion would begin. Nabokov would invariably take the lead as the good-humored but sarcastic professor. He once criticized the work of an older émigré writer named Matusevich in an apparently serious manner but actually making up spurious supposed lines such as "she was a luxurious woman" or "her divine bulges." When a young poet recited the line "the horse fell back," Nabokov interrupted and asked, "In one word, backwards *(nazad)*, or two, on its back *(na zad)*?" And before the poet could say anything, he answered his own question: "Well, I suppose it amounts to the same thing."

Piotrovsky was the only poet in the club whom Nabokov was willing to accept as his equal, in part because Piotrovsky, who was slightly older than Nabokov, alone never took offense at his critical remarks and on occasion would score a shot of his own against Nabokov. Once they nearly came to blows. In 1929 Piotrovsky published a cycle of unusual poems titled *Beatrice*, which are very strong. One of the few enthusiastic book reviews written by Nabokov in Berlin was an appreciation of *Beatrice*. Later, the Korvin was added to his name and he became Korvin-Piotrovsky, which was ironic, Nabokov thought, because he knew nothing about Baron Corvo and yet had something of Corvo in his personality. Nabokov thought Piotrovsky was a "commonplace liar" who told tall tales about his heroism in the civil war. It is quite likely that bits of Piotrovsky were used by Nabokov for Smurov in *The Eye*. Nabokov recalled that Korvin-Piotrovsky, after the war, published an unpleasant poem about him, but he still planned to do two translations of Korvin-Piotrovsky poems in an English-language anthology of Russian poetry that he planned to compile.

The meetings of the two Berlin circles with their unquestionable dedication to Russian literature and passion for the Russian language were probably more important for Nabokov than he would ever have admitted. He struck poses in both circles and played games (such as the party game of closing one's eyes after looking at a picture for two minutes and then recalling what one could remember of it—Nabokov always won, of course), but the main thing is that he was in Russia when he was in those circles. Behind his humor and his haughtiness there could only occasionally be glimpsed, for Nabokov wore a tightly fastened mask that concealed any sign of grief over all that he had lost, the powerful emotions that burned secretly within him. In one of his poems most often quoted in the emigration Nabokov defiantly declares: "We'll manage very well without Russia." But at one meeting of the Poets' Circle, Sirin recited a poem that appeared in *The Rudder* in July 1928. In this poem the poet turns away from a reading of his palm which is supposed to reveal all the paths, roads, and streams of his life. He will depend upon Russia, which is the source of his happiness. But he has dreamt already that his *"last hour, careless hour"* may come in a foreign land. "Why is it a 'careless' hour?" asked Piotrovsky. "Because," Nabokov answered, "it is the last. There are no more sorrows and cares."

13

IN THE DEEP STRUCTURE OF HIS LIFE NABOKOV'S TIES TO HIS
parents were, together with those to Russia, the all-important
ones. Their unabated adoration of him meant that he truly had no
need of Freudian conflicts and antagonisms. Freudianism claims
to speak to a fundamental and universally shared human personality. It was unthinkable that Narcissus should see Everyman in
the pool. Nabokov wrote his first attack on Freudianism in 1931.
It appeared in the excellent but short-lived émigré paper *New
Gazette* in Paris. That same journal, by the way, submitted a
questionnaire about the achievements of émigré literature to
leading writers and intellectuals: the name Sirin figured prominently—one writer called him the only true writer in the younger
generation, another said *The Defense* was the most important
Russian book of the preceding five years, and Khodasevich cited
three outstanding books since the revolution, Bunin's *Life of
Arsen'ev*, Olesha's *Envy*, and *The Defense*. In Nabokov's article
Freudianism is treated like a brand of shaving cream. Customer
satisfaction is guaranteed: "We have enthusiastic testimonials
from many writers and artists, from three engineers, from mid-
wives, and many, many more. Its effect is instantaneous and pleas-
urable. Every modern man must acquire this. It's extremely
interesting! Amazingly cheap!"

It was not too long before he wrote this article, after all, that
Nabokov had been tempted to use images taken directly from abnormal psychology in his depiction of Luzhin. Sensing the dan-

ger, he adopted an attitude of outrageous openness and derisive parody toward sexual matters. A short time before, in 1928, he wrote "Lilith," a poem in which a man is killed, has intercourse with a ravishing child who is very like a memory from his own childhood, and then discovers he is in hell when the child vanishes just as he is about to reach a climax with her. (The poem wasn't published until 1970 in *Poems and Problems*.) This boldness enabled him to leap over Freud's ground while at the same time affecting an air of smirking superiority. There is not, when you think of it, a single actual "sexual" scene in all of Nabokov, except for the one in "Lilith," though there are ever so many pages of sensual deep breathing mingled with muffled ventriloquial snorts of derisive laughter.

What sort of brazen compulsion, the ultimate gesture of contempt for everything Freudian, brought Nabokov to use a version of his mother's nickname for the heroine of his greatest novel? The nickname was Lolya. Photocopies of the letters by Nabokov to his mother that were given to me have one word cut out: the salutation. It is a word about seven letters long and with the tail or hat of Nabokov's Russian *t* often showing clearly below or above the cut-out space. Lolita, surely, it seems to me.

As regards his father, Nabokov was not overshadowed by him, because he moved deftly to the side. His father was a prominent politician, whose son disdained politics, turning political questions into matters concerning the philosophy of the self. But despite that, Nabokov took after his father in many ways. He grew a mustache exactly like his father's when he reached the age of his father's death. He considered that his personality was in certain respects like his father's, and that he sometimes suffered from the same awkward and overly formal way of speaking.

The murder of his father had left Vladimir as the titular head of a rather large family, and he was not temperamentally or emotionally prepared for such a role. That would have involved, among other things, staying in the bank and, when the Ullstein money came, not taking that long vacation in the Pyrenees. His brother Sergei managed to be self-sufficient, but his mother had extreme difficulties in Prague. He did send them money at first, but by 1934, when his mother was in desperate need, he had to confess that his own situation was similar and that he had absolutely no means to help her. Since he was Kirill's godfather, there was also a particularly strong obligation toward him. In his late teens and early twenties Kirill wanted to be a poet, and Nabokov wanted above all to prevent that, in one case writing to a friend asking that any sort of job be somehow obtained for him even if it was only as a garbageman. Nabokov also very much wanted to prevent Kirill's return to Prague, probably because of their mother's high-strung state. Kirill managed somehow (in a more quiet way, he is said to have had a measure of Vladimir's self-confidence) and became a Belgian travel agent before going to work for Radio Free Europe in Munich, where he died of a heart attack in 1964. He did publish poetry, and he made broadcasts about his brother's work to Russia on Radio Free Europe. There were rumors, probably groundless, that he had been murdered by Soviet agents at the radio station.

Nabokov was awkward, as can be seen in *Speak, Memory*, with his brother Sergei, and he found it difficult even to write about Sergei after his death. They saw each other for about two years before Vladimir left for America and Sergei was shipped to Neuengamme, a Nazi concentration camp in northern Germany. It is said that he had a German lover and so believed that he was safe, which was a very rash thing for a Russian homosexual to think. He was arrested on December 15, 1943. The sister of the composer Nicolai Nabokov was the last family member to see him before he was arrested and to have word about him before he was shipped to the camp. While he was awaiting arrest he told her that he had been denounced to the Gestapo for having simply said, "All the same, England is the most civilized country in the world." He was taken to a death camp where terrible experiments were being performed on the inmates. Sergei had converted to Roman Catholicism and, according to a Russian survivor of the same camp, spent all the time until his death in prayer and consoling other prisoners. Vladimir and Sergei were never very close, but the life of his brother was always a painful point in the family's history for Vladimir.

His father's cool passage through difficult times and especially his heroic death were things that his son could equal only in his fiction, and the performance of a heroic exploit by a character similar to V. D. Nabokov became the focus of Nabokov's 1931–32 novel *Glory*. Originally to have been called *Happiness* or *The*

Romantic Age, the novel had a profound effect on many members of the young émigré intelligentsia who, many of them have explained to me over the years, felt estranged from the experience of their parents and had themselves little or no recollection of Russia. They grasped the novel, its hero, and entire range of emotions, as the standard of their generation. *Glory* is a strange Nabokov novel in that it is entirely realistic and contains no stylistic tricks. Nabokov considered it the happiest of his fictions. The very title Nabokov finally chose is a clue to the personal aspiration to the bravery of his father that must have been, whether subconsciously or consciously, in Nabokov's mind, for the novel's title, *podvig*, or "heroic exploit," was the term widely applied to the way V. D. Nabokov had died:

> In Nabokov's fate, a fate full of high drama, there is a deeply engraved heroic meaning, and before this heroic exploit you must bow in reverence. This exploit was performed freely, consciously. It was the knightly action of a noble, courageous, and burning heart. The beauty of this exploit can never be forgotten.

Nabokov imitated his father in *Glory*. It was not, of course, an easy topic to discuss with Vladimir Nabokov: "Transference. *What?!* What do you mean?"

The hero of *Glory*, Martin Edelweis, is said to have a great resemblance to his dead father, but he doesn't like to hear others speak about his father. He himself remembers him as a man whose emotions were all but wholly concealed from view. Martin makes lunges, particularly toward emotional attachments to women, but he is essentially as reserved as his father. Martin feels disconnected from the other people in the novel, as though they were traveling on one train but in separate cars. He is émigré literature's most vivid contribution to the century-old great Russian theme of the "superfluous man" who appears in famous works by Griboedov, Lermontov, Dostoevsky, and Turgenev. Certainly the inability of Martin to form any sort of lasting relationship is one of the things that pushes him toward a seemingly mad, but for him logical, decision to undertake a daring "exploit"—a short foray into Russia. Deeds of this sort were always being talked about in the emigration. Sometimes the forays were made by double agents about whom there was always an air of great mystery. Martin is outspokenly apolitical. He has no real reason to return to Russia, which in the end is the reason he goes. When Martin was in the Crimea, he was almost shot, and the incident lingers in his imagination as a sweet and fantastic episode. Martin's rejection by Sonya—there is a lot of the romance with Svetlana here—is another important factor that causes him to turn toward performing his exploit, but there is a full pattern of small and large, intentional and chance, failures, which cause him to think of Russia more and more. Though Nabokov acknowledged the autobiographical character of *Glory* in regard to Martin, he said that the secondary character, Darwin, was wholly invented, which is not quite so, for his classmate Peter Mrosovsky, though not an Englishman, shared some characteristics with Darwin (such as the way he kicks doors shut with his foot against the top corner), and it is possible, too, that there is a degree of the future government minister Rab Butler, in Darwin.

The first clear sign in the novel of Martin's intention to go to Russia is a Tolstoyan excursion to live and work in a French workers' community. Martin never speaks about Russia or his intention to go there. Indeed, in jesting exchanges with Sonya, he invents an imaginary Zoorlandia, and the Zoorlandian motif is the sole customary Nabokovian complexity in *Glory*. Nabokov published a short poem as "a translation from the Zoorlandian" in May 1930. The theme of an imaginary land and/or language is used, casually or centrally, five more times by Nabokov before reaching its major expression in *Pale Fire*'s Zembla. Martin's Zoorlandia is not merely an ironic metaphor expressing the loss of Russia. It is also a simple recognition by Martin that he will not be able to live in Russia, which has become the "merciless Zoorlandian night." Even though he does protest to himself that, of course, he will return, Zoorlandia is death.

A 1936 short story, "The Annihilation of Tyrants," has a hero who is like Martin in his contempt for politics and patriotism. Faced with a tyrant, he will annihilate him by committing suicide. Everything is only in terms of one's self, and everyone has the means to destroy tyrants with a powerful arsenal ranging from ridicule to suicide.

Glory's abrupt and inconclusive ending was a source of bewilderment to émigré critics. Is it likely, as one critic suggested, that

Martin, like Ganin in *Mary*, will realize the futility (spiritual not practical) of attempting to bring his quixotic dream into being and will instead turn back at the border?

The open-ended narrative was a characteristic form for Nabokov. But *Glory* is a realistic novel, and I venture to suggest that its unwritten conclusion is carefully prefigured. In practical terms Martin's return to Russia is a return to the scene, a reenactment of his father's lonely death. Thus seen, *Glory* is Martin's unconscious imposition of a congruent pattern, his father's fate, upon the past. This must, of course, be simply speculation, but another poem, "The Execution," written in 1927, joins the themes of Russia and death. The poet's bed drifts off to Russia as soon as he lies down to sleep, and he is a little resentful when wakefulness returns him to the safety of exile and salvation from a gloriously romantic death by firing squad under stars in Russia.

The other novel that Nabokov wrote in the same period, *Camera obscura* (later changed to *Laughter in the Dark* and considerably reworked, even to the point of changing the characters' names), is one of his coldest studies of human isolation. Like *King, Queen, Knave,* it has non-Russian characters and is done in an Expressionist manner intended to make it suitable for film. (It almost but not quite made it then, too: there were two film options taken on the novel in the thirties.) The plot of the novel—Nabokov himself considered it his least significant longer work—is a variant of *The Blue Angel.* Vladislav Khodasevich was quite right to see that the plot is simply a literal application of the time-honored dictum "love is blind." The novel is about the cinema, and it is also about three failed artists. Until *The Gift* Nabokov would not write about a successful artist, and even there the real artistic achievement of his hero Fyodor lies in the future. There is, however, one minor character who stands out sharply from the others in *Laughter in the Dark:* a German artist exiled in France. He knows that it will be a century before he is appreciated at his worth and is convinced that there comes a time when the true artist ceases to need his native land. *Glory* and *Laughter in the Dark* are as different as any two Nabokov novels but share the vision of life at hand as a dull and flat Punch and Judy show. Reality for Nabokov is elsewhere, outside and beyond.

Nabokov's next novel, in 1935, was to be the most controversial of his Russian works. It is also the most fablelike of all his works:

this time it was the literal application of "life is a dream." *Invitation to a Beheading* also has a particular and personal reference to Nabokov and his father hidden in it. For the hero's name refers not to Lucius Quinctius Cincinnatus, who is a model of the simple and virtuous statesman, but rather to the statesman's son, who was censored by a Tribune of the People in 461 B.C. for his extraordinary oratory and excessive pride and forced to go into exile. This then is the real "politics" of *Invitation*, though the searchlights of Hitler's Germany could be seen in the night sky from the windows of Nabokov's apartment in Nestorstrasse as he wrote the book.

According to Khodasevich, the novel was "only the play of decorator-elves, the play of devices and images which fill the creative consciousness or, to put it a better way, the creative delirium of Cincinnatus." In the character of Cincinnatus we have the purest representation of Narcissus in all of Nabokov. It is interesting that this novel, unlike all his others until *Ada*, was written in a headlong frenzy. Ordinarily, Nabokov worked steadily and patiently to produce about 280 pages a year. *Invitation* is indulgent in the way it turns all of perceived reality into a trivial cartoon. It is clear now that Nabokov had, for all his denials, read Kafka—and read him well—in the thirties. Recent scholarship has shown very convincingly that there was a sufficient quantity of émigré essays on Kafka—some by friends of Nabokov such as Vladimir Weidle—to make it extremely unlikely that he wouldn't have known Kafka's work or been interested in it. Nabokov was firm in his contention that his knowledge of and affection for Kafka came later. He claimed that he was almost sure that he had once ridden the elevated railway of Berlin on a regular basis with Kafka, because he had a strong jolt of recognition when he first saw a picture of Kafka. There are certain clear echoes. The father-in-law of Cincinnatus attacks him with a vindictiveness that recalls Gregor's family in "The Metamorphosis." Like Gregor, Cincinnatus suffers from a rare and awful condition. In his case it is "gnostical turpitude"—he isn't transparent. His mother tells him secretly that his father suffered from the same disease. Although he understands his situation perfectly well, Cincinnatus still feels a powerful urge to rejoin his terrible family in their dreadful world. M'sieur Pierre, who tries to become the true friend and confidant but turns out to be the appointed executioner of Cincinnatus, is a complete reversal of the prisoner-hero. Pyotr Bitsilli (it is not a made-up name), one of the five or six best émigré literary critics and Nabokov's own favorite Russian critic of his work, wrote two articles on *Invitation*, both of which appeared in *Contemporary Annals*, and in one of them he makes just this point:

> Cincinnatus and M'sieur Pierre are two aspects of "man in general," the *everyman* of the old English outdoor mystery drama. There is a potential "M'sieur Pierre" in every man insofar as he lives, that is, insofar as he remains in that condition of a "bad dream," of *death*, that we call life. For "Cincinnatus" to die means to extract from himself the "M'sieur Pierre."

Bitsilli's judgment, though it may be somewhat loosely formulated—it would be better to say that Pierre is the vulgar everyman who controls and obscures the individual in each of us—is confirmed by the conclusion in which Cincinnatus walks away free, and it is the executioner who is dispatched. As Cincinnatus strides toward the giant beings who are akin to him, it has not been sufficiently noticed that Pierre is carried away by a woman dressed in black "like a larva." It is Kafka's metamorphosis applied with moral justice. Nabokov very likely read "The Metamorphosis" in the *Nouvelle Revue Français* (to which he later contributed) in 1928: he referred to Gregor Samsa using the French given name Gregoire. Nabokov's mind was like Kafka's in many respects, with the highly important difference that he possessed a fierce, sometimes hysterical, belief in the ultimate triumph of the individual artist (the two words were inseparable for Nabokov) over the absurdity of perceived existence.

Another wafting besides Kafka that can be felt throughout *Invitation to a Beheading* is the grotesque comic vision of Gogol. In Bitsilli's excellent comparison between *Invitation* and the prose of Saltykov-Shchedrin, he draws some most striking parallels. But the point is that Saltykov-Shchedrin also belongs in the Gogolian tradition. By "Gogolian" art one should understand not only a particular artistic style, but also a particular sort of primitive consciousness that accompanies the artist's genius. Nabokov put it very nicely in his book on Gogol when he said that Gogol had a special knack of planning his books after he'd written them.

For this reason writers in the Gogolian tradition—such as Dostoevsky, Sukhovo-Kobylin, Saltykov-Shchedrin, Sologub, Bely, Savich, Evreinov, Nabokov, and, most recently, Tertz-Sinyavsky—can really only be considered partially Gogolian. For all these Gogolian writers must write more or less deliberately as Gogol did in spite of himself. The cited important writers in the Gogolian tradition are those who have found a unique and personal voice and viewpoint to accompany and, in the end, form some new variant of Gogol's manner. Nabokov, of course, claimed that "desperate critics" had tried to tie him up and pigeonhole his work with Gogol, but that he got away every time like a literary Houdini.

All the same, several Russian critics pointed out that the secondary characters in *Invitation to a Beheading* were "more dead" than Gogol's famous dead-soul caricatures. Pierre is, like Gogol's Khlestakov, fond of eating whole watermelons, but more than that one of his two nipples has green leaves tattooed around it so that it looks like a rose, a strong instance of the sort of sublime *poshlost'* or vulgarity about which Nabokov instructed Western readers of Russian literature almost single-handedly for nearly thirty years in several books and endless interviews. When little Emmie, the twelve-year-old daughter of the jailer, is engaged in eating a large piece of watermelon at her father's house, M'sieur Pierre, sipping a cup of tea with his right hand, inconspicuously gooses her under the table with his left. The child jumps and giggles but—the Gogolian touch—doesn't miss a bite of her watermelon. Cincinnatus, who has many moments of weakness, hopes that Emmie will remain a nymphet but at the same time be a mature woman with burning cheeks who can lead him to freedom. Perhaps wild little Emmie is the craftiest trap of all. She herself suggests that they will run away together and marry, but then goes into a rapid pirouette that is suspiciously like the antics of M'sieur Pierre. Another obvious Gogolism is the way Nabokov lists things that do not belong together in order to set free a jack-in-the-box absurdity in the final item listed. Gogol's Chichikov dances by himself in his room. Nabokov's Pierre does it shamelessly in public. Sex is one of the most potent weapons by which Cincinnatus is bound to his dubious society. In her final visit to him his wife Marthe offers to copulate in much the same way a coin would be thrown to a beggar. Her main concern is that he do it quickly and get it over with. For Pierre, who is impotent, the bliss of sex and bowel movement are the same. Throughout Gogol sex is unreal or absent. In *Invitation* it is made absurd.

One enormous difference between Gogol and Nabokov is the manner in which the unreality of the characters in *Invitation to a Beheading* is constantly spelled out for the reader: "I thank you, rag doll, coachman, painted swine." Gogol believed that his fantastic creations were real people. Even more incredible, in the face of all evidence to the contrary, many readers accepted him as a comic realist. In his book *The Unnoticed Generation* (1956) the critic Vladimir Varshavsky remarks that "if Cincinnatus himself had not continually underscored the fact that he is surrounded by grotesque apparitions rather than people, very likely many readers whose tastes were formed on 'healthy realism' would not even have noticed how these personages, so credible and speaking just as in life, differ from real people." *Invitation to a Beheading* is about consciousness, and it also in a sense concerns the resolution of the problem that Gogol couldn't solve: how do you turn shadows into substance? Gogolian grotesques cannot by their very nature turn into "real" people. But, Nabokov shows, a real person may exist in their midst. Even Cincinnatus has another "more real" Cincinnatus deep within him who weeps when the larger Cincinnatus compromises himself.

There is one further work to mention in connection with *Invitation to a Beheading:* Zamyatin's *We.* There is much in common between Cincinnatus and D-503. The situation of the individual versus the mass is the same. Only the philosophical position is radically different in the two novels. If one considers the unquestionable lineage—Gogol, Kafka, Zamyatin (*We* first appeared in the Prague émigré journal *The Will of Russia*, in 1927, and so it is impossible to think Nabokov didn't read it)—then *Invitation to a Beheading* is actually far from the most original of Nabokov's fictions but is rather a Nabokovian rendering of a theme used by two of the most innovative artists of his time, with a cupful of Gogol thrown in.

Khodasevich was the first critic to insist that Nabokov's novels were all parables about the situation of the artist. Discussing the conclusion of *Invitation* he wrote:

> In the concluding lines the two-dimensional, pained world of Cincinnatus comes apart, and "amidst the flapping scenery,

Cincinnatus made his way in that direction where, to judge
by the voices, stood beings akin to him." This, of course, represents the return of the artist from his art to reality. If one
looks at it this way, at this moment an execution occurs, but
it is not the one or in the same sense that the hero and the
reader expected: with his return to the world of "beings akin
to him" the life of Cincinnatus-as-artist is cut off.

Varshavsky accepted Khodasevich's formulation only with reservation. He preferred to see in the novel a contrast between literary characters and language that possess the secret of life (as in
Tolstoy) and characters and language that are dead (socialist realist fiction). Varshavsky's variant reading doesn't have support
within the text, but it is possible to read *Invitation* as a struggle
between true art and dead art or caricature. The importance that
questions of art has for this novel is underscored by the very title,
which, Nabokov has acknowledged, refers to Baudelaire's "Invitation au voyage" and thus refers to the sacred function of art in
the Symbolist tradition.

Although it is true that the tale is complex and cannot be reduced to any simple point, *Invitation to a Beheading* is all the
same the most fablelike of all Nabokov's novels. Its weakness is
the disparity between the air of a fable and the story's rather protracted length. The exception to the rule of brevity for fables is,
of course, the greatest "fable-novelist," Kafka. But in Kafka delay
and protractedness are essentials of his tales. This is true to a
much lesser degree of *Invitation*. The matter can be put another
way: imagine, if you will, Gogol's Chichikov not traveling about
from estate to estate to purchase his dead souls but, with the help
of a few other of the dead souls, closeted up in one place where a
"live" person is being held by them. The absence of movement
from one place to another and the comparatively restricted number of characters require that the novel contain, in compensation,
a number of busy set pieces. One is the tunnel that is dug toward
the cell of Cincinnatus not, it turns out, by someone who is trying
to free him but by Pierre. These set pieces are frequently brilliant
in themselves, but an involuntary impatience with them begins to
gain control.

An interesting comparison to *Invitation to a Beheading* is the
1937 short story "Cloud, Lake, Tower"—translated into English
as "Cloud, Castle, Lake," very likely to preserve the first-syllable
stress on each word in the title that the Russian has—which

Khodasevich referred to as an "afterword" to the novel. It is true that even the phrase "invitation to a beheading" occurs in the story. It, too, is a fable stressing the primacy of individuality over social coercion. It is, comparatively speaking, a "realistic" tale, though its premise is fantastic enough. In the end the narrator lets his "representative" go at his urgent request, and, though one might hope that he will go back to his perfect and dreamlike lake, Nabokov explained: "He will never find it again. If I let him go, it is in the hope that he will find a less dangerous job than that of my agent."

Both Nabokov and his wife considered *Invitation* one of his four greatest novels, a masterpiece. It was certainly one of his most popular works among his Russian readers, probably because it is a novel of ideas and seeks to make a broad philosophical statement. The statement of the novel is a justification of narcissism as a rare summit of the personality that leaves lowly egotism and all things pertaining to the body and the physical world behind. That is why Cincinnatus, though he is not himself a dead soul, can remove his own head like a puppet. On a more immediate level, of course, it is a message that easily found resonance in an émigré audience that frequently had great difficulty in believing in the reality of the languages and cultures that came after Russia. To that extent, though it may be seen as central to understanding Nabokov and his work, the novel stands apart from his other work. It really has a message. It is also the first Nabokov novel in which humor emerges with fully sharpened claws. Another work of this period, and a personal favorite of Vera Nabokov's, which demonstrates this same spirit of triumphant solipsism, is the 1932 short story "Perfection." If "Cloud, Castle, Lake" is an afterword to *Invitation*, "Perfection" is probably its foreword. The story portrays a man who exists entirely within a single cell of his own body, totally unsupported by any other form of existence and yet absolutely in control of reality.

It scarcely needs to be stressed that Vladimir Nabokov is one of the most intensely literary writers of our century. Though many of his games are games of structure (these are the ones you must solve to understand the work properly), the majority are games of literary reference. It frequently happens in the histories of all literatures that the giants step forward at the beginning. It was so as the golden age of Russian literature began. Though great writers came after them, no one, not even Tolstoy and Dostoevsky, surpassed Alexander Pushkin and Nikolai Gogol. Gogol claimed that the mantle of Russian literature had been passed to him by Pushkin, but it was not really that way at all. No two writers could possibly be more different, in life as in art.

Pushkin and Gogol are polar opposites, and Nabokov's artistic personality is an electric arc oscillating between these two poles. Pushkin's sense of pure poetry and light irony as well as his heightened feeling of *amor propre* are to be found throughout Nabokov's Russian poetry, his scores of post-*Lolita* interviews, in the lyrical and emotional sentences that well up in his novels and contribute so much to their greatness, and in many aspects of *Speak, Memory.* His rough literary manners go back far beyond Gumilyov and are first to be found in Pushkin's correspondence. Gogol's solemn deviousness, his spectral vision in art, and the peculiar intensity of his comedy make him the main forebear of what we now in our time call Nabokovian. There are other features as well. Gogol said of himself: "In my dealings with people there has been much that put them off . . . In part this came about through deep self-esteem . . . There has never been another writer with this gift to portray the *poshlost'* of life so vividly, to know how to sketch the self-satisfaction of vulgar people so forcefully that this ephemeral aspect which escapes the eyes of most people is thrown in front of everyone." Gogol's *A Correspondence with Friends* expressed his hopes of communicating special secrets about life known to no one else. Particularly in his English metamorphosis, Nabokov's claim to special knowledge denied to other men was strong. The most famous statement was made in the 1964 *Playboy* interview in which he said: "What I am going to say now is something I never said before, and I hope it provokes a salutary little chill: I know more than I can express in words, and the little I can express would not have been expressed, had I not known more."

The young Dostoevsky parodied the prophetic Gogol savagely in his minor work *The Friend of the Family.* Which did not, as the great Formalist critic and novelist Yury Tynyanov showed, stop Dostoevsky from using the very same Gogol as a stylistic model and, ultimately, from behaving the same way himself. It is in this historical tradition of one aspect of the Russian psyche that we should see Nabokov's mockery of Gogol the man and dismissal of Dostoevsky the writer. Nabokov loved Pushkin all his life and aspired to his lightness and grace in writing, and to his careless Byronic bravery in the world. But it was Nabokov's greatness and his personal tragedy that he slept with Gogol's muse.

14

UNTIL 1933 NABOKOV AND HIS WIFE FELT COMFORTABLE enough in Germany. The extent of the dangers of nazism, and particularly its anti-Semitism, were still not clear to them. From the time of their marriage they had lived in a somewhat transient fashion, with no regard for furnishings or possessions. (So casual were the Nabokovs about where they were physically housed that they didn't even move into joint quarters until nearly two weeks after they were married.) German inflation went wild just when Nabokov was falling into his most mature and full stride as a productive writer, and the Nabokovs felt very much at risk. From 1932 until 1937 Nabokov and his wife had at least no rent worries, because they had moved into the four-room apartment of Anna Feigin, a maternal cousin of Vera Evseevna's. The apartment was at 22 Nestorstrasse. Their apartments before that final move were at 21 Luitpoldstrasse and at 29 Westphalischestrasse. Some years before Anna Feigin had become a kind of older sister to them after both of Vera Evseevna's parents died in 1928. Anna Feigin had typed the manuscript of *Mashenka* for Nabokov because she had always wanted to be involved in the production of a work of literature. She was in the fur business and modestly well-off. She suffered from a persecution complex all her life, and yet in spite of that she, too, failed at first to see the danger that Hitler presented to Jews. It is an exceedingly awkward subject, but in the very first days of Hitlerian rule there were some émigrés who responded positively to Hitler's alleged anticommunism and the strength with which he would supposedly put Germany's house in order. One source who knew Anna Feigin has indicated to me that she was one of these émigrés who was in the first years heedlessly oblivious to the true direction of nazism. Vladimir and Vera Nabokov, needless to say, were not in the slightest approving of what was happening, but after 1933 they were fairly dependent upon Anna and so stayed and stayed past all reason, though they did constantly lay plans for leaving. There were serious plans to emigrate to Australia together with Misha Kaminka (the son of Avgust Kaminka, coeditor of *The Rudder* with V. D. Nabokov and Joseph Hessen). They were on the verge of going in 1930, well before Hitler took power, but Kaminka and his wife separated, and the plan was scrapped.

Another intended destination after that was Belgium. Nabokov wrote to his friend and critic Zinaida Schakowskoi in 1932 about his intention to leave Berlin and Germany altogether. The problem, he said, was simply lack of money. There was also, however, the considerable difficulty presented by the green Nansen émigré passport, which granted permanent residency without citizenship and made travel from one's country of residence difficult. Generally speaking, other countries would accept a Nansen passport holder only if there was a firm contract for employment. In 1936 Nabokov asked Schakowskoi to rent an apartment for them, not in Brussels but in some obscure vacation town where they could count on getting two rooms and a kitchen very cheaply in the off season. One supposes that Nabokov's idea was to come first as a tourist and hope that better arrangements could be made once they were actually there. Nabokov (like millions of others, of course) felt quite powerless in the German economic situation. His feelings were aggravated by the knowledge that, beginning in 1936, his mother was living in bad health and near starvation in Czechoslovakia. For whatever reason, the Nabokovs abandoned their plans to go to Belgium as well.

Only a few years before, in 1929, the Nabokovs had felt secure enough about their future in Germany to have put a deposit on a small sliver of lakeside land near Kolberg, in an area of Germany (now it belongs to Poland) that had strong Slavic ties. The city had been founded as a Slavic outpost and had belonged to Russia as recently as the eighteenth century. There was a steady flow of Germans to the region during the summer months, but it was also the main area in which Berlin Russians spent their vacations. The Nabokovs had planned to build a simple cottage to which they could go for a month or so every summer. Misha Kaminka also had some land on the same lake. The land came from a large estate that was being subdivided. Nabokov thought in later years that the area of the land was no greater than the size of his suite at the Montreux Palace Hotel. They picnicked there frequently in the summer of 1929 and used it a bit in 1930 and 1931, too. But it became clear that they couldn't continue to meet the payments, and they let the land revert to the seller on the nonpayment clause. The land was "developed" by Nabokov as the setting for his 1936 novel *Despair*. Nabokov remembered the period around that land purchase much more positively than did his wife: "Darling, it was a good period. I had wonderful pupils."

The Rudder ceased publication in 1931. The days when it had had money and been able to pay more or less decent rates to its contributors were long gone, but there had all the same remained some payment, and the paper was, of course, exceptionally sympathetic to Nabokov. The modest but fairly assured income provided by Vera Evseevna's skills as a trained stenographer and an experienced simultaneous translator finally dried up when under the new Nazi laws she was forbidden to work any longer for the legal firm of Weil, Gans, and Dieckmann, where she had been employed since April 1930. When pressed about the danger and even folly of remaining so long in Berlin, Nabokov was vague and somewhat puzzled himself: "Yes, but we were always sluggish. Gracefully sluggish in the case of my wife, terribly sluggish in my case. We get accustomed to a place, and we just stay." Nabokov felt that it wasn't traditional Russian Oblomovism but rather his great fear that, since French was a language that he possessed fluently, France would inevitably impinge on the syntax and tone of his Russian if he lived there.

In May 1930, Nabokov made his first trip abroad for a literary reading, to Prague, where he read several poems and excerpts from *The Defense*. In the course of the next six years literary readings abroad assumed something of the formality of the professional lecture circuit. Invitations were given by local literary clubs, occasionally by universities where Russian was studied or where there were Russian scholars. There might be anywhere from two to five hundred people at such a reading, and, as stated earlier, Nabokov thought that his fee for such a reading could sometimes cover their living costs for up to three months. His wife thought he exaggerated.

Sirin was beyond question the outstanding young émigré writer by the early 1930s. He had been parodied in *Pravda*, and he had created a unique and strong style and voice. His use of German and English settings and characters in his novels made Sirin seem a very modish and international bird to his Russian readers. Thus, there was considerable curiosity among the émigré reading public to see the man.

When he gave his first literary reading in Paris in November 1932, Andrei Sedykh gave the following newspaper portrait of him:

> The curious will see a thirty-three-year-old young sportsman,
> very slender, nervous, and impulsive. His graceful manner
> and elegant speech with slightly rolled r's came to him from
> St. Petersburg; Cambridge contributed the look of a sports-
> man; Berlin gave him his good nature and a certain bagginess
> in his clothes—few people in Paris wear such macintoshes
> with button-out linings. He has a long thin face with a high
> tanned forehead and distinguished features. Sirin speaks
> quickly and with enthusiasm, but a certain sense of restraint
> keeps him from talking about himself.

Nabokov noted indignantly about these remarks that he had actually been wearing an English trenchcoat.

In his recent Russian memoirs Vasily Yanovsky recounts the sullen hostility that Nabokov faced when he gave his first reading in Paris in 1932. The older generation was highly suspicious of his surface polish, and the younger one thought his writing was insufficiently sincere and straightforward. Yanovsky, who had suffered a cutting Sirin review in *The Rudder* and so had his own reasons to be hostile to Nabokov, nonetheless found himself rooting for Nabokov in his struggle with a packed but unsympathetic hall:

> For me the sight of an extremely thin young man with, or so
> it seemed, a concave chest and the fleshy nose of a boxer,
> wearing a wondrously shabby smoking jacket, and reading

things he cared passionately about to people who were hostile to him, for me this sight had something glorious and triumphantly heroic about it. I gladly began to take his side . . . It was one against all, and he was winning. You had to be for him, and I found myself whole-heartedly wishing him to prevail. All this was in spite of the fact that Sirin combined the cultural level of writers like Kafka and Joyce . . . with the vulgarity of a second-rate movie actress.

Alas, few were fully won over by the performance as I was . . . Our poets didn't in the main give a hoot for prose, and as far as they were concerned Sirin stood in the dock for having produced poetry which was merely imitative of Bunin. All around me people were saying, almost in unison: "Wonderful, wonderful, but who needs this?"

The same opinion was expressed by Isaac Babel when he visited Paris shortly after *Invitation to a Beheading* had appeared. Asked what he thought about the quality of émigré writing, Babel, who must have been thinking of Nabokov, replied: "There are some who are writing extremely cleverly, even brilliantly. But what's the point of it? Among us in the Union such literature is simply necessary to no one."

In the mid-thirties the circuit of Nabokov's lectures traced a loose web back and forth across Europe. He read in Antwerp and Brussels (an excerpt from *Invitation to a Beheading* and the short story "The Aurelian"), where he went without a visa. He'd been instructed by the Social Revolutionaries of *Contemporary Annals* in how to disembark from the train at Charleroi and walk calmly across the tracks at a certain point in the underground station to the nearby subway system, as countless Russian revolutionaries traveling through Europe had done before him.

He read again in Prague, but by this time the Nazis were already becoming bothersome at the border, and so Nabokov went to Czechoslovakia by a roundabout route, carrying the manuscript of "Cloud, Castle, Lake," one of his several very sharp satires on the German character. Nabokov enjoyed telling the story of how the flabbergasted Ivan Bunin was forcibly given a purgative and shaken out in a search for the jewels that it was presumed the newly elected Nobel laureate might be attempting to smuggle away from the future German war effort. What Nabokov didn't tell interviewers was that shortly before this trip in 1934 he had

had coffee with Bunin at the Adlon in Berlin and had asked Bunin
if he could smuggle some money to his sister in Paris. Bunin refused. Nabokov's own favorite story about himself in this time of
troubles was how he and a friend named Cannac purposely went
into all the Jewish shops with smashed plate-glass windows to
demonstrate contempt for the Nazis the day after the Krystal-
nacht.

One of Nabokov's most fruitful lectures was given for the Russian Department of the University of Dresden, where he was invited by the talented philosopher of art Fyodor Stepun, who
taught there. There was a full hall for the reading in the arts theater of the university, and afterward the local Russian Orthodox
priest, Father Pyotr, played chess with Nabokov on stage. It is
not recorded who won or how long the match lasted. When the
evening was over, Nabokov and Stepun strolled along Mathema-
tician's Walk to Stepun's quarters, where they had a wide-rang-
ing discussion on questions of art that lasted until two in the
morning. Stepun made a remark about someone's face resembling
a cow's udder. Several years later that puckish observation furnished Nabokov with the description of Sebastian Knight's bad
biographer in his first English novel, *The Real Life of Sebastian
Knight:* "Mr. Goodman's large soft pinkish face was, and is, remarkably like a cow's udder." By artistic mutation Stepun's
strong image in turn generated the now-famous image at the end
of the novel of the writer removing his black glove to reveal a
multitude of tiny hands that spill about the floor.

Nabokov's wife said that until 1933 Germany was a "rather
democratic country," though Nabokov himself did not agree. By
1934 Germany was a dictatorship. The Nabokovs heard Hitler
speak and decided from the sound of his voice that they should
leave. Nabokov made several gestures of heedless disgust. Nabokov's friend George Hessen recalled going to a boxing match at
the Sports Palace with Nabokov and an émigré newspaper reporter named Boris Brodsky where Nazi signs and announcements were everywhere. On the way home either Nabokov or
Brodsky (Hessen's and Nabokov's accounts differ) amused himself by playing with the flowers or feathers on the hat of a woman
on their tram who was in obviously Nazi company. "I was scared,
and he was glad," said Hessen. Whoever played the reckless game
that evening, it is not unlike other things that we know Nabokov

did do. Hessen says he used to get phone calls from Nabokov asking unnerving questions such as: "When will our Communist cell meet?"

In 1933 and 1934 Nabokov, Hessen, and Brodsky were frequently in each other's company. On several occasions they went to the municipal swimming pool together, though the first time Brodsky nearly drowned after jumping in the deep end because he was trying to conceal the fact that he didn't know how to swim. Nabokov told me that many Russians can't swim, and that such gestures of suicidal pride are quite common among Russians. The comforting warmth of such specifically Russian incidents became more important as the din of nazism grew louder in Berlin. He chuckled as he recalled how Hessen started to fill a napkin ring with vodka and was saved from disaster only by the fact that he had also forgotten to take the top off the bottle before pouring.

In 1934 Vera Evseevna was pregnant, and while she was giving birth Nabokov played chess until three in the morning with George Hessen's half-brother. In January 1934, émigré Berlin feted Bunin for the Nobel Prize he had won a few months earlier. Nabokov and his very pregnant wife attended the festivities with Nabokov seated at Bunin's side at the head table. It was one of the last émigré occasions in Berlin. Nabokov told me that it was an example of the Russian failure to notice the ordinary facts of life that, although they continued to lead their normal social life until the eleventh hour, only George Hessen among their acquaintances knew that Vera was pregnant. Hessen agreed that no one else had noticed, but he gallantly defended the Russians' powers of observation, pointing out to me that Vera's dress and posture during pregnancy were both extremely artful—for certain Russians showing a pregnancy is a very bourgeois thing to do.

The period 1929–37 was in most respects an extremely happy one for the Nabokovs. He was a famous writer (though in an invisible nation) and their child Dmitri was born. But the steady, boring pressure of penury could no longer be waved away. In 1933 Nabokov applied for a writer's subsidy from the main émigré writers' fund. His application letter was a single sentence. He received 250 francs and did not say thank you but merely gave directions as to where the money was to be sent. His pride was enormous and probably worked to his detriment. Other writers received two and three times as much.

By 1935 the anti-Semitic Nuremburg Laws made Jews into nonpersons. In August 1934, after the birth of their son, Nabokov wrote to his mother explaining that he was surrounded by debts and was unable to say when he could help her. In May 1935 he continued on the same theme but told his mother that all the same they mustn't lose heart. In late 1935 Nabokov was written about in English for the first time in articles by Albert Parry in H. L. Mencken's *American Mercury* and in the *New York Times*. Mencken had asked Parry to do a provocative article naming émigré writers beside Bunin who were worthy of note, and Parry had fixed on Sirin as the most outstanding. Nabokov wrote to his mother that, although the *New York Times* had written that "our age has been enriched by the appearance of a great writer," he didn't own a decent pair of trousers any more and didn't know what he was going to get to wear to Belgium where PEN had invited him to give a reading.

Nabokov had a successful reading tour of England in early 1937, though he was embarrassed by a grammatical slip in the title of his English essay, *England and Me*, which was his first effort in autobiography, and he failed to obtain an academic appointment, which had been one of the purposes of the trip.

When Nabokov read for the second time in France, in 1936, the evening was the apogee of his émigré career. *Despair*, one of his finest Russian novels (and the one closest in spirit and tone to *Lolita*) had just been published, and what was to be his major Russian novel, *The Gift*, was shortly to begin serialization in *Contemporary Annals*. The finest literary critics of the emigration—Khodasevich, Bem, Weidle, and Bitsilli—had all within the preceding two years written about Sirin as a Russian and indeed European writer of the first rank. That evening, February 9, 1936, the Parnassus of Russian émigré literature was in the hall. Nabokov shared the evening with Vladislav Khodasevich, who read first. Tickets for the reading in a small auditorium on the rue Las-Cases were quickly sold out, and, though extra chairs had been added in the hall, people were still pressing in when Khodasevich had already begun to read. Nabokov sat beside Ivan Bunin, who, deathly afraid of catching cold, kept his overcoat and a hat on and his nose buried in his collar. Adamovich, who was even more hostile to Khodasevich than to Nabokov, was there, and Khodasevich read a poem that satirized him rather harshly. There had been an unpleasant incident prior to the reading, when Miliukov's *The Latest News*, for which Adamovich was the main literary critic, ran an announcement of the reading with Sirin's name printed in much bolder type than Khodasevich's, and Nabokov had had to complain on behalf of his fellow poet. It is ironic and sad that, once it had indisputably added something to the riches of Russian literature, émigré culture in its second decade turned significantly more sour and sullenly querulous. There had been intimations of it from the beginning.

After the intermission Nabokov read three short stories that he had recently written: "A Russian Beauty," "Terra Incognita," and "Breaking the News." He had a bad sore throat, but lozenges kept it sufficiently lubricated. It was, he wrote to his wife, one of the most successful literary readings he had ever had. When the reading was over, a large company of writers, some with husbands and wives, went to drink champagne at the La Fontaine café. Bunin, Khodasevich, Aldanov, Weidle, and Nina Berberova were there. Fondaminsky and another editor of *Contemporary Annals* sat at a nearby table. The group didn't disperse until three in the morning. Nabokov has denied Berberova's recollection in her memoirs of how he shocked nearly everyone, and Aldanov in particular, by his curt dismissal of some of Tolstoy's early work as juvenilia and his assertion that he had never even read *The Sevastopol Tales*. (In this instance a letter that Nabokov wrote to his wife the next day shows that Berberova did get it wrong.)

Aldanov was indeed indignant, but it had nothing to do with Tolstoy. It was a proper Russian scene in the style of Dostoevsky. They had all probably had a little too much to drink. Aldanov shouted at Nabokov: "You despise us all!" He then said that Nabokov was the first writer of the emigration and demanded that Bunin take off his signet ring and give it to Nabokov as a token in recognition of his superiority. Bunin didn't do it, of course, and then the Nobel Prize winner passed his affront on to the half-Polish Khodasevich, whom he didn't like, by calling out: "Hey, Polak!" Fortunately, the evening was gayer than these awkward moments. Though Berberova claims that Bunin could not hear the name Sirin without having a tantrum, and it is true that Bunin's pronouncement that Sirin was "a monster" was well known, the gruff but just Bunin is credited in the memoirs of Galina Kuznetsova, who lived with Bunin for many years, with having declared: "Nabokov has discovered a whole new universe, for which one must be grateful to him." But Bunin did predict, to Nabokov's face, that he would die in total isolation.

Nabokov gave one French reading. He was a replacement speaker, as a result of which some of the audience started to leave as soon as he began to read and they realized he was a substitute. But Nabokov had the consolation of attentive James Joyce in the audience that stayed. He was invited to dinner with Joyce once by mutual friends, the Leons, but Nabokov claimed that it was not a memorable evening. The only thing he could recall about it was that Joyce wanted to know the history of mead in Russia.

Perhaps because of the frequent readings he did, perhaps because they represented more accessible income, Nabokov produced a steady stream of short stories in the thirties. A noticeably greater note of cynicism is present in many of these last European stories. Typical is "A Dashing Fellow," written in 1930–31, which was rejected by both *The Rudder* and *The Latest News* because its hero has a premature ejaculation (there had never before been one in staid Russian literature). The story presents much the same treatment of the problem of moral duty versus sexual desire that confronts Humbert Humbert. A traveling salesman, a Russian émigré named Konstantin, meets a somewhat pretentious but very friendly German actress on a train. They get on very well together, and she readily agrees with his proposal that he get off the train with her and spend the night at her apartment. While she goes out to bring back some food, someone leaves a message for her that her father is dying. But when she returns, instead of telling her, Konstantin tries to hustle her to bed, which is when he has his "awkward, messy, and premature spasm." He tells her that he is going out for some cigars but heads instead for the station where he has checked his bag and leaves town. The tale is narrated by the salesman in a nonchalant "we." Konstantin realizes that he is going to go on traveling on trains, picking up women, going to cafés, "and, in several years, we'll die." Konstantin is the same sort of repulsive hero that Nabokov developed more fully in his 1936 novel *Despair*.

Not only his heroes, but also his heroines are quite off-putting in stories of this period. The most unattractive of the Nabokov women are unquestionably the non-Russian ones. The greatest eroticism is given to the seductive children like Emma who precede Lolita. His Russian women may be charming but are always sophisticated and sad. Olga, the heroine of "A Russian Beauty," is typical in this regard—within a very few pages she passes from being a young beauty for whom students are prepared to commit suicide to an awkwardly unmarried woman for whom a lusterless match is finally made, whereupon she dies in childbirth. None of the major Russian works by Nabokov has a woman as its main character. (And even in *Lolita* and *Ada* the primacy of the female characters is more apparent than real.) Women are accorded neither the madness nor the attractive romanticism that Nabokov's heroes in one degree or another all have. In this regard particularly, Nabokov is the exception to prove a rule about Russian literature. For Russian literature has been historically noted for the purity and moral force of its heroines. Nabokov doesn't give us women of this sort, with the exception of his first heroine, Mashen'ka. In fact, there is a valid question to be put: Did Nabokov like women? In his fiction, at least, by and large not.

In literature and life Nabokov preferred acerbic women. His greatest Russian heroine—from the point of view of being a fully realized and memorable character—is probably Nina in his 1936 short story, "Spring in Fialta." This story was Nabokov's own favorite among all his short stories, and it certainly is one of his handful of unquestionably great ones. The narrator tells of his many chance meetings over the years with Nina. They are both married to other people, and their affair takes place only from time to time in "the margin of my life." Her character remains as unfathomable as she herself is attractive, and, when she is killed in a car crash, the narrator learned with surprise that she "turned out to be mortal after all." Nina's reality depends upon the narrator's conveyed emotion, and that is intense. Not only in the descriptions of Nina, but in almost every line one feels a rich, tactile prose that perfectly conveys this feeling. The story is a verbal sun shower (more brilliant perhaps in the original Russian), and in the course of it one only occasionally notices the poignant sorrow in the narrator's voice. In Nina at least, and also in Liza Bogolepov in the later *Pnin*, Nabokov does show a link with classical nineteenth-century Russian literature.

In writing about "Spring in Fialta," Zinaida Schakowskoi said that Nina's husband has "a certain something in common with one of Nabokov's contemporaries but also has much in common with Nabokov himself." To that it can be added that Nabokov may well have had much in common with the narrator, who is periodically drawn into bed by the impulsive Nina. The husband— a tall, haughty Hungarian artist who is inclined toward puns and writes in French—would be the decoy character. This is one door of Nabokov's life that must remain sealed, for "Nina," I believe, is still alive. It is possible that "Spring in Fialta," though its plot is totally invented, may well be a tangential record of Nabokov's first serious extramarital affair. I initially learned of this aspect of Nabokov's life from George Hessen, who smiled at me quizzically when he saw that I was stunned by what he had just told me: "And did you think that he changed once he had got married? Volodya was always the same."

The most highly developed antipathy toward women in any of Nabokov's Russian works is to be found in the novel *Despair*, which he wrote between 1932 and 1936. We know now that this novel, with all its abnormal psychology, was composed almost in parallel with *The Gift*, which is classical in its serenity and which he also began to write in 1932. The juxtaposition of "pessimistic" *Despair* and "optimistic" *The Gift* in time of composition is one of the strongest demonstrations possible of a sharp dualism in Nabokov's narrative imagination.

Despair is a tale of a murder that goes wrong. Felix the victim is the necessary and complementary mirror without which Hermann, the murderer, cannot be seen in proper focus. Hermann is right-handed, Felix left-handed. In a key sentence added to the English translation of the novel, the relationship is neatly stated as "Narcissus fooling Nemesis by helping his image out of the brook." Nemesis is the personification of divine retribution for violation of sacred law. Murder is only one aspect of Hermann's transgression. His despair is predominantly sexual. In the original Russian the sexual despair—the threat of homosexuality, the repulsion felt by the hero toward women—was expressed only in marginal asides by Hermann, but the 1966 *Despair* has "an important passage which had been stupidly omitted in more timid times." The scene is Hermann's description of intercourse with his wife Lydia, who is pudgy and formless, but then that is the only sort of woman, Hermann informs us, who excites him. The dream involves schizophrenic dissociation. Hermann stands outside of himself and gains excitement by watching himself copulate with Lydia through strong binoculars from an ever-increasing distance. The aberration, which is distinctly narcissistic in character, is, Hermann tells us, "not as uncommon as I thought at first among high-strung men in their middle thirties." This reference, once again, is to the case studies of Havelock Ellis, which Vera Evseevna's friend, Magda Nachmann-Achariya, brought to Nabokov from the Berlin University library in 1931 when Nabokov was in bed for some weeks with severe neuralgia. His nervous rashes did not show above his neck but for a considerable period of time covered much of the rest of his body.

Despair is the first of Nabokov's novels in which he defies the possibility of any judgmental interpretation, particularly Freudian. Hermann leers at the "rat-faced, sly little expert" who will discover sure signs of psychic abnormality in his tale. There is a great deal of teasing and taunting of the reader by Hermann, rather in the manner—it cannot really be avoided—of Dostoevsky's underground man. It should be fairly self-evident in looking back over all of Nabokov's work that some of his strongest dislikes—Freud and Dostoevsky, in particular—are genuine enough but also involve a certain amount of territorial dispute and not a little unacknowledged borrowing. Of course *Despair* is a parody and a rejection of the terms of the classical "realistic" novel, but all the same Hermann is playing the part of Raskolnikov, and the novel is about the crime of pride and its punishment.

One particularly Dostoevskian dream in *Despair* is the one in which Hermann opens a door to a perfectly empty, newly whitewashed room. There is a chair in the room, as though someone was going to nail something up near the ceiling. This pure room is an obvious parody of Dostoevsky's famous spider-filled room. Hermann says that, since he knows whom he would find on that chair with a hammer and a mouthful of nails, he spat the nails out and left the door to the room closed. He may be talking about suicide, the alternative to the murder of Felix.

Hermann's assault upon Felix is really an assault upon the "refuse particles" of his own past, and he says that the real author of the tale that he is telling is his memory. As he waits for Felix in the dingy hotel room he thinks of "Christina Forsmann, whom I had known carnally in 1915" and then loses his way in a sand-storm of memory in which he cannot discover the kernel of his personality. But this is just one moment of Proustian sublimity. Hermann's past seems singularly devoid of love, the necessary catalyst, and there is nothing worthy of being *retrouvé*. Her-mann's false "twin" Felix is a simple soul in some ways, but he has exceptionally repulsive habits. Hermann has entrusted his diary to an émigré writer, the author of psychological novels, which, though they are very artificial, are "not badly con-structed." But Hermann, as presented to the reader, scarcely needs a ghostwriter. By his own admission Hermann possesses the gift of "penetrating life's devices" and also of "lighthearted inspired lying." Thus, whether Hermann is the character himself speaking through his diary or an émigré novelist playing games with the diary (and Hermann) becomes extremely problematic. It's a technique Nabokov had already used in *The Eye*, and which he would use more and more in his later years.

But there is also another "more real" story which can only be guessed at from the infrequent *lapses* in Hermann's commentary. Thus, Lydia leaves him a note saying that she has gone to the movies, but Hermann chances to drop in on her cousin Ardalion that evening and finds his wife lying half-dressed on his bed. Hermann, however, assures us that he has complete faith in his wife's fidelity and love. The possibility, indeed probability, that Lydia's affair with Ardalion is the realistic element of the novel leads to some most interesting further thoughts. For the meek Lydia plays a key role in Hermann's crime, and, if she is not in fact the submissive and loyal wife Hermann thinks she is, there emerges a good chance that the entire story is a madman's fan-tasy. This possibility is corroborated by a technical detail at the end of the novel, for Hermann is writing a description of what he is doing at the very moment he is supposedly doing it.

Hermann has his own interpretation of his tale, and it is a polit-ical one. He imagines a world where doubles are everywhere: perfect socialism, where all men are more than equal—they are in-terchangeable. Hermann's reading of *Despair* is only a whimsical bit of byplay on Nabokov's part, another deceptive chess move. There is no politics in the novel. Hermann gives the correct solu-tion in the first paragraph, where he compares himself to a poet.

Seen in this way, the murder becomes the artist's assault upon his creation, trying to fashion it to his will and to the appearance of reality, and Hermann's failure then is simply a matter of interpretation. Hermann is striving to achieve not merely a perfect crime but, more than that, the triumph of a perfect work of art. In this Nabokov is following the famous analogy of Oscar Wilde between the criminal and the artist. There are two basic principles at play in *Despair*. Nabokov gives one to Hermann and the other to Ardalion. The first is that every work of art is a deception, the second, that each face is unique.

The virtuosity with which Hermann changes his narrative voice and the thrust and hilarity of his literary parodies, ranging from Swinburne to Pushkin, constitute a semiautonomous work of art within the novel. What Nabokov and Hermann share most of all is their mutual contempt for the great Fyodor Mikhailovich, who ends as the second, unnoticed corpse of the novel; alternatively, Nabokov and Hermann may have carried away Dostoevsky's shell to use for their own purposes. Hermann speculates mockingly on having a Dostoevskian conclusion to his story in which something is told about the further fate of each character. In the English translation Dostoevsky is reduced to "Dusty." When Gallimard brought out the novel in a French translation, Jean-Paul Sartre attacked it but failed to see the parodic nature of Nabokov's relationship and spoke of the novel as being "of the old school" and under the influence of Dostoevsky. The real purpose of Sartre's review was probably to place the possibility of politically uncommitted émigré literature firmly out of view. For Sartre the difference between Dostoevsky and Nabokov is that,

> Dostoevsky believed in his characters, M. Nabokov no longer believes in his, nor even in the art of the novel. He does not conceal borrowing Dostoevsky's artistic method, even as he ridicules it ... Here, one thinks in closing the book, is a lot of noise for nothing ... I fear that M. Nabokov, like his hero, has read too much. But I see another resemblance between the author and his character. Both are victims of the war and emigration ... There now exists a curious literature of Russian émigrés and others who are *rootless*. The rootlessness of Nabokov, like that of Hermann Karlovich, is total. He does not concern himself with any society, even to revolt against it, because he is not of any society.

Sartre's essay is a splendidly low watermark in the non-Russian critical literature on émigré writing. Nabokov took his revenge a decade later when he reviewed the English translation of Sartre's *Nausea* in the *New York Times Book Review* and claimed that behind Sartre "looms Dostoevsky at his worst."

Despair is, measured against the outstanding fiction of this century, a major novel—the first one Nabokov wrote—but it has been its poor fortune to be overshadowed by some four or five later Nabokov novels. When it first appeared, Vladimir Weidle wrote in the occasional journal *Circle:* "Really, there is no point in writing reviews about *Despair*. Everyone who has not yet lost interest in Russian literature has read this novel or will read it. Everyone who has not yet lost sensitivity to literary innovation and freshness in Russian prose will acknowledge the enormous giftedness of its author."

Khodasevich's interpretation of the novel went farther than Weidle's, in the same vein as all his other reviews of Sirin:

> The theme of Sirin's art is art itself; this is the first thing that must be said about him ... The urge to transfer himself into his double, to turn the reality surrounding the narrator inside out, to achieve something like a frustrated suicide by means of murder, and finally the failure of the whole plan, the detection behind all the fictions and apparitions, behind the crumbling reality and the destroyed dream of the bare, trembling spiritual protoplasm which is condemned to death—does not all of this bespeak an intricate allegory behind which is concealed not the despair of a murderer scheming for money, but the despair of an artist incapable of believing in the object of his art? *This* despair constitutes the basic motif of the best things created by Sirin. It puts him on a level with the most significant artists in contemporary European literature, and moreover gives him a place occupied by no one else in Russian literature.

Partial as I am to this interpretation of Nabokov's art, it doesn't sufficiently take into account the one other important artistic innovation that made its first appearance in this novel before being developed to a much greater degree in *Invitation to a Beheading, Bend Sinister, Pale Fire,* and *Transparent Things.* That theme, which has already been touched upon, is the literary character's awareness or ignorance of the fact that he *is* a literary character.

Adam Krug in *Bend Sinister* goes mad when he glimpses the face of his creator through the mirror of a puddle. Hermann Karlovich, like Charles Kinbote, struggles against the control of his creator, striving to become his own man, and we can never really be sure how much Hermann does understand. This theme is, in essence, a theological joke, the modernist stage framework of a belief in God. The closing "movie rehearsal" scene of *Despair* is an insanely impetuous last effort on the part of Hermann to snatch the story away from his creator, Sirin, who smiles gently from behind the mask that is Hermann. For Khodasevich, Hermann corresponded to Salieri, the artist tormented by his awareness of his own inadequacies in comparison with Mozart. Was there something of this in Nabokov himself? It's logical to assume that it may well have been a factor in his literary personality in relation to, say, Pushkin and Gogol when one considers how intensely literary a writer he was, and how strongly his talent was denigrated—at the same time that it acquired passionate advocates, of course—at various stages throughout his career. Nabokov was, after all, a parodist, and a parodist at the end of a great literary tradition. He was a great writer, not a Salieri, but he was not a Mozart either, and, until the last years of his life, I think that his continued use of this theme and problem demonstrates that he knew it. Some of Nabokov's mad heroes end in wild laughter, suicide, or silence, but a few like Hermann, Humbert, and Kinbote can never stop talking, and it is from these characters that we have the proof of the importance of the theme of that last wild, hopeless push to the very summit of Parnassus: literary perfection and self-love perfectly requited.

Nabokov always dealt in extremes, and many of his works examine a truism or an idea in terms of its apparent opposite. Three years before *Despair* Nabokov wrote another fantasy about murder, "An Affair of Honor," but in this story the protagonist is the intended victim. A man returns home earlier than he had told his wife he would (recalling *King, Queen, Knave*) and finds a business acquaintance in his apartment getting dressed while his wife is singing in the bathtub (recalling *Laughter in the Dark*, as does another scene in the story). The man challenges his wife's lover to a duel, but the man is a former White Army officer who has boasted of killing over five hundred Reds. The husband's only

fault is that he is a total coward, and at the end of the story he has
fled to a cheap hotel room where he greedily munches on a sand-
wich like a hungry animal. He has had a fantasy in which his opponent has turned out to be a greater coward than he is, but he
knows that such things don't happen in real life. In the gallery of
Nabokov's characters this deceived and cowardly husband is perhaps superior to the central character of *Laughter in the Dark*,
who has lusts and absurd pretenses but almost no imaginative faculty, but he is inferior to the otherwise exceedingly unpleasant
Hermann, who at least has his highly developed imagination.

This obsession with cowardice, nastiness, and madness in his
writing in the thirties was not entirely detached play on the part
of a cool-handed and morally indifferent artist. In one of his
English interviews Nabokov allowed that in *Laughter in the
Dark*: "I tried to express a world in terms as candid, as near to my
vision of the world, as I could. If I was cruel, I suppose it was because I saw the world as cruel in those days." It is interesting to
note that, when he came to reprint that interview in his collection
Strong Opinions, he deleted those sentences.

And yet, at the same time, Nabokov was beginning, from 1932
(and in a major way, from 1935), to write *The Gift*, which is
characterized by serenity and positivism and accepts the émigré
world that has been given to the artists of his generation. Perhaps
the "yes" in that novel is a bit too artificially assertive. Almost
certainly it was taken as a motif from Molly Bloom's famous
speech in *Ulysses*, but it is a genuine and powerful aspect of Nabokov's true personality, too, attested to by almost everyone who
met him in these years.

The Gift is like Lermontov's *A Hero of Our Time* (although
its structural originality is far bolder) in that it is a novel of tenuously connected short stories and also, as Nabokov has taken
pains to stress in his English foreword to the novel, it is a kind of
unorthodox history of Russian literature. The novel came late to
Russia and, perhaps because of this, its form has always possessed
a certain tendency not to obey strict rules of structure. Starting
with Pushkin's "novel in verse," Gogol's "poem" novel, Lermontov, and proceeding through several dozen other major novels
right up to *Doctor Zhivago* with its appendix of poems by the
hero, Nabokov stands very much in a particular tradition of the
novel. In addition to the biography of Chernyshevsky and the life

of the poet Fyodor's father, the other most significant autonomous stories within the novel are, of course, Fyodor's romance with Zina, the patchy panorama of émigré literary life in Berlin, the imaginary discourses, virtual lectures, on Russian literature, and the strange death of young Yasha Chernyshevsky.

In his foreword to the English-language edition, Nabokov robustly declared that he has nothing to do with his hero Fyodor. Fyodor's explorer father is not his father, he never courted Zina Merz and was never concerned about the poet Koncheyev, or any other writer for that matter. The truth is: Nabokov is a closer analogue to Fyodor than to any other fictional character created by him in his mature prose. V. D. Nabokov was certainly not an explorer—that is what his son would have been had the revolution not occurred and had he been able to stage his planned entomological exploration of Siberia—but Nabokov's mother had been pressing Volodya to write something about his father for years. Those who observed them at close quarters over many years, such as Zinaida Schakowskoi, have insisted that in their view there is a great deal of Vera Evseevna in the portrayal of Zina. Koncheyev is most certainly Vladislav Khodasevich, for Nabokov used many of the same phrases in talking about Khodasevich with me that are used to describe Koncheyev in the novel. And even the student Yasha Chernyshevsky's name echoes nicely the name Chernykhovsky, a regular pupil of Nabokov's in those years. Nabokov intended to extend his chronicle of émigré life even farther by writing a sequel to *The Gift*, but the war and his escape into an entirely different culture prevented that.

The Gift as a whole is intended to have the character of an eternally not-yet-written novel. The biographies of Chernyshevsky, Fyodor's father, and Yasha are, we are told, raw material for a novelist. There is someone else within Fyodor who is filing things away for use in a future novel. The artist in Fyodor is able to slip into other people's souls at will. Nabokov acknowledged straight realistic representation only for Vladimirov (which is true, but all the same he is a decoy) and Goryainov, an official of the Berlin committee of émigré writers, who could recite classical drama with a marvelous accent. Goryainov portrays a certain Plaksin who was active in émigré organizations.

Various signs of the spectral reality of the novel are given to the reader, such as the way Koncheyev makes tentative efforts to-

ward composing a poem based on Fyodor's unspoken thoughts.
Like Nabokov, Fyodor declares that he either loves a writer fer-
vently or completely rejects him. Goncharov, Pisemsky, and Les-
kov are treated roughly. Pushkin, Gogol, Tolstoy, and Chekhov
are wholly accepted. With reservations Lermontov, Tiutchev,
Fet, and Blok are admitted to the Russian Parnassus, too, but
Turgenev and Dostoevsky are treated disdainfully. Other addi-
tions to the proper canon of Russian literature are sprinkled
throughout the book, such as the intense and crystalline turn-of-
the-century poet Innokenty Annensky. But of contemporary
writers and poets only Vladislav Khodasevich is admitted. In a
very real sense Khodasevich and Nabokov, the two foremost
writers of the emigration after Ivan Bunin (who already clearly
belonged to the past), were engaged in a conspiracy of two for
nearly a decade and a half. Nabokov had written a highly favor-
able review of Khodasevich, in 1927, and Khodasevich reviewed
Nabokov eight times, each in an extremely positive way. Nabokov repaid his debt after the death of Khodasevich by declaring
that he was the greatest poet the twentieth century had yet produced.

The Gift is plotted according to intricate analogy and coincidence. The misfortune of the Berlin Chernyshevsky family serves
as a parallel in Fyodor's mind to the loss of his father. The ridiculous parodic reviews counterpoint the serious literary discussions.
Fyodor's meeting with Zina occurs after a long series of unsuccessful tries on the part of fate to bring them together. Fyodor
suggests that their romance should be the theme of a novel, cur-
tained and surrounded by all his professional passions and cares.
Zina is concerned that such a novel will simply be autobiography,
but Fyodor assures her that he will twist and change everything
so that nothing is recognizable. This conversation about the novel
Fyodor will write is also a description of the novel Nabokov has
written.

The Gift has an open ending, and we can foresee that Fyodor
and Zina will be married, Fyodor will emerge as a major artist,
and, in the more immediate future, they will be unable to get
back into their house since they have both lost their keys. The
childhood poems of Fyodor Godunov-Cherdyntsev and the
somewhat excessive parody of Chernyshevsky each serve a definite and carefully calculated function. The poems are bland, the

biography is excessively sharp, but they both mark a necessary step in Godunov-Cherdyntsev's artistic maturation. Fyodor tells both Koncheyev and Zina that his previous faults will not be present in his next work. Nabokov's goal, in other words, is to present a major writer before he has attained complete mastery, but in such a manner that the question of his emergence as an important writer is never in question. In the early stages of Nabokov's work on the novel a few scattered Sirin poems occasionally appeared in *The Latest News* with the notation "from F. G. Ch.," but these poems weren't used in the novel. These poems, both in theme and mastery, belong to a fully mature poet and thus more closely resemble the later verse of Nabokov than the poetry of Godunov-Cherdyntsev. It would demonstrate too abruptly the gift that is meant only to be promised in the novel, and it may well be that these 1934 poems were meant to enter into the continuation of the novel that Nabokov planned.

In his review of *The Gift*, which appeared before the novel's serialization had been completed, Khodasevich stressed the natural slowness of the novel's development. It does indeed proceed at an old-fashioned pace, which is both necessary and natural to it, since its subject is in large part the history of Russian literature. There is a striking contrast with the perhaps too frenetic pace of *Invitation to a Beheading*. *The Gift* is written on the plan of a river serenely picking up its already subdued tributaries and, in the process, gradually but unmistakably expanding its shores. The novel occupies a singular place in Nabokov's art, and there is a case, I believe, for claiming it as the greatest Russian novel of this century.

Nabokov took the unfinished novel with him when he finally left Berlin in 1937, but his days as a Russian writer were already numbered. He was in France less than three years before the fall of Paris, and, while he did write six short stories (two of which were to have been part of a novel that was never completed), two plays, and some poetry, his time as a Russian writer belongs in the main to the Berlin period. In his time in France he was literally a trilingual writer, writing in French but also working on *The Real Life of Sebastian Knight* and preparing to become an English writer. In published figures of library circulation there is clear indication that the level of émigré reader sophistication in Paris in the thirties was not as high as it had been in Berlin in the twenties. The Turgenev Library, the largest Russian library in Paris, listed its two most-borrowed authors as Tolstoy and Dostoevsky, which is not surprising, but close after them there was a group of absolutely unimportant writers such as Amfiteatrov, Mintslov, and Princess Bebutov. Even Ivan Bunin was absent from the list. The sole serious émigré writer who figured on it was Mark Aldanov.

So Nabokov did not for various reasons really have a French period in the way that he had a German one. When he left Berlin, *The Gift* was largely completed, and his major prose works included the great short story "The Potato Elf," the novels *The Eye, Invitation to a Beheading, The Defense, Despair, Laughter in the Dark, Mary, King, Queen, Knave,* as well as scattered other short stories such as "The Return of Chorb," "Lik," and "Spring in Fialta." In just ten years he had created a body of work which may be compared in this century only to that of Chekhov and Bunin, and it is not too much to say that in all of Russian literature there are really only two prose writers against whose work Nabokov's Russian work may be measured in proper perspective: Gogol and Tolstoy.

15

THE REASON (ACCORDING TO A LETTER WRITTEN BY VERA) that Nabokov finally left Berlin was that Taboritsky, one of his father's killers, was released from prison in 1937 and almost immediately given a position in Hitler's government and supervision of émigré affairs. Vera Evseevna insisted that Nabokov leave at once. He had been able to lay claim to a small portion of the Graun estate, an antique snuff box, to be precise, that had been advertised for claimants. Fortunately, Nabokov knew that one of his great-grandmothers was a Graun. It was sold at once and produced the several hundred dollars necessary to prepare to leave Germany. A further forty-two pounds—a substantial sum—came at the last minute as the advance payment for the English translation of *Despair.*

In their last Berlin years Vera Evseevna was working regularly, while Nabokov stayed at home looking after the baby and writing in the bathtub with a board across it to serve as a desk. Behind his back, Fondaminsky called Nabokov an eagle caged in a bathroom. He was good-humored about his domestic duties and would show friends how diapers were wrung out with an elegant backhand twist of the wrist like in tennis. Unless the weather was bad, Nabokov would take Dmitri for a regular stroll at nine, returning at twelve forty-five. After lunch there was a nap that lasted until four, when the boy was given a cup of cocoa, and Nabokov took him out on the streets again. The mornings tended to be passed in parks and on bridges watching trains go by. The afternoons were the time for the pedal car. Nabokov took an active role in toilet training and bathing, too, though he told his mother at first that he was finding the whole routine quite exhausting. All the same, by all signs Nabokov was a devoted "modern"-style father.

It appears that there were strains in the marriage. When Nabokov went to Paris for the second time, he began a serious love affair. Her name was Irina Guadinini. She had lived with her mother and brother in Brussels before the family moved to Paris. Prior to the revolution her mother's first husband had been a prominent St. Petersburg Kadet. He was killed during the revolution. Guadinini-Kokoshkin and her two children formed an intense family unit. In Belgium they ran a little Russian restaurant. But her brother was a serious alcoholic and died prematurely.

Irina was a rather attractive (*khoroshen'kaya* in Russian) blonde with a finely chiseled face that was not unlike Vera Nabokov's in its contours, though her complexion and hair were darker. She was known for her irony. Irina married a Lieutenant Malakhov, who had become one of the "Congo Russians." They met when he was on leave from Africa. Malakhov was a solitary sort, and it was his intention to take Irina to the Congo immediately after their marriage. But Irina produced a doctor's certificate declaring that the state of her health would not allow her to live in a tropical latitude. He went back to the Congo without her, and they were divorced.

After the divorce Irina and her mother came to Paris, where they lived a reclusive life in Montparnasse. Irina wrote poetry, and she published a book of her work, *Letters*, which received praise from one critic, Vladimir Smolensky. She was a passionate animal lover and earned a meager living as a poodle trimmer. Irina and her mother were, however, frequently guests at Ilya Fondaminsky's luxurious apartment in the sixteenth arrondisement, and it was there, when Fondaminsky stopped in to pay a social call, that Nabokov met her in January 1937. The relationship of Fondaminsky to the Guadininis undoubtedly had its basis in his old friendship with Kokoshkin. Nabokov, who was living at the Fondaminsky apartment, was taken to the Guadinini apartment by Fondaminsky and Vladimir Zenzinov, one of the editors on the board of *Contemporary Annals*. Vera Guadinini's diary records that the meeting between her daughter and Sirin produced something of a *coup de foudre*. Irina was able to quote an enormous quantity of poetry by heart (even for a Russian), usually in a mood of ecstatic transport, and it may well have been that she recited some of the Sirin poems to Nabokov in this way. Nabokov phoned the next day. Irina was not there. He chatted for some time with her mother. Soon afterward they began to go out together regularly to cafés and to films, and it was not too long before they both began to come in extremely late at night.

It was rumored in émigré Paris, where the romance was evidently the subject of much gossip and speculation, that Fondaminsky became quite frightened about what was happening and wrote anonymously to Vera Evseevna in Berlin. (Vladimir and Vera held the belief that the anonymous letter was written by Irina's mother.) At any rate, she came to Paris and then went to Prague with Dmitri to see Nabokov's mother. During this period Nabokov was once again stricken with psoriasis, this time covering his face as well. Nabokov left Paris for Prague, after which he and Vera went to Frazensbad for a month and from there to the Riviera with Dmitri. It was the only time Elena Nabokov saw her grandson and the last time that Nabokov saw his mother.

The connection with Irina was not yet severed. Nabokov sent her seven letters, from Berlin, Marienbad (another stop on the way to France where Vera had gone to see her cousin Anna), and Cannes. They were love letters (in one he tells Irina that she is the only person he has), but they are written in a fearful way: "I am sitting on the beach and hurrying to get this written." He doesn't mention his wife by name but expresses terror that such a thing should have happened to him "after fourteen cloudless years of happiness." In one he recounts his extramarital love life: There had been one time when he had intercourse with a German woman in a forest on the outskirts of Berlin, after which he had had nothing more to do with her. Then there was the incident with the stout woman to whom he had been giving lessons. In addition to these German indiscretions, he had slept with one woman four times in France, presumably in 1936, "but always without love or even any affection." Nabokov told Irina that he had never had an experience such as the one he had had with her, and that, except for their son, he would like to divorce his wife. He told Irina about the four-page anonymous letter to his wife which led to his having to leave so abruptly. After the letter, according to Nabokov, "she" (he never names his wife) and he finally agreed that it would be a matter they would not talk about, but all conversation between them was now "unbearably difficult."

Nabokov instructed her to write to him *post restante* addressing the letters to Korf. He said that he was living in fear and told Guadinini that she must remain faithful to him. Then suddenly, in August, a seventh letter asked Irina to return the previous letters "which, anyway, have much writer's exaggeration in them." This letter was evidently destroyed by Guadinini, but its contents were registered in her mother's diary, together with the information that there was then an eighth letter, registered, which Irina refused to accept. She went to Cannes but, according to Vera, was rebuffed by Nabokov.

Irina left Paris and got a job producing assorted radio programs at Radio Liberty after the war. When she returned to Paris she lived in near poverty and was often unemployed. She lived for a time with a Frenchman whom she had met by chance and who did not understand that, among other things, she had reverted to a state of infantilism. In the end she had no one and was convinced that her neighbors were plotting against her and stealing things from her apartment late at night. A mutual acquaintance of Guadinini and Nabokov approached him with a request for some financial help to ease her poverty. He gave money but very little, explaining, "Yes, I've grown miserly in my old age." She was placed in a Russian convalescent home on the outskirts of Paris, where she died in November 1976.

Ilya Fondaminsky had been for several years in the early 1930s Nabokov's principal literary patron through his sponsorship of the quarterly *Contemporary Annals.* His support for Nabokov lessened considerably after 1936, but it was probably not directly connected with the Guadinini affair, for after 1936 Fondaminsky was drawn more and more to religious and philosophical interests, and he took less part in the editing of the journal. By 1937 the journal was effectively being edited by only one of the five original editors, a man whose primary commitment was to social rebirth through religion. This shift in editorial balance explains the rejection of the Chernyshevsky chapter in *The Gift.* The de facto managing editor of the journal wrote several letters to Nabokov expressing virtual ecstasy over *The Gift,* but he explained that one of the editors was threatening such a row over that chapter of the novel that it would have to be bypassed.

By 1937 the term of émigré literature was approaching twenty years, but one could no longer speak of a fellowship of Russian artists in exile. Hopes of ever returning to Russia had finally been surrendered by most of the émigrés. The audience for émigré literature now could be calculated not even in thousands but in mere hundreds of readers. The old combinations by which a literary livelihood might still be put together were less possible now. Pavel Miliukov's *The Latest News* (it was, with *Contemporary Annals*, the other major source of income for most of the well-known émigré writers) made a move to condense one of Nabokov's short stories. Nabokov protested loudly, claiming that the paper was seeking a pretext to free itself of him. *The Latest News* claimed that its first obligation had to be to a handful of workmen-authors who had entered into an agreement, refused by Nabokov, to turn out two stories a month. The fact that Nabokov was more or less obliged to turn to Miliukov's paper at least from time to time for a portion of his income, and that that paper spent a certain amount of its time trying to belittle his work, was an unhappy set of circumstances. Everyone in the editorial office of *The Latest News* was very angry with Nabokov over his literary parodies in *The Gift*. Miliukov also became one of the editors of another journal in which Nabokov's work had been appearing, *Russian Annals*. It was a kind of supplementary journal to *Contemporary Annals:* the contributors to the two journals were almost identical. Nabokov wrote to Fondaminsky seeking his intercession and suggesting that the dropped chapter be printed in *Russian Annals* instead, but Fondaminsky chose not to act.

Fondaminsky's brother had been sent into Siberian exile in czarist times and died there. He himself also became a committed revolutionary, and at the same time he was an expert on the Italian Renaissance. He had taken part in the unsuccessful revolution of 1905 in which he was arrested for his leadership of the July 20 naval uprising in Revel, one of the few fronts of the 1905 revolution which came very close to succeeding. It had been expected by other members of the Social-Revolutionary movement that he would be executed, but he was released by the Revel military court, and unofficially one of the judges whispered to his wife

Amalia that she should take her husband abroad at once. The (probably apochryphal) story that was reported in the Russian press at the time was that the Fondaminskys had left the court-room, hailed a cab, and that Amalia Fondaminsky had cried out: "Driver, abroad!" They had independent means (the family possessed one of the great Russian tea fortunes) and remained in France for twelve years, after which he returned to Russia briefly to take part in the provisional government with V. D. Nabokov. When he had to go into exile once again, his apartment in France was waiting for him. He also had a villa in Grasse, and many writers stayed there as his guests. Insofar as the West had any conception of the "White émigrés" during these decades, it was as wealthy revanchists, which was a caricature that may have fitted a handful but did not correspond to the situation or views held by the overwhelming majority of those who were active in Russian émigré life or politics.

Because he had spent so many years on French soil, Fonda-minsky grew to feel himself a part of France in a way that most Russians never could. For this reason, and perhaps in part, too, because of the heavy blow he felt on the death of his wife in 1935, Fondaminsky elected not to flee France when the Nazis came. Since he was a Jew this was tantamount to electing to go to a concentration camp. He died in Auschwitz in 1942 and is said to have been saintly in what he did there for others. Fondaminsky had lingered on the verge of conversion for years but only became a Christian in his last days in the camp. Nabokov remembered the touching way he had of attempting to steer a conversation to a religious theme and then asking whether one would be interested in reading a certain saint's life, and also the charming Russian way that a group of his friends would have of ganging up on him from time to time and literally manhandling him to the bathtub.

Fondaminsky was a man who would give himself to everything he undertook with wholehearted enthusiasm, and yet he was in no way aggressive. Although he was providing the funds, at first he did not even want to be on the editorial board of *Contempo-rary Annals*, but when he had agreed to be one of the editors he made the excellence of that journal one of the primary tasks in his life. He was fond of saying: "When they ask us what the justifi-cation of our émigré existence was, we shall point to the volumes of *Contemporary Annals*." And indeed, the seventy volumes of the journal between 1920 and 1940 can stand beside English-language journals such as *Horizon* or the best years of *Partisan Review,* and it surpasses the two venerable nineteenth-century Russian journals, *The Contemporary* and *Annals of the Fatherland* (after which it was named).

Two of the most important ways in which Fondaminsky shaped the character of the journal were his belief that culture and art were essential, independent means to any justifiable social or revolutionary end, and that, while the journal was to have a socialist viewpoint, its pages were to be open both politically and artistically. There were few people of any intellectual or artistic distinction in the Russian emigration who did not at some time or other appear there. When Fondaminsky solicited Sirin's work for *Contemporary Annals* in 1930, he told Nabokov: "Why, we like your work so much. We simply can't understand why you haven't, why you aren't publishing your work in *Contemporary Annals.*" Nabokov handed him the manuscript to *The Defense,* which he had completed not long before and said: "You're welcome," and, Nabokov continued, "He bought it then and there without having read it."

When Nabokov came to Paris for his first reading, in October 1932, and stayed for about a month, he visited Fondaminsky every day. Toward the end of his stay he was invited to transfer to their apartment, then on rue Chernoviz. The Fondaminskys extended themselves to the utmost for the young writer but did it all in such a way, Nabokov remembered, as to make it appear effortless and natural. He had a book-lined bedroom with a bottle of mineral water always at his bedside. Elegant scented toilet articles were laid out for him. Amalia Fondaminsky attended to the distribution and sale of the tickets for Nabokov's reading, and she also typed a portion of the manuscript of *Despair* for him, while Nabokov smoked too much nearby (in later years he feared he had been a difficult houseguest), and the Fondaminskys' stout Siamese cat, who reminded Nabokov of a kangaroo, warmed itself by the fireplace. One night when Nabokov came in very late, he accidently turned on all the lights in the apartment while trying to turn on the hall lamp, and then, after lying awake awhile and fearful that he might not have corrected the awful blunder, he went back to doublecheck his error and ended by pninishly repeating it once more.

Nabokov recalled with particular pleasure the time he spent with Fondaminsky and his friend and political associate Vladimir Zenzinov when he was in Paris in 1936. Zenzinov was the man who had been selected to assassinate his friend Azef for the Social-Revolutionary party in 1914, upon the discovery that Azef was a secret czarist agent. (The assassination attempt didn't succeed.) Another Social Revolutionary whom Nabokov met at Fondaminsky's was the assassin of Father Gapon, the priest who had played a prominent role in the 1905 uprising but had also turned out to be a czarist agent: "There he was sitting in front of me at the tea table . . . I looked at his red freckles, his red hands. He was supposed to have *strangled* Gapon with those hands . . . Those Social Revolutionaries were terrorists. They were also metaphysicians and intellectuals . . . But they were rather naïve in a way."

Nabokov got to know Alexander Kerensky, the former head of the provisional government, quite well at Fondaminsky's since Kerensky also lived there for a time before he married an Australian heiress and moved to Brisbane. (After her death Kerensky settled in New York for his last years.) Kerensky hadn't been on particularly friendly terms with V. D. Nabokov in St. Petersburg, and the two families had never been in social contact, but he and Vladimir Vladimirovich grew quite fond of one another in Paris, and years later they occasionally still saw each other in New York. Nabokov remembered that as a boy he had sat in the first row of a large auditorium with his father, while Kerensky made a speech. Nabokov said that when Kerensky said: "I swear on the heads . . ." two little boys came running out from the wings, and Kerensky placed his hands on their heads as he finished his declaration. "There was something theatrical about him. Pleasingly theatrical apparently," said Nabokov. "He would deliver a speech on any pretext at Fondaminsky's." Nabokov found it very pleasant to hear him talk about the imperial family or his adventures, or to listen to his views about Russia in general.

In 1936 Fondaminsky was in the midst of organizing a memorial volume for his wife. Nabokov wasn't eager to contribute, but he had to. It was the only patron's right that Fondaminsky ever asked of Nabokov. The essay that he wrote was decorous enough, not exactly a memorial article by usual standards but nothing out of the ordinary either. What was remarkable were two paragraphs that he deleted from the article that was printed. These two paragraphs, which have survived, express a clear and strong certainty in a mysterious deity and in life after death.

Fondaminsky held open house every Saturday, and these Saturdays (and the café located near his apartment on the rue de Versailles where Russian writers and poets would spend many hours) now constituted the spiritual center for the culture of the Russian diaspora. Nabokov said that he did not attend Fondaminsky's Saturdays, because he disliked the kind of group discussions that took place there, but Nabokov met most of the Russian writers whom he had not known before at the café. Fondaminsky had the gift of being able to draw together on a relatively amicable basis writers as far apart as the reactionary couple Dmitri Merezhkovsky and Zinaida Gippius and the (tragically) Sovietophile Marina Tsvetaeva, or the religious poet Mother Maria and the decadent Georgy Ivanov.

Nabokov met Teffi, the author of fine short stories in a semi-humorous vein about the nonintellectual emigration. She had something of the Dorothy Parker wit. Nabokov recalled how someone once complimented her on how youthful she appeared, and she replied sweetly, "To the eye, not to the taste." He met Sergei Sharshun, a talented minor novelist, and once by chance overheard him discussing the reading he had just given, a moment that Nabokov incorporated into *The Gift*. He met the aphoristic poet Baron Anatoly Shteiger and came to know him and his sister, who was also a poet, rather well. Shteiger is usually credited by those who know émigré poetry with being a unique and talented poet. Nabokov, however, did not think so: "I don't think he was. His talent has been greatly exaggerated. He was a very minor poet. *Very* minor poet. With a very limited gift and with a very limited emotional life. A nice person. A charming person. A well-bred person. That's all."

There were obstacles to Nabokov's appreciation of Shteiger, chief among them being that he was a close friend of Georgy Adamovich and one of the most important figures in Adamovich's "Paris school." There were other things they disagreed strongly about as well: Shteiger was a homosexual, and he had the easy anti-Semitism of the Russian aristocracy that Nabokov had fought against so bitterly for so many years. Shteiger had actually first met Nabokov on a trip he made to Berlin in 1935. In a letter to a friend Shteiger wrote:

I have met with Sirin several times and attended his evening at which there were 100–120 Jews of the purest sort, Aldanov characters, a milieu which gives me goose bumps but
without which not one line of Russian would have been published in the emigration. Sirin read poems, which were simply
incomprehensible to me, a very ordinary story, and a brilliant
excerpt from a *biographie romancée*—a caricature perhaps? a
pamphlet against "the idea of society"?—about Chernyshevsky. It was brilliant.

And what do you think about *Invitation to a Beheading*? I
know that the Social Revolutionaries on whose agreement its
appearance in *Contemporary Annals* depended nearly broke
their own hearts in agreeing to it . . . Sirin has something
about him which disposes one well towards him: he is a real
old-world landowner of a sort you very seldom encounter in
our literary waters, but you could meet him every day for ten
years and still know nothing conclusive about him. He has
produced an impression of almost tragic "lack of well-being"
on me, and I would not be surprised by anything he might
do. But after our meetings my previously modest interest in
him has catapulted.

On three or four occasions Nabokov was with Marina Tsvetaeva,
who was a close friend of Shteiger's, in Paris. Tsvetaeva, whose
main rival was Anna Akhmatova, had become the Poetess of
the White Guard, but she changed her politics (her husband
turned out to be a double agent) and generally kept aloof from
other émigrés. She had her own entourage. Tsvetaeva had a protracted romance with a cousin of Vera Nabokov's, but he was not
from a branch of her family with whom Vera maintained contact.

Nabokov recalled a literary stroll he had with Tsvetaeva on a
rainy gray Paris day discussing writers whom they mutually
liked or disliked. He met Dovid Knut, a talented Jewish poet who
in a few years would fight in the French Resistance (in which his
wife perished). Eventually Knut immigrated to Israel and became a Hebrew poet. He had published four books of poetry in
Russian. Mother Maria, a frequent guest at Fondaminsky's, was
another Russian poet who perished heroically in a German concentration camp. He met the frizzy-haired blond Dr. Vasily Yanovsky, whom he had ridiculed in one of his *Rudder* reviews years
before for an ineptly described soccer match. He struck Nabokov

as a "delayed *enfant terrible.*" (Yanovsky was another Russian who wrote in English, and many years later his writing was highly praised by Auden.) Vladimir Varshavsky, a poet and critic who had praised Nabokov, seemed to him "vaguely like [Gogol's] Chichikov."

Another very frequent visitor at Fondaminsky's was Nikolai Berdyaev, the foremost postrevolutionary philosophical opponent of communism. He had a horrible speech affliction. After every few words his tongue would throw itself out of his mouth, and he would have to replace it by hand. Another older writer whom he saw a deal of was Boris Zaitsev, a sort of minor Bunin. Nabokov recalled suddenly feeling pity for Zaitsev as he watched him being demolished in argument by Khodasevich.

The writers whom Nabokov saw most frequently at Fondaminsky's and elsewhere were those who were quite independent of any group—Bunin, Khodasevich, and Mark Aldanov. Of the four writers only Bunin was more or less free from attacks by various artistic factions. A fairly large and articulate group of readers was cultivated, largely by Adamovich and his group, who were ready to affirm that Sirin was a "middling" and even an "empty" writer. Khodasevich was virtually forgotten as a poet (Nabokov remarked upon this fact when he wrote a memorial article on Khodasevich's death in 1939 for *Contemporary Annals*), and that certainly had something to do with the bitter silence that fell on him in his last years.

Both Khodasevich and Sirin knew how to fight back. Khodasevich wielded a deft literary scalpel for the sake of strict literary standards as the regular literary critic for *Renaissance*, the other Russian paper in Paris, but its circulation was much smaller than that of *The Latest News*, and there was little of cultural interest in *Renaissance* besides Khodasevich's articles.

Nabokov was engaged in playing his Shishkov trap on Adamovich right up to the moment war was about to start. Aldanov reproached him bitterly, saying: "It's war! War! How can you waste time on such trifles?" But Nabokov had, together with Khodasevich in the emigration, that same deep-rooted feeling that one finds in James Joyce: that nothing in life is as important as art. In a letter to Nabokov that he wrote in January 1938, Khodasevich informed Nabokov that he was about to publish an article on "our friend Georgy Ivanov," and congratulated Nabokov on his parody of Adamovich in the installment of *The Gift* that had just appeared in *Contemporary Annals:* "Mortus was, as you observed, furious, but this is useful."

Referring to his generation of Russian writers and poets, Khodasevich once wrote: "One was allowed to be possessed by whatever one liked. The only requirement was that one be totally possessed." Nabokov belonged to the end of that same generation, and Khodasevich's proposition helps to place and explain from an historical point of view certain aspects of Nabokov's character. Both were in a tradition which sought to make literary venom into a delicate art. In 1936 Nabokov wrote to his wife in Berlin after he had paid a visit to Khodasevich, who was ill and reminded Nabokov somewhat of Pushkin: "He was in very good form and served me some of his playful poison." Khodasevich's face was long and bony, really more like a starving Pasternak than Pushkin, with that same shock of hair sheaflike across his forehead. But whereas Pasternak's Mongol features had perhaps a certain intimation of comfort and display about them, Khodasevich's angular face had simply the tired wariness and indifference to his appearance of the professional gambler, which he was. In his last years be became obsessed with the idea of absolute, relentless honesty in everything, and in so doing he naturally increased considerably his already large corps of literary enemies and set himself quite apart from the world, ready to meet posterity. Nabokov recalled how Khodasevich came to their apartment for tea and removed his dentures and placed them on the table before starting to eat. Before his death he yellowed to the color of old parchment. When he died, at fifty-three, a lock of his hair was sent to Nabokov by Nina Berberova, with whom Khodasevich had lived years before (he had subsequently married someone else). Nabokov told me that he immediately disposed of it with disgust. At the funeral Nabokov lunged at Nikolai Otsup, a critic whom he and Khodasevich both hated, and had to be pulled off by the shocked mourners.

At Fondaminsky's Saturdays there was one servant girl. Nabokov remembered that she was "a girl of incredible, theatrical beauty, deeply devoted to her gentle employer and married to an authentic apache who could be sometimes seen in the kitchen devouring bananas or ironing his silk shirts. Fondaminsky the old terrorist and new mystic was fascinated by that elegant hood. At his Saturdays she seldom served, the host and his guests taking over." Fondaminsky did his best to prevent a collision between Adamovich and Ivanov (they often traveled in each other's company) and Nabokov or Khodasevich. When he was first introduced to Adamovich in 1936, Nabokov wrote to his mother: "I said something so caustic to him that he will not forgive me." Fondaminsky actually asked Nabokov not to come into the living room during the Saturday meetings, and particularly when Adamovich and Ivanov were there. But once, when Gippius, Merezhkovsky, and Ivanov were there, Nabokov, who had an appointment somewhere else, passed ("just by chance") through the living room. Nabokov stopped and shook hands with everyone in the room except Ivanov, whom he left in a half-rising position. Fondaminsky was very nervous and kept repeating: "Will you have some tea? Will you have some tea?" A short while after that Nabokov and Ivanov passed each other on the street, and each turned his head away from the other.

Ivanov had made his name prior to 1917 as one of the most promising of the very young poets who trailed after Akhmatova, Mandelstam, and Gumilyov, but there was a drastic change of tone in what he wrote when he left St. Petersburg. Now his poetry was written in a totally pessimistic voice of a sort that had never been heard in Russian poetry before. For Ivanov Russia no longer existed, and everything was without hope and worthless. In many respects Ivanov represented a perfect contrast to Nabokov, as can be shown vividly enough in Ivanov's attitude toward Pushkin. "Pushkin's Russia, why did you deceive me?" he once wrote. "Pushkin's Russia, why did you betray us?" For Nabokov, of course, Pushkin represents the primary "gift" of *The Gift*.

When they left Prague Nabokov and his wife had spent June 1937 in Marienbad. After that they had stopped briefly in Paris in July but had immediately departed for Cannes in mid-July. They stayed at the Hotel des Alpes in Cannes until mid-October, when they transferred to a boardinghouse, Les Hesperides, in Mentone. Nabokov remembered nothing about that boardinghouse except that there was another Russian in it, a secret agent who was very nice to Dmitri. In early July 1938, they transferred to the Hotel de la Poste in Moulinet, and in August they went to Cap d'Antibes, where they stayed at the House of the Union of the St. George Cross for Disabled Veterans. In all Nabokov and his wife spent about fifteen months in the south of France. They had originally intended to stay only a few months but had extended the time when they received a largish sum from Bobbs-Merrill in the United States for the translation of *Laughter in the Dark*. Nabokov continued to do a lot of writing during this period, working on his plays and his next novel, *Solus Rex*, and he was also able to resume butterfly collecting seriously once again. When they finally returned to Paris in mid-September 1938, he was able to store his butterflies and moths in the elegant storage cabinet that he had purchased cheaply at auction in Berlin and which had been shipped to Paris where it resided in the Fondaminsky apartment. It's not clear why the Nabokovs shifted about so much between different small hotels and rooming houses during this brief Mediterranean period of their lives, and in general this is one of the most obscure years in Nabokov's life. While they were on the Riviera, they received official permission to remain in France but without work permits.

When they returned to Paris, they also spent nearly six months in quarters on the rue de Saigon until, in March 1939, they obtained a small apartment at 59, rue Boileau, where they stayed for a year. Two other émigré writers lived on that street. One was Nikolai Evreinov, the other was Alexei Remizov, one of the most famous of the writers who went into emigration. Remizov was a queer little simian man with medieval and Dostoevskian inclinations in his writing. Some ranked Remizov alongside Bunin, but Nabokov did not: "He detested me. We were very polite to each other . . . The only nice thing about him was that he really lived in literature." Nabokov would from time to time meet him in the offices of French journals. Once Nabokov was talking to Joyce at the *Nouvelle Revue Française*, and Joyce asked him whether he knew Remizov. "Why, yes, why do you ask?" Nabokov responded in perplexity which he reenacted for my benefit. "Joyce, you see, was under the impression that Remizov *mattered* as a writer!!" Neither Nabokov nor his wife would hear a good word said about Remizov's writing. There was very likely something more than literary taste involved, but the cause of the long-held grudge was never explained. When they were still in Berlin an old painter named Zaretsky, upon hearing Nabokov make a scathing remark about Remizov's writing, wrote a rejoinder that he read at a private literary soirée. In it Remizov was compared to

Pushkin and Nabokov to a notorious writer who was in the pay of Czar Nicholas I's police. Nabokov told Zaretsky that, if it were not for his age, he would slap his face—more than that, the Russian word for face that Nabokov used was the one ordinarily only applied to an animal—whereupon Zaretsky tried to call him out before a literary court of honor. Virtually every Russian literary organization had one. The matter went as far as the appointment of judges for the dispute (one of them was Boris Brodsky), but then Nabokov simply declined to take part in the affair, though he offered to fight if called out.

The querulousness and almost domesticated danger that lingered at the edges of émigré life were captured very well by Nabokov in his 1938 play *The Event*, which was presented in Paris in May 1938 and then in Prague, Warsaw, Belgrade, and even New York. Drama was, for obvious reasons, the weakest of all the literary arts in émigré conditions. *The Event*, as staged by the Russian Theater and directed by Petrunkin with a set by the famous illustrator Annenkov who had done the revolutionary drawings for Blok's *The Twelve*, was probably the most successful original play of the emigration. While it was running, *The Waltz Invention* was being prepared for production, but then the war came.

The Event is simply a reversal of *The Inspector General*. Whereas the real inspector comes only at the end of Gogol's play—causing general consternation among the officials who took the imposter Khlestakov to be the inspector—*The Event* is permeated with fear from the beginning: an old enemy has just been released from prison prematurely, and the hero of the play is sure that he is coming to kill him. But the real fear running through the play is of life that is quite insubstantial and can be seen through (an actual effect in the play) like stage gauze. The friends and relatives who have gathered around the fearful artist turn into caricatures of his imagination. But at the same time, the artist is vaguely aware that he is surrounded by people who don't really like him. In a different way this same bifocal effect is central to *The Waltz Invention*, where "a sudden thinning of the texture" allows another layer "to glimmer through."

The revenge of the man who never comes is precisely that he doesn't appear, so that, with no more reason to be afraid, the artist and his wife will, we assume, continue to lead their "real lives" but will also have a heightened awareness of the flat stageboard reality of their lives. Khodasevich, who wrote a long essay about the play in *Contemporary Annals,* saw it as a deeply pessimistic work in which everything is not only transparent, but also vulgar and soiled, and, moreover, "that's how it will remain—the inspector won't come, and one need not be afraid of him." Later, writing about the play in *Renaissance,* Khodasevich expressed an opinion somewhat at variance from what he had said in *Contemporary Annals:* "My love for Sirin has been evidenced so many times that I have a right to be very demanding of him, and it seems to me that Sirin has not succeeded in finding balance between the very gloomy subject of the play and its underlying comic style." The play suffers one other serious defect—too little happens, and it is overly static. The play is about a failed marriage and an artist who has to work in a puppet-show world. At the same time, it is a hilarious potpourri of literary pastiche and parody, with Gogol and Chekhov the main referents.

All of this means that while *The Event* is not successful enough as a play (Nabokov came close several times, but he was never really a playwright) it still remains one of the most intriguing of Nabokov's middle-year works, perhaps indeed his fullest expression of the problems of the artist in middle age. The extreme pessimism of the work corresponds precisely to what we know of his own situation and outlook at this time. Similarly, *The Waltz Invention* shows for the first time a Nabokovian Prospero gone out of control with both dream and real worlds flying out of Waltz's grasp. Subsequently, all of Nabokov's madmen/heroes would remain totally in control of their fantasy and their privileged position of godlike narrator in spite of all failures in and rejection by the "real" world. This basic premise for Nabokov is articulated very clearly in *The Waltz Invention,* not by Waltz himself but by one of the minor characters speaking to him. He tells him that it is useless to speak with him because "we are all only participants in your delirium." The difference is that in *The Eye* and in *Pale Fire* that delirium is defiantly asserted to be a state of happiness, whereas in the 1938 plays the world, the universe, in fact, is about to blow away leaving a void behind. That is true in spite of Nabokov's direction for *The Waltz Invention* that it should employ scenery "as rich and verisimilar as a Dutch painting." Such a contrast between rich reality and the despair of a spiritual void merely underscores the tone of the plays.

Due to *The Event,* on stage and in print, other appearances
both in *Contemporary Annals* and various French journals, the
last remnants of the Bobbs-Merrill money, and a small sum from
Gallimard for a forthcoming translation, 1938 was not a bad year,
at least from a financial point of view. He even had a few private
pupils for language lessons again. As late as 1939 the Nabokovs
were able to take vacations to Seytenex in the Savoy mountains
and then to a Russian pension, Rodnoy, at Frejus.

Though Nabokov had expressed a fear that residence in France
could impinge upon his Russian simply because he knew the language so well, in fact something like an awkward courtship with
French literature had begun in 1936. The noted philosopher,
dramatist, and Kierkegaard expert Gabriel Marcel, who had taken
a particular interest in Nabokov's writing, having learned about it
through mutual friends, spoke for nearly an hour introducing him
at the French lecture. The lecture was about Pushkin—it was the
centenary of the poet's death—and in the course of his reading, he
wrote to his mother, "applause came like bomb explosions." The
talk was later printed in the *Nouvelle Revue Français* in March
1937. The article, entitled *"Pouchkine ou le vrai et le vraisembl-
able"* is less about Pushkin in particular than about the art and
manner of biography in general.

For Nabokov the biographer is someone who cuts up correspondence to make a lovely paper costume for his subject. Without standing on ceremony the biographer makes free use of what
the subject has created to furnish the appearance of the subject's
own intimate thoughts. Ideas are pulled out of the subject's books
to stuff the biographer's book, and often there is added to this the
disgusting spectacle of "playful Freudianism." But then Nabokov
turns on his own point and confesses that he rather enjoys the
sight of a bad actor playing the part of Pushkin, which can serve
at least as a pleasing theatrical backdrop to the only real biography any writer has, his work. In effect, the emperor has too many
clothes, which are not really his anyway, and which prevent us
from seeing him properly. And yet, as indicated in the essay,
Pushkin is so alluring a subject that an exception may almost be
made in this instance. There are, according to Nabokov, popular
biographies of him which are quite revolting, but "Pushkin occupies a singular position, because even rumors about him can *seem*
plausible."

The other work that Nabokov did in French between 1937 and

1939 were some translations of Pushkin's poetry and "Mademoi-selle O," which appeared in *Mesures* and eventually was incor-porated into his autobiography. Nabokov first took this piece to a reading in Belgium, where he performed it in its entirety, but he didn't have an overly high opinion of its value at first: "In general this thing is quite second-class, perhaps even third."

While Nabokov was in Brussels he became very friendly with the Belgian French writer Franz Hellens, whose aesthetic views were in some respects rather close to Nabokov's and who had, moreover, a Russian wife. Hellens was one of the earliest writers noted for the technique of *realité fantastique*. Nabokov had known Hellens's books for several years before he met him and had admired in particular his 1925 novel, *OEil-de-Dieu*, which is, like Nabokov's *Despair*, in part a parody of a detective novel. Hellens wrote to Jean Paulhan warmly praising "Mademoiselle O." Back in Paris Nabokov met Jules Supervielle, then consid-ered by a few to be the hope of French literature, and he asked Nabokov to read "Mademoiselle O," about which Hellens had written to him. (It was Supervielle who told Nabokov about Hellens's letter to Paulhan.) Then he, too, recommended its pub-lication to Paulhan. Nabokov got on very well with Supervielle, but it was a friendship for which "the tape recorder of memory [forgot] to be turned on." Nabokov remembered him as a tall, gaunt Spaniard with a charming old-world manner ("which I also have"), though he appeared older than he in fact was and was in a state of great disarray and confusion prior to leaving for his native Uruguay. He had a number of daughters and a wife who looked like the eldest of them. Nabokov translated some of Su-pervielle's poetry into Russian.

Paulhan was one of the most powerful behind-the-scenes fig-ures in French literature in this period, and the way seemed to have been perfectly prepared for the acceptance of Nabokov. Moreover, Paulhan had a highly developed sense of whimsy well suited to Nabokov's narrative method. *Despair* was accepted for publication by Gallimard, and thus Nabokov joined Bunin and Remizov as one of three émigré authors accepted by the French establishment.

In addition to Paulhan, Nabokov came to know Edouard Du-jardin. He didn't know Jean Cocteau, but his brother Sergei was very friendly with him, and once Cocteau spoke to him briefly on the phone, thinking he was Sergei, and warning him that his phone was being tapped. Nabokov was invited to lunch by Edmond Jaloux, the tactful and kindly but overly polished critic, who, André Gide wrote, was more comfortable in a tailcoat than ordinary clothes. Nabokov described Jaloux to me as "totally second-rate and terribly influential." Nabokov tumbled into laughter as he remembered Jaloux and the lunch: "I think that even in this repulsive little *Larousse* . . . ye-e-e-s, he should be here. Good old Jaloux," and he read the *Larousse* entry aloud, punctuating it with snorts of laughter and appending to its end, "He was as fresh as a peach, I remember, and a com*plete* mediocrity." The lunch was saved for Nabokov by the presence of champagne, which Nabokov adored and Jaloux always had for lunch.

Perhaps failure to win the favor of Jaloux might have been the pivotal point at which the possibility of Nabokov becoming a French writer slipped away ("I might have been a great French writer," said Nabokov pondering that untraveled road). Raissa Tarr had been trying to get Nabokov a regular position as a newspaper book and drama critic. There was certainly enthusiasm for Nabokov's French writing on the part of some French writers and critics, but all the same there was a certain lack of ease and warmth toward Nabokov on the part of literary Paris. Nabokov wrote perfect French, and his pronunciation was also quite exact. But when he was speaking French, he had a tendency to confuse the gender of nouns, the one fault that a Frenchman rarely has, no matter how badly he speaks in other ways. These were the judgments of his wife. Nabokov tried to protest, but Vera Evseevna promptly recalled such a slip he had made the preceding day: "And it's not the first time. Sergei spoke much better French than Vladimir, but his English was much less rich than yours." It is more likely that the reason that he was accepted but with a certain clearly felt reserve in French literary circles was that his manner was that of the English snob, and there is nothing toward which the French are more antipathetic. And so, after the first flush of the French flirtation, the simple fact, according to Vera Evseevna, was clear: "There were no opportunities for a career for him there."

The logical choice of a country and language, Nabokov felt, was certainly England and English, but England was not particularly eager to praise Nabokov's novels or to furnish him with an academic position. "Your application will, however, be filed for future reference," wrote the vice chancellor of Leeds University after British Russian expert Sir Bernard Pares had made unsuccessful attempts to get Nabokov a position at Leeds. A previous attempt to get a position at Cambridge through a classmate who had obtained a place there had also failed.

There were problems in regard to France and French culture, too. Gabriel Marcel, in spite of his great enthusiasm for Nabokov, termed himself "allergic" to the epigraph to *Invitation to a Beheading* by an imaginary French philosopher: "*Comme un fou se croit Dieu, nous nous croyons mortels.*" ("As a madman believes that he is God, we believe that we are mortal.") That quote, which is so important in understanding Nabokov because of its compression of the themes of the madman/God and human immortality in a single sentence, could probably not have been written by any French philosopher or writer, simply because of its Dostoevskian sweep and assertion. Also, the French reverence for language is different from Nabokov's. If Nabokov had elected to become a French writer, there is reason to suppose that Sirin-Nabokoff would at best have found himself in much the same position as his friends Hellens and Supervielle, recognized and brilliant writers who all the same remained peripheral. Nabokov confessed to a fear of being "enveloped" by French culture.

In his approximately three and a half Parisian years, Nabokov, now himself the recipient of phantom fame (that is, only émigré fame), associated with all the most famous Russian writers in exile that he cared to see in a way that he had not done in Berlin (though he and Bunin had spent some time together in their last Berlin year), but Nabokov felt that "life in the Russian colony in Berlin was perhaps more interesting than in Paris." Paris itself he found somewhat dingy. Life had changed very much in that decade: "The thirties were pretty hopeless . . . I think that in the middle thirties we had just given up the idea of going back. But it didn't matter much because Russia was with us. We were Russia. We represented Russia . . . What had we lost? What had we lost? We had lost . . ." Nabokov's sentence trailed off and was left unfinished.

The second phase or decade of Russian émigré literature was fast coming to a close, and what came after was to be quite different—an émigré literature with no new names, no new movements, with absolutely no possibility (except for a few journalists) of even reasonably supplementing one's income with one's pen, with ever fewer possibilities to print books except at one's own expense. Russia was becoming hopelessly blurred by decades of separation and an émigré existence that few survivors could profess to understand and still fewer take pride in. Seen from a distance by a detached observer, even the unpleasant querulousness of the Parisian period would seem, all the same, a sign of life and creative energy.

Their last French apartment was on the rue de Saigon between the Etoile and the Bois de Boulogne. Its proportions recalled some of the places they had lived in in Berlin, although it was far larger. There was one gigantic room, with a large kitchen capable of also serving as a dining room to one side and a very large bathroom to the other. The flat was rather attractive (it was paid for by the last of the translation money), but it was intended to accommodate a young man on the town rather than a family of three. Because the apartment's one large room was perforce not only the living room but also the bedroom and nursery, it was necessary, when Dmitri was sleeping, to entertain company in the kitchen, and that is why Nabokov wrote most of *The Real Life of Sebastian Knight* on a suitcase placed across a bidet in the sun-filled bathroom with chessboard tiles.

The last two years in France were perhaps the most difficult period in Nabokov's life. It was now no longer possible to be casual about one's empty pockets and speak of poverty as though it were a chosen way of life, as Nabokov had regarded it in the days of his Berlin youth (*"my golden poverty"* he had called it in a 1925 poem). Toward the end of 1939 and the beginning of 1940 things became unbearably difficult. At last they simply did not have the money to exist on a day-to-day basis, and they needed money for their overseas trip besides, so Nabokov had to ask various friends for loans. Aldanov accompanied Nabokov on visits to various wealthy Jewish families in an effort to help his friend raise the money. One woman kept asking him: "Are you sure you're going? Quite sure?" It was a matter of about fifty dollars.

About twelve months earlier Rachmaninov, whom Nabokov had never even met but who admired Sirin's writing and who lent an occasional helping hand to émigré literature in the manner of Fondaminsky, had sent Nabokov the following brief note:

Dear Vladimir Vladimirovich,

*Only today, May 28, did I learn of your letter to L.
L'vov of May 10 in which your two words* Ghastly des-
titution *stunned me. I am sending you 2500 francs by
telegram, which you may repay me when these words no
longer apply. And if this should not be soon—though
God grant that this is not the case—it doesn't matter.
The mere thought that I have been able to help you in a
moment of need is sufficient repayment.*

I am afraid that the question of the publication of
The Gift *must be put off for a time.*

As it happened, the novel had to wait fourteen years for publication in Russian by the Chekhov Publishing House in New York,
using support from the Ford Foundation, and the novel received
scarcely any critical notice when it finally appeared in full.

But in 1939–40 in France there were matters even more fundamental than subsistence: everyone had to prepare to take a side,
lie low, run, fight, or collaborate. Under the Vichy government, a
Russian émigré was mysteriously transformed into a *prestataire,
n.m., a person liable to prestations, n.f. payment of a toll, etc.,
taking of an oath, etc.* No one could understand the decree,
though its potential dangers were clear to all. The Nansen passport had been exceedingly annoying (one had to lodge application to travel abroad at least three weeks prior to travel, and the
passport did not automatically include permission to work), but
the Nansen was not subject to cancellation, nor were its holders
deported in ordinary circumstances. Now denunciations were
being made and people were being arrested. Russians were called
before committees of émigré Fascists and reactionaries for questioning about possible Jewish blood.

The emigration, like most other social groups in Europe, was
dividing into four segments. There were those who went into the
underground to fight the Germans. Numerous contributors to
Contemporary Annals were in this group, and, in fact, the very
term "Resistance" was given to the movement by Russian émigrés,
who were specially honored for their heroism by the French government when France was finally freed. Then there were those
who chose to collaborate, and, surprisingly, there turned out to be

one or two *Contemporary Annals* people in this category, too. A very large group either decided to stay put or for various reasons simply had to remain and pray for the best. And lastly, there were those who, largely because of age, political affiliations, or religion, wished to flee Europe. Getting the necessary papers and bookings wasn't easy.

Nabokov's choice was to join the French army or to leave. He had both to raise the money and secure places on a boat. An official in one of the organizations arranging departures interviewed Nabokov and has drawn a harsh picture of him. She described Nabokov as being in a state of "panic and wild fear at the prospect of war." The woman, whose husband had died fighting in the Resistance, recalled that he was prepared to do anything to get away.

The situation was saved by a Jewish rescue organization that was run by an old friend of Nabokov's father named Frumkin (ironically, he was almost a perfect double for Nicholas II), who gave the Nabokov family not simply a place but a first-class cabin: "I had a lovely bath every morning. It was marvelous." Nabokov had been able to borrow the money to pay half the fare. The next step was to go through some harrowing red tape to procure the family's exit papers. It took Nabokov two months of trudging from office to office until a lucky bribe made "the last rat in the last rathole" finally issue the *visa de sortie*.

On the eve of their departure from Paris, Nabokov went to say good-bye to Ivan Bunin and found Zinaida Gippius and her husband Dmitri Merezhkovsky there. Gippius had made demeaning remarks about Sirin in *Numbers* and elsewhere, and Merezhkovsky had given a lecture in Paris in 1935 entitled "With Jesus or Sirin?" But Nabokov came to know them at Fondaminsky's, and in the end he was on rather amiable terms with them. Nabokov thought that the Merezhkovskys were miffed at the fact that Nabokov did not pay them due deference (Merezhkovsky had been tipped by many to get the Nobel Prize instead of Bunin) or attend their regular salons, which vied in popularity with Fondaminsky's.

While they held few views in common, toward the end of the Paris period Gippius seemed willing to acknowledge Sirin's talent, and Nabokov for his part never allowed other considerations to cloud his appreciation of her artistic stature: "I don't think he was a bad writer, but he hasn't written things that will endure. His wife, on the other hand, has written at least three or four poems which will always remain, shining like precious gems in the history of Russian literature." At this point Nabokov began to recite some Gippius poems by heart for me, while his wife, less tolerant of the talent of Gippius, made a strongly disapproving face and finally interrupted his recitation. Nabokov said that, when he met Gippius, "she would speak in a very, very squeaky voice and ask idiotic questions, idiotic questions which I don't even remember. And is it really true that you also write in Dutch? That kind of question." Thus circumstance, which had led to the awkward lunch with Bunin at the Parisian Russian restaurant Kornilov's, which is described in *Speak, Memory*, prevented once again any memorable conversation between Bunin and Nabokov at their last meeting.

Bunin sat deep in a stuffed armchair so that he appeared much smaller than he was and eyed his visitors through his round spectacles. Aldanov had once remarked that watching Bunin and Nabokov talk was like watching two movie cameras aimed at each other. Most of the conversation was supplied by Zinaida Gippius, who kept asking Nabokov: "You're going away to America? Why are you going? Why are you going?" Nabokov answered her shortly. Hitler was at that moment advancing on Paris. Before they left Berlin a religious acquaintance had asked the same question and had volunteered the advice that it would be better for their souls to stay and suffer. Then Gippius began to insist at great length that they must go by bus to Calais. There was a rumor that the railways had been taken over by the French army for troop transport. Nabokov said his good-bye to Bunin rather perfunctorily and descended the stairs with the Merezhkovskys, she still continuing to impress upon him the necessity above all of traveling to Calais by bus. It was a bright and gusty spring day. They went to Calais by train and used a considerable portion of their money for a first-class compartment because Dmitri was quite ill.

Nabokov's real good-bye to émigré literature was in the last issue of *Contemporary Annals*, which had appeared only weeks before. Sirin was represented in it by three pieces: a poem, a book review, and the first portion of his next Russian novel, *Solus Rex*, which he would never complete but which was more than made up for by *Pale Fire* twenty years later. It was time. The causes for their late departure were quite different from those that had pertained in regard to leaving Berlin, but all the same the ship that they sailed on, the *Champlain*, was the very last to leave France before the full terror and conflict began. They evidently did not associate with other refugees on the crossing.

Within a few days of their arrival in New York Nabokov wrote six paragraph-long philosophical sketches (a most uncharacteristic form for him) under the title "Definitions" in the New York émigré newspaper *The New Russian Word*. One of them is a definition of France from an émigré point of view. Nabokov's attitude is surprisingly warm, and he even forgives France her weakness before fascism. France, according to Nabokov, is an endlessly delightful country, where—and this is the main thing—it is easiest for a Russian to remember his lost native country. The same sort of emotional connection was later made in his last long Russian poem, *A Parisian Poem*, which was written in 1943 in America and published the following year. In spite of its title and passing scenery, it is not really a poem about Paris at all but a parodic quilt of Gogol and other Russian writers and poets. Another of the paragraphs in "Definitions" celebrates the "sinewy strength" of Russian literature in exile and the incredible freedom, never before known to Russian writers, that was enjoyed over a twenty-year period. For Nabokov correctly saw that an important historical period was at an end, and that the emigration would not be able to regroup effectively in America.

It isn't easy to have a vivid and living sense of the invisible country called Emigration, where Vladimir Nabokov resided in Europe for exactly twenty years. But a very minor older émigré writer, who wrote under the pseudonym Don Aminado, perhaps came closest to summarizing the entire European emigration by using the Russian trial-genre form. He called it *A Judgment of the Russian Emigration* (*A Humorous Scenario in Three Acts, Without Politics*). In the prosecutor's concluding speech, he speaks condescendingly of the way in which the Russians absolutely refused to meld into the countries into which they chanced to fall. They have begun to waste their lives with endless mooning over their lost country and the past. An apartment house taken over by Russians, the prosecutor claims, is worthy of study by a natural scientist with its notes pinned to every door: "Knock loudly, we're bathing," "Come back in an hour I'm asleep," and "They've evicted us. Come to our new housewarming party— we'll let you know the address." The Russians refuse to learn the languages of the countries to which they have come. They adopt strange ways of living in which people sit around on radiators and tables and beds, anything but chairs, and after midnight play sentimental Russian songs on the guitar.

The counsel for the defense points to the way in which Russians have gone to every corner of the earth, so that Parisian Russian literary journals are being read in Hawaii or in Singapore, while in the Belgian Congo Russians constructing the railway teach the natives how to cook Russian borscht. Sikorsky builds helicopters in America, while Alekhine plays chess in Argentina, and a Russian orchestra performs in Paris. To the charge of an inability to assimilate, he replies: "Turgenev spent twenty-five years abroad and created all his works in a language that is not French but the language of Turgenev!" In conditions of extreme material and psychological hardship, the Russians have carried on their culture and continued to believe in a radiant future while driving taxis and accepting tips for menial jobs. The jury is not out for long: the Russian emigration is wholly justified.

It is immediately apparent in contemplating such a debate that Vladimir Nabokov stands outside of its terms of reference in many ways. He worked very hard, had no difficulty with two other European languages, and indeed affected the air of an English sportsman (and occasionally dandy) not only for the Russian colony, but also for the Germans and the French. That was an essential part of his family heritage (Trotsky had called his father "an overstarched Englishman"), which made him far and away the most Westernized of the Russians in emigration. It was only in England itself that he was Russian. And yet, against all advice, he, too, remained obdurately Russian in his passionate attachment to the language until the last years of the emigration. He had used German subjects to try to break into film and win a wider audience; he had made attempts to gain a literary foothold in France. It was only in the final phase of the European emigration, with better foresight than he ever showed at any other time in his career, that he understood that a viable émigré literary community was no longer going to be possible. When he landed in America, he already had the manuscript of his first American novel, *The Real Life of Sebastian Knight* (begun in 1936), with him as well as his English lecture notes for the summer-school course at Stanford University where he was going as the replacement lecturer for Mark Aldanov. Put another way, when Nabokov landed in America his bags had been long and well packed with his English-language future.

16

THERE WERE NO REPORTERS WAITING FOR NABOKOV AT DOCK-
side when the *Champlain* landed in New York that misty morning of May 28, 1940, as there were to be when he sailed back to
Europe nearly twenty years later after *Lolita* had become a best-
seller in the United States. In fact there was no one there to meet
him at all. His old Cambridge friend Count Robert de Calry and
the ex-wife of his cousin Nicolai, Nathalie Nabokov, were supposed to meet the Nabokovs, but there had been some confusion
about the landing time. Their first hour on American soil was extremely pleasant, and Nabokov would maintain later that that
first impression was on the whole to be sustained throughout his
eighteen American years.

They had lost the key to a lovely but by now quite battered
trunk that had accompanied Nabokov from Petrograd. He stood
bantering with a diminutive porter and two quite large customs
men until another, quite merry little porter arrived and opened
the lock with a simple *thwack* of his iron. Unfortunately, the
locksmith-by-luck was so pleased by his simple solution that he
kept playing with the lock until it snapped shut again. When the
trunk was finally opened once more, there were two sets of boxing gloves lying on top. Nabokov, on his knees, had been giving
his six-year-old son boxing lessons. The two customs men
grabbed the gloves and began a mock sparring session, dancing
around Nabokov. "Where would that happen? Where would that
happen?" Nabokov exclaimed to me.

Unlike the hundreds of their fellow passengers milling around them, almost all French and German Jews who spoke little English, the Nabokovs felt quite at ease. He made a telephone call to the Tolstoy Fund, which was directed by one of Tolstoy's daughters, Alexandra, and which was the most important agency in resettling Russian immigrants. He asked his wife where she thought they might be able to get a newspaper, but, before she could reply, one of the men said he'd get one for them and returned in a moment with a copy of the *New York Times*. Then they hailed a yellow Checker cab and set out to Nathalie Nabokov's apartment. It wasn't a very long trip, though it seemed like the end of an epic journey to them.

"Then we looked at the meter, and we saw nine, o, oh God, ninety, ninety dollars." All the money that the Nabokovs had with them was a single hundred-dollar bill, which they gave to the cabby, who laughed and told Vera Evseevna: 'Lady, I haven't got a hundred dollars. If I had that kind of money, I wouldn't be sitting here driving this cab . . .' Of course the simplest way for him would have been to give us the ten dollars change and call it a day." Again, it was the kind of good-humored and lucky episode of the sort which, Nabokov claimed, might never have happened in Europe.

There were friends in New York whose presence had followed Nabokov along some part of the way from Russia to Germany to France and now to the United States. In addition to Nathalie Nabokov and de Calry, his good Berlin friend Bertrand Thompson had returned to New York. Nabokov again met Mstislav Dobuzhinsky, who had given him art lessons as a boy. He became friendly with Roman Grynberg, one of the last of his European pupils. He met the brilliant Polish émigré poet Julian Tuwim in New York. Tuwim was a man whose personality had the same general European cast as Nabokov's (Tuwim was passionately antibourgeois without aligning himself with any other class), and he was one of the best translators of Pushkin. There is, unfortunately, no record of their acquaintanceship. Kerensky had also come to New York, via Australia. But the number of friends and acquaintances was very much diminished. Nabokov finally met Rachmaninov, who had supplied some money for the portion of the boat fare that Nabokov had to pay when they left Europe, probably at the behest of Aldanov. This meeting had an awkward aftermath, because Rachmaninov sent Nabokov a package of his old clothes (including a fine but out-of-date tuxedo), and Nabokov returned the package.

So many had been left behind, how many had perished. The only other important Russian writer who had come to America was Aldanov, and he was to return to Europe after just a few years. Aldanov founded a quarterly, *The New Review*, in New York in 1942. It had contributions from many of the émigré writers still in Europe, but somehow the tone of intellectual urgency and freshness in *Contemporary Annals* was never recaptured by the new journal, which was dominated by writers whose names had flashed only occasionally in the previous journal and by many people who weren't writers at all. It was impossible for émigré literature to continue in its old terms in America. The size of the country and the fact that many Russian intellectuals soon drifted away to teach their native language and sundry subjects on far-flung American campuses dissipated whatever cultural cohesion there might otherwise have been among Russians in the United States. Five hundred copies of the first issue of *The New Review* were printed, and the issue sold out. As a result, a thousand copies of the second issue were printed. Five hundred and twenty were sold.

In New York there were no regular Saturday or Sunday gatherings for the cultured Russian elite. From the first, Nabokov moved among Americans as much as he could. He said that he never made any terribly close friends in America, but that he was quite friendly (much more so than he had ever been with Western Europeans during his first period of exile) with many people during his residence of nearly two decades.

In their first weeks in New York the Nabokovs stayed for a short time in Nathalie Nabokov's apartment on East 87th Street. Then they were able to get an inexpensive summer sublet of the apartment across the hall, which belonged to an actress, for two months. After that they lived for a while in the apartment of a niece of the Countess Panina who had given the Nabokovs their first sanctuary in the Crimea. During that same summer they accepted an invitation to visit the Vermont summer home of Professor Michael Karpovich, whom Nabokov had met at Fondaminsky's in Paris. Karpovich was a professor of Russian history at Harvard. He had immigrated directly to America in

1917. The Nabokovs spent two summers, 1940 and 1942, at his Vermont home. Another Russian family with a house nearby in West Brattleboro was that of Eugene Rabinowitch, the physicist who had been a member of the Berlin Poets' Circle. Karpovich became a coeditor of *The New Review*, and the little summer colony of endlessly arriving and departing émigré guests received its literary memorial in *Pnin*. Suitably surrounded by birches, it was the last capital of old Russian culture in exile. In fact, it was more the meeting place of last survivors. Nabokov claimed that he had had to magnify and embellish the scene considerably for *Pnin*.

When the Nabokovs returned to New York from Vermont they were rather hard up, but there were prospects. The job that he was offered through the good offices of the Tolstoy Fund as a bicycle delivery boy for Scribner's Bookstore was refused, but a less risible attempt was being made by a friend to get Nabokov an appointment as the head of the Russian section of the Voice of America. He was taken there and introduced to all the staff members ("Everyone bowing, I thinking: I will never take this job"), and a complete security check was done on him with interviews of all his relatives and acquaintances in the United States. A prophetically humorous mistake was made by Nabokov when he was being interviewed by the FBI. He wrote the wrong year for her birth, and the interviewer had to ask him: "Isn't it strange that your mother was only thirteen when you were born?" Nabokov lost that undesired job, which was given to his cousin Nicolai Nabokov, who had been one of his references. Nabokov snorted with good humor at the recollection: "He evidently told them, 'Why don't you give the job to me instead?'"

Nabokov then wrote to Avram Yarmolinsky, who was head of the Slavonic Section of the New York Public Library, announcing his desire to obtain a position in a Russian department in some American college or university. Though this did not eventuate at first, Nabokov did meet Yarmolinsky and his wife, the poet Babette Deutsch, and their friend Edmund Wilson. Wilson also knew of Nabokov through two other mutual friends, Bobby de Calry and Roman Grynberg.

His friendship with Wilson would prove to be absolutely critical in establishing Nabokov as a writer in English. Wilson was at this time the literary editor of *The New Republic*, and Nabokov received about twelve dollars apiece for a series of book reviews Wilson invited him to write for *The New Republic* and slightly more for those of another series he did, through an introduction provided by Wilson, for *The New York Sun*. And as a result of these reviews he was asked to write one for the *New York Times Book Review*, which paid well. All in all, the reviewing managed to see them through the summer. But by far the most important stroke of good fortune that summer was that Nabokov got himself placed on the lecture circuit roster of the Institute of International Education, which was run by a Mr. Fisher. One of his 1941 lectures was a March engagement at Wellesley College, which eventually led to an association with Wellesley that was to last for seven years.

In spite of the financial hardship of 1940–41 the Nabokovs were pleased with virtually everything in America, except perhaps the ways of some of their fellow émigrés. When they had first arrived, Alexandra Tolstoy had given Nabokov advice intended to help him "get on" in the new country, and she had specifically warned him that all Americans were completely uncultured, credulous fools. He was introduced to a Russian woman who taught at Columbia University and was immediately complimented: "All one hears here are Yids. What a magnificent aristocratic pronunciation you have!" It was not the only such unpleasant incident. Nabokov found the conversation at one émigré party at which he was the nominal guest of honor so offensive that he decided to shock his host in return by casually using an obscenity after the host said "yid." Then he left. In May 1941, Nabokov wrote to his friend George Hessen, who was having difficulty getting settled in America, and told him that he was in a cultured and exceedingly diverse country in which he would thrive so long as he took care to deal only with genuine Americans and not to get involved with the local émigrés. That letter was simply a confirmation of what was becoming an ever-clearer inclination on Nabokov's part.

In the winter of 1940 Nabokov returned with full energy to his entomological research. He worked at the Museum of Natural History in New York classifying butterflies, and he was able to publish two papers arising from this work in the following year. There was no position as such, but he was paid for various entomological drawings he did. He established a very good rapport with the museum staff, and he used to manage to drop in almost every time he came to New York in the succeeding years. There was a rather plain woman who used to be there fairly often when he was and who, he thought, spent a lot of time chatting him up and flirting with him. The woman was named Margaret Mead, but in subsequent years Nabokov said he could never be absolutely sure that it was the *same* Margaret Mead. In the fifties he happened to arrive at the museum just after the notorious "Murph the Surf" jewel robbery and was surprised by armed guards who were highly suspicious of his account of who he was until staff were found who were able to vouch for his identity. As Nabokov was telling me how he was taken upstairs by a stern armed guard, his wife cut in to tease him: "They had found you out. At last."

Entomology was not a hobby in Nabokov's mind, needless to say, but, particularly in the first year, another possible career path. And while he was not offered a job there, the benefits to him of his work at the museum in 1940-41 turned out to be real since the two lepidopterists with whom he was quite friendly in New York, Comstock and Sandford, were good friends of Samuel Barbour, the director of the Museum of Comparative Zoology. Nabokov eventually got a part-time job there to supplement his income and allow him to continue his entomological work when he went to Wellesley. It was not a fantastic coincidence, as related in *Speak, Memory,* that the director, Dr. Banks, happened to be reading Nabokov's 1919 Crimean article when he first dropped in to the museum. Comstock and Sandford had told the MCZ that he would be coming. And Dr. Barbour was, in turn, a close friend of the then director of the Guggenheim Foundation, which considerably eased the way toward the first of two Guggenheim grants that Nabokov won in 1943. Everything proceeded with magical smoothness in comparison with similar efforts in Germany, England, and France.

The prospect of the trip to California was momentarily threatened by the fact that Vera Evseevna was seriously ill through much of the winter, and there was some question as to whether they could go. They did go, and on their first trip across America the Nabokovs were fortunate enough to have a driver. Her name was Dorothy Leuthold, and she was the last of Nabokov's private language pupils, an unmarried American woman who had worked for years in the New York Public Library system. Nabokov had met her quite by chance, and she had expressed a desire to supplement her knowledge of Russian, which was very limited but included, for reasons Nabokov could never fathom, all the swear words, the meanings of which she evidently did not properly grasp. Then, when the Nabokovs told her that they were going to California, she offered them her car, a brand-new Pontiac that she had just bought. But neither Nabokov nor his wife had had any more occasion to know how to drive a car than to understand a bank statement—both were simple enough matters abstractly, but neither had obtruded upon their lives in the course of two decades. Their friend and pupil, when she learned that, said, "Oh, I'll drive you." Not only did she drive them, she also planned their itinerary, which took a southerly course and included a particularly memorable stop in Arizona, for it was there, on the south rim of the Grand Canyon on a very cold day in June (they had departed on May 26) that Nabokov walked down a path into the gorge and captured a new butterfly, which he gallantly named after their chauffeur, who had made the trip just to follow her whim and improve her Russian and be kind to some newly arrived immigrants. Over the years numerous butterflies were named after Nabokov himself.

Nabokov acknowledged that the impressions of motel-America that began then contributed significantly to the genesis of his most famous novel. He recalled, too, that his six-year-old son, who had grown up to such a large extent in *pensions* in Europe, had the impression that they had somehow "come home" when they began to change from motel to motel on the trip. They stayed at about a dozen in the drive westward. Dmitri somehow had the idea that this was the way all little boys lived, so that, Nabokov said, "when somebody at a garage would say, 'Sonny, where do you live?' he would say, 'In little houses by the road.' It was very exact."

When they reached Palo Alto, the house that had been rented for them at 230 Sequoia Avenue resembled a Riviera villa. It was the first real house they had had since Russia. Their friend did not stay at Stanford with them but immediately drove back to the East Coast. Nabokov didn't have many students, but they were exceptionally good ones.

Nabokov taught creative writing at Stanford. The fact that his course met in the student union building was perhaps a sign that the administration did not regard the subject as a serious one. When he arrived for the first class, fifteen minutes late, he himself further underscored the anarchic nature of the enterprise because he wore no socks and had on dirty tennis sneakers with holes. At Stanford, where the spirit of Herbert Hoover still reigned, that in itself was enough to make him "the Bohemian professor."

Nabokov's entire body was then vaguely concave. The outline of his ribs could be clearly seen through his shirt. But he was muscular and had acquired a tan that was very dramatic in combination with the shadows thrown down his face by his cheekbones. It was, after all, only a few months since he had been living in conditions of semi-starvation in Paris.

It might be thought that he would have appeared consumptive to the robust California young men and women he was to teach, but their main memory of him was of a man with more energy than he could contain. He didn't teach a structured course in writing. Instead, he mainly read from his own work, particularly *The Real Life of Sebastian Knight*, and made connected comments on artistic composition. He read with such sustained intensity that a white froth of spittle soon covered his lips, but he seemed totally unaware that it was there and never wiped it off. It was a sight that most of the students had never before witnessed in a classroom and, indeed, were never to meet with again.

One student wrote of the experience years later:

> I don't recall taking any notes in that class. It would have been rather like scribbling notes while Michelangelo talked about how he had designed and painted the ceiling of the Sistine Chapel. In any event, I don't recall that he lectured in any conventional sense of the term. He shared with us his creative activity and experience. Never was there richer fare in any course taught on a college campus, but it was as impossible to reduce to notes as to convert a Rolls-Royce into tin cans with a tack hammer.

The students were so in awe of this foreigner who spoke perfect English and wrote prose of a sort they had never encountered before that they did not work up the nerve to ask him how his name was pronounced. They were invited to tea once and served by Vera from a very large samovar, together with *petit fours* that were all sugar and given instructions on the proper way to take Russian tea. Oddly, Nabokov was a most undemanding teacher at Stanford and would be highly appreciative of anything even vaguely resembling acceptable prose. Only barbarous writing would occasionally provoke him to mild ridicule, though he would frequently ask the class for help when he could not understand what someone was trying to do in an assignment. Students occasionally would spot him wandering around in odd corners of the university, behaving rather like an avid eavesdropping anthropologist.

When the summer session was over the Nabokovs returned to New York by train. Nabokov had received eight hundred dollars for two months, a rather good salary for the time. During that summer Nabokov lectured (often he amused himself by calling on the opinions of the well-known Russian writer Vladimir Sirin) on class days, while on free days he would sit out in the sun in bathing trunks and write or go up into the mountains after butterflies. Two of his Stanford public lectures on drama have now been printed. Nabokov brusquely dismissed most of modern drama, and some ancient, too.

At Palo Alto he wrote his first poem in English for nearly twenty years, and almost every evening he played chess with the university's sole professor of Russian, Henry Lanz. Though born in Moscow, Lanz was able to come to America in 1917 because his father was a naturalized American. He had offered his services to Stanford to teach Russian on a private basis in 1918 and had gradually established a department and become a professor. When they played chess, every time that Nabokov offered Lanz a sacrifice, he would madly leap at it, then hold it and lower it back to the board horribly slowly, but the temptation would always prove overwhelming, and he would slip it away again just as it touched the board. Then he would invariably find himself in checkmate within several moves.

It will be clear that Lanz's play provided the prototype for that of Gaston Godin in *Lolita*, a "preposterous" insinuation to which Nabokov vehemently objected but which is considerably likely since Lanz suffered, Nabokov claimed, from nympholepsy. Nabokov found out about it quite accidentally. He felt that Lanz was both extremely strange and highly cultured, and that he was suffering from a tragic illness. Lanz evidently talked about his condition with Nabokov, because Nabokov knew that Lanz drove into the country on weekends to participate in orgies, and also, Nabokov claimed that he forced his wife to dress as a girl. Apart from that, the only thing Nabokov told me about Lanz was that once, when he was driving with him on a deserted road, he happened to say that Alexander Blok was Jewish but concealed the fact. Lanz brought the car to an immediate halt in the middle of the road without pulling over, turned to Nabokov, and exclaimed: *"Kak podlo!"* ("How loathsome!") Nabokov said that Lanz attempted to commit suicide once and succeeded on the second try.

The matter of Lanz's death is, however, somewhat muddled. A memorial statement from the university said that the shock of his death at fifty-nine was intensified by the fact that the day before his illness he appeared perfectly well. *The Stanford Alumni Review,* however, reported that his death was the result of a liver ailment aggravated by a long infection and peritonitis. The main scholarly work for which he was known was titled *In Quest of Morals.*

In any event, the characters of Humbert, Quilty, or, for that matter, Godin cannot be said to be drawn from Lanz. Lanz merely furnished Nabokov with the usual snatches and gestures from which he usually built a substantially new character. The theme of nympholepsy dates, as we have seen, after all, from 1928 in Nabokov's poetry and from about 1936 in his prose. From a purely literary point of view, the celebrated sexual novels of D. H. Lawrence have been given insufficient notice for the commencement of eroticism in Russian émigré writing, particularly that of Sirin and Bunin, especially after the appearance of *Lady Chatterley's Lover* in 1928. Lawrence's work was well known in both Berlin and Paris, and, of course, Nabokov would have had no difficulty in obtaining and reading Lawrence in the original, just as he had read *Ulysses* immediately upon its appearance. That Nabokov always reacted toward Lawrence with a vehemence otherwise reserved for Dostoevsky does not in the least remove the likelihood of this important foreign influence. In 1938 Georgy Ivanov had written a pessimistic and very pornographic "answer" to Henry Miller in a novella called *The Splitting of the Atom,* and in 1939 Nabokov wrote his short story called "The Magician" on the theme that he was to develop more fully in *Lolita.*

Nabokov stressed to me that in the course of his life he had

known five, perhaps six such people, so that there was no particular reason why Lanz should have figured particularly strongly in
his creation of Humbert: "No, no, no. I may have had him in the
back of my mind. He himself was what is called a fountainist, like
Bloom in *Ulysses*. First of all, this is the *commonest* thing. In
Swiss papers they always call them *un triste individual*. And I
was always interested in psychology. I knew my Havelock Ellis
rather well. There are many Australian case histories, as I remember now, in his book." At this point Nabokov's wife inter-
vened forcefully to change the subject: "*Why*, darling? It's . . ."
he protested. "Then do what you like. I don't object," she replied
and left the room, and he said, "Just a few words," and provided
the information that has been given.

When the Nabokovs arrived back in New York, there was a telegram waiting for him: would he like to come and teach at Wellesley? He accepted at once. When Nabokov had first visited
Wellesley in 1941, he had delivered a mixed bag of lectures, some
of which had been written to serve double duty at both Stanford
and as the Institute of International Education lectures. The talks
were: "Hard Facts About Readers," "A Century of Exile," "The
Strange Fate of Russian Literature," "The Artist and Common-
sense," "The Tragedy of Tragedy," "The Art of Writing," "The
Novel," "The Short Story," and separate lectures on Pushkin,
Lermontov, Gogol, and Tolstoy. The initial lectures on the art of
writing were so well received that he was asked to stay an additional fortnight, during which time he gave his other general lectures on literature and the one on the strange fate of Russian
literature. Once again he spoke about Sirin and Bunin, and in his
most charming European manner he delivered broadsides against
Hemingway and Gorky. When he left, it was strongly intimated
that a job might be offered to him.

Nabokov worked harder during his first American year than he
had ever worked before. He did virtually no creative writing, but
his scholarly and entomological work was exceedingly pleasing to
him. He worked on the assumption that he would soon have an
academic appointment and so prepared lectures for approximately one hundred teaching hours. Working on a calculation of
approximately twenty typed pages for a fifty-minute lecture, that
meant a manuscript of about two thousand pages. He would read
his lectures at a slightly subdued pace, and he developed early on

an extremely subtle way of glancing up and down, though he is sure that his more alert students were never in doubt of the fact that he was reading rather than speaking from notes, even including the little bits of local color (these alone were changed from place to place over the years) and dramatic improvisations with which he conservatively spiced his hours, such as the story about Gogol pleading with his doctors to have the leeches removed from his nose. The lectures stood him in good stead for nearly two decades: "The labor was tremendous, but I had no labor after that, thinking about them. I could think of something totally different while I was delivering my lecture." He had given lessons in Berlin in much the same spirit.

Laughter in the Dark had appeared in America in 1938, following which Nabokov had received many letters of inquiry from literary agents and agencies. All had fallen away save one by the time they came to America. She was a tall, strapping, and eccentric woman with bright red hair and—Nabokov thought—a gangster husband. She didn't last long as his agent. Nabokov thought that she was mad, and he feared that she had a yen to handle him in other ways as well.

The Real Life of Sebastian Knight was placed with New Directions with the help of Delmore Schwartz and Karpovich's friend Harry Levin of Harvard's comparative literature department. Both were on very friendly terms with James Laughlin, the founder of New Directions. Nabokov received a hundred and fifty dollars for the novel, which was even less than he got for the serialization of *The Gift* in *Contemporary Annals*. The acceptance came while he was at Stanford. Nabokov felt that his financial relations with New Directions were wild at first, though they eventually quieted down. As late as 1951 Nabokov was involved in a dispute with his publisher over the terms of the rights for a French translation of the novel. The novel did not have many reviews, but they ranged from respectful to enthusiastic. Kay Boyle, writing in *The New Republic*, found that the story was told brilliantly, with delicacy and venomous humor. Walter Allen in *The Spectator* called Nabokov a brilliant writer worthy of comparison with Pirandello, though he felt that the novel's power was damaged because of the impression it gave that "it was all done with mirrors." A review in the *New York Herald Tribune* called it "a little masterpiece of cerebration." In just a few years

The Real Life of Sebastian Knight was held in high esteem by writers such as Erskine Caldwell, Flannery O'Connor, Herbert Gold, and Howard Nemerov, but at the time of its first appearance the Boyle and Allen reviews were the only serious ones. In the Russian version of his memoirs Nabokov tells his émigré readers of the "unbearable imperfections" he now finds in his first English novel. Like his judgment of the inadequacies of *Mary*, this judgment is unduly harsh. At the time that the novel appeared he wrote to Vladimir Zenzinov that he was very proud of this novel as a tour de force.

Like *The Gift, The Real Life of Sebastian Knight* concerns the art of biography, for the novel is almost wholly about the research for and composition of the life of Sebastian Knight after his death by his half brother. The narrator—identified only as V— has had very little to do with his half brother since their childhood, but perhaps this very distance enables V to avoid the constraints of closeness that caused Godunov-Cherdyntsev to abandon his biography of his father. V self-consciously informs us that his mastery of English is unsure, and that he is writing the biography of his half brother to express the lifelong affection for Sebastian and his writing that he always felt but somehow never expressed. And yet V also warns us to "beware the honest broker." In the end, of course, the line that separates the biographer from his subject is often all but impossible to perceive. Is it possible that *The Real Life of Sebastian Knight* is not a fictional biography at all, but a fictional autobiography, another of Sebastian Knight's own novels? It is more than possible. It is explicitly stated at the end of the novel where the narrator says that he cannot remove Sebastian's mask from his face, and that either he is Sebastian, or Sebastian is he. The novels of Sebastian Knight given in plot precis in the novel are very like the novels that Nabokov had already written and was to write in the years ahead. It has been stressed as a major motif in Sebastian Knight's art that "the only real number is one, the rest are mere repetition," and this dictum serves very well to reduce the fraction of the half brothers to a single unit.

Another important Nabokovian idea is expressed as directly in this novel as anywhere else in Nabokov's art: At one point the noted author is lying spread-eagled on the floor, but he suddenly announces that he is not dead but is merely enjoying a Sabbath rest after finishing the construction of a world. And as V looks into the portrait that has been painted of Sebastian he notes that the face and eyes give the impression of being reflected "Narcissus-like" in water as though it were really a picture not of Sebastian but of his reflection in a pool. But what is by far the most arresting piece of autobiographical commentary, however, is V's critical judgment of Sebastian's art. An imaginary critic of the imaginary novelist is cited with approbation for proclaiming that Knight is like a clown developing wings or, alternatively, an angel mimicking a tumbler pigeon. Knight's art is seen as embodying a fanatical hatred for the live things that have 'died but continue to be accepted as fresh and bright by lazy minds. Knight's art is not representational but rather is concerned with demonstrating the various possibilities of artistic composition. It is the task of the reader to see through this scaffolding to the reality that can be imagined behind it. The art of Sebastian Knight is above all parodic. Knight uses parody as a "springboard" that is capable of throwing him up to the very highest regions of "serious emotion." That is as precise a profile of Nabokov's artistic method as there is. It is another way of talking about the leap from the realm of Gogol to that of Pushkin, though, in fact, the actual leap is from Gogol the comic to Gogol the prophet. Autocriticism had made its first appearance in Nabokov's art in a 1927 short story, "The Passenger," in which the narrator discusses his artistic manner with a critic.

The parodic element in Nabokov's writing increased considerably when he switched into English, though, of course, he also habitually parodied other writers and forms in his Russian works. In his first "English" novel and his casual reviews he began to use language itself parodically and to pun in a way that he had never done in Russian. It was the first thing that alarmed Edmund Wilson about Nabokov's writing as their friendship began, and he tried in vain to get him to hold back a little. In *The Real Life of Sebastian Knight* sexual urges are said to arise from a "sexophone" plaint in nature. The ability to see how words can be turned inside out or altered slightly is something one would expect in a writer, who, although he had full command of English, still saw the language with the creative strangeness of an outsider's eyes. Often the ability that Nabokov has to see English with completely fresh eyes is brilliant, as when, for example, he turns *merry-go-round* into *sorry-go-round*. At other times the linguistic games don't work and damage the tone and effectiveness of his writing. From the first Nabokov was not, in print anyway, willing to be diffident about his English. In one of his *New Republic* reviews, for example, he scoffed at Alexander Herzen when, in writing about England in the nineteenth century, he confused the words *bugger* and *beggar*. In his first English novel Nabokov had already begun to play with the craft of Russians speaking English badly for comic effect. An inclination to use queer and awkward words such as *condemnable* serves the same end: such words underscore the sense of strangeness and even unreality of the language.

A flirtation with the possibility of continuing to write in Russian remained in his first few years in America, but Nabokov's hand if not his heart had been given to English. While he was at Stanford Nabokov found that he felt an unprecedented passion to read Russian newspapers and journals at the same time that he was writing in English, and he frequented the Hoover Library, complaining of the fact that one was made to wait a month from the time of their arrival before the Soviet papers were available to the general readership. He gave the second part of his unfinished novel *Solus Rex* to Aldanov for *The New Review* (he was paid twenty-eight dollars for it), but that, of course, had been written in Europe. He did write two Russian poems in 1941, both of which he published in *The New Review*. One was a conclusion to Pushkin's unfinished dramatic poem, "The Water Nymph." It is simply an imitative exercise and not outstandingly successful. The long poem "Fame" is written in a slightly irregular three-footed meter. The poem shows the peculiarly strong influence of Pasternak, because its lines, like so many of Pasternak's, are really loose groupings of metaphors and images that refuse to submit to the autocratic yoke of mere grammatical meaning. Nabokov paid respects to Pasternak the poet in a series of remarks in poetry reviews in *The Rudder* throughout the twenties, though he violently rejected *Doctor Zhivago* in 1958 and said that on this subject he and Adamovich met for the first time symbolically as the only two émigré critics who recognized the sentimentality and vulgarity of the novel. Respect for Pasternak's gift is accompanied by fascinated astonishment at how he disregards or overcomes the most elementary grammatical precepts of the Russian language. Once Nabokov allowed his vexation to take the upper hand and wrote that Pasternak "has a rather poor knowledge of the Russian language" (*"plokhovato on znaet russky yazyk"*), but, more typically, he would speak of the "marvelous ungrammatical quality of the talented but murky Pasternak."

The Pasternakian manner of poetic speech is very much present in "Fame." In it a poet talks with an apparition, a sort of sooty ghost on wheels, about the ways in which he may pass like a candle between mirrors "to the fire-lit darkness of my native land." The apparition tells the poet that his leaves have no ground to fall to, and that no one in the great expanse of Russia will ever mention even one page by him. The poet's writing in English is mentioned, too, but in an entirely condescending way. But the poet has the last word and affirms that, even though he has had to mature without body and can have no resonance, all the same he carries a great secret within himself and has learned how to rise above himself.

Because of the ravages of the war on Russia, perhaps, but certainly because of the pain involved in his switch to a new language, the theme of Russia figures strongly once again in his Russian poems. The 1940s are, oddly, the "Soviet period" in Nabokov's poetry, for it is not only Pasternak, but also Mayakovsky who is both ridiculed and imitated in a Russian poem called "About Heads of State," which he wrote in 1945. His 1947 Russian poem, "To Prince S. M. Kachurin," is Nabokov's longest poetic treatment of the theme of return to Russia. The poem adopts the tone of some of his whimsical shorter poems on this theme written in the 1920s. He wrote one poem, "An Apparition" (1924), in which the poet returns to his native land to see *"the mother of all birches,"* and someone is carrying a child's coffin toward it: his Russia is in that coffin. A 1927 poem, "The Ticket," concerns a more specific and mundane subject, the ticket agent who will sell him the ticket for his return home. (This particular poem was picked up and mocked in the Soviet press.) In other poems, such as "Ut pictura poesis" (1926), the journey is presented as a whimsical possibility achieved by "stepping over there" in seven-league boots. In one of Nabokov's first works that deals with an imaginary land and language, *Uldaborg: A Translation from the Zoorlandian* (1930), the return is made but not to St. Petersburg, and the poet's reaction is laughter, at Uldaborg perhaps, but more likely at the very possibility of "return."

"To Prince S. M. Kachurin" presents this same pattern of reality that is skeptical of itself at somewhat greater length. The poet returns with a faked passport to occupy a suite on the Neva. But the poet finally asks himself how, really, he could be there in transparent form and with a Sirin novel in his hand. He wishes to go back to the America he dreamt of in his childhood. The dreamlike return to Russia has proved to be a nightmare.

Throughout his life Nabokov brooded and dreamed intensely about return, while at the same time fiercely mocking his own impulse. In the amusing 1933 short story, "The Admiralty Needle," the Soviet present actually reaches out for the narrator's Russian past. The narrator's childhood love has seemingly told the story of their youthful romance to a cheap novelist who has used it in a novel. Or, it might be, she herself is the novelist. The story is an angry letter to his past, imploring Katya to pause in terror at what she has done to their young love. It is, of course, a reversed projection of Nabokov's fears about his own uses of his past, and there was also an actual incident when the past threatened to come to him: Valentina Shulgina's sister turned up in the emigration in the thirties and was in touch with Sergei in Paris, wishing to pass on information about Valentina's fate. Vladimir didn't want to establish contact with her. "The Admiralty Needle" is a story that has certain things in common with the Tamara chapter of *Speak, Memory* and probably arose in Nabokov's mind as a result of this incident.

Nabokov's first mature English poem, which appeared in *The Atlantic Monthly* in December 1941, was called "The Softest of Tongues." It is a poem saying good-bye to the Russian language, which is seen as his true love, and facing up to the prospect of having to work with new and clumsy tools in his search "for heart and art." In April 1941, Aldanov had written to Nabokov reminding him that he had "firmly promised" *The New Review* a novel that was to be a continuation of *The Gift*. Nabokov recalled how Aldanov had scolded him harshly for his parodies in *The Gift* just a few years before and reflected how far off all of that seemed now. His decision had been made, his poems were being accepted in both *The Atlantic Monthly* and *The New Yorker*. Of the twelve poems that Nabokov wrote between 1941 and 1947, eight are in English. Aldanov told him that he was delighted that he was once again in circumstances in which he could write, though he was sad, of course, that he was not writing in Russian.

Contemporary Russia and Europe were nazism and Stalinism for Nabokov, subjects that he could barely bring himself to think about, much less deal with in writing. In an undated letter to Vladimir Zenzinov, which was written from California during the summer of 1941, Nabokov asked his help in obtaining visas for the people in France to whom he felt the closest ties. Nabokov had just received word from Zenzinov that Fondaminsky had been taken by the Nazis, and he wrote that he hoped that Zenzinov was right in thinking that knowledge of where he was might in the end prove useful in getting him freed. Nabokov said that he was so tormented by his letter that he was hurrying to dash off his reply, and he asked forgiveness for the brevity of his letter because his hand was aching from having written too much. He mentioned three people but only named one, Anna Feigin, Vera's cousin, who was left in Nice because she was waiting for her visa just when a completely new law was introduced. The second person may be assumed to be Fondaminsky. Who the third was, Nabokov did not say at all. He may have had his brother Sergei in mind, though Sergei was, of course, in Berlin. In 1941–42 Nabokov had a first taste of comfort and security of a sort he had not known in his adult life. It is true, as he says in numerous letters in these years, that he had no idea what lay before him after Stanford, but there were good prospects everywhere looming "hazily" around him. Yet recent personal and historical difficulties and tragedies were hanging over him. He felt, he wrote to Zenzinov on July 23, 1941, a certain coldness in his soul.

17

WHEN THE NABOKOVS CAME TO WELLESLEY PRIOR TO THE start of the fall term in 1941 they rented a house at 19 Appleby Road, several blocks from the campus. Wellesley has always been an exceptionally peaceful town. Nabokov wrote to a friend that he was writing and reading in conditions of "ecstatic quietude." He got the position, which paid three thousand dollars a year (a quite respectable salary for a visiting lecturer at that time). He was hired because of his successful lectures, and the fact that Wellesley's rare-book department had an *Alice in Wonderland* collection that included a copy of his 1923 translation of the tale. In addition, there was the very fortunate circumstance that Wellesley College's Assembly, a full participatory democracy that has long been a model for other educational institutions, had set aside funds for a visiting refugee scholar. He continued to feel insecure, however, and wrote to a friend that he would not remain at Wellesley and had no idea where he would be next autumn.

When he first arrived at Wellesley he gave his series of six general lectures on Russian writers. He offered the first half, on Pushkin, Lermontov, and Gogol, during the first three weeks of October. The final three, on Turgenev and Tolstoy, Tiutchev, and Chekhov, began at the end of February and concluded in mid-March. They all took place in the afternoon, usually the late afternoon, in Pendleton Hall. The lectures concentrated upon the

"Westernness" of each writer, as if to establish and underscore the intrinsically émigré quality of all of Russian literature. The titles were uniform: "Pushkin as a West European Writer" (October 1), "Lermontov as a West European Writer" (October 8), "Gogol as a West European Writer" (October 15), and so forth. Other lecturers in the series that year at Wellesley were the poet Stephen Vincent Benet and Harvard Professor John H. Finley, Jr., on Homer, though there were also lesser lectures on such subjects as "Marriage on a Budget" and "Pick Your Job and Land It." In all, Nabokov delivered slightly fewer than half the public lectures in the 1942–43 series.

The lecture on Pushkin explained how the great poet was an exile in his own country, unable to receive permission to go abroad, hated by officialdom, and always subject to the personal censorship of the czar. In his lecture on Gogol, Nabokov spoke of that writer as being one of the very first novelists to apply techniques of art to literature, and he saw Gogol's influence in Dostoevsky, Kafka, and Joyce. His remarks on Tolstoy are of interest, because, after he had told the sad history of the relationship between Tolstoy and Turgenev, Nabokov spoke of Tolstoy as the writer who possessed the deepest and most human concept of time. In his talk of Chekhov he emphasized the effect that Chekhov creates by his subtle interweaving of seemingly random and insignificant details. The lectures were well attended and created a small but absolutely vital (as it turned out) Nabokov coterie on campus.

In addition to these formal lectures, Nabokov was frequently invited to talk on various books and subjects in the French and English departments, and occasionally in other departments. Nabokov became quite friendly with Jorge Guillen, the eminent Spanish poet and one of the most illustrious Wellesley staff members in those years. Guillen, who was himself an exile from and a very outspoken critic of the Franco regime, happened to live near Nabokov, and they spent a fair bit of time together. Although Nabokov did not chance ever to refer to Guillen in any of his printed interviews, Guillen dedicated one of his poems to Nabokov, and Nabokov prepared a number of talks for the Spanish department on topics such as Spain in Russia.

In the first semester Nabokov was simply the visiting public lecturer. He had no students of his own at first nor any marking responsibilities. During the second semester he taught Russian to a group of interested faculty members. It was the only serious course in a group of peripheral "special courses" attended by both students and staff. Others included vegetable gardening, home nursing, and child care. That first course without credit was held in a basement room in Founders in the early evening. Regular Wellesley classes were not taught in the evening. The prospects were indeed not good: it was a temporary appointment from a special fund at a college that had no intention of offering Russian. A war was being fought, and the then president of Wellesley also served as the head of the WAVES, a division of the female armed forces, and was an adviser to President Roosevelt's cabinet. The study of the humanities was a low priority on American campuses, and there was even some question as to whether departments of language and literature would be maintained throughout the war. Wellesley did better than many institutions in mounting a defense of them. When this context is understood, it is clear that it was a considerable feat on Nabokov's part to win a foothold as a continuing lecturer in Russian. Beginning in 1944, he taught a course in elementary Russian that was open to all undergraduates and met for six hours a week. After 1945 there was enough demand for a second-year Intermediate Course. Nabokov spent at first two and then three days a week on the campus. By this time he had moved to an apartment at 8 Craigie Circle in Cambridge, which allowed him to be closer to his part-time job at the Museum of Comparative Zoology at Harvard, where he spent as much time as he could.

A quite substantial and even insistent faction of the faculty was fascinated by Nabokov and wanted him made a permanent member of the staff. At the end of 1942 there was a petition from the departments of French, Italian, German, and Spanish asking that he be kept. And a faction of the student body had also clearly decided that he was the most interesting man on the faculty.

A student of the class of 1945 has left us a sketch of the middle-aged Nabokov as a language teacher in the student magazine *We* (vol. 1, no. 2, December 1943). Nabokov is presented as a very shy and idiosyncratic teacher. He would timidly ask his students whether they had done their assignment and then later pour a torrent of guttural and fricative Russian upon them. He would plead winsomely with a class to "like" a word, and then he would stride to a student's notebook and despair with mock ferocity ("Ai-yai-yai!") over her poorly formed Slavic letters. The blackboard, according to the student, would look as though it was covered with Oriental letters after several uses and improper erasures.

Nabokov would handle his grammar with deadpan gusto: "And now we come to the saddest story ever told. 'She is here. He is there.'" Or: "How am I supposed to know 'Where is the book?'" As a preview of coming attractions, he would tell his students of exciting episodes in forthcoming chapters: "Those uncles are crossing these rivers." A difficult point of grammar would always be introduced apologetically, but then Nabokov would brighten and assure his students that, having crossed this hurdle: "You will know practically all there is to know about Russian!" It is doubtful whether any of the students could possibly have appreciated at the time the sarcasm behind the *Peterburzhets* Nabokov's praise of their recitations: "So good to hear Russian spoken again! It's just like being back in Moscow!"

A fair number of the students attended the course as much for the pleasure of the lecturer as for knowledge of the obscure subject he taught. Nabokov once calmed a distraught student who approached him in anguish about her forthcoming exam as he was setting off in pursuit of butterflies near the Wellesley lake by telling her, "Life is beautiful. Life is sad. That's all you need to know."

Nabokov became a well-known and popular figure on campus, to the point where he was "featured" in a little piece headed "Men on Their Minds" in *Mademoiselle* magazine in September 1947. A determined student was quoted as saying: "He's quite a guy! I'm going to write a book about him!" In later years Nabokov would shake his head in wonder and disbelief that many of these nice girls from his classes were now grandmothers.

When he arrived at Wellesley to deliver his very first lectures before he was hired, Nabokov had been housed in the guest room of Claflin Hall while he delivered his lectures. In the time-honored Wellesley tradition, which has always placed much emphasis upon visitors, the lectures were made compulsory for students in many departments, including those majoring in English composition, which meant writing a novel in one's senior year. Since there were about ten seniors who were composition majors living in Claflin, they were asked to entertain him at dinner and at coffee in the Great Hall afterward. Since it was the spring semester and the pressure to complete their novels for submission in order to graduate was growing, the students were at first less than delighted to have nightly social obligations added to a number of Russian novels that they had been suddenly assigned without warning. But they very soon warmed to the task, for the gaunt and opinionated Nabokov was a fascinating mystery man in the context of what many of them regarded as a rather bland faculty.

The Wellesley students, with few exceptions, found Nabokov very attractive, and all the more so since he seemed to them an almost entirely cerebral creature with little or no awareness of himself as physically attractive. He slouched and wore extremely shabby clothes with many patched places, but that was more than compensated for by his wistful and sensual expression. In later years many remembered his full lower lip, and some were quite outspoken about how stricken with him they were. "His effect was like adrenaline," one said. "How much one *wanted* him." A former student who published a sketch of Nabokov as a teacher in *The New Yorker* said that she and two friends came down to the front row at the end of one lecture and begged: "Do it again!"

At college dinners he enjoyed being bold in conversation with the Wellesley students. Once, it is recorded, he told the table emphatically: "I like small-breasted women!" His conversation was very funny in a cynical way. He disabused one of the creative-writing students of the notion that it was necessary to suffer in order to be a great writer, and he continued to tease her about her naïve notions of the importance of suffering. He seemed to enjoy conversations *à deux* with the girls, for he took a considerable number of them to The Well on campus for cups of coffee. There was, however, never a serious whisper of any romantic link between Nabokov and one of his students. He enjoyed the great attention they paid him; they enjoyed flirting with a genuine European intellectual. One student plied him with questions about his wife and child, but he wouldn't answer. On the other hand, something personal must have been said and misunderstood by someone, for a rumor that he had been married before persisted for years at Wellesley. He had never encountered young American women before and in general he responded very positively to the intelligence, exuberance, and self-confidence of the

Wellesley students, his only reservation being that they appeared to lead overly protected lives.

A French-speaking student in 1943 remembers Nabokov as a frequent visitor to the meals of the "French corridor" at Tower Court:

> It had the secret cosmopolitan feeling that made Wellesley seem less Ivory Tower. Then, here at dinner was this fascinating, *handsome* man who flirted openly with all of us (we never dreamed he might be married) and told enchanting tales. We all felt that he was "having an affair" with one of the "refugee" girls on the corridor. He was so informative and never pompous, and so full of little tales that didn't quite hold together, eating cakes and sipping tea at late sunlit afternoons in Tower's Great Room.
>
> But my most exciting adventure was the open sensuality of the man. He awoke in all of us the wonderful sensual possibility of poetry and literature: all the senses, not just sexual ones. Everything was always in an undertone, subtle, but stated in a thousand gestures. We, who were all trained as "gifted little intellectuals" before the "liberated" later days, would listen to him talking of poetry, music, *The Cherry Orchard*, always broadening and probing our awareness that everything in life could not always be "intellectualized." He taught me a wonderful lesson—you must "sensualize": smell, feel, taste—experience the things you read, hear, know . . . We were part of his fantasy I now see, just as he was part of ours.

For this student the specifics of the later Nabokov books were merely a sequel to what she termed the "hidden agenda" of the talk that so entranced all his Tower Court admirers.

Other students saw other Nabokovs. One of the students who encountered Nabokov when he first arrived recalled that "he seemed very small, thin, pale, and ill at ease when he first came into our Novel Seminar. As I recall he had very little to say and was reluctant to enter into discussions." He made no secret of the fact that he wanted to be invited to dinner in the dormitories and ate "as if he did not know when he would see food again." He always wore his trenchcoat and kept its collar up in all weather, so that he looked more like a spy than a visiting scholar. His appearance lent substance to the rumor among the students that he was a refugee scholar badly in need of a job whom Wellesley had decided to help, and that helped to draw students, too: "I never knew if any of this was true, but it made Beginning Russian a terribly special offering, for me at least, and I always looked forward to Tuesday-evening Russian." The biggest shock for most of his old Wellesley students was seeing his picture ten to fifteen years later when he became famous: by then he weighed over two hundred pounds, and most of his old pupils had great difficulty in discerning the lines of the face they had known in his new appearance.

As a language teacher Nabokov used the rather old-fashioned Potapova textbook. But his methodology was quite radical for his time. The story about how he instructed his students to say "I love you" by muttering "yellow-blue vase" (*Ya liubliu vas*) is true but not at all representative of what he actually did. A vase and flowers had happened to be in the classroom, and Nabokov had merely seized the occasion to make the interlingual pun, to which he added the charming footnote that this was the most important Russian sentence that he would ever teach them. The radical thing that Nabokov did as a language teacher was simply to throw his pupils into the deep water of Russian. He frequently told his class stories or recited passages to them, which he knew they could scarcely understand, but he would accompany these recitations with a great deal of gesticulation so that the sense of the anecdote or passage was at least clear in mime. Looking back on the experience one of his early students said: "It was interesting, but I wondered why he did this when we could understand very little. Later, after class, I realized I could hear those rhythms rolling through my head like music that returns to the brain some time after a hearing. He was right in his approach, as teachers of language now realize, too, since this is the way we learn our own native tongue."

After his first year at Wellesley, Nabokov had taken a year off, because he had his Guggenheim grant and also a commitment to tour again for the speaking bureau. When he was rehired in 1944, he was given the more permanent-sounding title of lecturer in Russian (though his contract had to be renewed yearly) and he was to teach a course in Russian literature in translation. This course, which could have twenty-five to thirty students in it, played the essential part in maintaining Nabokov's place at Wellesley. Once the fight to have Nabokov established at Wellesley had been more or less won, the numbers in his language classes trailed off. In 1947–48, his last year at Wellesley, for example, only three students enrolled in his elementary Russian class. That did nothing whatsoever to lessen his dedication as a teacher, or the devotion of his few pupils. One of those three wrote of him: "We were madly in love with him. He was a marvelous man. Kind, thoughtful, gentle. There was nothing he would not explain. He always started off the class with some marvelous anecdote. He was terribly poor then. He often had patches on his clothes. It was very difficult for him. I think he was the most charming man I have ever met. He was a perfect gentleman. He was what the word 'gentleman' meant." And though the number of his language students was not a large one during all the time he was at Wellesley, a reasonable number of them did go on to master and use Russian, though it has to be recorded as well that the man who eventually replaced Nabokov at Wellesley, a Polish historian, felt that his elementary students had not been very well prepared.

One thing impeded the growth of Russian studies under Nabokov. Many of the students who wanted to learn Russian were among the most radical in viewpoint in the student body. They felt that knowing Russian would help them to understand socialism better and were eager not only to learn Russian, but also to get to know a genuine Russian. There was inevitably considerable shock when they learned what Nabokov thought about the Soviet Union and how conservative he was in general. Surprisingly, however, Nabokov was a practical man, and one of the exercises he did with his students was to have them memorize and enact in class two Soviet plays.

Nabokov had made his antipathy toward Soviet literature quite clear in his initial public lectures. Wilma Kirby-Miller of the English department recalled that he was "brilliantly satirical about Soviet conformism." In an early college colloquium, "On What Faith Means to a Resisting People," Nabokov shocked many with his insistence that there was little difference between the brutish regimes of Russia and Germany. This was at a time when Russians were being slaughtered by Nazis on the Eastern Front. When Nabokov's determination to express these views became clear, his presence became an embarrassment to a few faculty members. While this faction numbered only three or four, unfortunately one of them was the president of Wellesley, Miss Mildred McAfee. In view of her connection with the government and America's relationship with Soviet Russia, Miss McAfee decided not to have Nabokov back for a second year. As a result, in addition to the official departmental petitions, about twenty-five staff members and faculty wives signed up to study Russian under Nabokov outside the auspices of the college. A kind of uneasy truce was reached after a few months: Nabokov returned to his official demi-position, but it became clear that the administration was not going to establish a Russian department while Nabokov was there.

Nabokov had only one direct encounter with Miss McAfee over the question. She approached him one day and said: "I want to ask you a great favor. Don't make these remarks about Soviet Russia. After all, we are allies." To which, of course, Nabokov replied: "I refuse. If you want me to lecture only on classical Russian literature, it's all right. But if I'm going to lecture on modern Russian literature, I'm *going* to make those remarks." "Look, Mr. Nabokov, a revolution has occurred in Russia, and we're hearing very interesting things about what's happening in art forms in Russia. Don't you think you could bring your courses up to date enough that we'd know something of what's happening there?" Nabokov's reply was direct: "There's nothing good, nothing good since the revolution!" As a result of this conversation, the essence of which was confirmed by both parties to it, Nabokov had a victory, but it was a limited one, for the final word in such matters is always said by the administration.

He remained a simple lecturer throughout his seven years at Wellesley, and he lost the chance for a professorship at Vassar when the word was passed that he was a *"prima donna* (with caprices)." It seems that it was not an apocryphal story that once Nabokov had handed the Recorder in Greene Hall his final grades before the students had taken the examination. "But Mr. Nabokov," the Recorder exclaimed, "you haven't given your EXAM yet!" Nabokov explained patiently that he knew perfectly well the level of attainment of each of his students, and that the exam didn't really matter at all. The Recorder didn't understand.

The struggle between Nabokov's freedom of expression and the administration's felt need to demonstrate diplomacy between allies continued into 1946. Nabokov tried to be as conciliatory as possible, but on the main point he remained obdurate. He told the president that he kept politics out of his language teaching, even though there were plenty of opportunities to air his views if he wanted to, and that he could easily keep politics out of his literature teaching, too. He stressed that there was a great difference between learning about a nation and learning about a literature. He said that, were he lecturing abroad on American literature, he doubted that reading *Moby Dick*, for example, would tell his students anything "about" America, nor would it do any good to try to claim great artistic merit for short stories in *The Saturday Evening Post* or *Good Housekeeping*. Nabokov felt strongly, he told her, that both contemporary American and Russian literature were "in a very poor way," and that he was not acting in a politically biased manner when he said that Konstantin Simonov's war stories were trashy. On the other hand, there were several Russian writers in the Soviet Union who were producing "fine work." He named Zoshchenko, Olesha, and Pasternak, and, while he did not actually say that he would teach them, one assumes that this was his compromise and counterproposal to readings in Soviet literature from writers like Simonov, Sholokhov, and Ehrenburg.

A little over a year later, in late 1947, Nabokov got a firm offer from Cornell and tried to use it as a lever to obtain a continuing appointment at Wellesley. President Horton (Miss McAfee had married) wrote to him assuring him of Wellesley's desire to maintain him on his current half-time status, but, she said, it would be unfair to make any further implicit promise to him or commitment on the part of Wellesley to establish a Russian department, while no decision had yet been made. The letter clearly implied that there would be no Russian department, since President Horton was concerned that the very fact of a continuing appointment would establish a *de facto* department. Nonetheless, she concluded, it was "our sincere hope" that he would find it possible to continue to do part-time work at Wellesley, and she assured him that Wellesley would lose him "with the utmost reluctance." The letter was signed "Very cordially yours."

Though the student numbers were admittedly sometimes small, Nabokov was a very successful and popular teacher. He had his Guggenheim, was contributing poetry, stories, and book reviews to the country's top magazines, and in 1944 he published

a book on Gogol in New Directions' Makers of Modern Literature Series. He was wildly popular with most of his colleagues.
But it was thought at the time that he never figured out how to
have a satisfactory professional relationship with the few powerful women who ran Wellesley. And they were powerful. It wasn't
really the Soviet Union, for Nabokov had indicated his willing-
ness to sidestep that issue. It was, more than anything, that there
existed a strong tradition of total commitment to Wellesley,
which Nabokov showed in many ways that he was not by nature
prepared to make. It was not too many years before Nabokov
came to Wellesley that it had even been considered unusual for a
faculty member to be married. Though he liked Wellesley and
Wellesley liked him, he was clearly not "the Wellesley type," in
some eyes at any rate.

Smoking was one of the minor but important ways in which he
infringed on the college's social customs. It was not generally
done and was actually forbidden in many places. Nabokov
smoked as much as ever, and while his students filed into the
classroom he could usually be seen puffing his last cigarette in the
hallway before going in to start teaching. He contested the administration's right to forbid him from smoking in class, a diplomatic blunder on which Wilma Kirby-Miller just managed to
intercede for him. To push further in the matter would have provided the perfect excuse to show him the door.

A student named Grace Pologe, who was a sculptor, was so
taken with the handsome lines of his head when she saw him
walking across the campus that she walked up to him and asked
him if he would pose for her. He said yes without a moment's
hesitation, and sittings were arranged in the sculpture studio in
the basement of the old art building. Smoking wasn't allowed
there, and he smoked incessantly as he sat for her. University administrators had offices above the studio, and the cigarette smoke
wafted up through the vents. The administrative officers came
rushing down to see who was breaking the rules but retreated
when they saw who it was. Junior though he was in status, his
reputation for being strong-willed was well-known.

Looking back on this series of sittings many years later Grace
Pologe decided:

> In a long career of working from models I have never had a
> worse one. In the time I refer to he was publishing occasional

Nabokov (*center*) at a family wedding. Berlin, 1923. (*Nabokov—His Life in Part*)

Nabokov and his first fiancée, Svetlana Zivert'. Berlin, 1923. (*Zinaida Schakowskoi*)

Nadezhda Gzovskaya playing in Wilde's *Salome* just prior to the Revolution (*New York Public Library*)

Nabokov and his wife Vera with their Berlin landlords, the von Dalwitz family. Berlin, circa 1930. (*Field collection*)

Nabokov and Beata Inaya from a newspaper photo in *The Rudder* at a literary gathering in honor of Pushkin. Berlin, 1924. (*Field collection*)

Irina Guadinini. (*Private collection*)

Nabokov's favorite picture of himself.
Berlin, 1934. (*Zinaida Schakowskoi*)

Nabokov (*left*) on the podium with Ivan Bunin and Joseph Hessen at an émigré ceremony honoring Bunin for the receipt of the Nobel Prize. Berlin, 1934. (*The Rudder*)

Nabokov. Paris, 1938. (*Field collection*)

Nabokov teaching at Wellesley. (*Wellesley College*)

Nabokov at the Museum of Comparative Zoology, Harvard, 1947. (*Joffé*)

Three of the houses rented by Nabokov during his years at Cornell. (*Field collection*)

Nabokov with his wife, Vera, and his son, Dmitri, at the piano, 1960. (*Wide World*)

Nabokov at the Montreux Palace, Switzerland. (*Copyright © Philippe Halsman 1968*)

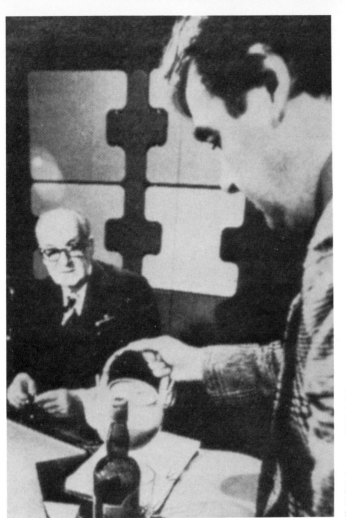

Bernard Pivot pours whiskey into Nabokov's teapot prior to his appearance on the French television program *Apostrophes*. Paris, 1976. (*Ledru Sygma*)

Nabokov with his brother Kirill and his sister Helene. Switzerland, 1959. (*Nabokov—His Life in Part*)

poems and short stories and used to come with galleys to
check. He would read aloud to me from them while holding
them up in front of his face so that I couldn't see him at all
and was always having to interrupt his reading. I liked the poetry and wanted to listen, and liked the head and wanted to
work, so there was a kind of schizophrenic quality to these
sessions. He read *An Evening of Russian Poetry* to me, and it
rolled off his tongue with a kind of gleeful unction. It was
captivating to have a writer of such quality and with such a
personality give one private readings, although I'm sure and
was sure at the time that he was doing it entirely for himself.
He certainly had an air of satisfaction about him.

Nabokov otherwise treated the student Pologe with kindness and
attentiveness.

Nabokov asked Grace Pologe whether one could learn anything about sculpture at Wellesley. When she replied not a great
deal, he asked her why she was there, and that led to a discussion
of the relations between parents and children, which passed into a
discussion of hostility in families. She was aware that Nabokov
seemed to have had endless affection from his parents and found
it incomprehensible that parents might feel any other way.
"There was a sunny quality about the way he talked of his own
family," she recalled. "One had the feeling of the much-loved little princeling. Clean linen and hot milk and never a scolding.
Perhaps I am romanticizing, but I do remember quite clearly
having that impression."

Nabokov was beginning to write his autobiography at Wellesley, and there are two interesting commentaries on that work
from his Wellesley days. The short-story writer Sylvia Berkman
from the English department was given early segments of the autobiography to read, and she remembers that he told her that he
was trying to *force* himself to write about his father. The subject
of brothers came up in his conversations with Grace Pologe because her brother was in the army at the time and she had always
been close to him and was worried about him: "It was on my
mind a lot, and I talked about it to a lot of people, including Nabokov, who made it crystal clear that he didn't want to discuss
brothers. I thought at the time that he was perhaps on bad terms
with his. When I mentioned my concerns about my brother, the
subject would change instantly. He was quite repressive about
the whole thing." And indeed it eventuated that the autobiogra-

phy, *Conclusive Evidence*, was devoted almost entirely to the peripheral people of his childhood and contained virtually nothing about his close family: in the final version of *Speak, Memory* several reverential but awkward pages about his father and a pained half page about his brother Sergei were inserted.

Nabokov participated in an informal car pool that took staff members who lived in Cambridge to and from Wellesley. Ordinarily he would only go back from Wellesley to Cambridge by car and would make the trip out to the college in the morning by bus and trolley. He was the lion of the car pool. The gas rationing meant that the cars usually had four, sometimes even five passengers. The charge was ten cents a trip, and Nabokov was the only passenger to pay his fare by the day rather than by the week. The car pool was to have figured in the second volume of his memoirs. Two moments are especially remembered by the other participants—Nabokov rubbing his forehead with his fingers one morning and saying, "My brother has perished in a concentration camp," and Nabokov standing in front of the car with Isobel Stephens, who taught in Wellesley's education department, and discussing his job dilemma with her. "All the same," he asked her, "shouldn't I stay at Wellesley?" It was very difficult for him to make the decision to leave, and, when he had gone to Cornell, he visited Sylvia Berkman in Cambridge shortly afterward and told her that he was already unhappy there.

In one of his early car-pool rides Nabokov sat on the unupholstered rear seat of the coupe belonging to the director of the Career Services Office. When the car finally reached his apartment, Nabokov declared from the back seat, "I cannot leave you. I am paralyzed." After that it evidently became traditional for him to sit in the front passenger's seat. The other riders learned to provoke him about his pet dislikes in literature or to nudge him into rhapsodies about *Madame Bovary* or *Anna Karenina*. He had no enthusiasm for Henry James. But in the main he simply chattered wittily, and sometimes he could be quite ribald. Sylvia Berkman had a keen awareness not only that she'd never known another person quite like him, but also that she probably never would know another such person. And so, on days when she had an exhausting teaching load, she would ride back in a later car pool, because she didn't feel that she could rise to Nabokov's wit. All the passengers felt a need to try to be more clever in his presence. One woman in the car pool had probably better not be identified. Sylvia Berkman said that Nabokov had never seen anyone quite like this woman before. She was very loud, rather vulgar, hearty, funny, and—in retrospect—"vaguely like Lolita's mother." There was one driver in the pool who Vera claimed was the only person ever capable of disciplining her husband: if he was not at the appointed corner at the proper time, she left without him.

The overwhelming portion of Nabokov's time was spent at the Museum of Comparative Zoology classifying butterflies. The main reason he moved from Wellesley to Cambridge had been so that he would be only a short walk from the museum. Nabokov would sometimes punctuate his day's investigations with more than a pack of cigarettes. He felt that his real life in those years was not so much in his teaching or even in his writing as in the enchanted stillness of the microscope and in drawing minute organs with the aid of the *camera lucida* (into which, he said, his *camera obscura* had been transformed). Virtually every day he would make some small discovery, and sometimes he had the intense pleasure of seeing some diminutive hook or thorn that no one had ever seen before. It was while working at the museum on June 6, 1944, D-Day, that Nabokov had a serious attack. The first of these attacks was food poisoning.

Vera was in New York with Dmitri, who was about to undergo an appendectomy, and so Nabokov was temporarily on his own. He had been spending his days working at the museum and his nights working on his second English novel, *Bend Sinister*. (His original title for the book was *The Person from Porlock*, but he had leaped at the phrase *bend sinister*, which had been used by Isobel Stephens on one of the Wellesley-Cambridge car rides.) But for the two days prior to June 6 Nabokov had closeted himself with his manuscript, which was close to completion. Living entirely on Rocquefort and pineapple, he had written eleven pages, which was an extraordinary amount for him: Nabokov calculated that on average he produced even slightly fewer pages a year in English than in Russian. He wanted to complete the novel before his wife and son returned from New York. That day, which was pleasant and breezy, Nabokov took a break from his writing and set off for the museum. He planned to spend the morning and early afternoon working, following which he had

arranged a late-afternoon tennis match. At about one he strolled
to Harvard Square and had Virginia ham and spinach with coffee
for lunch. He was back at his microscope at about two, and at
two-thirty the first wave of nausea hit him, and he barely managed to rush out of the building onto the street before he began to
feel faint and to have spasms and retch. A colleague had seen Nabokov's distressed exit from the building and followed him to the
street. He offered to accompany him home, but Nabokov thought
that he had sufficiently recovered his composure to make it home
by himself.

Nabokov had underestimated the extent of his illness. As he
staggered home he became so weak that he had to stop and sit
down on the sidewalk every few steps. People laughed at him
good-naturedly, because they thought that he was celebrating the
invasion. By the time he reached the apartment he was writhing
on the floor and quite unable to stand. He dragged the telephone
down from its stand and, sitting on the floor, called the Karpoviches. Earlier that day he had intended to pay a visit to Karpovich, who had himself just been taken seriously ill. They did not
live far from one another, and Madame Karpovich came at once.
She shrewdly called the police rather than an ambulance, calcu-
lating that that was by far the faster means to get Nabokov to a
hospital. The police did, in fact, arrive in just a few minutes, but
it was still to be some time before Nabokov got any relief. First
they had to work their way through a police farce: "Who is this
woman? What poison have you taken?" He was finally driven
into Boston to a "sinister hospital" (as he described it in a letter
to his wife), and it took still more time to get himself away from
that hospital and into a better one at Cambridge.

At the hospital he was promptly washed out with saline solution and then had to spend a sleepless night in a room with an old
man noisily dying in Canadian French. He was immensely
cheered at dawn by a breakfast of bacon, which, it turned out,
had been meant for another patient. By the next afternoon he felt
much better and had a tremendous appetite and desire to smoke,
but he was allowed nothing except water until that night. The
day after that, feeling still better but not well, he was transferred
to a general ward.

The ward itself was nice enough, but Nabokov was soon being
driven to distraction by the hubbub all around him. A radio

played ceaselessly, the sick moaned, the healthy laughed and talked loudly to one another from different ends of the huge ward, and a sixteen-year-old idiot followed the nursing staff about and played hospital jester, giving imitations of the groans of some of the older and more severely sick patients. Nabokov had drawn the curtain around his bed and was sullenly trying either to rest or to read in the semidarkness a medical dictionary that he had filched from a bookcase while being wheeled down a hallway. The staff, however, vehemently objected to the drawn curtains because they implied that a sudden death had occurred. The book was pronounced too technical and taken away from him. It was Wednesday, and the doctor had promised Nabokov that he could leave on Friday. When Madame Karpovich came to see him during visiting hours, he laid his escape plan. She left and waited in her car. Nabokov casually walked to an open side door, and, wearing only his dressing gown, which was all he had, he made a sudden dash for freedom and the waiting car, with two staff members in furious pursuit. He just made it, and they sped away to the Karpoviches' home, where Nabokov stayed for several days until he had completely regained his health.

In 1948 he had a second health crisis near the time of his planned departure for Cornell. Late one night, after Nabokov had taken Dmitri, who was home from school, to a wrestling match, he suddenly began to cough up tremendous amounts of blood. At the hospital no one could quite decide what was the matter with him. They began to perform a bronchogram and inserted a vulcanized rubber tube into his windpipe. Nabokov said the words "vulcanized rubber tube" very slowly, as though, it seemed to me, he could still feel the tube. He was fully conscious under local anesthetic during the whole operation, which lasted two and a half hours: "The doctors kept cracking jokes at me to keep my morale up. I remember one asking me, 'How do you feel?' I said, 'Controlled panic.' " Though he wasn't told at the time, the doctors were looking for and expecting to find cancer, but they didn't. One of his tests, however, showed that he had tuberculosis. It turned out to have been a mix-up with someone else's results. No definite diagnosis was ever made. Nabokov took the view that it was his body's ridding itself of the damage done to his lungs by thirty-five years of nonstop smoking. (He had stopped smoking abruptly nearly three years before on the orders of a forceful doctor.) While he was sick his wife taught his language classes and read his lectures for him at Wellesley. One of the complaints against him at the administrative level was that this happened a little too often. From that point onward Nabokov enjoyed better health than ever before in his life, though for two full years after that at Cornell he could sometimes taste the medicinal oil that had been used in his lungs during the exploratory operation. Nabokov viewed the way that he had stopped smoking forever in a single day as a heroic act, though Vera gave less importance to the deed: "Nonsense, that's the way everyone does it: all at once or not at all." After he gave up smoking, he asked people not to smoke in his presence.

Two important things happened in 1945: Nabokov stopped smoking, and the Nabokovs received their citizenship papers. They went for their examination with two sponsors, Professor Karpovich and Miss Amy Kelly, a very charming older woman and estimable scholar who taught English at Wellesley. She had published a serious book on Eleanor of Aquitaine, which to everyone's astonishment suddenly became a best-seller. She was one of the people Nabokov would cite in maintaining that in those years Wellesley's English and French departments were as good as one could find anywhere in the country. He had in mind, in particular, Harvard, where, he thought, a much more careerist and less purely scholarly spirit reigned.

As they all waited for the examination time Karpovich said to Nabokov: "Now look here, I want to ask you something. Don't joke, please don't joke with them. This is quite serious, you know. Don't joke." Nabokov agreed, but it was not to be. The examiner, who had a slight accent himself, gave Nabokov a phrase to read, *the child is bald*, which seemed a little silly to Nabokov, but he read it. The examiner, however, corrected him: "No, it is not bald. It is bold." To which Nabokov replied that babies don't have very much hair. (Nabokov subsequently used this phrase in *Bend Sinister*.) The examiner acknowledged the statement with mock interest and then asked Nabokov a question on American history. Nabokov didn't even understand the question, but within a moment the two men were kidding each other and roaring with laughter, while apprehensive Professor Karpovich stood looking at them both as though they were madmen. "You passed, you passed," the examiner was finally able to gasp. Nabokov remembered the day with great affection and cited the incident as an illustration of the Russian's lack of ability to understand the American sense of humor: "I had a wonderful time becoming an American citizen. That was an absolutely wonderful day. That's very characteristic, you know. This rather prim Russian who wants to be very serious, and this easygoing American way of settling things. He saw at once that I could read English. It was very soothing, very soothing." Nabokov played at being American with gusto. Harry Levin's wife Elena complained that he didn't fit in with their Harvard friends, because he would always begin to clown around the moment he was introduced.

Nabokov did not get on very well with the Slavic department at Harvard. When he first began to teach literature at Wellesley, a dean had submitted his proposed syllabus to Samuel Hazard Cross at Harvard for his approval without asking Nabokov first. Cross, who was then chairman of the Slavic department, did not approve. Nabokov was infuriated at what he thought was interference both uncalled for and incompetent. Nabokov loved to tell the story of how Cross dived desperately to erase his blackboard mistakes in a Russian grammar class when one of his colleagues chanced to come into the room about something. But, according to Nabokov, Cross wasn't able to erase what amounted to the Russian for "in the company of a stick" for the phrase which should have been "with a stick." There was an unkind rhyme that circulated about Cross that began, "There once was a *macher* named Cross/Had a yen to be everyone's boss." By character Nabokov was a self-assured and independent prince with no inclination to acknowledge fealty, and nowhere more so than in the case of someone such as Harvard's chairman, who did not really know Russian. Nabokov was not altogether fair to Cross, who was actually a medievalist and had edited a competent scholarly volume of the Russian *Primary Chronicle*.

Nabokov and Roman Jakobson had at first at least qualified respect for each other's abilities, but, after an initially friendly period when Nabokov accepted some of Jakobson's readings of the medieval "Song of Igor's Campaign," differences in approach, belief, and temperament made themselves felt. There is a tape recording that is perhaps symptomatic on which Jakobson and Nabokov are reciting stanzas from *Eugene Onegin* in order to illustrate the difference between the St. Petersburg and Moscow accents. At one point in Jakobson's reading a subdued but quite clear *Uzhasno!* (*Horrible!*) escapes from Nabokov in the background. Since Jakobson was essentially a specialist in linguistics and Nabokov thoroughly literary, they need not have had a clash of professional interests. The difficulty was that Jakobson had gargantuan academic ambitions—which he would fulfill, becoming within the decade the most powerful Slavist in American university life—and it was not likely that he would have encouraged another Russian star in the Harvard firmament so soon after taking his own chair. On a personal level it was noticed by many that Nabokov's anarchic intelligence and ready repartee made Jakobson distinctly nervous and ill at ease in his presence. Some years later Nabokov was asked to contribute to an anniversary volume *festschrift* for Jakobson. He at first agreed but then thought better of it and withdrew. Jakobson, who in his youth had been a friend of Mayakovsky's, was one of those émigrés who maintained warm relations with the Soviet government and frequently went back. Once he even approached Nabokov with a proposal to arrange a return visit for him. Nabokov deeply disapproved.

The two men became adversaries without quarreling. Nabokov's contingent consisted of Karpovich and Levin, who were both, of course, in other departments. Nonetheless, the struggle between the pro- and anti-Nabokov factions was close, and in 1946 it looked as though Nabokov was going to be appointed professor of comparative and Slavic literature at Harvard. One evening Renato Poggioli, an Italian comparativist with a special interest in Russian literature who was visiting Harvard, paid a courtesy call on him, and they spent a delightful evening discussing literature and all sorts of other things except the fact that Poggioli had, as Nabokov learned the next day, just been given the post that he was to have had. Jakobson had successfully led the opposition to Nabokov's appointment by rising in the committee room and sarcastically exclaiming in his richly Russian English (it was the standard witticism about Jakobson among his friends and foes alike that he spoke thirty languages, all, including Russian, with a foreign accent): "Gentlemen, even if one allows that he is an important writer, are we next to invite an elephant to be professor of zoology?" In the face of such hostility from within the Slavic department, Levin had to turn to his other favored candidate. Nabokov thought Poggioli a mediocre mind who had had very good luck in his appointments throughout his academic career.

Two years later, when another scholar of more modest academic ability was given a visiting Harvard appointment, Nabokov wrote to Edmund Wilson (November 21, 1948) expressing wonder at the "curious disinclination" on Harvard's part to take advantage of his abilities. In the end Nabokov was invited to Harvard by Michael Karpovich as a visiting professor, too. He gave the general literature lectures in Humanities 4 in the second semester of 1952, following which, in 1953, he used his second Guggenheim grant to continue his work on Pushkin in the richness of Widener Library. One of the books he lectured on was *Don Quixote*. An illustrated edition of the novel had been given to him as a present by his father when he was a boy. As a mature reader he was appalled by the jerrybuilt aspect of the novel, primarily the way in which Cervantes had thrown in fragments from his earlier writing. His highly critical lectures on *Don Quixote* eventually formed the basis for his posthumous book on the novel. At the time the lectures raised many eyebrows at Harvard. Nabokov told me that Professor Levin was rather taken aback and told him primly: "Harvard thinks otherwise." For his part Nabokov expressed dissatisfaction with the large auditorium of students, most of whom, he thought, had no real interest in reading the set books and wanted to be told about them at second hand.

However many hairs he may have raised on the backs of literary necks at Harvard, there was, Nabokov assured me, even greater hostility and opposition to him on the part of certain entomologists at the MCZ (as the Harvard museum was always called). For in his descriptive methodology of butterflies there was also an idiosyncratic approach, which won him some admirers but also frowns.

The unusual academic talents of Nabokov may, it seems to me, be profitably compared with those of Edmund Wilson. Both men may be described in the same terms as the famous definition of democracy: they were undoubtedly the worst sort of academics except for all the others. And though he was, of course, much more of a pedant than Wilson ever was, Nabokov fully shared his friend's views on Modern Language Association–type people. "I loathe them," Nabokov told me, saying it practically as a single word.

When he was first paid one thousand dollars by *The New Yorker* for a short story (a sum larger than he had received for many of his novels) he told Sylvia Berkman that he wished he could stop teaching and just write. "Why *don't* you?" she replied. Nabokov said that he didn't dare for fear that *The New Yorker* money might dry up. By late 1945 Nabokov had begun to put on a tremendous amount of weight, largely because he was compensating for his missing cigarettes by eating great quantities of molasses drops. But there was clearly in it as well something of the starving artist who has tasted the unexpected possibility of security. The point was underscored by Nabokov himself when he posed with his brand-new bulk for a photo at Wellesley in front of a poster that exhorted: FEED EUROPE.

He would have preferred most of all just to write, after that to have a tenured position at Wellesley (or Harvard or Vassar), but it was going to be Cornell. It was at least a professorship, though Nabokov did not know that Cornell did not have a Russian department as such. Nabokov's chair was the last remaining one in a round-robin: Jakobson had left Columbia for Harvard, Ernest J. Simmons, who was the author of popular biographies of Tolstoy and Dostoevsky and who had missed out on the Harvard position in competition with Jakobson, went from Cornell to Columbia, and now Nabokov would go to Cornell to fill the vacancy left by Simmons. One consolation was that there were some very good entomologists at Cornell.

While they were living in Cambridge, Vera Nabokov had been working as a part-time secretary to both the French and German departments at Harvard for several years, and some people were not even aware she spoke English. Their friends were people from Wellesley: Hannah French, the rare-book librarian who studied Russian in Nabokov's faculty class. Jorge Guillen. Isobel Stephens. Amy Kelly. Wilma Kirby-Miller, who was not only an admirer of Nabokov's, but also a minor dean and thus in a position to argue diplomatically for him with the president. Agnes Perkins, the chairman of the English department and the one credited by most people with having lobbied to have Nabokov hired when he gave his first visiting lectures at Wellesley and also to have him rehired after the 1942–43 hiatus. Sylvia

Berkman, with whom he felt he could discuss his writing problems seriously. He liked her as much as anyone at Wellesley, though he called her Sensitive Prose behind her back. Once he even invited her home for dinner, announcing as they came in the door: "Vera, I've brought a guest for supper . . . but it's a little one!" The dinner consisted of cold cuts, potato salad, and pumpernickel, all from the local deli. "Marvelous! Wonderful! What a great meal!" cried Vladimir in mock ecstasy. It was a joke and not domestic sarcasm. Wilma Kirby-Miller said of them: "I never knew any family who cared less about possessions, food, anything. Their only luxury was Dmitri. He had expensive toys and went to the best schools." And in addition to the staff, there were students, not many but a few, with whom he had established warm ties. He sent one of them an inscribed copy of one of his books when her first child was born.

As he was leaving Wellesley, Grace Pologe happened to be paying a visit to the college. She scarcely recognized him. The former lines of his lean face were hidden: "All those spare beautiful planes were softened, in fact turned to mush, and, I thought, coarsened." "Don't say it! I've grown fat!" Nabokov interjected when he encountered a Russian acquaintance whom he had not seen for several years, and in a letter to Mark Aldanov he described his new dimensions, saying that the only thing that truly astonished and surprised him about his new state was the fact that he suddenly possessed the breasts of a young girl. But in his own mind his portliness was simply another of his impersonations as he moved into a new phase of his life.

The admiring staff and students. The neo-Tudor and New England wood buildings set on gentle vales and dotted with substantial groves of trees, which might just (especially in winter) have passed for a Russian estate converted into an educational institution. There were difficulties at Wellesley, to be sure, but, when he looked back on those years, Nabokov declared firmly: "It was there that I was happiest, you know."

18

THE WELLESLEY YEARS WERE VERY PRODUCTIVE FOR NA-
bokov, though a great deal of what he wrote in this seven-year
period belongs to the time in 1941–42 when he was on the lecture
circuit and enjoying his Guggenheim grant. The real drama of
these years was the awkwardness he felt with his new language
and the painful bonds he felt with his abandoned one. In December 1942, he wrote to George Hessen telling him that the Sirin in
him was beginning to stir again, and that he felt too old to change
"conradically." He felt as though he had created a person who
had in turn created *The Real Life of Sebastian Knight* and *The
New Yorker* poems, but that it was all a game or sport. Even
when he was finishing *Bend Sinister*, he wrote to Aldanov that
the possibility that he might write another novel in Russian was
not to be excluded.

Nabokov was not enthusiastic about going on the tour when
the time came in the autumn of 1942, but it was too late to withdraw. He had no particular obligations at Wellesley in October
and November, and he arranged to have his wife perform one of
his rather delicate chores involving the transfer of several series of
specimens from one tray to another at the MCZ while he was
away. "*Perekolesh'*," he told me, examining the letter of instruction he had written to his wife at the beginning of the tour,
"when you pin them from one box to another. Wonderful verb—
perekolesh'. . . ." In another letter to Vera written on this lecture
tour Nabokov tells of going for a walk after a night at the movies

in a mood of wild boredom and suddenly being seized by a bolt of inspiration and a passionate desire to write in Russian, which he knows he must not do. In such a mood, he writes, English is something false, an illusion.

But although he was writing and speaking in English, virtually all the literary work that Nabokov did in the years he was at Wellesley, save a few short stories and the odd book review, concerned Russians or Russia in some degree.

One of his first stops on the tour was Wells College, where his cousin Nicolai was teaching. After that Nabokov's reading tour went south to the border of Florida and then swung north to Illinois and Minnesota. He traveled by overnight train. At the beginning of the trip he had had to wait because he found someone already asleep in his berth, but they conversed amiably about their situation "in men's room jargon," and after a while the porter found another berth for the first man. Nabokov didn't sleep terribly well because of the groans and bumps of cars coupling and parting in New York. His first stop, on October 3, was Florence, South Carolina, where he was to be met and driven to Hartsville, the home of Coker College, a women's school. The heat and the sun of South Carolina in October reminded him of coming to the Riviera from Paris. In the next few days he would learn that the American South also had the same sort of savage mosquitoes that are found on the Riviera.

The train from Florence was an hour late, and there was no one there to meet him. He called Coker and was told that they would call him right back about a car for him. He waited an hour and a half for that call in a little station café by the phone booth. He was irritable, for he had not had his bath or shaved, and he was tired from the night on the train. Finally a professor of theology from the college called and cheerfully informed him that he was in Florence on some personal business and would drive him to Hartsville in three hours. Nabokov indicated that he wasn't overjoyed at this prospect in view of how tired he was, but he was told that he would be taken to a local hotel to rest until then. No one appeared, and, after waiting a while longer, Nabokov learned that the taxi that had been sent to pick him up had had an accident. He was taken to the college by another taxi and finally united with his theology professor, whose business in town, however, was still not completed. Thus Nabokov had no prospects of reaching Hartsville until shortly before dinner at six fifteen, after which the lecture was to follow, and so he went to the local barbershop to get a shave. There was a howling five-year-old in the next chair, and Nabokov's barber was a nervous old man who attempted to aid his fellow-barber by shushing the child, as a result of which Nabokov was left with a bristly tuft on his Adam's apple and a slight razor cut under his nose.

The theology professor reappeared punctually in his car, but pulling away from there they were hailed by an emaciated woman who thought the car was a taxi—she needed to go to Hartsville and was terribly afraid she was going to be late for the Russian professor's lecture. The three had an animated conversation about Christianity and the war as they drove to the magnificent Confederate estate that belonged to the family of Major Coker, the college's founder. They arrived ten minutes before dinner was to be served. Nabokov dived through a bath in his haste to get groomed and dressed in time. Unfortunately, his shirt was overstarched, and one of his cufflinks fell and vanished. He made his appearance at twenty minutes to seven with one sleeve slightly rolled up in his tuxedo sleeve. His social sense prompted him to declare the disarray of his dress at once, and someone else's cufflinks were promptly produced and fixed in place for him by one of the ladies. From that point onward everything went beautifully: two days of lectures and a reading ("Mademoiselle O"), extensive butterfly collecting in the perfumed and blue-green Crimean lushness of the southern countryside with a Presbyterian minister, who turned out to be the son of an entomologist whose work Nabokov knew well, tennis with the local pro, and hospitality from the numerous Cokers who seemed to control half of Hartsville. He met with traditional southern warmth and as much interest as had been shown in him at Wellesley, for his pieces in *The Atlantic* were known not only to the Coker faculty, but also to the Cokers themselves, who were friendly with Edward Weeks, *The Atlantic*'s editor.

Nabokov's lecture stops were all different. The experience was tiring but pleasant and immensely educative, the further Americanization of Vladimir Nabokov. After Coker Nabokov was to have gone on to Richmond, but because of a wartime blackout there his lectures had to be canceled. In place of Richmond his tour organizer sent him to Spelman College, the black women's college in Atlanta.

It was to be simply a stopover of a few days with lectures in exchange for food and board, but it turned out to be one of his most successful receptions, and he was surprised at the end when he was given his usual fee, a hundred dollars. The college was, he thought, "a black Wellesley."

His first talk at Spelman was on Pushkin, with particular emphasis on the poet's African (Abyssinian) blood, and it was met with wild enthusiasm. Nabokov became especially friendly with the president of Spelman, Miss Read. She went to great lengths to surround him with interesting people, and even to see to it that he didn't run out of cigarettes and that his forward traveling arrangements were properly made. In later years she visited the Nabokovs on several occasions. While he was at Spelman Nabokov would breakfast with Miss Read each morning and discuss "the Negro problem" and telepathy. At nine o'clock he would be dragged to chapel for hymns with the entire student body. At first he tried protesting that he was a heretic and hated all music, but Miss Read knew that he would like theirs. They read prayers in his honor thanking God for poets and those who delight in making things and make them well, and Nabokov responded by reading his own translations of classical Russian poems exalted enough to suit the occasion. He deeply liked Spelman, and all the more because he had been more depressed than amused by the Uncle Tomism he had observed at the white college he had just left. The college magazine, *The Spelman Messenger* (November 1942), ran a long article on his various talks and readings. One of them was a "lightly Rabelaisian poem on Superman." It described the explosion of Superman's honeymoon hotel on his wedding night. (The poem had shortly before been rejected by *The New Yorker*.) The Spelman article closes by predicting that Nabokov might someday be a great writer.

The problem with the speaking tour was that people were so eager to please and kept him so busy that he was scarcely ever left alone. Miss Read understood his need to have some time alone, and at Spelman Nabokov finished writing his book on Gogol. The book was positively reviewed by Edmund Wilson and others, but Nabokov felt that it was a frivolous work that might have cost him the chair at Harvard, and it was one of the few of his works that he didn't later revise for reissue when fame came. The book is a joyful romp, half criticism and half artistic prose, and quite essential to an understanding of both Gogol and

Nabokov. It begins with Gogol's death, moves through numerous related diversions having to do with Gogolian themes or points about literature in general, and ends with an imaginary conversation with his publisher (drawn from a real conversation with James Laughlin) in which the plots of various Gogol works are spelled out for the first time. Gogol is shown to be the shadow of his books, and the biographical portrait that Nabokov gives of him is very close in many ways to the biography of Chernyshevsky, except that, whereas Chernyshevsky is shown floundering in ink, Gogol is shown with dirty hands, greasy hair, and pus coming out of his ear. It is a delightful book, though it is clear that, in retrospect, even Nabokov himself thought that he had gone too far. All the same, it is the first book that I would give to someone who knows no Nabokov at all. It is a lively and iconoclastic study of the essence of Gogol's literary genius, which is important in its own right, and, because it is a wildly funny book, it is also eminently suited to prepare the reader for Nabokov's novels.

By the time he reached the northern leg of the tour, Nabokov was extremely tired. He managed to cut short the tour in mid-November instead of mid-December as had been planned. In one city Nabokov went for a walk, got lost, and could not find his hotel. Another time, to his extreme horror, he arrived for his speech without the text that he thought he had in his jacket. Fortunately, the impromptu version was wholly successful. Though he had begun the trip in excellent health, toward the end he began to suffer attacks of brief but very severe pains in his rib-cage, intercostal neuralgia. Though *Pnin* had not yet begun to take shape in Nabokov's imagination, it seems clear that, just as the motels of Nabokov's collecting expeditions made their contribution to *Lolita*, so various incidents and observations on this lecture tour cast their shadow, albeit a much lighter one, on *Pnin*. The comic mural in Waindell, Nabokov's imaginary college in *Pnin*, for example, records an actual mural that he saw at one of his provincial stops depicting great figures passing on the torch of knowledge. His largest audience was at Macalester College in St. Paul, Minnesota, where he spoke to an audience of nine hundred on November 10. The talk was also broadcast on the radio. The enormous audience had resulted from a newspaper article that called him a "celebrated Soviet writer and a personal friend of Joseph Stalin."

Over the years Nabokov lectured at about thirty American colleges and universities, but he never undertook such an extensive single speaking tour again. He spoke at Cornell once before he came there to teach, and he was invited to speak at Yale. They were "looking him over," but it turned out that the person who was at that time in charge of the Russian program at Yale spoke Russian with an extremely strange regional accent, and Nabokov thought that he was not interested in the academic qualifications or capabilities of any new appointee so much as in finding someone who spoke Russian somewhat as he did.

One of his most memorable speaking engagements was at Dartmouth. He might have been warned when he received his letter of invitation, which was signed Vladimir Nabokov. The absentminded professor who had arranged the lecture completely forgot to have it advertised or even announced so that, when the time came, there were only eight people in the audience, and they had been dragged in from the hallway. Another, better-publicized lecture was being given by a visiting explorer at the same time. The nervous chairman pointed out to his speaker that, although there weren't many people in the hall, they were "very well distributed." Among the audience of eight were a lady with her son and dog and the noted popular scholar of Russian history, René Fülop-Miller. "Under the circumstances," Nabokov said, "I had either not to give it or to do the very best I could. It was a wonderful lecture." That was in spite of the fact that Professor Fülop-Miller appeared to be asleep throughout. Afterward the Russian group wandered over into the explorer's reception where Nabokov did rather better and considerably annoyed the explorer, because he gathered a large group around him including the explorer's wife. Much less often, but from time to time, Nabokov gave lectures on butterflies. He lectured on mimicry at the Museum of Natural History, and once, during the Wellesley period when Dmitri was at the Dexter School, he spoke on butterflies there.

At about the same time that Nabokov was experiencing his torments of withdrawal from the Russian language, he said that, somewhat to his own surprise ("that is what it was, one of my few idiotic moments") he found himself wanting to join the U.S. Army and fight against Nazi Germany. Nabokov told Vera that, if it were not for her, he would enlist and go to fight in Morocco. Always true to himself even in his moments of greatest altruism, there was a particular kind of butterfly in North Africa which he longed to capture. (Even more than that, he told her, he wanted to write a book in Russian again.) He withstood the Russian temptation, but, when he returned to Wellesley in 1944, he presented himself, a gentleman in his mid-forties, for active service. He said that he was told, "Go home and think about it, fellow," and finally classified out of service.

Nabokov had suffered from neuralgia from the time he was a young man, and he was briefly hospitalized with severe attacks both in Germany and in France. The pain from them could be quite disabling. Apart from these rather rare attacks, throughout his life Nabokov suffered from recurrent headaches that no pills could help enough, an occasional heart palpitation, and also a suspected shadow behind the heart. This caused him difficulty when he had to undergo the usual medical examination in 1951 prior to his term as visiting professor at Harvard in 1952. No firm diagnosis was ever established: "I have a shadow behind the heart, which I gave to one of my characters. There was difficulty at Harvard over this. I still don't know. There may be something to it. A shadow behind the heart . . . I could also talk to you at length, at length about my dental trouble." Because he played tennis and took long butterfly hikes, Nabokov was in reasonably good shape, but he believed that, without even realizing it, he had always been rather sickly until he stopped smoking.

There are no accounts or letters indicating that Nabokov took any notice at all of the war in his personal life, but the "Wellesley period" is by far the most political in Nabokov's art, particularly at the end of the war. Two short stories, "The Assistant Producer" and "Double Talk" (its original title was "Conversation Piece," 1945), one written about a year and a half before *Bend Sinister* and the other during the course of his work on it, are specifically concerned with politics. "Double Talk" is a story about an invitation that is accepted by mistake. The narrator has been followed across Europe by a disreputable and reactionary namesake whom he has never met. His first awareness of his namesake's existence was a request that he received while living in Prague to return his copy of *The Protocalls of the Elders of Zion* to a little White Army library. The narrator receives many such misdirected letters and telegrams over the years, but when he comes to America and settles in Boston he assumes that he has finally left his sinister namesake behind for good. He accepts the invitation not intended for him because of another doubling—the woman who has sent the invitation says that she is a close friend of Mrs. Sharp, and the narrator also happens to know a Mrs. Sharp.

The meeting to which he goes at a private apartment turns out to be a gathering of apologists for Nazi Germany. They are in the main Germans, but there are also Russians among them. Their conversation concerns such things as the need to intern Hitler in a sanatorium in a neutral country if he should turn out to be still alive and the fact that German soldiers have always acted in a gentlemanly fashion. Suddenly all of the characters, either murderers or fools, or both, in the narrator's eyes, turn into a kind of puppet show. The ironic ending is a complaint from the namesake about how he has had to suffer all his life by being thought to be the author of the narrator's "depraved decadent writings."

Bend Sinister was written in 1945–46 and published in 1947. It has strong and obvious ties, which Nabokov himself acknowledged, to *Invitation to a Beheading*. The novel is about a dictatorship in an imaginary country and the harassment of that country's leading thinker, the philosopher Adam Krug. There are in *Bend Sinister* bits of Lenin's speeches, satires on Fascist efficiency, and even a small portion of the Soviet constitution. Like the figures that surround Cincinnatus, the citizenry and political functionaries surrounding Krug belong to another, lower reality. He, too, lives in a dream world and wonders why he is where he is.

In the concluding scene of *Bend Sinister*, Adam Krug has been brought to a courtyard where his friends and colleagues are gathered together. The scene itself is not presented. Instead, we are given a "colored photograph" of it that has become animated. "You may move again," says the narrator. This, of course, is yet another variant on the basic Gogolian device of the frozen scene, used earlier by Nabokov in his play, *The Event*. The place of one character has been taken by an "extremely gifted impersonator," and the courtyard is the same one in which Krug used to play in childhood. All of the adults, including the dictator Paduk, whom Krug knew when they were fellow students, turn back into children. Krug may save the lives of everyone if he is only willing to submit to Paduk, but instead Krug turns the execution scene into a reenactment of old school attacks upon the repulsive and inferior Toad, as Paduk was then known. There is an explanation for all of this in reality: Adam Krug has gone mad. "Mad Adam" is what the Toad calls him, and his surname, Krug, is the Russian word for circle, indicating the hermetic self-sufficiency within which he lives. Krug has gone mad, because Nabokov felt "a pang of pity" for him. As the novel ends Krug and his world are removed, and we are given a glimpse of his creator amidst the manuscript and draft pages which are all there is to the world that is *Bend Sinister*. With his novel finished, Nabokov's attention is drawn to a moth that has been attracted to the window screen and is clinging there. The moth, of course, represents the author's hero on the other side of the glass that separates art and life. As the novel ends, the author sees the special spatulate puddle that appears on the footpath near his Craigie Circle apartment in Cambridge after every rainstorm. The novel began with this same puddle, and this pool is echoed and repeated throughout the book in various forms, such as an inkblot and spilled milk.

The reader may sense the author as an active participant throughout the novel. These manipulations are in the spirit and manner of Laurence Sterne. Frank Kermode has detailed the echoes of *Tristram Shandy* in *Bend Sinister* in his 1962 book *Puzzles and Epiphanies*. Kermode saw Sterne's ubiquitous Latin and the Russian in Nabokov's novel as mock bows to verisimilitude, and also as signs of superior linguistic powers. Other Sterne mannerisms in Nabokov noted by Kermode include notes to himself by the author and digressions used to indicate emotional evasion or stress on the part of the hero. Kermode's good comparison can be extended still further to locate many passages in *Bend Sinister* that are not merely vaguely reminiscent of *Tristram Shandy* but clearly ape specific moments of that playful book, such as Sterne's Uncle Toby going up and down the stairs in instant replay and Nabokov's announcement that a whole scene will have to be repeated, in reverse. The connection is not chance, for Nabokov, while casually denigrating several other prominent eighteenth-century English writers in a 1959 interview, acknowledged his special affection and respect for Sterne. Though his admiration for Joyce and Proust was more frequently repeated, Sterne stands on a level with Kafka as one of the most structurally and technically "used" non-Russian writers in Nabokov's art.

There is a passage in the third-from-last chapter of *Bend Sinister* that parallels the emotionally compressed opening scene of *Laughter in the Dark* in which the entire tale is told in a very terse fashion. But Adam Krug resists the servant girl who tries to tempt him by rubbing her thighs together in such a way as to imitate the chirping sound of a cricket. He is Adam Krug, we are told again, though we have long known it. It is an incantation of the spirit of the true individual. The novel itself is in many ways one of Nabokov's weakest efforts. Its primary faults were well described on its appearance in a review by Diana Trilling in *The Nation*. But Adam Krug is perhaps the best portrait of the true potentiality of man in all of Nabokov's fiction. When Cincinnatus walks away from *his* execution and police state toward those "beings akin to him," he is walking toward Adam Krug. Both characters, for all the differences between them, are variants on the theme of the poet bound and freed. The manner in which Krug doubles, forming "another Krug" in moments of great emotional stess, recalls Cincinnatus in similar moments of stress. He desperately wants his little boy David, whose life is the only power that the dictatorial regime holds over him. The loss of the child is a great, almost maternal force in Krug throughout the book.

There is a great distance between this novel and the immediacy felt in the major works of the period such as the novels of Koestler and Orwell that were fired by the flames of totalitarianism. It is not at all that Nabokov is any less opposed to totalitarianism. The difference lies in the way that Nabokov insists that the world of totalitarian dictatorship is an illusion, a flimsy stage set that can be swept away, and also in the way that Nabokov insists upon playing linguistic games as he tells the story. The playfulness irritated Edmund Wilson and was one of the first sources of serious discord between them. But this playfulness was merely the linguistic signature of a trilingual author who had read the four-volume nineteenth-century *Complete Dictionary of the Russian Language* by Dahl through several times and was accustomed to using russified English and French words with archaic Russian words to achieve startling juxtapositions and, always, to using words of his own invention. He even went so far in his Russian usage as to invent his own special application of the genitive case. Nabokov had had over twenty years to accustom his Russian readers to this linguistic rococo, which is such an important part of what one means when one says "Nabokovian." He hadn't done it in *The Real Life of Sebastian Knight,* and perhaps it was a misjudgment to play these games in a novel about totalitarianism written so soon after many millions of deaths. Odd words such as "rebounce" and awkward phrases such as "get at his guts" are mixed with French and Russian phrases and classical allusions. In *Bend Sinister* the playfulness is all somehow out of place in a way that it isn't in *King, Queen, Knave* or *Invitation to a Beheading.* The novel's gamesmanship was the primary reason given in readers' reports for its rejection at Random House, where it was submitted before being accepted by Henry Holt in 1947. Nabokov claimed that his Paduk was an amalgam of Lenin, Hitler, Stalin, and some other more minor dictators, but that is more a felt intention than an observable reality.

The virtue of the novel, on the other hand, may be said to derive from just this defect. The evil characters are made to be vulgar dolls, and evil itself, in the phrase made famous by Hannah Arendt many years later, is banal. In a letter to Edmund Wilson in 1945, Nabokov doubts that it is the real Stalin who is at Yalta and refers to whoever is impersonating him as a uniformed doll controlled by the supposed interpreter and clockwork movements.

The two most important works of Nabokov's Wellesley period were his autobiography and his long English poem, "An Evening of Russian Poetry." Nabokov had not attempted a poem of this length since his mock-Pushkinian "University Poem" in his Cambridge youth. Oddly enough it shares the whimsicality of that early poem, but it is far more successful because of the interplay of the light form and serious subject matter. The poem is ostensibly a lecture, but it is really the mimetic semblance of a lecture that has either already taken place or is yet to be delivered. A proper analogy to the organization and effect of the poem would be an epistolary novel in which the letters indirectly but clearly smile at the pretense of an addressee and wander off into hermetic monologue. There are numerous unmistakable signs that this is so: the poem has as its epigraph an extract from what purports to be a letter addressed to the visiting speaker, and yet the girls who pose questions are addressed familiarly by name. (When questioned about it, Nabokov, of course, denied that the poem had anything whatsoever to do with Wellesley.) At the conclusion the speaker answers the girls' coy compliments by shifting into Russian, and these lines point to the real subject of the poem: the poet who has carried his culture into another language, a fantastic "feat" but a source of great personal pain. What he has done is an "apostasy," and he asks forgiveness of the Russian language, which is referred to as "my love." The poem is, after all, an evening of *English* poetry.

"An Evening of Russian Poetry" has a deliberately disjointed progression. In the course of the lecturer's panegyric on Russian poetry (only Pushkin and Nekrasov are mentioned, however) someone else, perhaps tenuously related to the "lecturer," repeatedly snatches away the discourse. This figure is a stylized, almost cartoonlike monarch, an ironic representation of the exiled poet and his lost kingdom of words. But though he is melodramatically described, this monarch-in-exile has an air of far greater seriousness than the mocking, almost Soviet visitant of his Russian poem "Fame" written three years before. The lecturer is not only a poet himself, but also the representative of the fate of all Russian poets: exile in one form or another. There are two Russian words that remain untranslated for the lecturer's audience, and they are the center of the poem, for they tell how unbearable it all is for the poet/speaker. Both the speaker and the poet are, in different ways, conjurors. The poet's feat is to make his muse ventriloquize so naturally that the imitation equals the original voice, which becomes the vital but secondary double or "blotter" page of his art. The rhythm and warbling soundplay of a spectral Russian sounding through English is the extraordinary achievement of this quite brilliant poem. The poet provides protection for himself with his extravagant irony:

> *The conjuror collects his poor belongings—*
> *the colored handkerchief, the magic rope*

It is well known that Nabokov, who practiced conjuring as a child, had a deep identification with the figure of the magician, which, he thought, was essentially synonymous with that of the artist. None of the below-the-surface currents in "An Evening of

Russian Poetry" disturb its steady glide and rich sheen. The metaphors and the tone of voice of the three figures in one—the lecturer, the sad magician/poet, and the monarch—are perfectly balanced and modulated. It is clearly the most successful and important poem that Nabokov ever wrote in either Russian or English. But in the decades since it first appeared in *The New Yorker*, the poem has remained rarely anthologized and essentially unnoticed, except for John Updike's praise of Nabokov's English poetry, and F. W. Dupee's designation of "great" in his article on Nabokov in *The King of the Cats*.

The autobiographical project undoubtedly gathered force as a result of the unexpected enthusiasm with which his recollection of his governess, Mademoiselle Miauton, was greeted in *Mesures* in 1939. Nabokov himself had spoken of the piece as "second, perhaps even third rate." "Mademoiselle O" was the first portion of the autobiography to appear in English, in *The Atlantic Monthly* in 1943, and without any indication that it was not fiction, and it was reprinted in the same way with eight short stories in the 1947 New Directions collection *Nine Stories*. One other section, "Colette," which appeared in *The New Yorker* in 1948, also appeared as a short story, retitled "First Love," in a later collection, *Nabokov's Dozen*.

Portions of the autobiography began to appear in *The New Yorker* in January 1948, and stretched through until June 1950. The pieces frequently appeared with spacings of a month or two between them. Five excerpts appeared in 1948, four in 1949, three in 1950. Two remaining excerpts then appeared in *Harper's* and *Partisan Review*. This serial publication meant that Nabokov's income from his writing was almost as good as his teaching salary, still quite small, in the first years at Cornell. There were really only two major expenses in the lives of the Nabokovs in those years: private school fees for Dmitri (except for one semester, he was in private schools throughout his primary and secondary education) and the butterfly expeditions that they made every summer. On at least one occasion *The New Yorker* check saved them from having to cut their summer travels short.

The autobiography was written in quite a different sequence from the one in which it finally appeared in *Conclusive Evidence* and *Speak, Memory*. In the serial publication the chapter order was: 3, 4, 6, 7, 9, 10, 2, 11, 12, 8, 1, 15, 13, 14. That underscores one important aspect of *Speak, Memory,* namely, that its separate parts are autonomous pendants and do not in the least require narrative continuity. The other important thing about his autobiography is that the self and the past are evoked by means of a great deal of guile so that tutors, his eccentric uncle, the two girlfriends "Colette" and "Tamara," and distant ancestors serve as the puppets of memory to evoke the past while leaving Nabokov's intimate life and family untouched. When I put this to him, he exclaimed gleefully: "Yes, yes, exactly! I planned it that way!"

The exception to this rule is the glowing and detailed portrait that he gives of his mother in chapter 2. Her habits and her moods and, most of all, her full parental involvement in the upbringing of her favored son are all vividly conveyed. His mother had taught him to be so passionate about remembering, and he shared with her the ability to experience various fragmentary moments of mental telepathy. By comparison the late additional pages on his father are wooden and constrained. They were offered to but refused by *The New Yorker* in 1966. That is not to say that his feeling about his father is any less than that for his mother—we know from the poems that it was not—but merely that he suffered almost pathological difficulties trying to express it.

The other emotionally fervent chapter of *Speak, Memory* is chapter 6, on butterflies. This is an especially interesting chapter because of the open way in which the fictional is deployed with the factual. Nabokov's first butterfly, a swallowtail captured for him by a (future) perfidious family servant in a cap, escaped from a wardrobe at Vyra. Mademoiselle had imagined that naphthalene would kill it overnight, but it escaped through a window the next morning when the wardrobe was opened. But the swallowtail is "overtaken and captured" by Nabokov forty years later on an "immigrant dandelion" in the mountains of Colorado. The attic books of his maternal grandmother are summoned up with the precision expected of a library call card, and this is followed by a capsule history of the evolution of butterfly classification in modern times. From that Nabokov gives a mini-lecture on mimicry in butterflies, and in nature and in art, following which he cites the (extremely rare) precise verses on butterflies to be found in Russian, French, and English poetry. But this slightly precious progression gradually succeeds in conveying the intensity of his passion for lepidoptera, which is one of the objects of the chapter. After having named with enormous pride the four places in America where he discovered new butterflies, he bravely shows himself as a vain and ambitious boy decades earlier making discoveries that were not really discoveries. All of this builds up force in a low but insistent manner until the concluding scene, when he is about eleven and in the marshland beyond the Oredezh comes upon "a paradise of lupines, columbines, and pentstemons." It is a kind of ecstasy or epiphany, and Nabokov has artfully prepared his reader for this crest of an emotional wave. It is one of the most successful passages of the autobiography, and, if we cannot understand how the boy Nabokov betrayed a friend to go on his obligatory morning hunt, we can see how important the mixture of memory, solitude, beauty, and passion became for him after Russia. In one of his best Russian poems, "In Paradise" (1930), he imagines himself after death as a provincial naturalist in paradise.

Nabokov has said that there were few things in his life to match the emotion, ambition, or excitement of his entomological explorations. It is a great loss that he had not completed the second volume of his memoirs before his death. It was to have been called either *Speak On, Memory* or *Speak, America* and to have contained a chapter on his butterfly collecting in America for nearly twenty years. By 1944 Nabokov had visited twenty-three states in his summer travels, and, before he left America, he had visited nearly all. Nabokov posed as a steely scientist, but his articles on butterflies always reveal an intimate sympathy with as well as great knowledge of the world in which butterflies live.

There is, too, another volume of Nabokov's memoirs, the Russian one, called *Other Shores*, which he published in 1954. It is not precisely a translation because it differs from the original in hundreds of little details. When one considers that there are effectively three slightly differing English versions, that means that Nabokov's autobiography exists as four different books. In English, for example, Nabokov relates how, as an adult, he was undergoing an appendectomy, and the smell of ether caused him to dream of the time he found a spectacular moth in the corner of a window at Vyra, and his mother killed it for him with ether. Nabokov being operated on dreams that he is fixing a moth on a mounting board and being helped by a Chinese lady whom he recognizes as his mother. In *Other Shores*, however, the woman isn't Chinese. She is simply his overexcited mother. There is additional detail on how he looked when the moth was caught. Even more surprising, the rising ground at the end of the marsh in *Other Shores* is not a "paradise of flowers" but simply the flaming of local flowers, and it is at this point that the Russian reader is taken to the exotic places in America (but the list is slightly different!) where Nabokov has captured entirely new species.

The curious thing about the variances in his autobiography is that there is no logical forward progression of detail as one would expect. There are, true, things that only a Russian readership would need or understand, such as the passage in which he names the insignificant Russian poets whom "Tamara" can quote endlessly by heart. There are contradictions that needed correction such as the early statement that he had written his first poem in the toilet as opposed to a different account of that first poem given in another section of the book. But there are also many things, such as the fact that Nabokov worked writing commercial (guidebook?) descriptions of various countries in the Berlin days, that are not then carried forward into the new English edition.

The logical explanation for the ever-shifting text of Nabokov's autobiography is probably, at a subconscious level, that the life described cannot be confidently "possessed" by any person other than Nabokov himself. A scholar working with all four texts can only have a heightened sense of how much of the detail must be classified as circumstantial evidence because of the other and sometimes conflicting details. Languages attempt to describe what can never be more than tangentially grazed by mere words. "Reality" is a personal and private treasure, and Nabokov smugly (more so in *Other Shores* than in *Speak, Memory*) adds that it is none of his business whether an "esteemed visitor" trips on his folded magic carpet or not. The autobiography was completed at Cornell in 1950.

Starting from the time of his first teaching at Stanford, when he felt great dissatisfaction with the competence of the English-language translations available to him for teaching purposes, Nabokov involved himself actively in the craft of translation. His first translation was of Pushkin's play *Mozart and Salieri*. He collaborated on this, without incident, with Edmund Wilson, and it was published in *The New Republic* in 1942. The primary translation was done by Nabokov with Wilson making stylistic changes. He also translated three poems for a New Directions anthology of poetry and prose edited by James Laughlin, and, in 1943, two poems by Fet in *The Russian Review*, which was then the leading English-language journal concerned with Russia in America. His major translation effort was a 1944 book, published once again by New Directions, called *Three Russian Poets: Translations of Pushkin, Lermontov, and Tiutchev*. These early translations were rhymed and in meter and quite brilliant, particularly the translations he did of his friend Khodasevich. In 1945 Nabokov published three rhymed stanzas from *Eugene Onegin* in *The Russian Review*.

In the early years Wilson tried to arrange for Nabokov to write regular articles in *The New Republic* on Russian literature, and Nabokov did begin work on an article about Soviet drama that was never finished. A previous review he wrote, which touched on Russian politics and anarchism, had been refused. Wilson explained to Nabokov that the magazine had been scared of it politically. Although Wilson disagreed with the article's remarks about Lenin, he thought it too good not to be printed and graciously offered to assist in its publication elsewhere.

Wilson was tremendously active on Nabokov's behalf in those early years. He eased Nabokov forward at *The New Republic* and *The Atlantic Monthly*. He supported him for the Guggenheim grant. And at all the campuses that Wilson visited to give talks he made representations on Nabokov's behalf and tried to set up academic appointments for him at Bennington, Yale, and, some years later, Princeton.

Wilson was aware from the beginning that Nabokov had produced a large *œuvre* in Russian, and it is clear that he was fascinated by Nabokov both personally and as an artist. He met Nabokov's friend from Cambridge Bobby de Calry and quizzed him at length about Nabokov's past. He also questioned his cousin Nicolai. He even met Nabokov's Cambridge roommate Kalashnikoff, though he told Nabokov that he remembered almost nothing of him, and there was Nabokov's old roller-skating companion from his first days in England who lived nearby on the Cape. Wilson chanced upon and purchased a rare copy of Nabokov's 1923 book of poems in New York, and he also read *Mary* (which he liked enormously) and *Invitation to a Beheading* in Russian (he found the Russian of *Invitation* too difficult and did not much like it) as well as the two Russian novels that were available in English, *Laughter in the Dark* and *Despair*. In a series of letters written in 1945, 1947, 1951, and 1953, Wilson announced to his friend that he was on the verge, first for *The Atlantic*, later for *The New Yorker*, of doing a comprehensive study of him. Even as that intention slipped away with time Wilson would from time to time declare that he was going to read Nabokov's complete works.

Sadly, that overview was one of the last things that Wilson wrote before he died, as a superficial note attached to his attack on Nabokov's translation of *Onegin* for the 1972 collection *A Window on Russia*. Seven novels are mentioned, several of them tossed away in a line or two, and only *Lolita* is praised. Wilson acknowledges at the beginning of his note that he has been moved to write it in order "to correct any possible injustice that I might have seemed to have done to Mr. Nabokov's work in other departments of literature than the scholarly." He is obviously made awkward by Nabokov's latter-day fame. His remarks are ill-tempered and yet somehow half-hearted. Their overall tone is somewhat kinder but all the same harks back to the kind of comments that used to be made by émigré critics such as Adamovich, Gippius, Ivanov, and Merezhkovsky.

In spite of his comments on the inadequacies of Wilson's Russian during their Pushkin controversy, Nabokov once thought well enough of him to propose, in April 1942, that Wilson become his translator. He also proposed to Wilson that they do the *Onegin* translation together! It was a mistake in judgment and perhaps also symptomatic of the flaw in their friendship from the beginning, for Wilson had just entered the stage of his career from which he could make or single-handedly hobble the reputation of any of his contemporaries, and it would have been unreasonable to expect that he would have taken on a literary relationship in which he would be subservient to a brilliant but impudent intruder into American literature. Wilson declined, saying that he would gladly become his translator but did not have the time, and, moreover, that his still uncertain Russian would probably cause Nabokov more difficulty than if he were to do the translation himself.

About a year and a half later (November 10, 1943) Wilson wrote to Nabokov with a proposal of his own: he wanted them to collaborate on a book about Russian literature in which he would

contribute an essay on a particular poet and Nabokov would supply a series of translations from that poet. Nabokov was then
under contract to give New Directions a book of his translations
of Russian poetry, but Wilson suggested that Nabokov could
perhaps withdraw from New Directions, and that he could procure a substantial advance from Doubleday, which they would
divide evenly. He also said that he hoped that Doubleday could
be induced at the same time to contract for Nabokov's second
English novel, parts of which he had already read and praised in
its first draft. And finally, Wilson reckoned that several of the
paired pieces would certainly be used by Weeks in *The Atlantic.*

Nabokov accepted the proposal by return mail. He could not
be released from his New Directions contract, but there were,
of course, other translations that he could do for the Wilson-
Nabokov book. But in the end only a single one of the pairs of
what they called their "Siamese connection" appeared, in *The
Atlantic* in 1944, and the project was put aside, first for the summer and then forever. Wilson did make the arrangement with
Doubleday, and they divided the advance equally, but the publishing house insisted, Wilson informed his friend somewhat
awkwardly, that the book was to be *by* Edmund Wilson *with
translations by Vladimir Nabokov.* Wilson assured Nabokov that
he would take care to see that Nabokov's name was set in the
same size print.

Then, not long afterward, Wilson's editor at Doubleday informed him that there had been a house decision to deemphasize
highbrow books and concentrate more on popular titles. Wilson
was told that in view of this he had no future with Doubleday. As
a result, Wilson began conversations with the Oxford University
Press to take over (or, he hoped, even raise) the Doubleday advance, but now the connection had been broken, and Wilson
wrote to Nabokov (July 18, 1947) that instead of the combined
volume Nabokov had wanted there would be a separate volume of
Wilson essays on Russian literature and a volume of Nabokov's
translations. However, the OUP editor turned down the poetic
translations on economic grounds, and that was the end of it.

In Nabokov's estimation 1946 marked the decline of the rather
close relationship that had developed between Wilson and himself, though they remained friendly as late as the early fifties. To
be sure, there were potentialities for awkwardness from the very

beginning. In his eighth letter to Nabokov, Wilson (who probably learned the nickname from Nicolai Nabokov) addressed him as Da-rogue-oy Val-odd-ya. In turn, Nabokov called Wilson "Bunny," at Wilson's request.

In their relationship Wilson seems often to have chosen to play the Russian, while Nabokov played the part of the American. When Nabokov visited Wilson at Stamford, Connecticut, in 1942 (Wilson's fridge is the hero of Nabokov's poem "The Refrigerator Awakes"), they went for a long stroll during which Wilson initiated the conversation by asking whether or not Nabokov believed in God. "Do you?" Nabokov replied. "What a strange question!" muttered Wilson. Nabokov, for his part, could not always withstand the temptation to fool around in the American manner. Once, for example, he reached over from the back seat of a convertible being driven by Mary McCarthy and took off Wilson's brown hat, impersonating the wind. Wilson ignored him and turned to Vera Evseevna: "Your husband has a rather strange sense of humor." On another occasion the Nabokovs arrived unannounced at the time when the separation between Wilson and McCarthy was beginning. Wilson greeted them in a rather flustered fashion at the door, and Nabokov foolishly attempted to "put him at his ease." "Don't worry. It doesn't matter—we're only going to stay for a few minutes," said Nabokov. "As a matter of fact, it does matter," said Wilson and gave them to understand that he couldn't ask them in. Something very like that had happened once before, in New York, when Nabokov had arrived at Wilson's at the wrong time, and he had a mistress awkwardly concealed in his bedroom.

When Wilson and Nabokov first met, *To the Finland Station* had just appeared. Wilson presented Nabokov with a copy inscribed: *To Vladimir Nabokov in the hope that this may make him think better of Lenin.* Nabokov sent Wilson a long letter praising the book but detailing what he felt were Wilson's misconceptions of Lenin the man and politician. In reply (December 19, 1940) Wilson acknowledged the weakness of his Russian background and gallantly allowed that there were weaknesses on the German side as well, but he held his ground about his judgment of Lenin. That is the way intellectual discussions between them usually went. Nabokov said that, when he visited Wilson at Wellfleet, they would have long arguments in which Nabokov had the impression that he had finally worn Wilson down and gained acquiescence on whatever point was at question, but that Wilson would always appear with fresh arguments the next day as though their previous conversation had never taken place. Particularly in political matters in the early years (later on, more and more in literary matters as well) Nabokov and Wilson found themselves almost inevitably at friendly odds.

If, given his views, Nabokov showed considerable restraint in regard to his political convictions with Wilson, Wilson for his part must have been extremely careful in regard to the expression of his anti-Semitic views (known to those who have worked with Wilson correspondence in archives), and he told a friend that he lived in terror of forgetting to include a warm greeting to Vera every time that he wrote to Nabokov.

For all their arguments, Nabokov considered that they were alike in certain ways and not so very different in taste. Both men were intellectually and artistically aggressive. The intrinsic need for a constant adversary can clearly be seen in Nabokov's career. The difference between them may be observed in the way that they walked. The younger Wilson was described (by Scott Fitzgerald) as walking briskly through New York crowds thoroughly wrapped in his own thoughts and looking straight ahead. The younger Nabokov was famous for his almost ethereal flying gait and seemed to some always to be looking at a far-off point. What is clear in both these impressions of the two men is that each to a large extent inhabited a world of his own.

Nabokov had many skills that had been given to him by the great procession of tutors and governesses enumerated in *Speak, Memory*, but Wilson compensated for that to some extent by the range of his interests, which was broad even in comparison with that of Nabokov. There cannot be the slightest doubt that Nabokov looked upon his friend's efforts at catholicity with a certain amount of condescension. He smiled disdainfully when he told how Wilson had specially asked him to include entomologists among the guests at a little party he was giving, and how Wilson immediately went into a corner with them and attempted to "talk shop." But the entomologists had not turned up at the party, and the guests from Wellesley were more than a little puzzled by Wilson's sudden interest in insects.

Nabokov particularly admired Wilson for his knowledge in

those areas such as lower-level early American literature where it seemed to him that Wilson really did have rare and deep knowledge. Nabokov sometimes accepted and followed Wilson's recommendations in English and American literature. It was through Wilson that Nabokov's respect for Melville grew, and Wilson also introduced him to Austen's *Mansfield Park*, which eventually became a staple of one of his courses at Cornell. Most of all they shared an undimmed boyhood admiration for H. G. Wells. Russia and Russian literature were always a problem. "These were the two mirages of Wilson," said Nabokov. "That he knew Russian history better than I because of his Marxism, and that he knew at least as much about Russian literature as I." For many years, at least until 1948, Wilson simply classified his friend as a White Russian to explain his political views. Then, once Wilson had abandoned his former political sympathies, he called Nabokov an ascetic, an austere worshiper of Pure Art, a monk, and a man with no experience of women. Wilson and Mary McCarthy and he, according to Nabokov, used to have conversations like this: "What exactly are you? You're not a Red, so you must be a White." "In a certain sense, I suppose so." "Then you're a Fascist." "I come from a family of Russian liberals." "There were no Russian liberals." Gradually politics did become less of an issue, though Wilson never stopped objecting to Nabokov's superpatriotism: "You new Americans with your enthusiasm. What a bore!"

In addition to their exchange of letters, Wilson and Nabokov would usually see each other several times a year, in Cambridge, on Cape Cod, in New York, and later in Ithaca. Nabokov sometimes stayed in Wilson's cold-water flat in New York when he visited the city. It was there that he met Allen Tate, with whom he grew quite friendly, and a young poet who would come to see Tate, Robert Lowell. He would also meet Wilson in Cambridge at Harry Levin's and at the home of Billy James, the son of William James. Billy James was a tremendous admirer of Nabokov's writing and promised Nabokov one of Henry James's desks, but he died before the desk had been passed on to Nabokov. He met Robert Lowell once more at Billy James's house. They talked about Lowell's school, St. Mark's, and Nabokov flabbergasted Lowell with the extent of his knowledge about the school. Dmitri had attended the school for a number of years, and Nabokov had been studying it for use in *Pnin*. Nabokov once wrote to Wilson lecturing him for drinking with Billy, who was under doctor's orders to abstain. For his concern he received a telegram from them in the old literary tradition: WE DRINK TO YOUR HEALTH BUNNY AND BILL.

When Nabokov was sick in 1948, Wilson played an important supportive role. There was a very real question for some time as to whether Nabokov would have to cease all work and take a prolonged period of complete rest. For nearly four weeks Wilson was extremely active on his friend's behalf and initiated a plan whereby *The New Yorker* would pay Nabokov, who by that time was a reasonably regular contributor to the magazine, a modest "pension" during the time he was recovering. In the end Wilson went too far on behalf of Nabokov, because he even turned to friends with requests for loans, which embarrassed Nabokov, because, as had been the case when he was leaving France, not all the requests were successful.

Nabokov and Wilson had roughly parallel experiences as fellow contributors to *The New Yorker* over the years. Nabokov was brought into *The New Yorker*'s stable on Wilson's recommendation by Katherine White, a senior editor who had followed and admired his work in *The Atlantic*. Each writer found that he frequently strained the air of gentility that was the journal's hallmark in those years. Wilson much more than Nabokov displeased comfortable readers with his provocative and often cranky essays after he replaced Clifton Fadiman as *The New Yorker*'s regular book reviewer. Nabokov always felt that it was a pleasure and a privilege to be a *New Yorker* author, both for the overall level of the magazine and, especially important to him in the forties, for the fees plus generous cost-of-living, or COLA, supplements, which were unequaled by any other serious magazine of the time. However, Nabokov periodically found that pieces of his were returned with what must be some of the most regretful and eloquent rejection notes in the history of literature. Two chapters of *Pnin* were rejected, on political grounds, he thought. The phrase "applesauce in your pants" in the short story "Lik" occasioned a pained explanation of the magazine's traditional policy in regard to bodily functions. It is characteristic of the relationship between Nabokov and *The New Yorker* that he accepted occasional editorial changes, something he never did for any other publisher or journal. In *Transparent Things* Nabokov stresses an author's duty to stand firm against any editorial changes.

In 1947 Wilson supported Nabokov in connection with some editorial difficulties that had arisen from one of his short stories, "Signs and Symbols," and a chapter from the autobiography. Writing to Katherine White (November 12, 1947), Wilson complained at length about the resistance encountered at the magazine by certain aspects and portions of his own and Nabokov's work. "Signs and Symbols" had been accepted but treated as an overwritten parody, which had angered Nabokov, who viewed it as a very serious work. Wilson expressed surprise that he had not challenged someone to a duel. He thought that Nabokov's story was "everyday" and suggested to Mrs. White that its editorial treatment showed a morbid fear on the part of a magazine that had come to an age when it was loathe to print anything that might jar its audience or seem unintentionally funny. Wilson recalled some short stories of his own that were rejected by the magazine because, he thought, they were not silly and empty and pale enough. As regards the autobiographical chapter, "My English Education," Wilson said that it was perfect for the magazine because the piece didn't get anywhere and was just the sort of little reminiscence of which *The New Yorker* had already printed any number. The root of the difficulty, according to Wilson, was that *The New Yorker* always objected to any manifestation of an idiosyncratic style or difficult content. *The New Yorker* had turned down Wilson's *Memoirs of Hecate County*. But these occasional little difficulties did not matter very much to Nabokov. What was significant was the unqualified recognition of his talent on the part of certain *New Yorker* editors. This was certainly no less important to the first half of his career as an American writer than his association with *Contemporary Annals* had been to the second half of his Russian career.

Wilson could not resist little clashes with Nabokov. Throughout their correspondence he corrected what he took to be Nabokov's stylistic or grammatical errors in English. Though he liked the novel, he pointed out weak spots in the language of *The Real Life of Sebastian Knight* and referred to other weaknesses in language in a slightly condescending *New Yorker* review of *Nikolai Gogol*. *Bend Sinister* initiated something very like real antagonism between them, though ironically (and characteristically) it was Wilson who finally found a publisher for it. Although he had liked the first bits that he had read, Wilson did not like the novel and said as much quite bluntly. He appended to his letter an extensive list of grammatical mistakes. Nabokov patiently explained the rationale for all the items Wilson raised, but Wilson found a few of these explanations to be worse than the supposed errors, and he reprimanded Nabokov for his silliness and bad taste.

Wilson performed many favors for Nabokov; Nabokov, none for Wilson. But Wilson simply was unable to do the essential thing, which was to recognize Nabokov in print as a major talent. This, in spite of the fact that several of Wilson's literary friends such as Allen Tate did not hesitate at a very early date to use the word *genius* when speaking of Nabokov. Recognition of his contemporaries was not Wilson's strong suit. He made every effort to contain his admiration of Nabokov within the bounds of a personal literary friendship. In March 1945, he wrote to Nabokov saying that their conversations had been among the few consolations of his literary life in years when old friends had been dying, petering out, and growing more and more neurotic. Wilson was not, Nabokov told him, a Nabokov fan. Wilson professed not to understand what he meant.

In the end Wilson and Nabokov had singularly similar positions in American culture in spite of all the differences between them. This similarity may be seen especially clearly in the attitudes toward and the experiences of both men in regard to universities. The distance that Edmund Wilson kept from the American academy has perhaps been somewhat exaggerated. Wilson was willing enough to attach himself to a college or university. In the Nabokov/Wilson correspondence there is reference to an appointment at Cornell on which Wilson was counting and which was lost at the last minute by the personal veto of Cornell's president. Very much like Nabokov, Wilson was happy to associate with the academy and academics, both of which he thought provincial and restricting, but on his own terms. The university that each man felt was his due place if he was to have an academic position at all was Harvard. Their experiences with that university were quite similar. Both had friends at Harvard, and yet most of the scholars there were not accustomed to and did not enjoy being slightly looked down on from the position of intellectual superiority that both Wilson and Nabokov tended to occupy.

19

AFTER THEY LEFT MASSACHUSETTS IN 1948, THE NABOKOVS lived in New York on West 70th Street for the month of June and arrived in Ithaca on July 1, 1948, the exact day on which his Cornell appointment commenced. Professor Morris Bishop of the Romance languages department had chanced upon a Wellesley publicity brochure that championed the college's part-time lecturer in Russian at just about the time that he had been asked to recommend a replacement for Ernest Simmons. Bishop had been following and admiring Nabokov's work in *The Atlantic* and *The New Yorker*. Nabokov was invited to Ithaca in late October 1947 and made a very good impression, especially on Bishop. The formal offer came a fortnight later. He was not offered a full professorship and the salary was only fifty-five hundred dollars, which was not terribly good, but the position was full time and relatively secure. He didn't learn until after his arrival that Cornell didn't then have a Russian department as such. Languages were taught under the aegis of the Modern Languages Division, and Russian literature lived administratively under the wing of Romance languages. That turned out to be a good thing for Nabokov, since, as at Wellesley, he did not attend a single faculty meeting during the entire decade that he was at Cornell, which might have caused difficulties for him had it not been for the powerful and beneficent Bishop above him, who handled and smoothed all the administrative problems for him.

Morris Bishop arranged the rental of a house for them when they arrived in Ithaca. It belonged to a professor of electrical engi-

neering and was at 957 East State Street. They only had that
house until September, though, as it happens, they were to rent
that same house again, and it was there that he finished writing
Lolita. It was difficult to find a furnished house for rent in September, and at the last moment they managed to get a "dismal"
house on East Seneca Street. Nabokov gives that house to Charlotte Haze in *Lolita*. After that they became extremely proficient
house finders. It has been said that, in never owning a home while
they were at Cornell, they had reverted to their European boardinghouse days. Some said they were the cuckoos of the campus:
always occupying other birds' nests. But that was so only in a
limited way. One should bear in mind that from a very practical
point of view the ten professorial homes that they rented in the
course of their Cornell decade ranged from comfortable and unpretentious middle class to several rather grand houses. Their
best Cornell house was at 880 Highland Road, where they stayed
for a year and a half. Occasionally, though, they would live in a
house for as little as four months. It was said that Vera Nabokov
could sometimes know that a house was going to be for rent before the owners knew it. As they were very good tenants, it soon
reached a point where staff members going on sabbatical actually
used to vie with one another to have the Nabokovs as tenants in
their absence. Victor Lange, who was then professor of German
at Cornell, told me that certain faculty members who were more
or less friendly with the Nabokovs and used to be invited to their
occasional afternoon gatherings for wine (Nabokov in those years
had a preference for very sweet wine and used to drink a flask of
Tokay) would play a game the object of which was to observe
and catalogue, as the Nabokovs shifted from house to house,
which objects actually belonged to the Nabokovs themselves.
There weren't many.

Once a cat to be tended came with the house, and they cared
for still another cat when Nabokov visited Harvard and rented
May Sarton's house on Maynard Place in Cambridge. Her cat
was named Tom Jones. When Tom became sick they took him to
the veterinarian and visited him there regularly until he was better. Tom Jones eventually came to live in *Pale Fire*.

The most plainspoken explanation of the Nabokovs' pattern of
living is furnished by a student whose major in Russian linguistics required him to take a full-year course in Russian literature.

He found himself the only student enrolled for Russian Literature 315-316—Pushkin. The course was taught in the study of the Nabokovs' house, which that year, 1954, was at 101 Irving Place, within walking distance of the campus. In the fall semester, the course consisted of several of Pushkin's shorter poems and *Eugene Onegin*. Nabokov set passages for translation every week and then would offer commentary on the translations and background information on Pushkin and Russia during that period. (Notes taken by the student often correspond quite closely with the published commentaries on *Onegin*, though there were asides that didn't go into print, such as Nabokov's assurance that Salieri didn't poison Mozart, or that the fatal dueling bullet that entered Pushkin's hip and lodged in his stomach might have been successfully removed had Pushkin had an operation, thus sparing him the gangrene and peritonitis that killed him.) Quite often the hour would end with Mrs. Nabokov bringing them a tray of tea. On one occasion the student asked him directly why he declined to buy a house: "He explained to me that his reluctance to own anything of a permanent nature, such as a house, was caused by the loss of his family's great estates at the time of the revolution. He did not want ever to risk such a loss again."

Although they never owned a house, in 1948 Vera took driving lessons, and they purchased a car. The distances and the lack of public transportation in Ithaca made driving a necessity. Even more, they needed a car for their summer collecting expeditions. Nabokov declared himself totally inept with "things" and drove a car only twice in his life: The first time was into a ditch on their estate in Russia, the second on a huge and empty parking lot in Hollywood, and he nearly collided with the only other car parked on the lot. In the Wellesley years Nabokov would often take a ride for collecting purposes with a fellow staff member who was going somewhere not too far away, but, Isobel Stephens reported, it could be terribly difficult to have Nabokov as your passenger in this way, because he would continually ask you to stop the car by the roadside and wait for him. Among the Nabokovs' cars at Cornell were a 1940 Plymouth, a 1946 Oldsmobile, and—their best car—a 1954 Buick, which Nabokov dubbed his *buicka*, when someone called it his troika. Among themselves the Nabokovs called it their *lyagushka* (frog), because the Buick was green. These cars caused difficulties in their recollection of their collect-

ing summers: "We *never* went west in the Plymouth!" declared
his wife after he had started to tell me about a trip in it. "Wait a
minute, darling," he said. "I have a note. A Plymouth four-door
sedan, six cylinders, eight years old, which we acquired on August 19, 1948. Wait a minute, I'm quite certain of all this. At
Canandaigua we picked up my student Dick Buxbaum, who took
turns driving the car to Salt Lake City." But Nabokov's victory
was a short-lived one: "It was not the Plymouth. It was the Olds.
We sold the Plymouth because it wouldn't go to Chicago." Their
four-door Buick with a dazzling white interior was the car in the
back seat of which, parked in shady roadside nooks, Nabokov
wrote much of *Lolita* during their tours around America and
across Canada.

Shortly after their arrival in Ithaca, the Nabokovs were visited
by Michael Karpovich and his wife. Nabokov was slowly recovering his strength after his operation for lung trouble in Cambridge, but his weight was continuing to increase at an alarming
rate and before the end of the summer had gone over 210 pounds.
Nabokov thought that he looked like a blend of the portly poet
Apukhtin and General MacArthur.

Nabokov was to have taught two Russian courses and one section of what Bishop had called a "stimulating blather" course, Introduction to Literature. It was an established course, and he
would have no part in choosing the set books. The authors studied included Cervantes, Thucydides, and Voltaire. Nabokov was
not pleased, but he accepted the obligation. However, when an
effort was made to get him to offer one of his two Russian courses
in English, he used this as an excuse to bargain his way out of Introduction to Literature by proposing instead that he teach a
course on Russian literature in English plus his two Russian literature courses in Russian. The proposal was accepted, and the
course in Russian literature in translation became his minor staple at Cornell, ordinarily having an enrollment of somewhere between thirty and forty students a year. The seminars in Russian
never had more than a handful of students, and he frequently
taught them at home.

Nabokov told some that he was very pleased that fate had led
him to Cornell. The East State Street house had very large
grounds and bordered on a stream at the back. Though Nabokov
was not in good enough health to go collecting (it was, anyway, a

poor summer for butterflies) he could sit in his own yard and observe butterflies while working. The library was large. The town
was exceptionally peaceful. When he was still in Paris and had
written letters to America in search of a permanent academic job,
he had said that he was competent to teach Russian or French and
was prepared to do it in any provincial backwater. At Cornell he
was in just such a backwater but at a good university. He said
that he was pleased that he no longer had to piece together a living out of two part-time jobs as he had had to do at Wellesley and
the MCZ.

Gradually, however, Nabokov came to feel vague dissatisfaction with his situation there. In 1950 he wrote to Roman Jakobson
at Harvard, with whom he was still supposed to be working tangentially on a mutual translation and commentary on the "Igor"
tale (Nabokov, of course, eventually published his own version in
1960), and told him that he was dissatisfied with Cornell. There
were several reasons: the language instruction was, he thought,
very poor and so did not allow him to plan courses at an advanced
level for his students, there were not many students of Russian
literature anyway, and, last but not least, his salary was far too
low. It was a period of low academic salaries everywhere, and
Cornell's were exceptionally low for a university of its standing.
Nabokov asked Jakobson if he could inform him of openings in
any of the other large American universities, but Jakobson did
nothing. In an undated letter to Aldanov that was probably written in the same year, Nabokov complained that at both Wellesley
and Cornell he worked for the wages of a provincial peasant.
That year Nabokov had an enrollment of seven for his two
Russian courses, and some of those seven were registered in both
courses.

It was Nabokov's third year at Cornell, and the number of his
students in his three courses had actually dipped slightly from a
little over forty in 1948 in all his courses to just over twenty in
1950. Many in the Division of Literature felt that Nabokov was
not pulling his weight, and he was unsuccessful in obtaining a salary increase. There were, in any case, constraints upon his promotion prospects, because he had been hired from a limited fund
pool that derived from a Rockefeller Foundation grant to Cornell.
The chairman, David Daiches, wrote to Nabokov that he could
help the department if he were to agree to take over 311–312 Eu-

ropean Fiction, and he gave him to understand that this might help his chances for better pay and promotion. The large course usually had about two hundred students, and it was traditionally called "dirty lit" because it taught *Madame Bovary* and *Anna Karenina*. This was the course in which Nabokov became famous at Cornell. He began to teach it in the fall of 1950, with a large contingent of Russian works, which gave way subsequently to Dickens, Austen, Stevenson, Kafka, Proust, and Joyce. The enrollment of 311–312 under Nabokov reached four hundred toward the end, and colleagues who had resented him because he had too little to do resented him because he was so popular.

As a lecturer Nabokov demanded two things from his students: strict passion and rare attention in regard to the texts he taught. He was a genial but very aloof professor, who was by then, moreover, attended by a secretary/wife. In fact, she had been given a job as Nabokov's marking assistant both because the course was so large that it required one, and also in order to improve their income slightly.

Professor Nabokov was theater. We know now that certain words were underlined for stress as he spoke, and he even wrote out the instruction to himself: "Look at the clock" at one point in a lecture, evidently to make sure that his performance was not running too far ahead or behind. Other important stress marks in his lectures were the parenthetical remarks and strange little expressions and modifiers that peek out from behind the smooth velvet curtain of professorial prose. Thus, Joyce's *Ulysses* first appeared in the "so-called *Little Review*," as though its very existence were in doubt, and motion pictures are "shown in places called theaters." In one lecture the students are warned that "all reality is comparative reality." He rejected one set text's paperback cover by calling it a "monstrous, abominable, atrocious, criminal, foul, vile, youth-depraving jacket—or better say straightjacket." No matter that a paperback cover is not called a jacket, and suppress the thought that that edition may have been chosen for the irresistible temptation to have that tirade against its cover. Nabokov was indeed an intellectual dandy performing in the provinces, but the students loved it. Although real writers, he told his students, are not to assume that they have any obligations to a national or universal community, literature itself constitutes a "magic democracy" in which the most minor character may "live and breed." The students were asked to "bask in Dickens" and "bathe in *Mansfield Park.*"

When Nabokov asked his students to "bathe" in a work of literature, he was simply asking them to immerse themselves in it and only in it. If Nabokov had a Golden Rule as a teacher it was "stick to the text." He acted like and was in truth a natural scientist turned loose among novels. The love of detail that he demonstrated and which he demanded of his students was the source of his greatness as a teacher. He taught more than three thousand Cornell students how to read slowly and to reread.

A colleague who lectured on Shakespeare in the hour before Nabokov's lecture would often chat with him for a few minutes in the interval as he left Goldwin Smith lecture hall B and Nabokov arrived. Nabokov knew that his colleague set five-minute factual quizzes on the day's play before the lecture began. One morning he quizzed his colleague: What were the names of Lear's three dogs? The colleague was able to answer but realized afterward that he hadn't given any thought to the fact that this passing detail, the three little dogs, exactly reflects the three daughters of Lear, and thereafter he would always insist in his lectures on *King Lear* that one could not understand the play if one didn't know Lear's dogs.

One of Nabokov's students claimed that she was so mesmerized by the terms of the course that she read one of the set books eleven times. Another, that to her surprise she found herself attending the lectures even when she was running a high fever. Nabokov continued to fraternize with students as he had at Wellesley, though now he tended to have his cups of coffee with postgraduate students in entomology and, less often, the little circle of young writers on campus. The Nabokovs did try at first to entertain the undergraduates, but there were simply too many of them. The core of the serious Nabokov cult on the campus consisted of the outstanding science-fiction writer Joanna Russ, Roger Sale, Whitney Balliet (later of *The New Yorker*), Richard Fariña (the author of *Been Down So Long It Looks Like Up to Me*), and Thomas Pynchon, though evidently there was no personal acquaintance between Pynchon and Nabokov. Two of Nabokov's students who became academics, Stephen Parker and Alfred Appel, have devoted a large portion of their academic careers to matters Nabokovian, and another student, Matthew Bruccoli, who eventually was instrumental in publishing Nabokov's university lectures. His colleagues were slower in the main to lionize him, and it was really not until the days of *Lolita* that Nabokov became a presence on the campus for anyone except a very small handful of the staff and a very large number of students of literature.

Professor Nabokov's affable severity didn't seem to matter at all to his students. He didn't pretend to love them: he loved his subject, and that was enough. He was certainly now a sterner teacher than he had been at Wellesley. Though he had, as he reached fifty, achieved much and had some stirring recognition in some quarters, he seems to have grown somewhat irritable, perhaps at his proper fame still withheld, perhaps at his less-than-thronelike academic situation. At the beginning of a term he would tell his students, "The seats are numbered. I would like you to choose your seat and stick to it. This is because I would like to link up your faces with your names. All satisfied with their seats? Okay. No talking, no smoking, no knitting, no newspaper reading, no sleeping, and for God's sake take notes." Before the first examination was too near in 311–312 he would say: "You have almost a month to reread *Anna Karenina* twice before the midterm," which always raised the expected roomful of groans. At the exam he would say: "One clear head, one blue book, ink, think . . . Do not pad ignorance with eloquence. Unless medical evidence is produced, nobody will be permitted to retire to the W.C." Nabokov claimed that it worked like a charm. He had an occasional variant on the no-bathroom theme that invited students who wished to leave the room to hand in their blue books for marking up to the point to which they had gone, and to return from the toilets to a set of specially prepared new and more difficult questions with which to finish the exam. The problem was that Nabokov was convinced that his students cheated a lot, though he also thought that he was very good at catching them at it. He rarely budged when students tried to get their grades raised. In one quite extraordinary recollection for the 1966 Robert Hughes television interview, Nabokov compared the attainment of grades with the survival of Resistance fighters in Europe. This rather strange thought was edited out of the interview.

The students could have had no idea of the cold clinical eye that Nabokov was casting on them, most likely in preparation for the academic chapter of his already planned second volume of memoirs (*Conclusive Evidence* had been completed on May 14, 1950). As students sat for their exam in the Masterpieces of European Fiction course on January 26, 1951, Nabokov made notes on them in one of the little black leatherette pocket diaries that he intermittently kept in America from 1946 through 1952. The character of these diaries is similar to that of his autobiography: they are not fictional, but they frequently use some of the devices and caprices of fiction. Very often a day's entry was a thought or observation that Nabokov wanted to file for future use. But sometimes, as in the winter examination, one has an opportunity to witness Nabokov the observer at work.

He describes the "young females" as well-groomed, whereas the "young males" are unwashed and unshaven. There are about 130 students, all giving little coughs, clearing nervous throats as they file in in little groups. When they sit down, there is a rustling of papers, a certain number of arms go back behind the head in meditative posture, and some stares fix upon him as the identifiable source of their "hideous boredom." In a corner of the lecture theater Nabokov notices some suitcases, which must belong, he judges, to girls ready to fly off to a wedding immediately after the exam. The snow outside the windows is falling slowly and somehow also involved in the atmosphere of boredom. There is now silence except for the odd rustle and creak of a seat. Nabokov, who calls himself Professor Kafka in his diary, answers a few questions from naïve or persistent students who are brave enough to come up to his desk. A pretty girl catches his eye and at once looks up to the ceiling piously with the end of the arm of her glasses hanging from the corner of her mouth. A girl is writing very quickly with a blunt pencil. An athletic type is shaking his wrist vigorously. The mist has by now begun to cover the windows, so the students cannot see the leaves of trees (from another diary entry, this one in January 1959) gesticulating to them in sign language from another world. The girls are either deep in thought with hands propping up cheeks or they are writing very rapidly while rhythmically chewing. They are frightened by the advancing arms of the clock. Blue-book pages are turned in unison, ink runs out, deodorants begin to fail, students look at Professor Kafka and then down at the floor "in specious thought."

Nabokov dreaded reading the blue books, because his disciplined thoughts and descriptions came back to him mangled and crippled. However, that was not always the case. He gave A's to students in his Russian courses who did their work intelligently and with great diligence, and once he even gave an A+ to a girl, John Updike's future wife, in the Masterpieces course. He was always quite clear about what would be rewarded—the complete mastery and faithful reproduction of his own system.

The greatest fault of all his lectures was closely connected with their virtue. For approximately seven-tenths of each lecture is nothing more than a patient retelling of the story. But what can be accomplished by this "simple" approach may be seen in the conclusions that Nabokov is able to reach by literally drawing sketches of the layout at Mansfield Park or the Samsa flat in "The Metamorphosis." For Nabokov is able to demonstrate that *Mansfield Park* is actually a play in disguise that must be understood in terms of its clusters and action groupings, and that "The Metamorphosis" is not only a play, but also a clearly delineated three-acter.

There were special moments throughout each lecture when workmanlike recapitulation was put to the side, and Nabokov would speak passionately as an artist to the subject of art. His trinity was enjoyment, magic, and style, and they are strongly interrelated. The importance assigned to these three things gives the lectures the cunningly casual air of the 1927 lectures by another writer/critic of his generation, E. M. Forster, which became *Aspects of the Novel*. Beneath the often whimsical surface of both Forster's and Nabokov's lectures there is a sophisticated and very tough defense of art by an artist. Nabokov in various ways and contexts frequently makes the point that art is quite useless, and yet it is far more durable than human beings. One can see the crafty pedagogic magician manipulating these assertions by sleight of hand.

The Nabokov lectures do not often add startlingly new insight or information to the best established critical works on their subjects. The weakest of his Masterpieces lectures are probably the ones on Austen and Dickens, undoubtedly because Nabokov had reservations about them as artists. In his Austen lecture he spoke of the duty of the artist to search for precisely the right word in each situation and gave the carefully qualified praise that "there are worse teachers than Jane Austen." Dickens fares slightly better. He is a great writer "despite certain faults." There is considerable judgmental tolerance for Robert Louis Stevenson, a favorite from Nabokov's youth. Flaubert and Proust are much more fully appreciated, and the intricacy of the analysis increases accordingly. The high points of the course were his lectures on Kafka and Joyce, each of which is as good as the best single essay on either author by anyone. The latter-day reader of these published lectures must, of course, bear in mind that their secret subject is always the artistic method of V. Nabokov. His detective search after the Man in the Brown Macintosh in *Ulysses*, who is revealed on circumstantial but convincing evidence to be Joyce himself flitting through his own narrative and being glimpsed by Bloom, is an open statement of one of Nabokov's own beloved motifs.

After the 1951–52 academic year, Nabokov had to give up one of his courses in Russian because the enrollment had fallen to two. He was, anyway, having to teach the course in English, though the students used readings in Russian. That was how Russian Literature 301–302 (in translation) came into being. It was taught in much the same spirit as the comparative course, except that there was a degree of student participation in this much smaller lecture group. The syllabus consisted in large degree of Nabokov's own translation material, some of which had not yet appeared in print and was kept in the library on reserve in manuscript copies for the use of students. Among this material were the *Igor* tale, *A Hero of Our Time*, and *Eugene Onegin*. The class served as a sounding board for Nabokov's commentaries on *Onegin*. Students were made to do things like memorize the full line of the princes of Kiev as they appear in Nabokov's "Igor" commentaries. Although the course was termed a "survey" in the handbook, he made it clear to his students that he was not in the least interested in literary tendencies or schools, much less groups of literary mediocrities gathered together under a flag. His target was books themselves, and in the evolution of the Russian literature course over the years the amount of time devoted to specific texts grew steadily. Nabokov boasted that he gave ten minutes to Dostoevsky in his course. That was eventually expanded to nearly two hours as a result of student grumbling, but his remarks on Dostoevsky are Nabokov at his critically weakest and most childishly petulant.

He was not always fair. He nearly failed one student for dragging in categories from an academic study that he considered particularly idiotic. He was extremely touchy about his name, and once he asked a student to leave the class because he had instructed the class carefully on the proper pronunciation of Vladimir during discussions about the old Kievan princes and yet the student continued to mispronounce it. He hadn't noticed that the student had been absent from that class the previous lecture. Nabokov would have had trouble teaching in this way on most American campuses in the radical decade that followed. He had only one taste of student radicalism, a student who stood up in class and said, "Mr. Nabokov, if you're not going to talk about Dostoevsky in this course, may I talk about him for one hour?" The student proposed that Nabokov open with the case against Dostoevsky, following which he would speak in favor of Dostoevsky for the rest of the hour. Nabokov told him to sit down. After that the student didn't attend the lectures in protest against Nabokov's treatment of "committed" writers. He failed the final exam sensationally. The story is not apochryphal, because after this class Nabokov was heard shouting in the office of the department of literature: "I want that boy expelled! I want him out of here!!" The prospect of a good postgraduate student in Russian was also lost over the issue of Dostoevsky. There was a student named Ed Sampson, who actually knew Russian and whose father, moreover, was a Cornell benefactor. He wanted to write a thesis on . . . the influence of Dostoevsky in Soviet literature! He went to see Professor Nabokov, who told him: "Dostoevsky is not an influential writer. He has had no influence." "What about Leonov?" the student protested. Nabokov threw up his hands and declaimed histrionically: "Poor Leonov!! Poor Leonov!!" That was the end of the interview. Cornell didn't produce a thesis in Russian literature during Nabokov's decade, though one of his undergraduate students did go on to become a professor of Russian, ironically, at Wellesley, and another at Kansas.

When Nabokov was leaving Cornell, it was widely said among many people on the faculty who were not Nabokov partisans that, though Cornell was losing a celebrity, it was gaining the possibility of having an undergraduate and postgraduate program in Russian language and literature that could begin at last to grant some degrees in the subject. There was undeniable truth in the complaint, but there was as well a below-the-surface current of resentment. As early as 1952 Nabokov had complained to Morris Bishop that colleagues from the "lower depths" were voicing discontent with his emphasis upon structure over ideas in literature. He had not the slightest intention of changing his ways. A young academic who was there said: "I distinctly recall the considerable jealousy on the part of other faculty members over Nabokov's notoriety. After all, from their point of view, here was a colleague who had been aloof and antisocial, strong in his convictions and not academically bent, who now was becoming rich and famous. It just wasn't fair. There was a great deal of this pettiness in regard to him around."

In his final two years at Cornell he had to abandon his last course in Russian, because no qualified students presented themselves. (Once again, there were cynics who asked aloud what exactly might satisfy Nabokov as adequate knowledge of Russian.) Three students who appeared for the seminar could not successfully complete a simple, short fill-in written quiz. That was Nabokov's side of the story. One of the three students has testified that the fill-in passage was taken from *The Gift*, and thus was not in the least a simple test! Nabokov wrote a letter of complaint about the situation of Russian at Cornell. In the letter (September 30, 1958) Nabokov said that the teaching of Russian at Cornell had been "steadily deteriorating" and had now reached a point where it would be disloyal to Cornell to remain silent. He said that there had been three excellent Russian instructors when he had arrived at Cornell, but two had left and now only one instructor of high competence, Avgusta Jaryc, remained. In their place, he claimed, were "ludicrously incompetent" instructors whose field of study was linguistics rather than Russian and who actually did not speak Russian at all.

At Cornell the Division of Modern Languages was kept separate from all the departments of literature. It was responsible for all language teaching and was headed by Milton Cowan, who was one of the originators of the army language program in World War II and had brought many of these techniques with him to Cornell. These included things such as memorization of pattern sentences with great reliance upon audio-visual techniques. In addition to this, Cowan's director of Russian, Professor Fairbanks, was a kindly and talented linguist who knew Russian quite

well from a linguistic point of view (he coauthored a grammar of
the language that is still used) but did not actually speak the language, or very much of it at any rate. Thus Nabokov felt that
students were taught to make seallike noises that were supposed
to be Russian sounds but were far from that in fact. (Professor
Fairbanks's real languages were Hindi and Urdu, and he eventually dropped Russian to concentrate upon teaching them at another university.) In theory a well-trained linguist was supposed
to be able to teach any language without need of either a large vocabulary or the ability to speak it. Nabokov was right in regard to
Russian. It didn't work. Cornell did produce some competent
language students in other languages, though the teaching of languages from a heavily linguistic point of view has now long
passed from favor. That is the full context of the dispute over
Russian. The necessary footnote, for those concerned about this
issue, is that Nabokov waited until he was on the verge of leaving
Cornell before registering his complaint formally.

When Nabokov first came to Ithaca, Milton Cowan was his
regular tennis partner. Cowan lived just a few houses away from
the Nabokovs' and knew from Avgusta Jaryc that Nabokov had
coached tennis in Berlin as a young man. Cowan asked him if he
would like to play. When he came to pick him up the first time
Cowan was driving the diminutive fire-engine red convertible
Crosley that he had purchased in order to teach his two sons to
drive. Nabokov stood and eyed the little car: "Eh heh! A bathtub." It was the means by which they regularly wended their
way to and from the faculty tennis courts passing across the
Cascadilla Creek bridge after which they drove a quarter of a mile
along a footpath through the woods with light branches slapping
the car and their sides. The very large Nabokov adored this part
of the ride in the very small Crosley, and it became their standard
route to the courts, although it was not actually the shortest way
there.

Cowan remembers Nabokov as a very good tennis player, with
the clear stylistic mark of a teacher used to returning the ball to
his pupil rather than attempting to place it beyond his stroke.
Nabokov had good ground strokes and was superior to Cowan if
he remained on the baseline. But Cowan soon discovered that
Nabokov didn't much like to run when a sharp volley developed,
and so he could gain the point he needed when he fell behind by

going to the net for short shots. Nabokov always played with four cans of balls, so that he never had to run after a ball. They would have enormously long volleys and often a deuce set that went on until they were ready to drive home in the red bathtub. Cowan recalled: "We never proceeded to set all the time we played tennis, for the simple reason that neither of us felt the need to win." Nabokov thought that Cowan had a winning smile and manner, but they never became friends, in all likelihood because of the issue of language instruction.

As regards chess, Nabokov's main opponent was his wife during the Cornell years, and thereafter, too. His wife has gracefully conceded that he was the better chess player. His one chess combat with a Cornell colleague ended badly. It happened that in one of their houses they lived next door to Professor Max Black, a professor of philosophy who was a very advanced chess player who frequently played and won games against multiple opponents in which he made split-second moves. Black won their first game in fifteen minutes, and Nabokov immediately asked for a rematch. Black won the second match in twelve minutes. The subject of chess was never mentioned between them again.

Cornell had a very strong entomology department. Nabokov had corresponded with John Franclemont, one of Cornell's entomologists, before he came to Ithaca. William T. M. Forbes, the leading entomologist at Cornell, had met Nabokov at Harvard and once suggested to Franclemont that he write to Nabokov at the MCZ about a type specimen of a particular moth. At the time Franclemont happened to remark to Forbes that, if one followed Nabokov's method of classification proposed in a 1944 paper on his specialty, blues (Lycaenidae), then butterflies would become a phylum, an independent major zoological grouping such as mollusks. Forbes related the gently sharp remark to Nabokov and when they met in Ithaca the first thing Nabokov said to the discomfited Franclemont was: "Here is the man who thinks that I believe the butterflies constitute a phylum." Forbes saved the day by joining in a conversation about novel systems of classification and the people who had invented them. Nabokov and Franclemont got on well together. He spoke of Nabokov as "among the very best" field collectors and observers of butterflies, which neatly sidestepped the issue of Nabokov's idiosyncratic methods of description and classification.

Opinion about Nabokov and butterflies, as in everything else, could be strong and widely separated. One of his Cornell colleagues said,

> He cannot be called one of the ranking authorities, but his work had weight. If he had devoted more time to his work in this field, he almost certainly would have been a major figure in the field . . . There is general acceptance of his work and admiration for its thoroughness. It is not eccentric. Work in this field falls into a certain mold of reporting facts. If his treatment were not standard, he would have been thrown out, that is, his work would not have been taken seriously.

Another Cornell natural scientist, Professor William Brown, Jr., has expressed a sharply differing view. He argued frequently and heatedly with Nabokov on the question of race. Brown stands within a modern school of thought that holds the very concept of "race" to be of dubious scientific use, for butterflies and people, proposing instead greater descriptive attention to unique individual types. Nabokov the antiracist, paradoxically, disagreed strongly. His whole entomological career had been dedicated to finding and describing new races of butterflies. In the same way that in *Speak, Memory* he described how German collectors were psychologically unable in the early years of the century to move beyond the philatelic description of butterflies by their markings to the new mode of classification by microscopic examination introduced by the English, so now Nabokov himself could not consider questioning the rigidly fixed categories of species and subspecies with which he had done all his work. According to Brown, Nabokov invented a system for naming the underwings, which other people had done before him, but he didn't know about their work. "The trouble with Vladimir Nabokov," said Brown, "was that he didn't bother to read the theoretical papers, and his own papers are idiosyncratic as all hell." Brown pointed out that Nabokov even insisted on using different abbreviations than those accepted by everyone else for place names. His method of spreading his specimens for display was also distinctive. Because he was primarily interested in the undersurfaces of wings, he spread many of his butterflies reverse side up, and, for this reason, it is relatively easy to spot the Nabokov butterflies in the Cornell butterfly collection room even though they are intermingled with all the others. But Brown was also quick to point out that, although Nabokov was frequently out of step with the rest of the scientific community in regard to format, his work was remarkable for its detail and the successful way in which it introduced little bits of human description into what was often too dry and lifeless a form of writing.

In addition to his specialized knowledge of lycaenidal butterflies, about which he may have known as much as anyone in the world, Nabokov excelled in another, descriptive specialty: butterfly genitalia, which are extremely important because there can be great differences in the genital structure of butterflies which otherwise look quite alike. The organs in question are tiny sclerotic particles. The work of preparing the genitalia for slides with a fine needle, is very difficult and tedious. After removal from the insect the organs are usually kept for a few hours in a certain solution (Nabokov, however, made the discovery that a brand of dental cleanser does the job much more quickly) until the fleshy portion dissolves away. After proper preparation the piece is dipped first in alcohol, then in an organic solvent before mounting. But mounting prevents the genitalia from being freely examined under the microscope, so Nabokov developed the technique of keeping each specimen in a weak solution of alcohol together with a little glycerine in corked vials. For one of his major papers Nabokov might do nearly a thousand such examinations, representing months of patient work. One difficulty about Vladimir, his cousin Nicolai once complained, was that, when he was working on his butterflies, there was always a faint smell of ether about him.

In their first decade in the United States the Nabokovs spent one summer in California, two summers in Vermont, one in Wellesley, one in New Hampshire (at "a horrible lodge on a dismal lake"), the first summer in Ithaca recuperating at home, and the rest in the Rocky Mountains. They were virtually all excellent collecting summers. The one in Wellesley was a miraculous collecting summer for Nabokov, during which he caught many butterflies that hadn't been observed in the environs for years. It was only when they went to Cape Cod that they found collecting not so good. Until 1949 they had traveled by train or taken a ride from someone. But with their own car they began to meander across the country, staying in hundreds of motel rooms. The

rates, even in relative terms, were not at all high during this period. On their 1949 trip their destination was Utah, where Nabokov had been invited to join a writers' conference.

Their Salt Lake City stay in 1949 was very pleasant and comfortable. In the Alpha Delta Phi fraternity house they had a good
room with a private bath, a condition stipulated by Nabokov in
agreeing to participate in the conference. Other staff members at
this conference were Oscar Williams, John Crowe Ransom,
Martha Foley, George Davis, Wallace Stegner, and Dr. Seuss
[Theodore Geisel] ("A charming man, one of the most gifted
people on this list"). Nabokov spent a deal of time with Ransom,
and on several occasions they spoke together on live radio discussions that were broadcast locally. Then—the conference lasted
only two weeks, though it seemed longer, because the intellectual
company had been so good—on July 16 the Nabokovs, still with
the Cornell student who was sharing the driving with them, made
a series of collecting stops, on one of which they had some rather
strange neighbors. They were, Nabokov said, "playboys," "gentle people, but in their cups they could be dangerous," who
owned a surplus World War II machine gun. One morning Nabokov came upon the awful stench of a machine-gunned horse by
the roadside. He told them, and "they laughed. They chuckled
and confessed that it was one of their neighbor's horses, and
sometimes their 'aim wasn't too good.' " Nabokov remembers
that returning from his collecting hikes he was far more concerned about the *ra-ta-tat* of that machine gun than about the
rather ugly moose that lived in the surrounding willow bogs. In
late August, on their way back to Ithaca, Nabokov captured some
rare specimens on a pile of bear dung.

On several occasions during their summer trips the Nabokovs
visited a ranch (half house, half resort—the rent was very reasonable) owned by James Laughlin of New Directions. The
ranch was in Alta, Utah, and Nabokov did some of his most important collecting in the Wasatch Mountains of the region.
Laughlin was tremendously impressed by Nabokov's energy, the
pace at which he attended to both his collecting and his writing.
But he was always very secretive with Laughlin about what he
was writing. Laughlin was, however, invited to go on a collecting
hike with his author. The two hiked for four and a half miles in
nine hours, a fairly average day's hike for rough terrain. Nabokov

was seeking a butterfly that has a symbiotic relationship with ants, and another one that would always go to the summit of Lone Peak, a mountain near Alta, just before it died. He got both butterflies. Nabokov wore white shorts and sneakers. There was snow on the top of Lone Peak. On the way down he slipped and slid about six hundred feet. He was quite bruised, but he didn't care: he had his butterfly. On level ground Nabokov could cover about fifteen miles a day. Then at night he would collect moths attracted in large numbers by the brilliantly illuminated plateglass windows of the Alta lodge.

Colorado and Utah were two of the states in which Nabokov spent protracted periods of time. In 1951 the Nabokovs spent July in Colorado while waiting for Dmitri, then a high-school senior, who had won a New England debating championship and had gone to California to compete in the national finals. In other years Nabokov climbed and collected in the mountains of Wyoming, and he and Vera rented homes for weeks or months in Yellowstone, in Oregon, and in Arizona, where they stayed one summer until Vera had had enough of the rattlesnakes. There were encounters with many bears on their trips as well. They tripped over a sleeping baby bear behind a log once, and another time they came across a bear with a condensed-milk can stuck on its nose. They contrasted the American bears favorably with the meaner variety of Russian bear they had both seen in their youths. "It was on one of those trips," Nabokov recalled of a period they spent at Babb Cabins in Montana, "that I discovered that *War and Peace* is really a very childish piece of writing." Nabokov intended to include a chapter in *Speak, America* that would re-create a day's collecting in each of his two favorite entomological places, the Rockies and the MCZ.

On February 18, 1951, Nabokov noted down nine out of a planned fifteen chapters for his second volume of autobiography, then provisionally called *More Evidence.* He was going to begin it with criticism of *Conclusive Evidence,* though the note doesn't make clear whether this means his own criticism or printed criticism of the book. Following that there would be chapters on differing forms of consciousness and dreams. The planned chapter on the MCZ and collecting would merge back into Russia, in the same way that the first volume merged forward into America. There would be a chapter on St. Marks School, and then two short stories, which were perhaps tangentially related to reality. He was in the process of writing one, which isn't named. The other is "Double Talk." The last two putative chapters are one on Edmund Wilson and one called "*the assistant professor who was never found out,*" which was to be based upon Cross and a Cornell professor who is still alive.

The pattern then would be continued: an autobiography in which the purely personal is skirted and the emphasis is placed upon peripheral places and people. The exception might have been the chapter on dreams. Nabokov had begun to write down his dreams in his diaries and noted that in doing so he seemed to be having sharper recall of them. It can hardly be likely that he intended to use many of his diary dreams. In one he dreamt of cold, joyless fornication with a fat old woman whom he knew only slightly and for whom he felt no desire whatsoever. Recollections of Prague flit through several dreams. One dream is about "V" and "A." "A" may or may not be a reference to a woman about whom I heard (from a member of the Nabokov family) "she was the one who nearly split them up" in Prague. I put the matter to Nabokov, who exploded and said it was a despicable lie. The truth will probably have to wait until Nabokov's Don Juan list is released from the closed papers of the Library of Congress archives near the end of the next century. In this dream Nabokov and "V" and "A" are living in the palace of the old Rumanian queen on the first day of the revolution. Troops are parading by the palace and the weather is gray. The queen is indifferent, "V" is contemptuous of the way the soldiers look, and "A" protests in awe that they are after all the former *Royal* guard. "V" says she doesn't care and pulls the portrait of the dead king from the palace wall. In his notes on the dream, Nabokov says that he can explain every element of the dream in terms of some recent chance impression, and yet there is a mystery about it in his mind that he cannot decipher. The street in the dream was rather like the view from his mother's apartment in Prague in the twenties.

In his most moving dream he is walking past a doorway when he hears the low and unsteady sound of a piano being played. He looks in and recognizes a room of their St. Petersburg house, which did not, however, have a piano in it. His father is the melancholy and awkward player. His father, though a music lover, did not play in life. The melody is uncertain, but Nabokov seems to recognize a Mozart sonata. Though his back is turned to him, Nabokov knows that it is his father by the bald spot on the back of his head. He sees that the bald patch is very like that on the back of Michael Karpovich's head, and this is unpleasant to him. He reflects that if he were indeed in his boyhood, he would now go up to his father and kiss him on that bald spot, but he merely stands there and observes him in his dream. Nabokov is slightly embarrassed to see his father, who was always so gay, in such a depressed mood. He begins to explain to his father about the work he is doing now, and how hard it is for him to determine the exact age of the characters in *Madame Bovary*, how vexing it is to read in Turgenev of "a little old man of about forty-five." Nabokov's father doesn't understand what he is talking about and just looks at him in a puzzled and listless way. Nabokov tries to explain cheerily that that vexes him because he himself is now almost fifty-two. His father is still sad and perplexed. At that moment Nabokov wakes up and suddenly understands that he himself is now exactly the age of his father when he was assassinated.

The sort of dream Nabokov would have been more likely to use in *Speak, America* would probably have been his far less intimate collecting dreams. In these dreams the butterflies always stayed conveniently perched on plants where they were easier to catch. Nabokov had begun to write at least the butterfly portion of *Speak, America*, because in 1973 he wrote to me that he was at work on it.

In 1951 Nabokov had five major projects under way, and that is not to speak of short stories either in progress or in an advanced stage of planning. These projects were *The Kingdom by the Sea*, which was the original title for *Lolita*, "The Double Monster," which he intended to be a novel but which was reduced to the status of a short story (it appeared in 1958), a book on the structure of *Madame Bovary*, and the translations of *Onegin* and the "Igor" tale. "The Double Monster" furnished the only recorded instance of a public disagreement between Nabokov and his wife. Nabokov announced to a group of his colleagues: "I am now going to write about the love life of Siamese twins," to which his wife at his side instantly added: "No you're not!" The subject of nympholepsy then may be viewed as a retreat into positively reasonable subject matter.

This list of projects does not even take into account the relatively simple but still time-consuming work of proofreading *The Gift* (Nabokov was almost a medieval nominalist in that he would go into fits of agony over a misprint) for its first appearance as a book in Russian and with the previously deleted chapter 4 restored. Two of his poems were printed in *The New Yorker* that year, and he wrote several short notes and book reviews about butterflies, including two reviews (one appeared in 1952) on butterfly books for the *New York Times Book Review*. Copies of *Conclusive Evidence* arrived at the end of January 1951. He grieved about two little errors he had found. It is clear that Nabokov, whose entire working life bristles with energy, was exceeding even his own usual pace as the fifties commenced. As the work on *Onegin* gathered momentum, he would work still harder. When the translation of and commentaries to Pushkin's novel-in-verse were finally completed, the manuscript consisted of eleven thick notebooks containing three thousand typed pages. It was a matter, in other words, of about five or six printed volumes of material rather than the three (the fourth was a photoreproduction of the *Onegin* edition published shortly before Pushkin's death) that did appear in 1964. And finally, perhaps because of this immersion into Pushkin, Nabokov felt stirrings to write in Russian again. It had reached a point where he would write to old Russian friends in English, and he had even sold his precious four-volume Dahl dictionary to Karpovich.

In 1952 he spoke on the centenary of Gogol's death, but he was violently sick in the men's room only a few minutes before he was due to speak and had only a vague recollection of what he said. His main memory of the occasion was that he had had to fish his wallet out of the toilet.

He did write a Russian poem-cycle in 1953. The theme was the usual one: a nostalgic but highly ironic search for the Russia that was gone forever. A small part appeared under the title *Irregular Iambics* in the first number of a New York Russian almanac published by Nabokov's former pupil Roman Grynberg. As a professional writer Nabokov insisted that his friend pay him for the poetry. Grynberg reluctantly gave him two dollars, shouting at him from across the street as they parted in half-English émigré Russian: "*Kak token!*" ("As a token!") The other seven poems appeared in *The New Review* three years later.

In the 1950s Nabokov effectively severed all contact with Russians in America with the exception of Michael Karpovich, Roman Grynberg, and Albert Parry, who had become a professor of Russian at nearby Colgate University. In his praise of Nabokov, Parry had called Sirin the outstanding émigré writer, giving him polite but clear preference over Bunin, who had just received his Nobel Prize, and said that his work should be watched and translated. Nabokov felt that this unrestrained praise opened important doors for him in regard to publication in America, and he chose to overlook or forget the fact that Parry had discussed him as a literary follower of Freud.

Parry and Nabokov met for the first time in the spring of 1951 when an academic conference was being held at Cornell. Nabokov spoke at the conference on the subject of translating Pushkin into English. It was the only time in all his years as an academic that Nabokov attended an academic conference. In anticipation of their meeting Parry brought all his Sirin editions with him to Ithaca to be autographed. Parry was invited back to the Nabokovs' house with a group of other academics after the conference sessions of the first day were over. Parry spread his Sirin collection out on the low coffee table in the living room—they were first editions in excellent condition—and both of the Nabokovs gasped at this unexpected display. He began to sign them all and placed a little butterfly drawing beside each of the signatures (this would become a constant feature of his signed books). Then he suddenly turned to Parry and said, "Listen, I don't have this first edition. The Nazis burned the entire stock of this first edition. Give this book to me!" Parry protested that he had just inscribed the book to him and asked him to search and make sure that he did indeed lack that edition, in which case, of course, he would give it to him. The matter was never raised again.

There were more than a few anecdotes of a Pnin-like character surrounding Nabokov at Cornell. Nabokov acknowledged to me that Pnin's interest in gestures was really his own. A book on gestures was yet another book he had considered writing but put aside.

Colleagues recalled that Nabokov walked along the corridors of Goldwin Smith together with Vera, lost in his own thoughts and oblivious to his surroundings. She would often give him a sharp dig in the ribs when they were passing someone they knew, and his face would immediately be animated into a gracious smile. Alfred Appel, Jr., tells the story of how, as a student, he saw Professor Nabokov wander into the wrong lecture hall and start to give his lecture to a group of completely befuddled undergraduates waiting for a lecturer in another subject. When the mistake was discovered, he gathered up his papers and told the students as he left: "You have just heard the coming attractions for Literature 325. If you are interested, you may register next fall." Another example of slightly unusual behavior concerned the wallpaper in the Bishop house, which was floral with the occasional butterfly. The butterflies were anatomically incorrect, and so Nabokov "corrected" one and drew his own, proper butterfly beside it.

Not all the eccentricity in *Pnin* is Nabokovian or even Russian. Nabokov followed popular American culture avidly and russified many things for the purposes of his novel. For example, Pnin's obsession with the washing-machine window in chapter 2 and his compulsion to throw odd objects, including tennis sneakers, into the washing machine is pure Americana, deriving from a syndicated newspaper column, "Heloise's Work and Money Savers," in which housewives were exhorted to wash their tennis shoes on a weekly basis together with their towels.

Occasionally Nabokov played the polymath, an ability he always admired in people and a role that many Russian intellectuals strive to fulfill. Nabokov approached the professor of fine arts with a commission from the family of another colleague to design two stained-glass windows for the local Episcopalian church. The windows were to be of St. John, and Nabokov reeled off fifty-five different St. Johns, major and minor saints, discredited saints, saints who were popes. He further astonished and impressed the professor of fine arts with his knowledge of how stained-glass windows are made. When a colleague came upon him descending the library steps with a pile of volumes of the nineteenth-century *Edinburgh Review* under his chin and paused to comment on how much wonderful material there was in that journal, Nabokov brightly cut him off: "Oh, but I do not want the articles. I am interested in the advertisements!"

Nabokov's polymath pretences did not always come off perfectly. A fair number of mushrooms sprouted at various spots on the Cornell campus, and once Nabokov went to pick some with that same professor of fine arts. As a Russian Nabokov claimed full and intimate knowledge of the art of mushroom gathering. There was a cluster of mushrooms growing on the grass strip by a sidewalk. Professor Kahn warned Nabokov that those mushrooms contained high traces of acid and were dangerous. Nabokov retorted: "Well, if you won't pick them, I'll pick them and take them home." Kahn, fearful that he would consume the inedible mushrooms, put them in a small paper bag so that their pungent odor would be concentrated and discernible. Nabokov inhaled the odor from the bag and pronounced obdurately: "There's nothing wrong with them!" But when they went to the coffee shop near the dam after they had finished picking, Kahn observed that Nabokov left the brown bag of dubious mushrooms behind on his bench when they left.

The self-observed oddities of Nabokov himself, however, are only tangential to *Pnin*, the work of Nabokov's that is most intimately connected with Cornell. It is the only novel that Nabokov ever published with the traditional disclaimer that any resemblance to living persons was purely coincidental. The book is teeming with people from Cornell, and some of the cutting stories and portrayals are close enough to reality. After 1955, thanks to *Pnin*, Nabokov was at last known as a writer on campus, and many students who took his courses also read his books.

And the genial, eccentric Professor Timofey Pnin himself? He is a fictional character but closer to a life model than many of Nabokov's characters. It has been long suspected and talked about in Ithaca, and the main suspect was indeed the model. Pnin is, in large degree, drawn from Professor Marc Szeftel, who then taught Russian history at Cornell. This was confirmed to me by Nabokov while riding in the elevator of the Montreux Palace. He told me that he was once riding in an elevator with Szeftel at Cornell at the time that the first parts of *Pnin* were appearing in *The New Yorker*. Szeftel gave a deep sigh and said: "Ve arre all Pnins!" "He had forgotten that I was writing that book and did not see that he was a character speaking to his author!" Nabokov was wrong to think that Szeftel did not know who the author of *Pnin* was, or that he played a part in the formation of that character. Szeftel's wife Kitty has said that she and her husband saw immediately that Pnin was based upon him but took no particular offense at the portrayal.

Pnin is a fictional character. It is only certain broad coordinates that correspond to the personality of Szeftel: a whimsical manner, fabulous absentmindedness, and a certain eccentric genius with the English language. Nabokov once told Szeftel that he spoke "ugly English." He took the principles of missed articles, transferred turns of phrase from other languages, and a rich but discontinuous train of thought and elevated it into his greatest comic character. Nabokov took a great deal of interest in Slavs speaking their own special sort of English in these years. (For that matter, when he returned from the summer collecting trips, he would do imitations of midwestern Americans for a few friends such as Albert Parry.) When a Cornell colleague did an imitation of a Russian speaking English, Nabokov told him with disdain that he sounded like an Irishman. Nabokov was convinced that he himself had no Russian imprint on his English, which he thought he spoke with a British accent.

There was very little similarity of either physical appearance or circumstance of life between the character Pnin and Marc Szeftel, who was small but rather handsome, not at all an "albino porcupine." There was just one very important congruity between fiction and fact: Marc Szeftel was, like Timofey Pnin, a victim of campus politics and could not get a promotion at Cornell. One person who was there at the time said that Szeftel's failure to get a promotion paralleled Pnin's, though Szeftel stayed at Cornell until 1961. The "fascinating lecturer" who is also the narrator and Pnin's not-quite friend is, of course, Nabokov himself, scarcely concealed at all. In chapter 7 one is given an only slightly kaleidoscopically rearranged version of the known life of Nabokov from his autobiography and early poetry: the new lecturer grew up in a rosy-stone house on the Morskaya, rode an English bicycle, listened to the barges scraping rhythmically against the embankments of the Neva. The narrator in his youth watches Pnin play in Schnitzler's *Liebelei*, the play that Nabokov himself acted in in the Crimea. The visiting lecturer is being invited to Waindell by the English department. Here there is a departure from reality, for the Cornell English department was very concerned that Nabokov might impinge on its territory, and he was never invited to lecture outside of his general literature course. One of the most venomous portraits in *Pnin* is drawn from the English department at Cornell.

The unnamed narrator of *Pnin* actually figures in the action of the novel, yet, if one is not alert, he may appear and disappear again without being noticed. Liza's marriage to Pnin had its initiation in the depression she was in "because of a rather silly affair with a litterateur who is now—but no matter." This aborted sentence is fully explained in the very last pages of the book, where it is revealed (strongly implied) that the narrator seduced Liza while devastating her poetic efforts. We know that Nabokov had Misha Gorlin and Raissa Blokh and their fate very much in mind while writing *Pnin*. We know that Blokh's poetry was praised by Adamovich and savaged by Sirin. What we cannot know is whether there was an affair between Nabokov and Blokh, or whether that element in the novel is simply an imaginative addition. Though *Pnin* belongs, together with *The Gift* and *Glory*, to the less complicated line of Nabokov's art from a structural point of view, it seems certain to remain a work that will continue to present complexities on the level of intent and biographical reference.

When Liza marries Pnin, she tells Timofey everything, and it is clear that the eccentric hero has not forgiven his narrator, for Pnin refuses his offer of academic protection at Waindell. Pnin was too wonderful to leave to harsh fate, however. He drives off "to where there was simply no saying what miracle might happen," and the miracle that indeed transpires is revealed in *Pale Fire* when Kinbote informs us that Pnin is now a departmental chairman.

Though they were not personally close, when Szeftel's contract wasn't renewed Nabokov registered a complaint with the administration. He did demonstrate a certain amount of émigré solidarity at Cornell. It is recorded that he once announced to a table of colleagues, "Do you realize the four of us at this table have been kicked out of our respective countries?"

The narrative movement of *Pnin* is a form of emigration: the flight of a character from his author, and, like the clerk in Gogol's "The Overcoat," Timofey Pnin finally succeeds in escaping . . . with the help of his author, of course. The suspiciously acting narrator is a *diabolus ex machina*. Nabokov uses the technique of an account by an interested party as a device to establish Pnin as a serious character as well as merely a campus character. To put it in another way, the narrator has two voices, and only one of them is serious. The first, supercilious voice is the one from which Pnin flees and the one which collects and relates all the hilarious misadventures of the little "assistant professor *emeritus.*" The second narrative voice, under cover of the other's jocosity and meticulous recounting of anecdotes, creates and describes a real and finely drawn character. The same split in narrative voice may be found in "The Overcoat," but it is curious that, although Gogol's second, serious voice is virtually buried beneath the brilliant verbal and narrative façades of the comic first voice, readers of Gogol's tale, under the tutelage of Russia's nineteenth-century critics (among them, Chernyshevsky) have for the most part heard only the "compassionate," "humane" (and largely nonexistent) second voice.

The title of Gogol's tale is particularly indicative because the overcoat is indeed considerably more substantial than its hero. But whereas Nabokov's character, like Gogol's, also has a joke instead of a name, the second, serious voice in *Pnin* is strong and central to the story. There is a very real person in the overcoat into which Pnin struggles with such Slavic artful awkwardness, despite the fact that almost all of the novel's critics have perceived him only through the voice of the novel's first narrator. And insofar as we give ourselves up to enjoyment of Pnin's zany speech and ways, the reader is also drawn into the circle of those characters in the novel who gently mock and taunt him, as indeed Pnin's own language mocks him.

Timofey Pnin's overcoat is his language, and it is well to remember that there are not only two narrative voices, but also two Pninian voices: one is his grotesque semblance of English, but the other is a natural Russian voice. The narrator's two voices then are a necessary stratagem to deal with the "two Pnins." On a philosophical level at least the serious narrator and the "real" Pnin are kindred spirits. The most serious statement in the novel is a plea for Pnin's essential privacy and discreteness. We are told that man does not exist except insofar as he is separated from the rest of life: "The cranium is a space-traveler's helmet. Stay inside or you perish." Pnin himself follows this precept in regard to much of his own past. He has taught himself rationally never to think of his childhood sweetheart, because he knows that he cannot bear the thought that that graceful and fragile girl was taken to a concentration camp in a cattle train. For this reason, much of Pnin's past is largely forbidden territory to him. When he sees the people of his Russian past gathered all together, an hallucination as he is about to address an academic audience in Vermont, he is very close to a heart attack. The scene of this hallucination is taken from one of Nabokov's speaking engagements, at the Middlebury Summer School for Russian, where, it is remembered, the director had strictly instructed all students and staff to appear properly dressed for the lecture, and Nabokov had delivered it in shorts and a sportshirt.

Pnin is full of esoteric Russian jokes. The most vital of these is Pnin's very name, which is taken from the name of the late eighteenth-century Russian poet Ivan Pnin. This real Pnin was the illegitimate son of Prince Repnin. At that time such truncated surnames were quite common for the bastard offspring of noblemen. Pnin's most famous work, *The Wail of Innocence*, is a passionate protest against his position as "half a person" in the eyes of society. In his frequent moments of great emotional stress, Nabokov's Pnin almost always "wails," and Pnin's one constant characteristic is certainly his innocence. Paired with this cruel and funny name taken from the eighteenth century, Pnin's Liza is also a meaningful joke. Liza is the heroine of Karamzin's famous eighteenth-century sentimental tale, *Poor Liza*, and so, when the narrator exclaims: "Poor Liza!" he is indulging in a joke at the expense of his English readers. The original title of the novel was *My Poor Pnin*.

One should not let the real-life vectors from Berlin and Cornell intrude overly on what is a perfectly self-contained and remarkably successful work of art. But the recollections of Albert Parry that were published in the New York *New Russian Word* (July 9, 1978) show clearly that the novel was, among other things, a very conscious final break on Nabokov's part with the community of America's Russian lecturers. When Parry saw Nabokov after the appearance of the novel, Nabokov asked him: "Aren't you angry with me for *Pnin*?" "I? Why should I be?" asked Parry. "After all, every Russian teaching Russian subjects in America can see himself in Pnin and is furious with me." "No, Vladimir Vladimirovich," Parry replied, "I don't see a bit of your Timofey in me, and so I have no reason to be angry with you." Nabokov frowned, and it seemed to Parry that he was very dissatisfied with this answer.

In addition to Karpovich and Parry, Nabokov had a friendly
connection at the University of Toronto as a result of which he
gave a lecture there every year in April. He grew more and more
distant from his academic friend of longest standing in America,
Gleb Struve. Struve was the son of a political associate of his father's with whom he had been friendly in Berlin and at Cambridge and to whom he had dedicated a short poem in 1923. In
America he taught Russian literature at Berkeley. Nabokov wrote
Struve a haughty letter in which he asked why it was that he
found himself on a high ridge looking down at the émigré intelligentsia in America. When Struve's Russian-language literary history *Russian Literature in Exile* appeared in 1956 Sirin was
given reasonably prominent space, twelve pages, in the section
"Younger Prose Writers." But Nabokov occupied just one of
thirty-odd chapters dealing with all manner and sort of émigré
novelists, and the book merely lays out a scrapbook of review
cuttings rather heavily weighted toward negative opinions such
as those of Adamovich and ending with the author's opinion that
the autobiography, *Other Shores*, consists of "unbearable, and
unusual for him, treacly sentimentalism." Struve also noted that
Nabokov's Gogol book had discovered too many Americas (a
common Russian expression) without giving credit to the previous Columbuses. Nabokov wrote to a friend that the Struve book
was workmanlike but coarse (*grubovataya*). What Nabokov
never did say but must have been on his mind was that, after fifteen years in America and with ever-growing notice as an English
writer, the attention paid to him as a writer by those whose profession was Russian literature in America was negligible. Nabokov had one highly successful Russian literary reading in New
York in 1951, but he never made gestures toward the fellowship
of émigré letters after that and indeed recoiled in horror from the
suggestion that he might participate in an émigré writers' conference in New York. They were all, in Nabokov's eyes, mediocrities.

Surrounded by and feeling such enmity and indifference in the
community of Russian scholars, Nabokov was naturally enough
apprehensive when it came time to submit his translation of *Onegin* and its massive commentary to a publisher, knowing that the
manuscript would inevitably be sent to "outside readers," and
those outside readers would, of course, include American Russian

scholars. He told Parry that in his opinion the majority of Slavists in both America and England either envied him or actually hated him. "Let them read it when it is published," he said. The manuscript was submitted to the Cornell University Press. There were to be three readers before a decision was made, and Nabokov had negotiated with them that only one of these readers was to be a Slavist, and that the press and Nabokov were each to prepare a list of proposed readers from which the final list would be compiled after mutual discussion, with the right of mutual exclusions. Nabokov's Slavist was, of course, Parry, and he had asked a friend to suggest Parry's name to the press as their Slavist as well. Parry's report said that Nabokov had "oversalted" his dish with his harsh criticisms of all previous translators of Pushkin, and he pointed out a handful of errors in the commentary that he had found, but the bulk of his report was a panegyric to the work's originality, freshness, and scholarly merits. He assured the press that, although it would be very expensive to publish the work because of its vast apparatus, expenses would eventually surely be recouped. It was accepted, and it is unclear exactly how and why Nabokov extricated it from Cornell for eventual publication by the Bollingen Foundation, though the published version was still very much in its "oversalted" form.

An incredible amount of intensive labor went into the *Onegin* and *Pnin*, leading into *Lolita*. An important thing always to remember about Nabokov is that he was an insomniac, with a recurring prick of light pain in his forehead, and, though he had not been a frenetic child, he was a frenetic adult, even if his manner, particularly with his new weight, was so measured that it was difficult to tell. When Dmitri was a student at Harvard, Vera and Vladimir would occasionally come to stay at the house of Harry Levin in Cambridge on holiday weekends. The Levins were stunned to realize that he always worked through the night with very short periods of actual sleep and many catnaps. In the years when they were at their Craigie Circle apartment in Cambridge, one of the two bedrooms was occupied by Vera and Dmitri, the other by Vladimir, so that he could nap and work through the night. When Edmund Wilson visited Nabokov in Ithaca, in May 1957, as negotiations were under way for an American edition of *Lolita*, he, too, was shocked by the amount of work that Nabokov did, for, in addition to entertaining several people (there was a

visiting editor who had come about *Lolita*) and writing, Nabokov
had a hundred and fifty essays to mark, which he did during the
short time Wilson was there. Wilson noted that Nabokov was
exceptionally genial as a result of the success of *Pnin* and the
looming success of *Lolita*, but that he would lapse into semidisa-
greeable moods. Another of the sources of Nabokov's high spirits,
according to Wilson, were the many little glasses of faculty port
and sherry that he kept consuming. On the second day of his stay
in Ithaca, Wilson records in his journal (published as *Upstate*),
that Nabokov seemed depressed and irritable after spending the
morning proctoring an exam.

They began to argue about Pushkin and languages, whether
Merimée knew Russian or Turgenev could read an English newspaper. Both men enjoyed their intellectual sparring, but it had
come to have an unpleasant edge to it, and Pushkin had become a
subject almost certain to lead to harsh words. Wilson wrote in his
diary:

> Vera always sides with Volodya, and one seems to feel her
> bristling with hostility if, in her presence, one argues with
> him. She had revived our discussion of metrics by inquiring,
> with a certain deadliness, whether it wasn't true that I had
> said that *Evgeni Onegin* was written in syllabic verse, and
> when I answered that this was absurd, she seemed to intimate
> that they had letters of mine which could prove the untruth
> of this disclaimer. When I attacked the subject of controversy
> from some angle—such as Greek and Latin—about which Vo-
> lodya knows nothing, he assumes an ironical expression.

Wilson had a bad attack of gout while he was with them and
had to be served dinner away from the table. Wilson had the impression that Vera was resentful of having to take any time away
from her attendance upon Volodya. In addition to that, he had
brought Nabokov a copy of *Histoire d'O* of which Vera much
disapproved. He recalled another occasion when he had brought a
magnum of champagne, and Vera had disapproved of that, too.
As he was leaving, Vera wanted to make sure that Vladimir had
given him back the offensive book, but Nabokov had leaned
through the car window and, burlesquing *Histoire*, told Wilson
in French: "I use lipstick on the lips of my belly."

When Nabokov read *Upstate* there was a short but furious exchange between them in the pages of the *New York Times Book Review*. Nabokov was indignant that Wilson, while his guest in Ithaca, was putting thoughts into his diary that would have caused him to ask Wilson to leave the house if he had dared utter any of them at the time. Nabokov uses phrases like "repulsive blend of vulgarity and naïveté," and Wilson is described as his former friend. Wilson probably won that exchange by means of his very brief rejoinder, which quoted Degas to Whistler: "You behave as if you had no talent." Once upon a time (1944) Wilson had told an editor friend, Robert N. Linscott, that Nabokov was the most brilliant man he had ever met, and that someday Nabokov would write a great modern novel.

A curious footnote to the strained next-to-last meeting between the two writers is provided by the Cornell postgraduate student who delivered the medicine for Wilson's gout on two occasions during those four days. On the occasion of the first delivery the student heard Nabokov shout out: "Freud knew no Rumanian, Michelangelo was a heterosexual, Dostoevsky had the handwriting of a child, Napoleon doted on chives!" Unfortunately, Wilson's reply—Nabokov may have been standing in the doorway of Wilson's bedroom—was inaudible. Two days later, Nabokov was talking with Morris Bishop in the front hallway when the student arrived with more medicine. Nabokov was showing Bishop a butterfly net with its bottom ripped out. "Surely you can't suspect Wilson of this merely because you met the wrong train," said Bishop. "We have had serious differences of opinion on Russian prosody," said Nabokov. "His condition makes him quite non-ambulatory . . . Still, he brought a pair of nail scissors. I cannot be certain."

The first irreparable rift in their friendship occurred in 1954 when Wilson read *Lolita* in manuscript. The novel had been given to Farrar, Straus, which was then Wilson's publishing house, with strict instructions that the manuscript was not to be shown to anyone, but a copy found its way into Wilson's hands. Roger Straus thought that the novel was publishable, but he backed away from Nabokov's insistence that the novel be published under a pseudonym in order to protect his position at Cornell (Nabokov had just been made a full professor in July 1954, and was enjoying a decent salary, nearly ten thousand dollars, for the first time in his life), because he thought the anonymity would make the legal defense too difficult for the firm. (For the record, Vera Nabokov has disputed this account, claiming that anonymity was merely an idea that had been toyed with but dropped before the manuscript was submitted anywhere, but Straus remains obdurate that it was under those terms that he received the manuscript.) Wilson wrote to Nabokov (November 30, 1954) and told him that he liked it less than anything else of his that he had read. The situation seemed to him too absurd to be tragic and too unpleasant to be funny. He felt that the novel had too much background and description of places. Wilson enclosed two notes with his letter. One was from Mary McCarthy—she was writing to Wilson not Nabokov—and she took what she termed a midway position. There were various things in the book she liked, but she concluded by saying that she thought the writing was terribly sloppy throughout, worse perhaps in the second part. The other note was from Wilson's fourth wife, Elena, who wrote that she could not put it down and thought it a very important book. Nabokov later would claim that his contempt was excited not by Wilson's opinion but by the fact that Wilson had read only half the novel before delivering his verdict.

As was his custom, Wilson, notwithstanding his own opinion, offered to help find a publisher for the novel and enclosed a little list of grammatical errors that he had noted. Besides Farrar, Straus, the book had been turned down by Doubleday, Simon & Schuster, The Dial Press, and Harper's. Frequently editors were wildly enthusiastic about the novel but frightened when they received opinions from their lawyers. The Dial Press, for example, saw the book as an opportunity to catapult the small firm into being a major publishing house, but they also had sadly to recognize that it could just as well give rise to ruinous litigation. It took four years for the book to appear in America. When *Lolita* finally became a best-seller, Wilson told Nabokov that he understood what his purpose had been: to write a modern *Fanny Hill* that would enjoy runaway sales because of its sexual theme. Wilson himself, some years before, had had very high hopes for his own *Memoirs of Hecate County*, but the book was banned by court order in New York, and, when the ban was lifted years later, the literary climate had changed drastically, and *Hecate* was no longer sensational. He made only about thirty thousand dollars from the book, a considerable sum then but, Nabokov thought, less than he had been hoping for. Nabokov's first earnings for *Lolita* were two hundred fifty thousand dollars, to which was added one hundred fifty thousand for the movie rights, and forty thousand to write the screenplay for Stanley Kubrick. The money was not tendered in lump sums but spread forward for tax purposes, but it still was more than sufficient to give Nabokov the independence that he had always wanted.

Over the years the literary exchanges between Wilson and Nabokov usually began with an enthusiasm of Wilson's. After reading Malraux while staying in Nevada in 1946, where he was waiting for a divorce and preparing to remarry again, Wilson wrote to Nabokov (November 17, 1946) that he had decided that Malraux was the greatest contemporary writer. Back came the reply, a four-page letter on the clichés, imprecisions, and pretensions in Malraux's writing. Wilson's reply to this was that he had been counting on getting a rise out of Nabokov (an important part of their relationship), and that, moreover, inaccuracies, clichés, and clumsiness do not in themselves invalidate a writer. They had similar exchanges about Genet and Faulkner, and again they agreed to disagree, though Nabokov's heavy assault upon the syntactic tangles in Faulkner's prose may have had something to do with Wilson's reservations on that score when he subsequently praised Faulkner in print. Their disagreement in 1960 on the merits of *Doctor Zhivago* then was only to be expected, though Wilson phoned Nabokov long distance in California (where he was at work on the screenplay of *Lolita*) to discover what he thought of the novel, on which Wilson was then writing for *The New Yorker* perhaps the most enthusiastic essay of his critical career. On a charitable day Nabokov thought *Zhivago* was a third-rate sentimental novel inexplicably written by a rather good poet. Marc Szeftel recalled seeing Nabokov following the best-seller lists in the library as *Doctor Zhivago* slowly crept up on *Lo*. During that year Nabokov took every opportunity to make snide remarks about Pasternak and *Zhivago* in the course of his lectures. Among Russian friends he compared the novel to the works of Charskaya, a novelist who had been popular with prerevolutionary Russian boarding-school girls. At one point, when *Lolita* was number one on the best-seller lists and *Zhivago* was number two, Nabokov encountered the Cornell professor of clas-

sics and, with a dramatic Roman downward thumb gesture, proclaimed theatrically in a paraphrase of Cato's call for the destruction of Carthage: *"Delendum esse Zhivago!"* We know now that
at the height of the political crisis over Pasternak's novel in the
USSR, Nabokov was put forward as the only man equal to the
job of translating the Zhivago poems into English, but that Pasternak himself rejected the suggestion, saying: "That won't work.
He's too jealous of my wretched position in this country to do it
properly."

Chief among Nabokov's complaints about *Doctor Zhivago* was
his conviction that the novel was a Soviet plant, because it approved of the Bolshevik coup and had surfaced by means of an
Italian Communist publisher, which meant, he declared, that
there was some manipulation from within the Kremlin involved
in the novel's appearance. Friends tried to explain to him that the
publisher was an *Italian* Communist, which was quite a different
thing, but to no avail. In addition to that he detected what seemed
to him to be notes of concealed anti-Semitism in it.

Real or imagined anti-Semitism became the focus for sporadic
irritability in Nabokov in the mid-fifties. He claimed to see it in
both the faculty and the student body at Cornell. He was friendly
with Cornell's best-known writer, Arthur Mizener, with whom
he nearly fought seriously over alleged anti-Semitism. (Mizener
liked Nabokov enough that he had invited him to his daughter's
wedding. Nabokov spent the ceremony studying the details of the
church.) In 1954 Mizener was one of a group of faculty friends
invited to a cocktail party by Nabokov, and at that party Mizener
told the story of an argument he had witnessed between Delmore
Schwartz and Robert Lowell over the award of the Bollingen prize
to Ezra Pound. Schwartz accused Lowell to his face of being an
anti-Semite like Pound. In telling the story Mizener expressed
confidence that Lowell, who had been one of the three judges
who had made the award, had made his decision on the basis of
the quality of the poetry alone, and he expressed sympathy for
the very difficult position that Lowell found himself in. Nabokov,
who had been listening to the story at a slight distance, paled and
took another guest, Professor M. H. Abrams, with him into a
nearby room. Nabokov expressed consternation at the dilemma
that faced him: Mizener was his friend, but he was going to have
to throw him out of his house for talking in an anti-Semitic way.

Abrams was astonished at Nabokov's interpretation of what Mizener had said and only just managed to calm Nabokov down. Nor did Nabokov let the matter pass. He consulted Philip Rahv of *Partisan Review* to discover if there was anything anti-Semitic known in Mizener's past. The matter concerns only Nabokov's extreme hypersensitivity in regard to the question. Nabokov's allegation was wholly unfounded.

At least Nabokov did not have the irritation at Cornell of being asked to say nice things about the Soviet Union and Soviet literature. For in his second decade in America McCarthyism was very much in the air, and Cornell was in the main a very conservative campus. The search for subversives in American universities stifled intellectual freedom, and more than a few innocent careers were ruined. To a White Russian such as Nabokov the struggle against communism was a just cause, in spite of the unpleasantness of McCarthy. (Hitlerism was another matter: Nabokov had written to Wilson during the war telling him that, difficult as it was for him to support Soviet Russia in any way, he hoped that it would succeed in wiping Germany from the face of the earth.)

Cornell was relatively fortunate in the McCarthy period. Only two professors there were cited for Communist affiliations, and, while one of them had been denounced before the Senate Internal Security Subcommittee as having "one of the most incriminating pro-communist records in the entire academic world," that professor had resigned from the party in 1939, and the other one had never been a card-carrying Communist. Both testified quite openly about their past political affiliations and beliefs. If there had been an actual Communist on the campus, or if either of the two men cited as subversives had attempted to conceal their radical connections, Cornell would probably have dismissed them. The president of Cornell, Deane Waldo Malott, defended intellectual freedom and stood by both men publically, even while privately he threatened both with dismissal if they embarrassed Cornell by having anything further to do with radical groups.

Cornell was a large and important enough university to warrant its own secret FBI bureau in Ithaca, and Malott worked very closely with it. As a professor of Russian, Nabokov had a great deal of contact with the FBI and even became friendly with one of the agents, a man who, he said, felt shunned by everyone be-

cause of the kind of work he did. Nabokov gave him warm support and told him that he would be proud to have his own son
become an FBI agent. Nabokov's anticommunism, of course, was
a secret to no one at Cornell, nor was his wife's. The story is told
of how Vera Nabokov, taking a cross-country stroll with the wife
of one of Nabokov's colleagues, passed a particularly pungent
barn: "Ah!" she exclaimed. "It smells just like Russia!" There can
be little doubt that, in the eyes of President Malott, who delighted in describing himself as "a rock-ribbed, reactionary Republican," Nabokov's impeccable anticommunist credentials did
much to compensate for the facts that he was not a committee
man and that there were almost no students of Russian when the
time came to consider granting him a full professorship.

Morris Bishop was the man on campus to whom Nabokov was
closest, and he was Nabokov's champion in the university. Nabokov noted in his diary that Bishop paid him the robust compliment of saying that his prose often gave him an erection, which
wasn't easy at his age. Bishop had an exceptional command of
French, Italian, and Spanish language and literature, and he could
speak Latin as well. Moreover, he was a prolific author of light
verse of the sort written by Perelman and Thurber. His verse suffers from academic archness, but some of it is quite good. He, too,
wrote for *The New Yorker* and published three collections, followed by a fourth called *The Best of Bishop*. He was also a reso-
lute man of the sort that Nabokov liked. At the Cornell
graduation ceremony in 1950 a former student tried to rush the
dais and disrupt the ceremony. Bishop stopped the intruder by
swinging the university's fourteen-pound, silver-and-gold mace,
which he was carrying, from the shoulder, landing a direct hit on
his ribcage. Bishop and Nabokov understood each other intui-
tively on most levels, and Bishop and his wife Joan were united in
their conviction that Vladimir and Vera were the two most extraordinary people they were ever going to meet.

But Bishop and Nabokov did not understand each other on the
matter of *Lolita*. Bishop was afraid that Nabokov had a 60 percent chance of being fired for the novel and saw himself in the
unenviable position of having to be his defender. Bishop wrote to
his daughter (May 28, 1957) that Nabokov was trying as hard as
he could to make a huge scandal of the book. He was saddened by
what he saw as a fall away from the "shimmering delight" of

Pnin. He wouldn't be budged, though Nabokov insisted that it was far and away the best thing he had ever written. Bishop would never admit to having even finished reading the novel. It was, in fact, Bishop who first put the proposition to him that Nabokov was endeavoring to live off a little girl's earnings, something that is looked on poorly in some places. Nabokov was not pleased at all, but he finally grew fond of saying himself that he was being supported by Lolita.

Nabokov was proud of Cornell for the sophistication with which it took *Lolita* in its stride. He was invited to give a public lecture at Cornell on April 10, 1958. The title he chose was "Readers, Writers, and Censors in Russia," and his position was as rock-firm as ever. The lecture is best remembered for the histrionic imitation by which Nabokov demonstrated a Soviet worker in a socialist realist novel declaring his love to a comrade worker while manning a jackhammer: "I luh-luh-luh-love you." All of Ithaca, from President Malott down, was at the lecture. There was never any question of Nabokov's job being in peril when the Olympia Press edition of *Lolita* appeared in 1955 and generated considerable rumor, nor was there any question when the Putnam's edition was finally released in 1958. The files of Cornell University actually contain only one (anonymous) letter of complaint from Two Concerned Parents: "Frankly, we have forbidden our youngster to enroll in any course taught by Nobkov, and we would be in fear for any young girl who consulted him at a private conference or ran into him after dark on the campus!"

Nabokov was careful about *Lolita* on the campus. A very few copies of the Olympia edition were sent on his instructions to friends at Cornell. When The Book & Bowl, an informal literary association that met in members' homes, decided to have a session based on the Olympia edition of *Lolita*, Nabokov at first wanted to attend, but the host for the meeting, Professor Abrams, dissuaded him. Selections from the novel were read by Richard Fariña and Marc Szeftel, following which Szeftel gave a talk on the book. Nabokov reconnoitered the substance of the talk afterward from various people who had been there. It was Szeftel's intention to write a book on *Lolita*, but Nabokov did not encourage him, which was probably prudent. Szeftel's talk was on the motifs of destiny, the double, and games in *Lolita*, with particular reference to the Sirin works unknown to his American readers, but he also had some very critical things to say about the novel, and it was subsequently revealed (in an article that Szeftel wrote about Nabokov three years after his death) that he saw a personal aspect in the novel: "... in a conversation about it with Morris Bishop I told him about a friend of mine, a great Polish writer who, approaching old age, complained of the unexpected physical attraction he suddenly felt for his teenage daughter's girlfriends. But he brushed the attraction aside, I said, without transferring it to a novel. This was not necessarily Nabokov's case, but the story was suggestive, and it struck Bishop as a 'little revelation.'" There were evil tongues ready to say that Vladimir took an unnatural interest in his son's dating. A much-told anecdote at Cornell is that some parents sent their small daughter to the Nabokov house on Halloween night with a sign reading LOLITA pinned across the front of her dress. Nabokov, it is said, exploded in fury and sent the girl away with an instruction to tell her mother that the prank was an obscenity.

The strongest support for the novel at Cornell came from Arthur Mizener, who saw in the novel Nabokov's great feeling and love for his adopted country and said that it was even quite possible that Nabokov could turn out to be the greatest American writer. Other colleagues in the French, German, and English departments were less generous. The most common criticism was that the novel sprawled or trailed off in the second half. The most hurtful comment, because Nabokov prided himself on having got the idiom and manner of the American teenager right, was the comment of a philosophy professor who protested that no American girl would have submitted passively to Humbert's long imprisonment of her as Lolita had. She would have gone to the police at some stage. When Szeftel assured Nabokov that it seemed clear that he would have no academic difficulty over the novel, Nabokov replied: "It is not yet sure! People might still comment on *Lolita* perverting the coed's purity. Ah, the pure coeds! An American myth!"

When he did talk of *Lolita*, Nabokov would have only two things to say about it: that it was a work of art, and that it had a high moral content. He pointed out with pride that he had received a letter from a man who said that he had abandoned his homosexuality after reading the novel, and he told of how, after one of his lectures in the European literature course, a student walked up to him with the Olympia edition in his hand and made a deep bow to him. When Vera Nabokov talked about the novel to people in Ithaca, she would stress the pathos of Lolita's utter loneliness.

The savage response to *Lolita* came from the Russian émigré community in New York. Nabokov was indignantly tried and found wanting in conversations at the doorway to the reading room of the Slavonic section of the New York Public Library, for many years a meeting place for New York's Russian intelligentsia. The stories quickly got back to Nabokov in Ithaca. A minor poet took an ad in *The New Russian Word* condemning those who abandoned their native tongue, and a savage epigram circulated: *Having lost his native soil/Nabokov has found new soil between his legs.* Nabokov felt that he was being unfairly cast as the sinner set against Pasternak's sainthood, and he responded with a Russian poem that parodied the poem Pasternak had written in response to the Soviet government's attacks on him for *Doctor Zhivago*.

It is fair to say that, though *Lolita* wasn't banned (except in New Zealand), there was much unpleasantness and stress involved in the book's appearance. Philip Rahv had agreed to use some of the novel in *Partisan Review* in order to help prepare the way for its appearance in America, but he declined at the last minute on legal advice. A portion did appear in *The Anchor Review*, with careful deletions, thanks to a young editor named Jason Epstein. He was very enthusiastic about the novel but could not get his publishing house to accept it, but that little prepublication helped the novel's American prospects considerably.

Nabokov was on leave from Cornell for a short time and living in Cambridge, where he was using Widener Library to complete the final draft of his Pushkin commentaries, when he chanced to see an item in the *New York Times Book Review* stating that *Lolita* had been cited by Graham Greene as one of the three best books of the year for 1955 in *The Sunday Times* (London). Nothing happened immediately, but a journalist on *The Sunday Express* had a copy of the novel which he gave to the editor of the paper, John Gordon, who proceeded to denounce both Greene and *The Sunday Times* for recommending pornography. That started a light-hearted romp that was ultimately to be responsible

for Vladimir Nabokov's fame. Greene formed a John Gordon Society, and a meeting of about sixty people was held on March 6,
1956. Greene was immediately elected president, but it was decided that it would be inappropriate to use the term vice president. Greene made a motion that in the future the manufacturer
of Scrabble should be asked to include a pledge for purchasers to
sign committing them not to use any words not included in the
Oxford Concise Dictionary. Publishers would be invited to use a
book band that proclaimed "Banned by the John Gordon Society." The participants in the John Gordon Society's first meeting included Christopher Isherwood, Angus Wilson, A. J. Ayer,
Peter Brook, and some of the best editors in London, including
David Farrer. The "society's" second meeting in May invited
John Gordon himself to speak on pornography and was even better. It had considerable newspaper publicity, and a Putnam's editor in London at the time looked into the outrageous novel that
was the pretext for the amiable raillery. This was how Putnam's
came to publish *Lolita*.

When it had become clear in 1954 that *Lolita* was not going to
find a publisher in New York, the manuscript had been sent to
Nabokov's French agent, and it was she who had arranged the
publication with the Olympia Press. Transferring the rights for
the novel wasn't easy. Olympia was eventually given one-third of
the royalties, which was a considerable step-down on their part
from what they originally asked. The (Russian) lawyer Liuba
Sherman, who succeeded in obtaining the divorce from Olympia,
became and remained the Nabokovs' European lawyer in gratitude.

There was a news conference at Putnam's at which Nabokov
spoke. Later he heard himself on WQXR in his hotel room and
was indignant: "They didn't ask me! They didn't pay me! Cha-
liapin said it—only the little birds sing for nothing!" There were
prominent articles about Nabokov, author, aristocrat, chaser of
butterflies, and he was famous. One of the more interesting interviews, which was long forgotten but has now been recovered
on tape, was filmed in New York with Lionel Trilling on the
CBC television program "Close-Up." Trilling had once visited
Cornell and attended a party where the guests grouped around
him at one end of the room and Nabokov at the other. Trilling
and Nabokov were like two queen bees ignoring one another.

They had met at the door as they were leaving, and Nabokov said to Trilling: "I understand, Mr. Trilling, you don't like my little *Lolita*." Trilling said that that wasn't so, and that in fact he was just putting off rereading the novel until the summer so that he could really come to grips with it. The essay that Trilling wrote was one of the strongest in support of the novel, which he saw as the last of the novels of grand passion. On "Close-Up" he declared: "I found it a deeply moving book. Mr. Nabokov may not have meant to move hearts, but he moved mine. He may not have meant to affect minds, but he affected my mind." Their television discussion is exceptionally important because it is perhaps the first and last time that Nabokov was to speak freely when he was being recorded in interview. His natural speech patterns are as interesting as what he says about the novel. Nabokov tended to puff and stutter a bit. His conversation proceeds by means of rhythmic repetitions: "I have invented in America my America and just as fantastic as any inventor's America." Or, at another point: "My baboon Humbert Humbert, for after all Humbert Humbert is a baboon, a baboon of genius but a baboon." He states caustically that the people who hate *Lolita* think in clichés and are "just common scolds and old philistines." Such people, Nabokov thought, are not only unable to recognize love, but also "perhaps they don't know what sex is either."

Comparatively little serious response to *Lolita*, apart from Trilling's article, appeared when it was first published in America—that would come later—but the book was certainly helped by an indignant and stuffy denunciation of it by Orville Prescott, the then chief book reviewer for the *New York Times*.

There was considerable expectation that *Lolita* would be banned in England. Serious political ramifications were possible because Nigel Nicolson of Weidenfeld & Nicolson was in Parliament, and he was having difficulty with his constituency over the prospect of publication, which was the talk of London. The possibility of damage to the Conservative Party was also very real, and the matter was being discussed in cabinet. The attorney general, Manningham-Buller (later Lord Dilhorne), conferred with Nicolson and Prime Minister Macmillan and said that Weidenfeld & Nicolson risked prosecution if they went ahead with publication. Edward Heath, the then chief whip, asked Nicolson to drop publication in the interest of political peace. Nicolson refused, but he made a speech in which he proposed that a single copy would be published and given to a member of Weidenfeld & Nicolson's staff. In this way the attorney general could prosecute the firm for a technical publication without any member of the public at large having been corrupted, and the question could be tested in court. The attorney general's department made no response to that plan, and the book was printed. During a very nervous launching party at the Ritz a messenger delivered a note to Nicolson that he climbed up on a table to read to the party: the government had decided not to prosecute. A cheer arose. *Lolita* was to be the number-one best-seller in England for many months and required two large reprintings in as many months. Nicolson lost his Bournemouth seat on the issue, but Weidenfeld & Nicolson became a major publisher in considerable measure because of the profits made on this book.

Nabokov had come to London for the publication and was at the party, though he stayed in England only three days. He no longer had acquaintances in England apart from his cousin de Peterson and his classmate Mrosovsky, but his brother Kirill came to London to be with him at the party, and one old girlfriend from the Cambridge days who the publishers knew had known Nabokov was invited. "Who is that corpse?" Kirill asked his brother in Russian, gesturing over his shoulder at the woman. To pass such remarks between themselves is not uncommon for Russian émigrés at English-speaking social gatherings. Kirill couldn't have known that the woman spoke Russian.

When Nabokov first arrived in London and met George Weidenfeld and Nigel Nicolson, he avoided the subject of his novel for hours. His publishers joined him in this strange omission, as if by mutual consent. He finally began to talk about *Lolita* when they were in a taxi going from one party to another. He said that he intended the book as a tragedy. Its point was that it was only when Humbert rediscovered Lolita that he realized for the first time that he loved her. But by that time she has lost her beauty and her charm, is pregnant, utterly destitute, and is virtually reduced to a slut: "The tragedy of the book is that having started the affair from purely selfish motives, he falls in love with her when she is beyond loving." That is the most direct statement made by Nabokov about the novel. He repeated this idea in an interview in 1964, but for some reason he did not choose to include that interview in his collection *Strong Opinions*. Another direct comment was a remark to his cousin Peter de Peterson, who visited him in Ithaca shortly after the novel appeared. Nabokov told him that he believed that love could exist in the form in which it is shown in the novel, and that such love could last longer than most people assumed. That, in personal terms, would mean that the novel can also be seen as time out of joint: the mature man desperately searching for his first love, who has somehow not aged at all. That Humbert lusts after not Lolita, but an ur-Lolita, is made very clear in the novel. In the Canadian interview Nabokov acknowledged that Humbert was like him a European and a man of letters, ". . . but I have been very careful, I have taken great care to separate myself from him." Humbert, he said, didn't know the difference between a hawk-moth and a butterfly, which is a mistake he, as an entomologist, would never make!

It was 1959 and time again to change, not cultures (Nabokov's was his own and portable) but countries. When the sum of the sale of the movie rights for *Lolita* was printed in *The New Russian Word*, Marc Szeftel congratulated Nabokov on his freedom now to resign and become a full-time writer. Nabokov said that he loved Cornell, and, besides, it was still too early to tell. The invitation by Stanley Kubrick to write the screenplay for the film and the ever-growing sale of substantial translation rights throughout Europe lessened doubts. Nabokov did not resign. He took a leave of absence and put his papers in storage in Ithaca. They were now a "possession." When it came time at last to ship them to Switzerland, it was discovered that they weighed nearly a ton and would cost three thousand dollars to ship. Finding a replacement for himself at Cornell was difficult for two reasons: he knew no one among the American Russians whom he would or could ask, and he did not, really, want a permanent replacement. The task was made much easier in that, for all intents and purposes, he had become a professor of comparative literature at Cornell rather than of Russian. A perfect temporary replacement was found in Herbert Gold, a young writer whom he had met and liked through Jay Laughlin and *New Directions*. He phoned him in New York and Gold came to Ithaca, where Nabokov carefully coached him on his interview and the ritual cocktail party afterward, at which he would have to show that he could drink but not too much and still remain in perfect command of himself. Gold passed the test, and on February 23, 1959, Nabokov and his wife set out on a leisurely last motor trip through the States to California where the movie script for Lolita would be written. Shortly before they left Ithaca, Vera Nabokov finally received compensation from the West German government for her loss of employment when the Nazis came to power.

The prospect of working on the film delighted Nabokov in several ways. Not only was it a long-overdue opportunity to work in the cinema (in the Cornell houses where there was a television set, Nabokov followed all the old movies and the soap operas as well), but it also afforded Nabokov the chance to even the score with Olympia Press. Maurice Girodias, in negotiating the release of rights for the novel, had grandly told Nabokov: "You can have the movie rights. They'll never make a movie of *that*!"

As they left Ithaca, the Nabokovs had a horrible skid on a frozen road and were lucky to escape a serious accident. Nabokov always praised his wife for being both a very fast and a skillful driver. They took a leisurely "lepping" route (a Nabokov neologism) through the Great Smokies, Tennessee, Texas, and Arizona. In Hollywood they rented a house at 2088 Mandeville Canyon Road. "Mandeville" would be used in *Pale Fire*. It was the kind of triple-bottomed allusion Nabokov loved—the house where he lived, man/devil, and Bernard de Mandeville, the author of an early-eighteenth-century verse satire that de Mandeville published together with a prose commentary on it. Nabokov grew tanned and noticeably more seignorial. The writing of the filmscript did not satisfy Kubrick. It was extremely self-indulgent (Nabokov had himself making an Alfred Hitchcock-style cameo appearance), far too long, and, most important, it lacked dramatic life. Drama was always Nabokov's weakest genre. Some of the dialogue was dreadfully corny and wooden. Very little of what he wrote was actually used in the film. When the screenplay was published in 1974, it attracted little interest.

In the spring, work on the screenplay finished, they drove back to Ithaca, where they stayed only briefly to pack. They sailed on the *Liberté* on May 28. Nabokov bantered with the reporters but would not be drawn into saying anything substantive. He left America with his own prediction (and his wife's decades-long conviction) to Albert Parry fulfilled. When the first European

translation of *Lolita* appeared, made from the *Olympia* edition
(Parry could not remember whether it was Danish or some other
language), Nabokov had waved it in his hand and told his friend:
*"Pomyanite moe slovo, vot otkuda nachnyotsya moe voskhozh-
denie!"*—"Mark my word. Here is where my ascension begins!"
The Russian word was the one used in the Orthodox service for
ascension into heaven after resurrection.

20

IN 1954, NABOKOV NEARLY DESTROYED THE MANUSCRIPT OF *Lolita*. He had been working on the novel for about a year and had come to find it very difficult to continue. The backyard incinerator was alight, and Nabokov appeared with the manuscript. "I think I could destroy this," he told Vera. "Don't burn it. Wait till tomorrow," she told him.

The subject was treated before by Nabokov in not one but two unpublished Russian short stories, one of which may, in fact, have been destroyed by Nabokov. The one story that has become known is "The Magician," because Nabokov wrote about it in the afterword to *Lolita* where he says that he wrote the story in 1939 and read it to a small group of friends including Aldanov, Fondaminsky, Vladimir Zenzinov, and a woman doctor named Kogan-Bernstein. Nabokov said that he was dissatisfied with the story and destroyed it after his arrival in America.

But another copy most certainly of "The Magician" did survive, because Nabokov gave me two pages of the story, which he said had come to light after he read the first draft of my 1967 book about him, and I translated and included those two passages in the book. As it happened, Vladimir Weidle, who knew English and was one of Nabokov's keenest émigré critics, had continued to follow Nabokov's career after he became an American writer, read the book, and remembered the short story quite differently. Weidle said that he had been given a typescript of the story to read by Nabokov in Paris. The manuscript, he said, was already marked with instructions for the printer. But it was not called "The Magician." The story that Weidle read was called "The Satyr." It also had one radical point of difference from "The Magician" and *Lolita* in that the young girl was not twelve but not more than ten, before puberty and without any feminine body characteristics. She was in every way a tender child. The main character, Arthur, is, like Humbert, described as a "central European." He has married an unhealthy Frenchwoman anticipating that, after her death, the girl will be entirely in his control, which is exactly what happens. (Weidle could not remember whether or not the girl is named in the story.) Arthur takes her to a remote little hotel in Switzerland, where, exhausted from their trip, she immediately falls asleep on the large double bed. Arthur begins to caress her whereupon she wakes up and, not understanding anything, begins to weep and scream. Everything has gone wrong. Arthur has a sexual spasm in his pajamas and furiously throws on his dressing gown. He rushes out of the room and the hotel and is immediately hit by a large truck on the street. His death is conveyed in three lines. Nothing is said about the fate of the little girl.

Like "The Satyr," "The Magician" is narrated in the third person. In both stories the girls are, unlike Lolita, innocent, but the girl in "The Magician" has an air of angelic semiacquiescence. Thus, the two short-story seduction scenes have a much graver aspect than the corresponding scene in *Lolita* in which Humbert is himself "seduced" by a very unvirginal little nymphet. When Arthur takes the girl to the hotel in "The Magician" she sinks down in his lap in an armchair:

> "My darling, my poor little girl," he murmured in a sort of
> general mist of pity, tenderness, and desire, observing her
> sleepiness, fuzziness, her wan smile, fondling her through her
> dark dress, feeling the stripe of the orphan's garter through its
> thin wool, thinking about her defenselessness, her state of
> abandonment, her warmth, enjoying the animated weight of
> her legs which sprawled loose and then again, with an ever so
> light bodily rustle, hunched themselves up higher—and she
> slowly wound one dreamy tight-sleeved arm around the back
> of his neck, immersing him in the chestnut odor of her soft
> hair.

Such highly erotic passages from "The Magician" have the same poetic and sensual intensity mixed with ordinary middle-class detail that characterizes *Lolita*. When Arthur first sees the little girl at the Tuileries Gardens she has been roller skating:

> Chewing rapidly, she undid the straps with her free hand, shook off all the heaviness of steel soles on solid wheels—and, descending to us on earth, having straightened up with a sudden sensation of heavenly nakedness which took a moment to grow aware of being shaped by shoes and socks, she rushed off.

Aldanov called the story a masterpiece after the reading. Nabokov remained dissatisfied with it. He diagnosed the problem as being that he didn't know any young French girls, and so the story had an inadequate realistic basis. The important difference between the short stories and the novel, as Weidle was quick to note, was that the stories had a thoroughly moral ending, and no Russian journal would have hesitated to print them in spite of the pedophiliac theme, which, anyway, never come to pass whereas *Lolita* is, well, a much more complex love story. "The Satyr" and "The Magician" may be seen as mere prologues to *Lolita*.

Nabokov's often-repeated story of how the theme that finally became *Lolita* came to him in September 1939, when, ill in bed with another severe attack of neuralgia, he chanced to read a filler item about a chimpanzee who was taught to draw and drew the bars of its cage, must now be reconsidered. He thought that the newspaper in which he saw the item was *Paris-Soir* ("somewhere in the middle of a page"), and, when it could not be found there, he named three other newspapers that he occasionally also read at the time, but they did not contain the story either. It was a strange time for such a light *entrefilet* to appear in a newspaper. The animal stories in the French newspapers for this period are about the evacuation of dangerous zoo animals so that they would not be let loose in the event that bombs fell on the zoos. A man has invented a gas mask to be worn by dogs. Even the question of which zoo in which the event took place remains uncertain. In the *Lolita* afterword, Nabokov thought it was the Jardin des Plantes, but some years later he told a reporter that it had been the Zoo de

Vincennes. At the Parisian Department of Zoos none of their older employees could recall the incident.

The newspaper item may or may not exist, but it becomes clear now that that "inspiration" was probably one of Nabokov's false trails. The tale is not told by Arthur himself in either version, and so the anecdote of the chimpanzee drawing the bars of his own cage has no relevance whatsoever to the original inspiration and execution. The basic plot of *Lolita* is sketched out in *The Gift*, which means that it was in Nabokov's mind as early as 1936. There the situation is put very modestly, for in the stepfather's story the man never makes an advance, and the girl grows into a woman who (having guessed his feelings?) simply looks at him with contempt. Zina's stepfather calls this "a Dostoevskian tragedy," and ultimately Nabokov's story does go back to the suppressed chapter, "Stavrogin's Confession," from Dostoevsky's novel *The Possessed* in which pedophilia figures.

When Nabokov, or anyone else, for that matter, plants a false trail, it is reasonable to suppose that there is a hidden, correct trail. The discovery of the correct trail belongs to Donald Rayfield, who is otherwise a Chekhov specialist at Queen Mary College, London. Rayfield followed a passing reference by Nabokov in *Speak, Memory* to confessions of pedophilia in the multivolume Havelock Ellis ranging from "Anglo-Saxon industrial centres to the Ukraine," where, according to Nabokov, a particularly interesting confession is given by a landowner. The obstacle to discovery of this confession was that it is not included in the English *Studies in the Psychology of Sex*, because the American publisher had warned Ellis that its inclusion could jeopardize publication. It appeared in the French edition, however, even though it was concealed in the section on sexuality during pregnancy in volume 6 and printed in type minute enough to make it almost unreadable.

The confession was written in 1912 by "Victor X," a member of a wealthy and intellectual Russian-Ukrainian family. Besides native Russian and fluent French, Victor says that he has a good command of six other languages. He is not a writer, and his confession, written in middle age, is his sole work. His perversion is not only little girls, but also the fact that he turns into his own double while having intercourse with them and stands to the side clinically watching himself. But the most truly Nabokovian thing about Victor X is his self-assurance and sense of his own innate superiority. He gives an extended analysis not only of himself, but also of Russian sexuality in general.

Donald Rayfield refers, almost correctly, I think (there are, after all, Tolstoy's diaries), to the confession of Victor X as a virtually unique commentary on Russian sexuality in the nineteenth century. Victor X says that the West makes a great mistake to believe that Russians, women as well as men, are in the slightest restrained in their sexuality by conventional morality or religion. He quotes the memoirs of a French professor who served as tutor to the young Alexander III in which he says that the atmosphere at Alexander III's court—and it was an extremely reactionary court—was very loose. He claimed that even the most virtuous ladies in the best Russian society had very broad ideas of sexual morality, and that an unmarried mother in Russia did not feel in the slightest ashamed of the fact in society. Rayfield gives extremely heavy weight for the purposes of social history to Victor's confession, claiming that the wealthy intellectuals in Russia tended to give their male children excessive freedom, both in terms of access to books and to the favors of peasant girls who could be easily seduced with little gifts. They supposedly did this with their children because of frustration owing to the political freedom that they lacked in public life. "Very often," claims Rayfield, "the more regimented political life, the more anarchic private life becomes in Russia," and he sees applicability of Victor's confession even to Soviet life today. From an historical point of view, according to Rayfield,

> The Russian intellectual gentry disowned the social structure
> on which they depended for their own prosperity and free-
> dom of thought and action. Historically, they wrote them-
> selves off as surely as did Victor . . . Victor is more than a
> relic of a bygone age. He may provide us with a window into
> the back rooms of a house which we used to know only by its
> façade . . .

On the one hand, Rayfield's conclusion is an extremely broad generalization based on the most limited possible sample, but on the other, it is in perfect concord with what we know of Nabokov's own grandfather and grandmother and great-grandmother.

The following, then, are the factors that contributed to *Lolita*. A parodic but very important analogue to incest in the Nabokov family tree. A large family that was inclined to favor itself romantically—besides using his mother's nickname for Lolita, Nabokov used the nickname of a cousin with whom he was madly in love as a little boy, Dolly, for her nickname, and Nicolai Nabokov proposed to Nabokov's sister Elena (she refused him). Nabokov's own passionate attachment to his memory of "Colette." The "five or six" pedophiles whom he said he had known personally during his life. (The dubious sixth was a staff member at *The New Yorker* with whom he had never discussed the matter but about whom he had strong suspicions.) His reading and rereading of Havelock Ellis at various points throughout his career. The address to the jury by the young Nabokov in the trial of Nikolai Evreinov's play. And finally, his hate/take relationship with Dostoevsky and the lure of Dostoevsky's most daring undeveloped theme coupled with the use of open eroticism by his contemporaries Ivan Bunin and D. H. Lawrence in the thirties. Considering all of these vectors, *Lolita* was not a chance but virtually a fatidic development in Nabokov's career.

The story of the artist-chimpanzee and his bars is very useful when we consider the novel that Nabokov actually wrote in 1953–54. His impulse by that time was to create a portrait of a man imprisoned in passion, but not in (we remember *Laughter in the Dark*) "blind passion." In his interview with Alain Robbe-Grillet, Nabokov said that for him *Lolita* was really "a certain problem" that he wished to solve in an elegant and economical fashion. The problem that Nabokov sought to resolve was threefold in nature. First, the protagonist as victim of his own or someone else's passion (*King, Queen, Knave* and *Laughter in the Dark*) had to be joined with the theme of the protagonist-artist (*Despair* and *The Eye*) who both controls and conveys the story. This synthesis, which presented a challenge far more difficult than it might first appear, required in turn that, while the narration would reside with the hero, the course of the story itself had to proceed according to inexorable rules. In such a synthesis, the hero's game must be both won and lost at the same time. And finally, there was the challenge and delight of allegorically resolving a theme, love, in terms of its extreme and seemingly mutually exclusive opposite, lechery. To put it in another way and more simply, *Lolita* is Nabokov's most mature novel and the meeting ground and perfect blending of all his habitual themes.

As a novel *Lolita* carries on where "The Satyr" and "The Magician" broke off. It is Charlotte Haze who is run down by the truck, leaving Humbert to be seduced by Lo.

Lolita is a novel of prisons. Humbert Humbert is in prison as he writes the book. Lolita was Humbert's prisoner, but he was hers, too, in quite a different way, and he was also the prisoner of Charlotte during their brief marriage. The motels where Humbert and Lolita stay are transient prisons, where they are asked to feel at home but warned that their license number is on record. But most of all, Humbert is a prisoner of his own past, the idyllic and brutally disrupted childhood romance that he is sentenced to repeat in his grotesque longing for nymphets. Nymphets themselves are eventually imprisoned in "the coffin of coarse female flesh" that is maturity. When Lolita escapes (is kidnapped) from Humbert with Quilty, it is because she has been momentarily transferred from the captivity of Humbert to that of a provincial American hospital where she is guarded from him by an imperious young nurse. And in the end Humbert imprisons and executes Quilty in his own house, after having carefully removed all the keys from the doors beforehand so that the prisoner cannot lock himself away from his executioner.

The natural correspondence to these various cagings is chess, the game of cell-like squares. Though *Lolita* is not a chess game, it does utilize the playing of chess at several important points, and the overall pattern of the novel suggests a chess simile. One of the important articles on *Lolita*, by Edmond Bernhard (*L'Arc*, no. 24, 1964), makes too great an effort to speak of the entire work as a match, and this frequently leads to strained analogy. Lolita as a pawn promoted to queen after Charlotte's death corresponds neither to chess nor to Humbert's vision of her. Bernhard's chess references are somewhat more helpful in explaining the forward tempo of the plot. Humbert's initial fault is, like premature use of the queen, a beginner's error, as a result of which he is thrown into the thick of play before he is ready for it. The death scene with Quilty is compared to a king blocked by his own guard and proposing in vain a series of exchanges, which amount to all his powers, for the chance to slip out of his own fortress. Humbert keeps the murder weapon in a chess box, and the poem he gives Quilty to read plays on chess terminology.

There are three actual chess games in the novel. Before his first marriage, in Europe, Humbert plays chess with his future father-in-law while his fiancée stands at her easel nearby working on a silly cubist painting. The second game occurs in America when Humbert plays chess with a homosexual friend while Lolita dances on the upper floor. His homosexual opponent seems to Humbert to be confusing the distant sounds of dancing feet with the menace of his queen. In the third game, played against the same opponent, Humbert receives a phone call that is his first clue that Lolita is deceiving him, and it immediately finds reflection in the chess game: his queen is at risk. This signals clearly, as does much else in the novel, that one of the important subjects in the novel is Humbert's struggle against homosexuality.

There are other games, too. The list of Lolita's classmates at the beginning of the novel corresponds to the twenty-five basic classifications of insects, and at one point Lolita's eyes are described with exactly the coloration of the underside of the wing of Nabokov's speciality, the Lycaenidae. The author of one article, Diana Butler (*New World Writing*, 1960), has written a detailed article on the butterflies in *Lolita*, based in part on an examination of Nabokov's butterflies at the MCZ. Another study finds that *Lolita* is basically a parody of *Eugene Onegin* (this "discovery" has also been made of *Ada*), and still another sees the paramount importance of Edgar Allan Poe, with particular reference to the circumstances of Poe's life, Annabelle Lee, and Poe's "The Cask of Amontillado" in relation to chapter 35 of *Lolita*. (A colossal irony is that Poe had behaved like Nabokov's grandfather: he had married the girl to ensure his tie to her mother!) None of the quests for an ultimate key are exactly wrong, but they cannot in themselves do the job, because the level of parody and reference, always rich in Nabokov, reaches new heights in *Lolita*. The allusions are there, but their uncovering must supply a self-sufficient pleasure for the reader who likes that sort of thing rather than an "answer." It is the strategy of James Joyce.

The stylized configurations and references in the novel can be important. Ultimately, however, *Lolita* depends upon the reality and urgency of Humbert's voice, and much of the artifice in the novel diverts the reader's attention from the pretence of reality. F. W. Dupee was only partially correct when, in *King of the Cats*, he saw *Lolita* as being about "a real wolf howling for a real

Red Riding Hood." If the book is realistic, it is, in Martin Green's happy phrase, "realistic rococo."

Humbert, who did not seduce Lolita and who is in prison for murder rather than child molestation, is concerned in the book he writes with two things—his human failure toward Lolita (every night while he was with her, when he pretended to be asleep he could hear her sobbing into her pillow) and his very real love for her, which has nothing to do with sex. Dolly, however, has not been completely broken by her relationship with Humbert. At the novel's end she is married to a steadfast if unexciting mechanic. Her eventual death in giving birth to his child does seem both fated and natural and recalls Nabokov's 1934 story "A Russian Beauty," in which the heroine also dies in childbirth. It is not Humbert's intention to rationalize what he has done. When he addresses the "gentlemen of the jury," he places himself in the dock.

The possible objections to *Lolita* were countered most cogently by V. S. Pritchett writing in *The New Statesman* when the novel first appeared, and they stand equally well today:

> I can imagine no book less likely to incite the corruptible
> reader; the already corrupted would surely be devastated by
> the author's power of projecting himself into their fantasy-
> addled minds. As for the minors, the nymphets and school-
> boys, one hardly sees *them* toiling through a book written in a
> difficult style, filled on every page with literary allusions, lin-
> guistic experiment and fits of idiosyncrasy.

Pritchett also makes another very telling point about the object of all the outcry over *Lolita*:

> The book ends with a murder which makes our "respectable"
> murder mongers and classy writers of sadistic thrillers (never
> threatened with prosecution) look like the fakers they are.
> Being comic, Mr. Nabokov's murder is horrible. Murder is.
> By what perversion of moral judgment does society regard
> murder as "clean" and sex as "dirty" as a subject?

There was a broad spectrum of response to the book's morality or lack thereof. The American Catholic magazine *Commonweal* stated firmly: "It has been said that this book has a high literary value; it has much more; a style, an individuality, a brilliance which may yet create a tradition in American letters." Adolf Eichmann was given a copy of the novel to read in his cell in Jerusalem and declared: *"Das ist aber ein sehr unerfreuliches Buch"* ("That is quite an offensive book").

The moral aspect of the novel can be most clearly observed in the opposition of two Humberts, which is probably the sense behind the lugubrious double name. Though all Nabokov novels have doubling, none has quite as much as this one. There is the Humbert everyone knows. But there is also the one who, when he confronts Clare Quilty, calls himself Dolores Haze's father. This Humbert not only murders this image of his darkest self, but also retraces everything that has happened to him and mercilessly cauterizes himself at every "kumfy kabin" in which he abused Lolita and deprived her of her childhood. The murder he commits is seen by him to have been morally necessary, both in itself and so that he, the other Humbert, could live to give his Lolita refuge and immortality in art. For the rest there is no possibility of mercy in his own eyes. Humbert declares that, if he were his own judge, he would give himself thirty-five years for rape and dismiss the remaining charges. The novel opens with an incantation of Lolita as the fire of Humbert's loins and ends with a declaration of pure love. The facetious introduction by JR, Jr., makes precisely this point. It is, really, addressed to the judge who may rule on the novel, and the judge is told that even those scenes that "a certain type of mind" might find aphrodisiac are absolutely necessary to a tale that proceeds "to nothing less than a moral apotheosis."

The first sexual story that Sirin ever published was "A Fable," which appeared in 1926 in *The Rudder*. It is an unassuming and almost disarmingly simple little fable about sexual desire written in the manner of E. T. A. Hoffmann, who is alluded to at one point, but it has links with *Lolita*. One of the pseudonyms that Humbert tells us he considered taking was Otto Otto, and the devil in "A Fable" appears in the guise of Madame Ott. In this story a timid little man named Erwin has made a ritual as he travels to and from work every day of "selecting a harem" from among the women he sees from the window of his trolley-car seat. Once he had summoned up the nerve to approach a woman whom he took to be a prostitute, but he had erred in that judgment, and since then he has avoided women except for his harmless trolley fantasies. Then one day in a café, after he has just made a mental choice through the window, a woman sitting opposite him says aloud, "That can be arranged." It is Madame Ott. The devil tells Erwin that she was drawn to help him by the rare combination of timidity and fierce desire in him, and that he may select himself a harem between noon and midnight the next day.

Madame Ott allays all of Erwin's doubts and fears. He will not be required to sacrifice his soul in the old-fashioned way for this pleasure, Madame Ott will provide a much better place of assignation with his chosen women than his meager little room, and he may choose as many women as he wishes as long as the final total sum is an odd number. It is this, as it must in any fairy tale, that proves his undoing, for in his rush to achieve his odd number just before the time is up he by mistake selects as his thirteenth choice the same girl who was also his first, and this time she reproaches him in the same way as the woman he had once taken for a prostitute. Erwin and Madame Ott chat familiarly and indifferently, like two office workers, and go their separate ways. Erwin did not trip himself up on numbers alone. His twelfth choice was a nymphet, and so he might have had his harem had he not chosen her. What "A Fable" demonstrates is that Nabokov's interest in certain extreme states of sexual desire is virtually as old as his writing career. For the story appeared a little over three months after the serialization of part of Nabokov's first novel.

One of the devices by which Nabokov separates his novel from the possibility of pornography is the vulgarity which, Humbert confides, is often found in the true nymphet. (The term, by the way, was indignantly claimed by French critics as belonging to French: *nymphette* occurs as far back as the seventeenth century in such poets as Ronsard. What they failed to note is that Ronsard is mentioned in Nabokov's novel.) Lolita is not an idealized young girl. She has a sticky hot neck, a strident voice, and a dreadful vocabulary. In the course of their cross-country trip her passion for comics, soda, chewing gum, and other Americana will prove to be the only means Humbert has to keep her. When, after he has had intercourse with her, Humbert tells Lolita that her mother is dead, his consoling gesture to her is an orgy of trinkets and gadgets. Critics have noted that the ritual of bribe and banter between Humbert and Lolita is in essence an extreme parody of the normal American man's materialistic and emotional collusion with his child. Nabokov objected violently to readings of this sort, but the objective reader can hardly deny that such a satirical element figures in the novel. If not "extreme parody," one might at least say that there is much persiflage in *Lolita*. Nabokov was quite lucky that his theme was held back by historical circumstance for so long, for in dealing with the relations between some fathers and daughters in America he had put his finger on a vital but until-then quiescent corner of American life.

There was, let it be said, more than a little sophistry in the way in which Nabokov pressed the case for *Lolita* as a work of pure art. It was that, but he also knew perfectly well what he was doing in presenting such a theme. Girodias of Olympia reported that Nabokov explicitly said that he would be deeply hurt if *Lolita* were to obtain a *succès de scandal*. Girodias, who was eventually hounded out of France by the de Gaulle government, had serious difficulties with the censors over *Lolita* (as well as many of his other titles such as *White Thighs* and *The Sexual Life of Robinson Crusoe*) and published a book of assorted documents, letters, and materials relating to the general topic of censorship under the title *L'Affaire Lolita*.

After the fact, Girodias wrote: "I sensed that *Lolita* would become the one great modern work of art to demonstrate once and for all the futility of modern censorship, and the indispensable role of passion in literature." But in spite of this high value placed on the novel, *Lolita* was not treated any differently from the steady run of Olympia titles, and in the first year of its publication it sold poorly and received no reviews. The book's reputation spread slowly by word of mouth. Nabokov and Girodias quarreled, naturally, and they each wrote about it in *The Evergreen Review*, Girodias in September 1965, Nabokov in February 1967. There was one clear misunderstanding between them: Nabokov had no interest whatsoever in using his novel to lead a crusade against censorship, and he was quite relieved when the U.S. Customs Bureau made the decision to release confiscated copies of *Lolita* to their owners, which meant in effect that the book was free to be published in America with no danger to author or publisher.

Much has been written about Humbert's nympholepsy as a kind of perverted idealism. Denis de Rougemont attempted to see a Tristan and Isolde pattern in the novel but had finally to admit that Lolita is no Isolde, and that the novel is, at best, a *"Tristan manqué."* Humbert himself constantly exercises his scholarly skills in what purport to be historical asides, but many of the comparisons he makes are not really applicable—Beatrice was eight when Dante saw her, but he himself was nine—and many that are applicable, such as Swinburne and Baudelaire (both writers whose work Nabokov knew very well) and Dowson, are not mentioned.

Lolita is basically neither the elaboration of a specific literary myth nor of a Freudian myth. But the story does proceed *on its own terms* over paths that Freud had also followed. Nabokov's technique is to attempt to, quite literally, by ridicule exclude the possibility of a Freudian reading. It is particularly important in this regard that in the second half of the novel the fairy-tale aspect challenges and at time overpowers the novel's realistic base. The play of myth is a powerful countervailing force preventing the novel from falling into the category of case history.

All the same, one cannot understand the novel at more than a surface level unless one grasps that Humbert's perversity is very close to homosexuality, though Humbert is not homosexual—his doubles assume that role for him. At one point early in the novel Humbert tells the reader about one of several occasions on which he lapsed into insanity and spent some time in a sanatorium. He bribes a nurse to gain access to his file where he gleefully discovers that he has been labeled potentially homosexual. Humbert boasts that he amuses himself by leading on the psychiatrists without letting on to them that he knows all their tricks.

Humbert claims that the basic appeal of a nymphet is the perilous indefiniteness of her form. He sees a third sex in nymphets. The nymphet is a female caught at that moment in her life, between nine and fourteen, when her sexual development has begun but she in many ways resembles a young boy much more than a mature woman. The true nymphet, moreover, can't be picked from a group of girls by any such simple outward sign as mere prettiness, and Lolita's tomboyish personality and manner of dress lead one to suspect that *this* is the true criterion by which nymphets are determined. Since the nymphet herself is a form of sexual displacement for Humbert, there is no difficulty in doubling the displacement: "What I had madly possessed was not she, but my own creation, another, fanciful Lolita . . ." There are many statements hinting at or clearly suggesting masturbation in the novel's first half.

In his dreams Humbert sees his two wives, Valeria and Charlotte, crossing and combining into one ghostlike creature who settles on a narrow board (in Nabokov's Russian translation, it is made more specific: a gynecological table) with legs apart, revealing something like "the rubber valve of a soccer ball's bladder." Humbert is not a man who loves women, and often he is quite impotent with them. To have intercourse with Charlotte, Humbert must try to imagine traces of Lolita in her figure. Humbert's abandoned urge to drown Charlotte while they are swimming in a local lake expresses a desire for free access to Lolita, but Humbert's wish also reaches much further than that, to the destruction of all mature women. He has done horrible things to Valeria, is spared by fate from actually murdering Charlotte, and, when he is called into the Beardsley School for a conference with Miss Pratt, who is concerned about Dolly's morbid *dis*interest in sexual matters and thinks that she is still in between anal and genital development, the thought flashes through his mind that he should marry Miss Pratt and strangle her.

One mature woman is an exception for Humbert. She is the second most important female character in the novel, the drunken divorcée Rita whom Humbert picks up in a bar shortly after Lolita disappears and who only occupies six pages in the novel. But those few pages span a period of time exactly matching the time—two years—that he lived with Lolita, and it is with Rita that his love for Lolita moves beyond perversion and the "second" Humbert moves downstage at last in the novel. Rita is smallish, but Humbert does not say that she has any of the essential attributes of a nymphet. The key to her success with Humbert is to make absolutely no demands of him. It is precisely compassion rather than passion that Humbert requires, and Rita, who is herself an outcast, is able to give him everything freely: companionship, sex that keeps him out of mischief, sympathy, and approval of his intention to find and kill the man who has stolen his Lolita. She even leaves him as painlessly and naturally as she first joined him, and Humbert addresses his warmest words to her.

Once Rita and Humbert awaken to find a strange amnesiac

man sleeping with them. He is taken to a hospital, yet another
sign that Humbert has finally been able to discard his past, and it
initiates a chain of actions that will take him back to The Enchanted Hunters, where he first stayed with Lolita, and set the
stage for another journey, which will involve his final meeting
with Lolita and his revenge upon his grotesque past. Humbert
has been a voyeur, observing himself, and at the same time being
watched and followed by others. Sex is "that leaping epilepsy."

Dissociation in *Lolita* is essential to understand the role and
place of the mysterious Clare Quilty. Quilty is Humbert's perverse *alter ego*, and his dark standard is perversion of an extreme
kind that demonstrates where Humbert's own perversion will finally lead. It is when Quilty and Humbert track each other in
turn that the realistic pretense of the novel is dropped, and *Lolita*
becomes either a madman's fantasy or an artist's surrealistic rendering of a deadly, sexual chess match. The reader who pays
careful attention to Quilty's appearances must, in the end, question the entire realistic basis of the story. Humbert does win the
seemingly impossible struggle by transforming the symbol of his
perverse passion into an object of actual love. To cross this bridge
Humbert must lose his old self and his nymphet, for, as has happened with so many Nabokovian heroes before him, Humbert's
love for Lolita can only be realized in her absence, in the pain and
purity of memory and of art.

Such a discussion of *Lolita*'s underlying sexuality should in itself bring to mind the true literary forerunner and partial model
for Nabokov's masterpiece: Proust. An excellent long article by
Octavio Mello Alvarenga, after twenty-five years still one of the
best pieces written on *Lolita*, compares Nabokov's narrative patterns with Proust's. Entitled *"Proust e Nabokov: Aproximaços,"*
it appeared in the Brazilian journal *Revista do Livro* in June
1960.

The similarity between the two works that Alvarenga calls attention to is, of course, that between the pairs Lolita and Humbert and Albertine and Marcel. Both Lolita and Albertine are
held prisoners, and both attempt to run away from their captors.
Humbert does not at first question Lolita's purity, but when she
becomes his paramour, her kisses make him suspect her of lesbianism, just as Marcel comes similarly to suspect Albertine. Both
Marcel and Humbert are seduced, and both are subject to fits of

intense jealousy. They each enjoy considerable financial power over their lovers, in spite of which each is deceived behind his back. After Albertine dies her lesbianism is confirmed: in their last meeting Lolita tells Humbert that she really loves not him or her husband Dick but the perverse Quilty. As Lolita had a predecessor in the Annabelle of Humbert's youth, Albertine, too, had one in Gilberte. Both *Remembrance of Things Past* and *Lolita* are told in the first person, and memory is the primary motive force in each. The clear intent behind all or most of these parallels is attested to, as Alvarenga points out, by Humbert's passing remark that his story could be called *Dolores Disparue. Albertine Disparue* was the title Proust used for two volumes of his masterpiece.

There are differences as well. Proust's novel proceeds at a deliberately and beautifully slow pace, the aim of which is poetic contemplation, whereas *Lolita* is a whirlpool of journeys and chases. The most important difference of all, which Alvarenga doesn't note, is the vast one in narrative forthrightness between the two works. To write about homosexuality, Proust adopts what Stanley Edgar Hyman has so aptly dubbed "the Albertine strategy." In place of Albertine we must always read Albert, for *Remembrance of Things Past* is, among other things, a covert glorification of homosexual love. Proust suffers to a degree from the coyness and archness that must necessarily accompany such an artistic approach. *Lolita*, though it is not without archness and has extremely complex narrative patterns, is an overt novel: Lolita is a girl-child, and Humbert Humbert is driven by a very heterosexual, if perverse, desire to possess her. Of course the *real* stakes in the novel are quite another question, but this remains secondary to the main action, which should be and has been taken to be the tragic story of a man's passion and love for a nymphet. The greatness of Nabokov's novel lies primarily in the extraordinary fullness and subtlety with which the subconscious and the conscious, the realistic and the fantastic play themselves out in perfect parodic harmony. Incest is parodied. Society is parodied. Literature is parodied. Sex is parodied. Women come off badly, homosexuals don't do too well either, and Humbert can hardly win one's sympathy because of the relentlessness of his self-serving argument. For Humbert what happens in his mind is precious. Flesh always fails him. Yet, more than in anything he wrote before or after, Nabokov succeeds in having it six ways at once. That is because of the genuine passion with which the novel is written, Nabokov's and Humbert's.

The murder of Quilty (Kilt in the French translation) is a ghoulishly comic dream, and not a murder so much as a partial suicide or an auto-assassination. When Humbert enters Quilty's castle, he is wearing a black suit and a black shirt, the color of the enemy forces. As he first enters and looks around, Humbert sees a number of used drink glasses, the only clue, undecipherable, when the amnesiac man made his appearance in Rita's bed. Quilty is wearing a purple dressing gown, which is, Humbert tells us, "very like one I had." As they spar verbally, Quilty makes every possible effort to confuse the question of both his own and Humbert's true identity. When they wrestle for the gun, they momentarily blend into one rolling person. Before he kills Quilty, who confesses that, like Humbert, he, too, is nearly impotent, Humbert declares himself innocent. Clare Quilty, with his "strange feminine manner," is at last brought to beg for his life, but, since he has no life apart from Humbert, the question of "life and death" is only a convention that Humbert observes with himself. As is appropriate to the farce they are enacting, Quilty greets every shot with mimicry, a fake accent, a joke. He suffers only as Punch suffers (Humbert has called him that), and he bleeds the blood of Alexander Blok's Pierrot, cranberry juice.

But Quilty has another important role in the novel. While Humbert is being seduced by Lolita in The Enchanted Hunters, Clare Quilty is there, too, writing his *The Enchanted Hunters* in which Lolita will play and meet the playwright. *The Enchanted Hunters* is *Lolita*, and in it the Poet points out to the other characters that they are all creatures of his imagination, and that the message of his play is that in love imagination and reality must merge. It is the premise and the message of *The Waltz Invention*, and of many other Nabokov works.

The brief incident of Quilty's play defines the novel and shows how it is in perfect concord with Vladislav Khodasevich's basic formulation about Nabokov's art. One would have thought that a stranger allegory of the artistic process than the murder in *Despair* could not be found, and yet lust and child molestation as a tale representing the tragic pain and entrancing beauty of art and the tremendous price it exacts are just that. If we choose to read

Quilty's play as a precise critical reflection, then all of *Lolita* becomes as fantastic a world as that of *Invitation to a Beheading*. The fatal hotel room at The Enchanted Hunters is a panoply of mirrored surfaces whose many reflections seem to take away the reality of the room that is held within them. But that reality, above all the superbly living portrait of Lolita, is not really taken away. Lolita eludes Humbert's grasp in art as she does in life (not really, she lives only because of his "fancy prose style"!), and the novel is hers just as much as *Anna Karenina* belongs—though Nabokov didn't think so—essentially to Anna. *Lolita* is mirrored, like all of Nabokov's art, but it can claim preeminence over all his other novels (and that was his own judgment, too), because its central reality remains ever firm and vibrant, even while its diabolically artful reflections play around it. It is curious, however, that Russia is not one of those mirror reflections in *Lolita*.

21

PALE FIRE WAS WRITTEN WHOLLY IN SWITZERLAND, BUT ITS evolution is located mainly in Ithaca. The conception of the novel, moreover, may be fixed quite precisely not only in his unfinished Russian novel *Solus Rex*, but also in a small newspaper item in Miliukov's *Latest News* that appeared on July 30, 1939 (page 3):

> *The Daily Telegraph* recalls that, in the first days, after the creation of The League of Nations, each nation had a right to five places for its delegates. Those who were not officially in a delegation could sit on side chairs from which one could neither see nor hear.
>
> A member of the Italian delegation . . . decided to use the free places for his compatriots who were seated behind the Venezuelan delegation. He made his way into the hall of delegates late at night and wrote on one of the display cards used to indicate a country: *Zemblya*.
>
> The next day the experts glanced at the card and solemnly nodded their heads: Zemblya. Thus, throughout the session five delegates of "the Republic of Zemblya" occupied their places, and it never entered their heads that such a republic didn't exist, and that its representatives were pure-blooded Italians.

The news filler was titled "The Republic of Zemblya." Of course this seed fell on an imagination, for hadn't Nabokov himself already invented Zoorlandia? "The Republic of Zemblya" is one of the best demonstrations of how Nabokov, like Joyce, actively used the daily press for artistic inspiration.

It is a commonplace to say that the form of the novel parodies Nabokov's own work in writing his Commentary on *Eugene Onegin*. So it doubtless does. Nabokov worked for nearly a decade on his Commentary, and it would have been surprising if the use of footnote for fictive purposes had not suggested itself to his fertile imagination. But that observation by itself is as useless as it is self-evident in plumbing the origins and workings of the novel.

The notion of fiction that is not only a world unto itself but one that also contains wholly separate worlds within itself—in other words, fiction as a solar system—was, as we have seen, first tried by Nabokov in *Solus Rex*. In addition to the two parts that finally did appear in print, there was a third chapter, equally disconnected and concerned with games, which Nabokov said that he destroyed. The specific paradigm of a scholarly commentary by someone who is very serious and (probably) at the same time slightly loopy was suggested to Nabokov by a playful piece written by his friend Morris Bishop. Given its subject matter, it is likely that it was written specifically for Nabokov. Titled "A Note on an Old Lewis Carroll Ms. (Not for Publication)," the poem purports to have been copied out at high speed from a heretofore unknown manuscript. This original "uncorrupted" text is not written in Jabberwocky but "Jakobsony." It is explained that Jabberwock—a nice dig at the Jakobson method of commentary—is merely a verbal corruption that has occurred through metathesis. The incomprehensible lines have accompanying footnotes that explain that certain words, for example, are "loan words from Old Bulgarian." Bishop dates his poem and commentary Barclay, Allophonia, September 31, 1958.

Cornell also furnished an important prototype for Charles Kinbote. The Nabokovs occasionally had lodgers in their Cornell residences. Only two were at all notable: The "honeymooners," as the Nabokovs called them, because of their nuptial noises, and an instructor from the French department who moved in with them in the beginning of 1951 and left at the end of January. The only information about him comes from Nabokov's diary, which means that it can only be accepted obliquely because of the way he mingles the fictional and the factual in his notes to himself. The entry for January 30, for example, has "Atman" (a fictitious name blending adman and the Sanskrit for universal self) dead in his room. When I asked Nabokov about that, he said that that simply meant that X——— had moved out. He complained that

Nabokov was observing him and using him, and Nabokov did confess to his diary that he had expected much from his colleague and lodger.

Nabokov described "Atman" as being bald with fuzz on his head and as having bulging eyes and a mottled complexion. On his second day the lodger asked if he could keep some fruit in the refrigerator. Nabokov said no. He thought that Atman spoke good French but not French French. By the second week Nabokov had begun to chat with him and began to realize his oddities. He complained about the floral pattern on the quilted bed cover with which they supplied him. The red of the roses had been printed out of alignment so that the color lopped over on one side and left a blank on the other. He said that it produced the impression on him of little worlds that had fallen out of orbit. He also was irritated by the way coats were piled on the beds when guests arrived for parties in Ithaca. He said it was symbolically rather like the way savages offer their wives to guests as a sign of hospitality. He and Nabokov had a good time discussing the vulgarity of American zipper and underwear ads.

During the third week of "Atman's" tenancy, Nabokov went up to Atman's room, thinking he was out, to leave a magazine that he wanted Atman to read for him. Atman was there wearing pajamas and a sleeveless pullover pulled up to his waist with his legs through the armholes. The day after that Atman, while he and Nabokov were discussing Joyce, said, "We think not in words but in the shadow of words." The next day Nabokov startled himself by repeating Atman's phrase during his Friday lecture. It had no connection at all with what he was talking about, and, more than that, he said it in French. At home he suddenly felt a powerful urge to rush out of the house. He walked to the corner where he picked up a coin and then returned home. Nabokov either feared or pretended to fear in his diary that Atman might be hypnotizing him. Bishop told Nabokov that there were rumors circulating about Atman. Eventually Atman got into considerable difficulty when he took, too quickly, a psychiatrist's advice that he needed direct experience with women and made a plainspoken sexual proposal to a librarian whom he scarcely knew. One of the rumors about Atman was that he was a convert to Catholicism who had been expelled from a Carmelite monastery. Those who knew him on campus thought that he was mad, and he was, in fact, eventually institutionalized.

At about the same time Nabokov read a newspaper story about a student who had taken potassium cyanide after an examination at Northwestern University. In the final question of his exam the student had written in French that he was going to God because life did not have much to offer him. Nabokov planned to combine the student with Atman. What the student wrote would have to be changed, and there would have to be some pathetic grammatical error in the declaration as well. Then he (or Atman) would be the lecturer, who had taken some blue books with him to read on the train.

Suicide is an element in both the poet Shade's "Pale Fire" and Kinbote's Commentary to it. Kinbote struggles with an impulse to commit suicide, and Shade's daughter Hazel does. Shade's own death is planned for that matter, since the death provides the necessary conclusion and—a conscious device—circles back to the beginning of the poem. In one of his notes Kinbote remarks that Hazel Shade is like him in some respects. Kinbote's last words are addressed to the question of his own suicide, and a strange thing happens. His voice changes, and just for a moment he speaks to us in the mocking tone of Clare Quilty.

In *Pale Fire* we must read a poem and a madman. The most cogent argument for the essential unity of poem with commentary are the rejected draft portions of Shade's poem, which Kinbote cites and which, if they are in fact Shade's, would prove—in direct contradiction to the poem itself—that the old poet was indeed originally on the verge of writing a poem about the country of Zembla. In Shade's discarded variants for lines 70 and 130 there is a goodly portion of Kinbote's story as he himself tells it. It is conceivable that John Shade might have used the fantasies of his boring and intrusive neighbor in a poem, but there is no logical reason to suppose that such themes could have an integral place in *this* poem. There must be more than just a suspicion that one of the two voices belongs, in ventriloquial fashion, to the other. Is it Kinbote speaking in the voice of Shade, or Shade speaking in his natural, craggy poet's voice as well as in the projected voice of a character he has created? The primary author—even without Nabokov's acknowledgment that Kinbote really does not know what is going on in Shade's poem—must be John Shade.

In all, considerably less than a quarter of what Kinbote writes is even ostensibly concerned, much less actually connected, with the Shade poem. Shade, a poet, could create a madman. A madman such as Kinbote could not possibly create a glacially serene poem such as "Pale Fire." What Kinbote writes falls into two categories: his conversations with Shade, and his account of his miraculous escape from Zembla and the subsequent hunt for him by the Extremist assassin Jakob Gradus. Both of these lines of the Commentary are to a great extent concerned with death, which is the unifying bond between the poem and the Commentary—in a word, the subject of *Pale Fire.*

Shade's poem, published seventeen years later in 1962, is not as imposing a work as "An Evening of Russian Poetry," but it is an important poem by Vladimir Nabokov that deserves consideration by itself. It has not usually been given this consideration, for several reasons, chief among them the poem's clear proximity to the poetics of Wordsworth. John Shade, like Wordsworth in "The Prelude," is trying to track the development of his own mind. But Wordsworth, with a touch of Robert Frost thrown in, was a disconcertingly out-of-phase poetic voice for the 1960s. Critics were bored by it, thought the poem stodgy. It is a serious imitation, and, if one wishes to dismiss it, then perhaps one should dismiss Wordsworth as well. One qualification may be made—the poem does need to be read aloud in Nabokov's manner (it can be heard on a Spoken Arts recording) in order to come alive. The pairing of the old-fashioned poem and the manic Commentary reflect perfectly the two voices of Nabokov, the poet and the writer. His two basic styles are indeed that far apart.

A comment should be made here about Nabokov's reply to critics who saw Robert Frost in the figure of Shade that he only knew one short poem by Frost. Nabokov did meet Frost. Moreover, the apartment that Nabokov rented in Cambridge in 1952 belonged to Frost. A Wellesley friend who knew Frost suggested that Nabokov would be a good person to rent his house while Frost was in Florida. But the apartment was stone cold—the Nabokovs called it the Jack Frost house—and they moved out after only three days and stayed in a hotel until another house was found. Seven years earlier Nabokov had second billing in a poetry reading he gave with Frost at Filene's department store in Boston. Nabokov was displeased that his "Evening of Russian Poetry" did not enjoy much favor with the audience in comparison with Frost's poems. It is thus rather inconceivable that Nabokov did not know Frost's poetry. The disclaimer has to be taken in the same spirit as his claim to be little acquainted with the work of Nikolai Evreinov.

However Wordsworthian or Frostian its tone, the poem is, in another way, nothing if not "contemporary American" to the core. If one is interested in such things as Nabokov's attitude toward ordinary middle-class American life, it is here, rather than to *Lolita*, that one should turn. Shade's poem turns and shifts its focus to provide a collage of the essential, and quite ordinary, coordinates in the poet's life. He tells of his childhood, in which he was reared by an aunt after the death of his parents, his high-school courtship of his future wife Sybil, their everyday life together, his process of creativity and his literary career. The one dramatic event, Hazel's suicide, is rendered in a very low-key way. The idea of giving John Shade a daughter probably resulted from a reunion Nabokov had in France with his Tenishev school-mate Shmurlo shortly before he began work on *Pale Fire*. Shmurlo had spent his life in Africa, and when Nabokov saw him he was quite sick and had been drinking heavily to reduce the pain. Vera Evseevna was annoyed and bored with the visit, but Nabokov was glad to see his old friend and interested to hear the many African stories he had to tell. As it happened, Nabokov's sister Elena (she now calls herself Helene) was with them. Shmurlo in his slight haze insisted on taking her for Vladimir's daughter.

Its 999-line length makes "Pale Fire" Nabokov's longest poem, though "A University Poem,"at 882 lines, is nearly as long. He wrote the Shade poem while on vacation in Nice, taking long walks in the hills or walking along the Promenade des Anglais. He thought it the most difficult thing he had ever composed. (Kinbote's Commentary was written over a longer span of time, largely under a particular tree in the garden of the Montreux Palace Hotel.) The poem "Pale Fire" is stubbornly matter-of-fact in the suburbanity of its surface subject matter. When John and Sybil are at the senior-class outing together she offers him "a thimbleful of bright metallic tea," which is to say, a thermos cup. Shade's passionate love for Sybil is seen, as though by a third party, against the pattern of typical American teenage romance. The mature poet asks his wife how she could have let him slobber all over her in a car parked in a lover's lane when they were young. Their forty-year marriage is measured against the suc-

VN

cession of free kitchen calendars, and the signs of his mature love for Sybil are tied to the necessary business of life in middle-class America such as packing for a car trip. The most important piece of Americana, however, both in itself and in the way it is used, is the television set. Shade and Sybil sit watching it while waiting for Hazel to come home from the blind date from which she will never return. Sybil plays Russian roulette with the dial, and as the set is finally switched off, the little light in the center of the screen fades, and, we gather from the next lines, Hazel's suicide occurs.

Hazel's ungainly appearance and her morose, hypersensitive character do not require analogy with other literary characters, but there is perhaps a loose tie between Hazel's suicide on the thin ice of a neighboring lake and the (accidental) death of Lucy Gray in Wordsworth's poem. The poetic presence of Wordsworth in "Pale Fire" is necessary and useful to keep in mind, even though the emotional tone of most of Wordsworth's poetry is not that of "Pale Fire." But some of the reproaches leveled at Wordsworth for introducing "common" elements into serious poetry, for example, parallel criticisms of "Pale Fire" for departing from the canon of high modernism.

Hazel has a strange interest in the supernatural, and once she spent several nights investigating sounds in a barn. Her strangeness has its projection in past time in old Aunt Maude (rhymes with God) who died at eighty. Her death was a painfully protracted guttering out, and Hazel in her childhood mutters in monotone. Maude's death causes Shade to speculate skeptically on the standard notions of death and afterlife. He disputes the precise boundary between life and death for Aunt Maude, and later he muses cynically on the inevitable complications of immortality: the widower who has remarried and must deal with both jealous wives throughout eternity. Canto 3 touches upon spiritualism, and in that same section Shade dies and comes to life again. It is a stroke, which he suffers when a querulous man in the audience which he is addressing stands up and points his pipe at him as he asks his question. (The biographical element of this moment scarcely requires explanation.) Life is a ludicrous show staged in a "most artistic cage," but that very fact presents the possibility of a kind of immortality in art.

Shade's parents died when he was still an infant. Because of the efforts he has made over the years to evoke them from certain chance words and attributes he has retained, he now feels that he possesses images of a thousand possible parents. In the initial portion of his poem the poet plays with reflected realities. His room is hung above the grass or snow—a common optical illusion at night—and he boasts of his Wordsworthian ability to take photographs with his eyes. The equality of illusion and reality for Shade is shown by his remarks (line 41–48) on a view of the lake that could just be made out from the house, but which can no longer be seen because something has caused a furrow in space. Similar notions of space and time are present, of course, in "An Evening of Russian Poetry" and *Speak, Memory*.

Hazel Shade continues to live, flying on like the waxwing in a reflected sky. The entire poem pulls toward this sense of permanence. In the concluding Canto Shade writes that a man's life furnishes the commentary to an unfinished poem. The fact that the first line of "Pale Fire" supplies the necessary thousandth line to complete the poem strongly suggests that the poet's end is a conscious one. That circularity symbolizes the ability to circumvent time itself. We have already seen Nabokov use it in *The Gift*. Shade ends with a note of promised continuation, just as V. D. Nabokov once did in the article that appeared only after his murder. Shade knows that it requires his death to complete the poem.

Wordsworth's masterpiece, "The Prelude," is an autobiographical poem, and one of its central concerns is conveying an essential metaphysical secret that Wordsworth felt he had discovered. The role of nature in "The Prelude" is very much akin to that of art in "Pale Fire," and, what is most important, "The Prelude" was a posthumously published poem, since Wordsworth felt that it might somehow still be incomplete and never could make the decision to submit it to print. This point is far more important than formal, metrical similarities with Wordsworth's verse in understanding what "Pale Fire" is about.

John Shade shares many views with Nabokov, though I know of nothing else to suggest that it is profitable to seek autobiographical parallels. The question that needs to be put is whether there are any meaningful links between Shade and Kinbote. There is really only one possibility of a connection, and it is not conclusive. Shade had a fit of madness or a stroke when he was only eleven (lines 140–156), and at the beginning of Canto 2 he refers to his "demented youth," when he felt that his ignorance of death was the result of a great conspiracy of all other people to keep the truth from him. Lastly, he ponders whether his stroke after the lecture might not have been "one of my old fits." That is all, but this information may be used as one of the essential determinants to establish a relationship between "Pale Fire" the poem and the novel *Pale Fire*, of which the poem is but a part.

Kinbote is quite as sure as Shade that he will continue to exist. He tells us that the assassin Gradus who kills Shade by mistake is a member of a Zemblan regicidal organization, and also that "grados" is the Zemblan word for tree. Thus, Shade has been felled by a tree. Kinbote doesn't realize that he has nothing to fear from Gradus because he is already on the other side of the false azure in the windowpane. His death lies in the past, in Zembla, which is now only a land of semblances. That Shade is the intended victim is made evident by the perfect synchronization of Gradus's advance on him. Gradus sets out on the very day that Shade begins his poem and arrives just in time to complete it for him by murder.

Using the image of the window with which the poem opens, this is what happens in the novel: Shade peers at himself (that is, he writes a self-reflective poem) in the reflection of the windowpane through which he dimly and intermittently sees Kinbote who lurks after him. Kinbote, for his part, sees Shade through the same windowpane but mainly sees the fabulous and deadly kingdom of Zembla, which is reflected from behind. In creating Kinbote as the reflection that flies on after his (artistic) death Shade more than substantiates his own speculation that, though life is a great surprise, death could be an even greater one.

The complex relationship of the disparate sections of *Pale Fire* may be seen more sharply by examination of the major episode of the second portion of *Solus Rex*. After he has completed his work on the no longer necessary illustrations to *Ultima Thule* (supplementary troops for the Zemblan army, by the way, come from Thule) the artist Sineusov turns to the only other expedient he now sees open to him to go beyond his grief for his wife who has just died. It happens that the artist has an old casual acquaintance about whom he hears a remarkable story very shortly after his wife's death. This man, Falter, whom Sineusov remembers as an essentially ordinary and even slightly vulgar man, suffers a fit one night in the little hotel where he is staying. Falter's screams are so unnatural that they seem like a woman with a man's voice in labor and about to give birth to a giant. When Falter finally comes out of his room, he refuses to make any comment about what happened to him. He merely steps out of his room, urinates profusely down the stairs, and then returns to his room and goes to sleep.

From that time on Falter is a more or less quiescent madman. The way that the madness began, however, draws the interest of an Italian psychiatrist who happened to have been visiting someone at Falter's hotel. This is the ur-Freudian psychiatrist who believes that all mental illnesses may be explained by the misfortunes of one's distant ancestors. But the psychiatrist drops dead from surprise when Falter explains the mystery of life to him.

Falter's story is promptly taken up by the press, and that is how it finally comes to the attention of Sineusov, who, because he happens to know Falter and thus can believe that what he says may not be the usual fakery, plans to see if he can scientifically or logically verify the madman's experience. This attempt in Nabokov's unfinished Russian novel is quite like John Shade's three-hundred-mile drive to talk to Mrs. Z in order to verify his own mystical experience. The conversations that Sineusov has with Falter are strikingly similar to the theological and philosophic exchanges of Shade and Kinbote. In *Pale Fire*, nearly a quarter of a century later, Nabokov combined with heightened skill and precision the three narrative threads in *Solus Rex:* the mysterious kingdom, the artist's quest for "ultimate truth," and the madman in art in whom that truth resides. Both works have as their fundamental conception the depiction of wholly separate narrative worlds in whose precise conjunction, as in astrology, fate is played out. That interaction is the chief reason why Kinbote's Commentary should not be considered something that has been "glued on," even though on the most obvious level, of course, it has. Just as the noises that Hazel heard in the barn were, in Kinbote's judgment, "an outward extension or expulsion of insanity," the figure of Kinbote himself is simply that same outward extension of insanity in relation to John Shade.

In *Solus Rex* Sineusov has little luck with Falter. They have a long intellectual sparring session in which Falter talks freely enough but refuses to allow himself to go to the "Italian precipice" again, because he doesn't want to have more difficulties with the authorities. He merely leads Sineusov on and then stops, stating that he has found the key to all knowledge but has no reason to use it. During their long discourse Falter turns away questions such as whether or not God exists by answering "cold," as though he were playing Twenty Questions, and sometimes he wanders into highly complex and impenetrable statements. One must be struck (and instructed) by the way in which both Sineusov and the madman Falter make statements like those Shade makes in his poem. The statements are usually connected with an evasion of mortality and terror at the prospect of the loss of memory.

When Sineusov, still trying to prod Falter into some sort of meaningful statement, compares life to a confused foreword with the main text still to come, Falter tells him: "Skip the foreword, and you've got it!" The statement means nothing to Sineusov, but it has great meaning for a reader of *Pale Fire* and is a major point in pursuing the argument that there *is* a connection between poem and commentary, at least in terms of authorial intent. Kinbote promises Shade that, as soon as he has joined the glory of Zembla with his verse, he will reveal an "ultimate truth" to him. In the end Falter's remarks strike Sineusov as being as deft as those of any streetcorner sophist, but Falter says that, all the same, he has let slip "a little corner of the truth" in the course of his nonsense. The repetition of a few stray words by the mysterious foreign poet, which have also been said in jest by Sineusov's dying wife, show that the poem in a strange language is evidently the map Sineusov requires to chart and unravel his own life. The twin metaphors text/commentary and image/reflection serve as a means by which the cliché of the writer as creator is put in upper-case print and, in its reflection, of course, also inverted. The Writer as Creator. The Creator as Writer. The metaphysics of Narcissus.

There is one other important world in "Pale Fire," and it is as inaccessible to the reader as it is to Kinbote, though Kinbote points the way to it in one of his footnotes. That is the relation between Shade and his wife which is presented as sacrosanct and hermetic. One of the most interesting of the "second generation"

of Nabokov critics, David Rampton, describes (in his 1984 critical study of Nabokov) Sybil's identification with a red admiral
butterfly in Shade's poem as "a hovering emblem of the love between husband and wife" and then properly points out, "Like the
moth associated with Krug's wife at the end of *Bend Sinister*, its
last appearance marks not just the end of a story and the end of a
life, but also the promise of something ephemeral that endures. In
these ways then their relationship is quietly and movingly presented for our approval, but if it is the key to the entire work
there is surprisingly little of it."

Kinbote's Zembla—apart from what *he* thinks it is—is also a
mapping of man's subconscious. Nabokov's work, and *Pale Fire*
above all, is proof that the subconscious does not only exist in
Freud's version of it. In Nabokov's representation of the subconscious there is not necessarily any connection between the real
self and the inversion by reflection. In another context, Nabokov,
in one of his interviews, says that his queer and nasty characters
have nothing to do with him but are like gargoyles that have been
put out of the church. Thus, Kinbote's Zembla is a homosexual
fantasy, but it has no connection with the John Shade we know
from the poem.

The sexuality of Zembla does not signify only itself. It is a poetic coefficient of death, which comes when the surface of the
mirror is broken. As Kinbote crosses the mountains to escape
from Zembla, he recites to himself, in both German and Zemblan, the opening lines of Goethe's poem "The Erl-King," in
which a sinister fairy king or wood spirit continually beckons to a
terrified child riding in his father's arms on horseback. The poem
combines perfectly the images of perversion and death. It is a
strange poem to be reciting as one goes into exile. Kinbote either
does not notice or does not say that in the last line of Goethe's
poem the child lies dead in his father's arms. Perhaps Kinbote is
reaching out to make Shade the child in his arms. Certainly Lisa's
son Victor, who has a fantasy that is not unlike this one in chapter
4 of *Pnin*, and his imaginary father, the king who has refused to
abdicate after the revolution, look rather alike, and it appears that
it is the son who is, through a cheerful American, about to rescue
the father.

The political spectrum of Zemblan life is divided into shades of
sexuality, and a man is a "Zemblan patriot" in Kinbote's index

only when he is a homosexual. There are some exceptions, most
notably the "heterosexual man of fashion and Zemblan patriot,"
Count Otar, whose patriotism seems to consist of having taken
little Fleur, Kinbote's bride, as his teenage mistress. Fleur is a
girl-boy, and the best thing about her as far as Kinbote is concerned is that she doesn't seem to mind when he abandons her for
"manlier" pursuits. Even so, Charles can only "dislike her less"
than other women, and—one of the typical lines in the novel—
"the sight of her four bare limbs and three mousepits (Zemblan
anatomy) irritated him."

All the Zemblan patriots have doubles who are traitors, and for
this reason *Pale Fire* has almost as many doubles as *Lolita*. Kinbote's page, for example, is himself a patriot, but his cousin,
whose name is an anagram of the page's, is an "experimentalist,
madman, and traitor." It is this page and his cousin who are
named Mandeville, and this refers not only to the eighteenth-century Bernard de Mandeville, but also to another one, Jean de
Mandeville, a fourteenth-century author of a popular book describing his visits to countries where he had never been.

The trick names, anagrams, and little Russian jokes that sprout
like mushrooms throughout *Pale Fire* are in turn useful and
amusing and then dangerous and distracting. If the good reader
"gets" them, they may help provide a satisfactory reading, or
they may lead one quite far astray. The little puzzles and tricks
have their place in the fictional landscape but only after the forest
and its fantastic lakeside distortion have been fully perceived.

Howard Nemerov once noted that Eliot forced poets and other
literate Americans and Englishmen to acquire at least a cursory
knowledge of Italian to read Dante, and, in the same way, Nabokov made many of his most serious readers learn at least some of
his own exotic Zemblan, the Russian language. For the English
reader Gerald Emerald, the teacher of freshman English, cannot
at once be recognized as the Zemblan Izumrudov, the superior officer of Gradus in the Shadows who gives Gradus the death order.
The reader with Russian is alerted at once, because *izumrud* is
emerald in Russian. Kinbote assures the reader that, even though
the name appears to be Russian, it actually derives from the Es-
kimo Umruds. Even this joke takes some Russian to appreciate
fully: in Russian "from the Umruds" would be *iz umrudov*. A
second good instance of the way in which Nabokov makes Rus-

sian necessary to the reader are the names of the three lakes near the campus in one of which Hazel takes her life: Omega, Ozero, and Zero. These are Indian names, Kinbote tells us, which were garbled by the early settlers. In fact, there is only one lake, or *ozero* (the Russian word for lake), which corresponds to the glass between Shade and Kinbote, and hence is neatly set between the other two O-ish obeli (Omega and Zero), which signify the two possibilities after death, nothing and everything—*omega*, the last letter of the Greek alphabet, is a symbol for infinity.

Games and puzzles in Nabokov have been occupying certain readers for more than twenty years now. Of his best-known novels they seem least obtrusive in *Lolita*, somewhat excessive in *Pale Fire* but ultimately acceptable because of the novel's radically revolutionary structure, and finally unbearably irritating in *Ada*. Hoaxes and puzzles must be recognized as essential to Nabokov's artistic manner. In overprofusion or used self-indulgently they signify a certain immature streak in his art, and one is justified in feeling irritated by them. The games are a sure means of keeping critics and academics busily occupied. The Nabokov-deciphering industry is fast gaining on the Joyceans. In *Pale Fire* the most important game is Word Golf. It is played by both Shade and Kinbote. One is allowed to change one letter in a progression from one set word to another in a fixed number of moves. Kinbote gives his best scores as: "hate-love in three, lass-male in four, and live-dead in five (with lend in the middle)." Mary McCarthy solved the first two in her June 1962 essay-review on the novel. I solved the third: live-line-lene-lend-lead-dead. The key was lene, an obscure verb meaning to conceal. Nabokov's Word Golf is actually the game of Doublets and is taken from Lewis Carroll's 1879 book *Doublets—A Word Puzzle.*

The danger in *Pale Fire* is that solutions become interpretations which cannot otherwise be sustained. Is *Pale Fire* about love and hate, men and women, and life and death? But of course, and how pointless. Critics may even be tempted to carry on playing Word Golf on their own. One of the most successful of these game players was R. H. W. Dillard, who took the first word of Kinbote's foreword and the last word of his index, and on the basis of the four words pale-pane-lane-land introduces suitable passages from *Pale Fire* to unlock the novel. Dillard's comments on the novel, however, do not really depend upon such gamesmanship. He knew what he was looking for and got his ball to the right place by putting it in his pocket. One of the things that Nabokov mastered in the second half of his career was the trick of writing the self-generating text, his only "contribution to postmodernist practice." But he really used the device to protect his own meanings. One of the interpretations of *Pale Fire* is that it is a demonstration of the impossibility, indeed the ultimate lunacy of literary criticism. This is one possible partial reading, to be sure, but it is not a notion that Nabokov entertained in regard to anyone's writing but his own.

The name Kinbote is worth explanation. We are told by Kinbote that in Zemblan it means regicide (and so we know that we can discard that possibility), and there is mention in the Commentary of a certain V. Botkin, "American scholar of Russian descent." Kinbote tells us—again, falsely—that the "king-bot" is the "maggot of extinct fly that once bred in mammoths and is thought to have hastened their philogenetic end." In fact, the bot is the larva, often parasitic in sheep and horses, of the bee-sized insect called the botfly, and this progression from internalized embryonic form to an insect buzzing around the "parent" animal is yet another reference to the orbital mechanism that is *Pale Fire*. V. Botkin is the "real" person out of whom Shade fashions Kinbote. The direct anagram of Botkin is *nikto*, the Russian word for nobody, with the same superfluous "b" of Alexander Pope's poetic reference to Zembla, referred to by Nabokov in one of his early Russian poems: "Nova Zembla, poor thing, with that B in her bonnet." B is the Russian letter corresponding to the English V, so VB is an interlingual monogram, and V. Botkin translates neatly as Nabokov & His Invention. The signatory of the official expression of grief on behalf of the Russian community in exile that appeared after the assassination of Nabokov's father by mistake was Botkin. Nabokov, of course, strongly denied all of this.

Above Shade and Kinbote and the poem and its Commentary is Nabokov himself, the sun high above the moon that circles the earth. It is he who imposes his patterns on both Shade and Kinbote. Vladislav Khodasevich was the first to point out that Nabokov really writes only about artists—failed artists, mad artists, even "businessman-artists"—though more often than not in allegorical form. Khodasevich expressed the hope that Nabokov would one day write about a writer as such. Nabokov began to do just that in *The Gift*, where his subject is a major writer in his youth. In *Pale Fire* he treats the mature writer as subject. (The writer at the end of his life is the subject of *Look at the Harlequins!*)

Shade and Sybil show the possibilities of love in *Pale Fire*, while Kinbote and Queen Disa, Duchess of Payn, demonstrate its impossibility. Their love is essentially not that different from the powerful but unconsummated love of Ganin in *Mary*. Insofar as it exists, it exists by means of distance. After the revolution Disa remains faithful and wants Kinbote to live with her, but he feels that he is in danger from the Shadows and leaves her to live in America. As Ganin had two Mashenkas in his mind—one idealized and splendid, the other an ordinary wife of a very vulgar émigré—so Kinbote has two Disas, Disa and para-Disa. It is only the para-Disa of his mind that Kinbote adores, and she is, in a manner of speaking, a homosexual's fantasy. Kinbote's torment and longing is weighted by a past admission to her that he does not love her. It is one of those Nabokov passages in which *commedia dell'arte* stylization and unreality blend perfectly with intense passion. An audience somehow separates him from her, and hands pass him notes telling him that she has married, is inaugurating a fire, has become a character in a novel, has died. The doomed love for Disa of Great Payn and Mone is a gambol, but it is also a moving statement of love accentuated through parodic form.

Frank Kermode has written that Kinbote's homosexuality is "a metaphor for the artist's minority view of a bad world." Though Nabokov faced life with obdurate optimism, the world (as opposed to the Self) shown throughout Nabokov's art does not contradict Kermode's view. Certainly in terms of *Pale Fire*'s comic sexuality (and this novel has the greatest amount of sexuality of any Nabokov work until *Ada*) Nabokov satisfies one of the basic precepts of comedy from the time of Aristophanes: the world turned on its head, tragedy and pain softened, but not lessened, by the presence of the absurd and the ludicrous.

The most notable response to *Pale Fire*'s appearance in 1962 was Mary McCarthy's essay-review that appeared in *The New Republic* in June and then in *Encounter* in October. The novel *was* rather frightening. It needs to be said that many other major critics ran for cover. Not only did Mary McCarthy grasp the net-tle and praise the novel in the highest terms possible, but also she rose to its challenge and accomplished some of the most essential first feats of deciphering. She was the first to get the Pope allusion to Zembla and the Extremist Party (the clue was that John Shade is the author of a book on Pope), the fact that pale fire is a phrase taken from *Timon of Athens* (the full passage confirms the basic constellation that the novel sets), and, in many ways her best find of all because it was the most difficult, the source of Hazel's name in *The Lady of the Lake* ("in lone Glenartney's hazel shade"). Her essay, reprinted in her 1973 collection, *The Writing on the Wall,* is an exemplary instance of critical generosity and will remain alive with the novel as one of the essential commentaries on it. Her overall perception of *Pale Fire* was as precise as it was full of the excitement merited by such a totally different apparition of the novel form:

> *Pale Fire* is a Jack-in-the-box, a Fabergé gem, a clockwork toy, a chess problem, an infernal machine, a trap to catch reviewers, a cat-and-mouse game, a do-it-yourself kit . . . Pretending to be a curio, it cannot disguise the fact that it is one of the very great works of art of this century, the modern novel that everyone thought was dead and that was only playing possum.

Looking back on *Pale Fire* from a vantage point of more than two decades, it is clear that the novel's history of perception is analogous to that of the Eiffel Tower, which, apart from a small band of enthusiasts, met both silent and active resistance at the beginning and only with time acquired acknowledgment of the simplicity, grace, and even necessity that it possessed all along. The novel displays better than any other of his works all the internal structure and theme of Nabokov's art, and it stands with *The Gift* and *Lolita* at the summit of his art, above a "lesser" six or seven novels that would, had he written nothing else, still have assured Nabokov an important place in the history of literature.

22

ONCE MORE: THOUGH *PALE FIRE* WAS WRITTEN IN THE FIRST years of Nabokov's Swiss residence, its main gestation was in America as much as was that of the *Onegin* Commentary, which was only edited in Montreux. Whether it was the momentum of the Cornell period, which had been the most productive in his life, or the stimulus of his long overdue fame, the first years in Switzerland were the golden ones. In addition to his novel and the translation, Nabokov began to work on a massive butterfly book. Although the project took three years of very hard work and in the end was laid aside and finally would have required too much updating to bring to publication, Nabokov remembered the time spent on this stillborn project with great warmth. And there was the duty and pedantic pleasure of correcting the French and German translations not only of *Lolita*, but also of the previously untranslated American and Russian works. The Nabokovs attended as best they could to the languages that they did not know as well. They had particular trouble with Swedish publishers, and some editions were forcibly withdrawn and destroyed. There was extreme difficulty in trying to trace and control pirate Indian and Arabic translations. There were at least five unauthorized translations of *Lolita*. Nabokov, who had never given much of himself to letter writing, now almost stopped writing personal letters, although he still wrote some. His wife conducted a voluminous business correspondence in regard to permissions, translations, and new editions, and she wrote their personal correspondence, too, sometimes with Nabokov dictating a paragraph over her shoulder. Eventually a part-time secretary was hired. Nabokov had become a light industry.

Nabokov had almost no "literary life" in Switzerland (as opposed to editorial dealings), but, when he first arrived, he spent a congenial few days with Alain Robbe-Grillet, who interviewed him for *L'Art*. Nabokov said that Robbe-Grillet's wife, a diminutive actress, dressed like Lolita every day as a joke. Once, when they were dining, a waiter asked her if she would like a Coca-Cola. Robbe-Grillet was the French writer Nabokov most admired.

Nabokov had gone to the Montreux Palace Hotel on the advice of Igor Markevich. The hotel is gigantic and did not in those years have many guests except in the high season. A quiet luxury hotel, it also offered good value for their money, although the Nabokovs did not at first lease quarters. But the hotel suited them very well, and so they made semipermanent arrangements. They had begun to live in a hotel even shortly before they left Cornell. In an age when servants are hard to get there is nothing at all eccentric about people of means and of a certain background and age residing in a hotel. Indeed, it is difficult to imagine an alternative mode of existence that would have been half as suitable for the Nabokovs.

In a Nabokov festival that was held at Cornell in 1983, his former colleague Avgusta Jaryc explained that the Nabokovs had shown that they could live domestically and even entertain, but, she said, the strain of it could always be felt. It was necessary to understand how that generation had been brought up in Russia: "Even the poor people had servants." Many years before, Nabokov had been asked what his greatest desires in life were, and one of his replies was that he wanted to live in a hotel de luxe.

When the Nabokovs first came to the Montreux Palace, Peter Ustinov was living there with his family in the old wing. The Nabokovs moved in on the third floor below the Ustinovs and then moved up to the sixth floor, to a suite of six rooms with a very diminutive salon or living room but with enough spare interior rooms to have a room of records with manuscripts and correspondence and, across the hall, a small library and study. They investigated buying a suite of rooms in the Eurotel across the road when it was being built but didn't. They looked at various houses and apartments in the Montreux region, also without success. They came very close to buying an elegant villa in France, but, as Nabokov was fond of explaining, it had a drawbridge and drawbacks. The Ustinovs moved on to Les Diablerets, half an hour from Montreux, and the Nabokovs followed them to the extent of purchasing a thousand square meters high in the hills. The Ustinovs eventually built a chalet, but the Nabokovs remained at the Montreux Palace. Another celebrity who lived nearby was James Mason. Nabokov had admired the way he played Humbert in the film of *Lolita* and was much amused over the years to watch Humbert aging before his eyes.

When summer and the American tourists arrived, Nabokov would go into voluntary exile. Enthusiastic as he was about America, he could not abide the Americans in Montreux, or so his wife wrote in a letter to a Russian friend. The Nabokovs had a Lancia, but they would often go to some of the less-peopled corners of Switzerland by long-distance taxi or by train to France, Italy, or Portugal. Butterflies were an important consideration in where they went during the summers. Nabokov fancied Iran, Morocco, and Chile as places where he would like to collect, but his wife held him back from such vagaries in much the same way that he held her back from ever acquiring a permanent abode, and with every year it seemed less and less likely or necessary, though there were always plans. The Israeli ambassador visited and asked Nabokov to come to Israel. He agreed but then put off the trip. There had been more or less firm plans to return briefly to the United States in 1972—it would have been only the third visit in twelve years—but then Lerner's *Lolita, My Love* folded in Philadelphia, and there were health problems as well.

Both of Nabokov's trips to America were brief ones. He came to New York for the world premiere of Kubrick's *Lolita*. He dined with Sue Lyon and Shelley Winters and on the evening of the opening passed unidentified from his limousine into the theater through the crowd of fans who were asking each other who that was and hazarding guesses as to his identity. In 1964 Nabokov gave a triumphal evening reading before a full house at University Memorial Hall at Harvard, the same hall where he had lectured in 1952, and he went back to Ithaca to see the Bishops and arrange to have his papers taken out of storage and shipped to Switzerland. The Nabokovs traveled to Ithaca on a long dirty train with a single parlor car at the rear. As Vladimir and Vera emerged from the car, it was obvious to both of the Bishops that the new European phase of their existence suited them very well. Vera seemed a little more regal: "I think she was somewhat reduced by falling into the bourgeois life and a difficult one at that. Now she looked very well and more beautiful than ever." The Bishops greeted their old friends, and then Nabokov raised his hands and clapped smartly for a porter. They were perhaps hundreds of miles from the nearest porter. It was clear that Nabokov, though politically an American patriot, had in terms of his life reverted wholly to being a European.

In the beginning Switzerland had seemed a particularly good place to be because their son was studying singing in Milan, and Nabokov and his wife each had sisters who came to live in Geneva. Nabokov reckoned that Montreux is on the way for American publishers traveling to and from other places in Europe, and, of course, also a convenient location to meet one's English, German, and Italian publishers from time to time. Later, Dmitri's singing career often kept him in New York for months and traveling around Europe much of the rest of the time. Nabokov's sister went to live in a modern condominium on the far outskirts of Geneva, and whether for reasons of health or location they saw each other less often. Thus, the original aims of the Montreux residence came to be no longer so well served, and the excellent manager of the hotel, with whom they had become quite friendly, left to direct a new hotel. They lunched with him once to discuss transferring, but in the end they stayed put. Really, for Nabokov Montreux, or Berlin, or Ithaca was neither here nor there. A certain domiciliary indolence caused him to remain for surprisingly protracted periods in those places into which he had happened to fall.

The town of Montreux had its Russians before Nabokov. The grave of Praskoviya Nabokoff, who was the widow of a first cousin of Nabokov's grandfather, is in the Montreux cemetery. But there were much richer associations than that. Nikolai Gogol once strolled by the Montreux lakeside as he prepared to write *Dead Souls*, and Tolstoy came there, too. Dostoevsky stayed at a slight distance from Montreux, in a lowly boardinghouse. Tiutchev, whose poetry Nabokov translated, wrote poetry about the mountains at Montreux. In the past one could have quickly formed an alternative government for Russia with the Social Democrats and Social Revolutionaries living by the side of Lake Leman. The town of Montreux is one of the wayside stations in the chain of an old tradition in Russian culture and literature: exile.

Russians of the nineteenth century had a passion for Western Europe. The artist Alexander Benois, who was one of the editors of the prerevolutionary journal *World of Art*, described Western Europe's attraction for the Russian artist and intellectual in his memoirs: "I don't know how they look upon 'abroad' now in Russia, but in my childhood, in St. Petersburg and in our circle, abroad appeared as the most alluring earthly paradise." Of course the Nabokov family was too sophisticated to permit one to speak of a passion for Europe. Simply, there have been Nabokovs in Western Europe constantly for over a century. When Nabokov left Europe, it was, he wrote (but only in his Russian memoirs), "with a feeling of boredom and disgust," but he returned and remained the moment he had achieved financial independence.

Those from other cultures have also paused at Montreux. Byron set "The Prisoner of Chillon" in a castle at the lake's edge. The castle is the principal tourist attraction of the region. The only previous resident *doyen* of the region was Romain Rolland. Though he translated Rolland as a young man, the mature Nabokov included Rolland among celebrated mediocrities in need of critical reduction. Rolland was not celebrated in Montreux, and Nabokov, too, despite the occasional television crews and the features about him in magazines, lived there more or less anonymously. One does not notice it at first, but there are some strange people on the streets of Montreux, and Nabokov confessed ("I should not do it, but I cannot help it") that he sometimes followed and observed them.

His sister felt that her brother's social horizon was too narrow and artificial in Montreux—publishers, journalists, academics, film people—and she wanted him to move about more. Nabokov said that his sister didn't know any of his many friends in Switzerland. His sister had gone back to the Soviet Union and visited the local museum at Rozhdestveno and the ruined site of Vyra, from which she had brought him back a broken piece of foundation brick that she had found in the ground. She claimed that he intensely wished to visit the family estate but would not admit it. She sparkled with pleasure as she said it:

I don't think he would ever do it. But we discuss very often
this problem. First of all I cannot imagine him walking the
streets of Leningrad or Moscow. It would be impossible. He
would attract attention, you know. The way he walks and the
way he's dressed and everything. What would happen? . . .
Vera. Vera says that he would be taken immediately . . . I
told her, but, Vera, listen, this would be a scandal for the
whole world. He is an American citizen, and what profit
would they have from this? . . . I don't think that he would be
afraid himself to go, but Vera would certainly be afraid.

Nabokov had to be satisfied with his piece of brick and some
photographs. He was always on guard against any signs of political softness and once accused his nephew of being "pink" for ar-
guing against the Vietnam War at the dinner table. While
virtually the entire American intelligentsia said no to the war,
there was one American writer, permanent resident of Switzerland, who sent Lyndon Johnson a telegram urging him to carry
on his good work. The attitude of *The New York Review of
Books* toward the war caused him to become estranged from the
journal. He also grew distressed at the editorial line of *The New
Yorker*.

Nabokov devoured papers and journals. He subscribed to the
*International Herald Tribune, The Times, The Observer, The
Telegraph, The New Statesman, Time, Playboy*, and *Lui*, the European imitation of *Playboy*. Once he wrote to the IHT urging
them to give more space to boosting American achievements.
From time to time a French newspaper would be thrown in. He
received *The National Review*, the journal closest to him politically, with the compliments of William Buckley, a sometime ski-
ing partner of his son's. Publishers sent him a steady stream of
novels, hoping for an endorsement that rarely came. He praised
the work of Edmund White and also the prose of the émigré son
of a Soviet diplomat, Sasha Sokolov, who writes so much in the
manner of Nabokov that he must be ranked as the foremost Nabokov epigone. He has said that he didn't have much time to do
reading that wasn't connected with his work.

Whether cunningly or not, he cultivated ineptness in the simple mechanics of living. Sometimes he would go to the local bake-
shop, but the indigestible bounty with which he returned was
almost never eaten. An unlucky impulse purchase of a piece of

jewelry became a running household joke: "I am going out. Can I bring you back something? Some bread? Milk? Pearls?" But their domestic life was conducted in good humor, and such banter was evidently an important component. "Such lovely pearls!" sighed Nabokov.

The hotel staff shielded them beautifully from tourists who wanted to include the Nabokovs among their sights. A man who asked at the desk was requested to write a note rather than telephone, and, as he stood hunched over writing the note, Nabokov came out of the elevator and started to walk through the lobby. A bellboy discreetly but swiftly approached him, said something, and motioned with his head toward the man who was still writing. The European gentleman in camel-hair overcoat smiled, shook his head from side to side, and continued out for his walk. Once some young American ladies even made an immodest proposal by means of hotel note, but, since Nabokov was not aware of their sex until the staff informed him later, he thought that he was being pointlessly abused rather than propositioned. There was a certain amount of oddity in the mail, some of it amusing but most of it merely a bother. They learned that they did not have to return unsolicited books that were sent to be autographed, but still the ethical annoyance was debated every time one came. Nabokov liked to tell of how they did send one back signed because of a touching letter from a father who thought it might be some comfort to his son, who was dying. Then, in a year, the miraculously recovered son wrote requesting an autographed edition for his dying father.

From about 1967, four years after the appearance of *Pale Fire*, discussion of Nabokov escalated from sporadic praise of the brilliance of a particular novel to the contention, beginning with an article by Eliot Fremont-Smith in the *New York Times*, that Nabokov was the world's greatest living writer. When *Time* magazine did its cover story on Nabokov in 1969 a deluge of covers for autographing (all unreturned) strained the homely butterfly-shaped mail catch hanging between the double doors through which one entered their rooms.

The annoyances of fame, carefully held at a slight distance, pleased Nabokov, though he would not admit it. I was with the Nabokovs when a young man, who had, he said, traveled across the ocean especially to see him, somehow made it through on the phone. Mrs. Nabokov set about discovering who he was and what precisely he wanted with her husband. While this bit of testing was going on, Nabokov paced up and down the little rectangular parlor with his hands behind his back. Finally, he took the phone from her and questioned the would-be intruder himself. His face was half aglow, and it was clear that he wanted the stranger to be clever enough to fake his way in, but he wasn't, and Nabokov explained that he was terribly busy.

In the sixties Nabokov would ordinarily begin his working day at about seven thirty. In the seventies he began at eight or eight thirty. Sometimes a particularly pure dose of his lifelong isomnia would cause him to sleep in later once he finally did fall off, but not very much later. One day he told me that he had been fully awake until six in the morning the night before but had then fallen asleep until nine and felt fine. Nabokov took a bath in the morning, every morning, always, and this practice was one of the small but essential steadfast features of his entire life. When he left Russia and lived in Berlin rooming houses, Nabokov used a portable rubber tub that one could step into rather like a vertical sleeping bag and bathe in by pouring in just a few glasses of water. His brother Sergei used one, too, and had won a shipboard bet while going into emigration by betting that he could take a bath with a single glass of water. (I found the device hard to visualize, and so Nabokov drew a picture of a man using one on one of the index cards on which I was noting down our conversation as we spoke.) His Swiss bath was a long steeping affair during which, with any luck, a sentence or two might emerge from the steam. He would tend to correct proofs—and it reached a stage when there were very nearly always proofs to correct from something and somewhere or other—as the first job of the morning.

When Nabokov finished his morning of writing, he puttered around a bit rearranging his desk, which tended toward disorderly, though that never interfered with his actual writing, since he wrote standing up at an old lectern that had been discovered in the hotel's basement. The first part of the day was the best as far as he was concerned, because then he felt young, there was the pleasure of creativity, and the very soothing view of the mountains across the lake as he wrote. Lunch and dinner arrangements depended upon whether a visitor was due that day. If the day was free, there could be a stroll in the afternoon, and then perhaps a short nap. Nabokov went to bed very early, usually by eight thirty. Sometimes the pattern was broken, and it did not apply at all during the summer, when butterfly collecting eclipsed writing. These were the fallow months, and what little work was done took place deep in deck chairs.

New editions and translations often exhausted him, because Nabokov possessed a terror of typos and mistakes in translation. He was capable of howling and moaning and requiring much comforting when confronted by a typo, and he once told an interviewer that he was less concerned about his literary status at some future time than that all the typographical errors be eventually corrected in future editions. He should not have devoted the energy he did to such things, but he felt that he must. Nabokov continually generated sidecar projects that were patiently but firmly opposed by his wife because of all the time and energy she could see they would require. He particularly threatened to compile a personal anthology of his own favorite Russian poems in neo-Spartan translations. Once, in the middle of a conversation about something else, he declared that henceforth he was going to write only in Russian once again. His wife reacted to this sudden public announcement with amused lack of interest.

Nabokov played his game quite well. After all, he invented it. He said of himself that, whenever a stranger asked him if he was Vladimir Nabokov, he would reply: "And what do you do?" because obviously he "did" Nabokov. It was, though, a wonder that he did not tire of it, for he was too good an actor to be satisfied with such a character part. How good his dramatic ability was could be glimpsed when he played someone other than himself in telling an anecdote. One of his best set pieces was Edmund Wilson speaking Russian. Nabokov used to ask Wilson to repeat something he had attempted to say in Russian and would then fall about laughing. All the same, when he spoke to me of Wilson, he weighed their long and often troubled relationship and finally decided that, in spite of all that happened between them, he was a very old friend, "in certain ways my closest," and, having said that, he tilted his head and looked at his wife in an owlish and arch manner. He had enacted this same scene before for other visitors, concluding with the arch look at Vera Evseevna.

Wilson visited Nabokov for the last time in 1964, shortly before the appearance of the Bollingen edition of *Eugene Onegin*.

Nabokov did not forgive the fact that Wilson had already written
the attack on his translation that was to appear in *The New York
Review of Books* at the time that he visited Switzerland but did
not say anything about it. They were in touch only tangentially
after their press clashes over the translation, chiefly through
Christmas cards sent by Wilson. I was present when the last one
arrived, a black butterfly powered by a rubber band. It didn't fly
but went straight to ground in a throbbing fit and then was still.
Nabokov answered the card in a reserved but chilly fashion. The
friendship had died, really, in Ithaca.

Nabokov's *Onegin* had an ill-starred beginning in that, shortly
before its publication, there appeared a fine poetic translation of
the poem by Walter Arndt. Nabokov wrote a scathing attack on
it, which appeared in *The New York Review of Books* (April 30,
1964). The Arndt translation had come into his hands as his own
was going to press, and Nabokov had been able only to insert a
one-line mention of it in which he said that it was "even worse"
than previous efforts. That was absurd. Nabokov found a few
errors at which he aimed his cannon and allowed the review to
sink to the level of uncontrolled abuse. He had, after all, been
working on his own Pushkin since 1950. The ironic punishment
for Nabokov was that Arndt's translation received the Bollingen
(!) prize for the best translation of poetry into English for 1964.

Wilson's attack on Nabokov came several months later, also in
The New York Review of Books (July 15, 1965), and was even
less fair to Nabokov than Nabokov's own attack on Arndt. The
clash provoked replies, counterreplies, letters, press commentary,
and—especially—personal passions and loyalties. Robert Lowell,
for example, was moved to write that "both common sense and
intuition tell us that Edmund Wilson must be nine-tenths unan-
swerable and right in his criticism of Nabokov."

The telltale imbalance in Wilson's attack on Nabokov's Pushkin may be easily demonstrated. Wilson's essay was slightly over
165 column inches long. Nabokov's translation is 345 pages long,
while his Commentaries in two volumes are 1,087 pages in length.
In other words, the translation is almost exactly one-third the
length of the Commentaries, and yet Wilson does not get around
to the Commentaries until the 115th of his 165 column inches:
"And now for the positive side. The Commentary, if one skips
the *longueurs*, does make very pleasant reading, and it rep-

resents an immense amount of labor . . . " Even in this conclusion
Wilson wanders off into many other areas so that, in sum, he de-
votes only 10 percent of his space to what is two-thirds, and far
and away the most important part, of Nabokov's work. What
should have been discussed at great length is passed off virtually
in one sentence: "Nabokov has also studied exhaustively Pushkin's relations with his Russian predecessors and contemporaries,
and there is a good deal of excellent literary criticism." Wilson
had told friends at Harvard that he was going to challenge
Nabokov on classical ground, where he felt Nabokov was weakest
in understanding the background of Pushkin's poem, but he
somehow abandoned this idea.

The main thing Wilson challenged Nabokov on was the question of how much English Pushkin knew. Nabokov answered su-
perciliously and not as effectively as he should have. Meaningful
evidence in such a matter would be personal reminiscences of
Englishmen who spoke with Pushkin in English (there are none),
comments on works that Pushkin could have read only in English
(there are none of these either), and the active uses to which he
put English in his writing. It is here that Wilson's case falls, and it
is odd that Nabokov, perhaps because of his great anger, did not
use the obvious proofs. One of Pushkin's "English plays" had as
its title in English *The caveteous Knigth*. In manuscript it was
"cuvetous." The other had as its English title *The city of the
plaque*, which shows that Pushkin adapted his play from a real
eighteenth-century English play but through a French translation
of it. But that skirmish is just an incident in the massive critical
and scholarly campaign that Nabokov was waging.

In essence Nabokov is putting the point, again and again, in his
Commentary that even Russians are not adequately prepared to
read Pushkin's masterpiece properly. For Pushkin did have full
mastery of eighteenth-century French, and he was widely read in
French literature even of the distinctly second-rate sort. As
shown by the Russian spellings that he gave to names, Pushkin
was almost wholly dependent upon French translations for his
knowledge of non-French European literature. Before Nabokov
Russian readers and Russian Pushkinists, too, simply did not
have the French or the necessary knowledge of French literature
of the time to deal adequately with this. One of Russia's foremost
Pushkinists, Boris Tomashevsky, concluded his modest 1923

essay, "Pushkin—Reader of French Poets," with the assertion that French poetry was the measure against which Pushkin's poetry should be seen, and he stressed that an enormous amount of study still had to be done before the matter of French influence upon Pushkin could be satisfactorily resolved. Nabokov resolved the question of the direct echo of scores of specified French texts and also the question of gallicisms in Pushkin's very language. It is not, when you think of it, at all surprising that Nabokov should choose to lead Pushkin across a French bridge to English culture. *This* is the great accomplishment of Nabokov's work on Pushkin.

Nabokov deftly and firmly traces the probable origins of Pushkin's variant on the sonnet form in La Fontaine (and his popularity in Russia), Moliere, and Malherbe. Frequently the comparisons with French writers are mere juxtapositions that enable the reader to see for the first time how much in the mainstream of French intellectual and artistic life Pushkin really was. The ability to have found the hundreds of pertinent analogies, comparing, for example, two stanzas in chapter 7 of *Onegin* with passages from Chateaubriand and Senancour, shows not only a thorough knowledge of French literature, but also virtually total recall of what he has read. The work on the Gallic influences in Pushkin's phrases and epithets is the most subtle of all. We learn that the line "having forgot the somber scapegrace" is close to the French *tenebreux* and derived from the type of *le beau tenebreux* (Amadis de Gaul) that was a fashionable term and model for young men in the late 1820s. Through hundreds of pages Pushkin's comments on writers he could not read in the original are traced back unerringly to the French translations he read, and the way in which he constructed his Russian sentences is linked back to the great French writers he knew and loved so well.

Nabokov tried very hard (sometimes too hard) to establish the specific weight and sound of every word that Pushkin used. When he spotted a rich leather binding on a word or phrase, he would use an equivalently obscure or archaic word to translate it. It was this aspect of Nabokov's translation that most infuriated Wilson, who thought that Pushkin was clear and simple, Nabokov, murky and affected. In essence Nabokov was right: Pushkin made a polished and elegant monument out of the rough stuff of the Russian literary language of the eighteenth century, and the illusion of simplicity came later as Pushkin's poem became intimately known to all educated Russians. Nabokov responded passionately to Wilson on the writer's ability and right to resurrect old words, which would continue to live as long as that writer's work survived. Nabokov was a passionate reader of dictionaries, and one of his hobbies was coining words—in fact, before his death he compiled a list of words he had invented.

If Nabokov was right in essence, Wilson was correct on the level of effective language. It is true that Nabokov declared that he only wanted to produce a "pony," and it is a brilliant pony that transports one back and forth into the groves of Nabokov's footnotes. But it is also true that Nabokov had a deep intrinsic need to do things differently, to shock, and as a result the translation is undeniably odd. Wilson did spot the "inner needs" at play in Nabokov's Pushkin, but he exaggerated their part considerably. The faults of Nabokov's Commentary are fairly obvious. They are written in a spirit of such total freedom that it sometimes seems that Nabokov has not had the discipline to leave anything out. He shows literary condescension and commits assassination casually, often in footnotes to his footnotes (in fact, the reader of the Commentary is strongly urged to pay most attention to these footnotes within the notes, which is where some of the greatest action takes place), and he finds occasion to perorate on subjects ranging from Soviet literature to the stature of Mickiewicz or Virgil, sometimes, as in instances like these, where there has to be doubt whether his firm opinions could possibly rest on firsthand knowledge of original sources. The two appendixes, one on Pushkin's great-grandfather and one on comparative prosody, are in the one instance historically willful and in the other far too dependent upon Andrei Bely. And all the same, there is no more imposing work of scholarship on Pushkin in any language, and, long before the novels of Sirin and Nabokov are recognized in the Soviet Union, Soviet Pushkinology must come to terms with Nabokov's *Onegin.*

It began with Wilson, but it did not end there. Nabokov became quite querulous in Switzerland. He fought with Stanley Kubrick to snatch back his original filmscript of *Lolita* for publication. He got the rights on very strict conditions that he was not allowed to say anything derogatory about Kubrick's film either in writing or verbally and was, moreover, not to conduct himself badly in public situations. Nabokov exploded with laughter as he told me about that alleged clause, which meant, he said, that he "wasn't permitted to screw a cow in a public square."

He demanded that both the questions and the answers of interviews be in writing. He was not only famous, he was rich. He would have total control over what an impertinent world said about him. The Italian reporters were the worst as far as he was concerned, because they recorded even telephone conversations, which made it awkward to deny something he had said. Nabokov's law firm was one of the most expensive in New York, Paul, Weiss, Rifkind, and his personal attorney was one of the most distinguished attorneys in that firm, Joseph Iseman. There was a four-year legal struggle over my 1977 book about him. Nabokov was furious about what he saw as a breach of faith. The author was upset because, he contended, he had been given assurances about the general outlines of the life of Nabokov that proved to be untrue. Yet though Nabokov's stance was menacing (when he was not being very genial), he never actually went to court over anything.

There were, however, more serious ways in which he wore his fame badly. Nabokov saw himself as being on Olympus and yet had an irritating awareness that not all the world agreed. One of the most painful of his many interviews is one in which he pedantically enumerates all the lackluster Nobel Prize winners there have been and openly boosts himself for the award. Bunin, he said, had written hundreds of letters lobbying for his prize.

His writing was affected by his circumstances. While he was working on *Ada* (which was first titled *The Texture of Time*) he wrote at a speed three times greater than he ever had before. Suddenly Nabokov's prose became an imaginative torrent, and it showed. He wrote the novel on twenty-five hundred index cards, which, typed by Mme. Callier, became a manuscript of more than 850 pages. The novel, published in 1969, was sprawling and self-indulgent. The erotic stakes of *Lolita* were upped slightly, to sibling incest. And he added sexual embellishments to nearly all the republications and new translations of the old Sirin novels as well.

While *Ada* was being written, Nabokov entered into a new publishing arrangement with McGraw-Hill in which he was to be paid handsomely on a words per year basis, and the yearly tally could include translations of old works as well as new work in English. The first McGraw-Hill book was *King, Queen, Knave,* and it was a dual selection of the Book-of-the-Month Club. Nabokov's advance was two hundred fifty thousand dollars—a considerable sum in 1968—and the blanket arrangement was effectively a million-dollar contract. Nabokov had indicated that he was dissatisfied with Putnam's lack of promotion for his other books after *Lolita.* There was both personal and business antipathy between the Nabokovs and the then president of Putnam's, Walter Minton, who did little to stop Nabokov from leaving, though Nabokov wanted to take all his books with him, and Minton, understandably, wasn't too keen about this. About a dozen American publishers sent delegations to Switzerland. McGraw-Hill's president, Edward Booher, and editor-in-chief, Frank Taylor, showed the most interest and made the best offer. The deal was sealed by handshakes between Vera Nabokov and Edward Booher and Frank Taylor. *Ada* was the Literary Guild spring selection in 1969 and was reviewed gushingly in the *New York Times.* There was not going to be any mistake in failing to recognize Nabokov's greatness again . . .

Ada is, in fact, a litmus test for those who approach Nabokov's art. It is the weakest novel he wrote, and the most overpraised by many critics. It is supposed to be a parody of the nineteenth-century family chronicle novel, which presents problems as a subject for parody. More, the presence of Nabokov within the text amounts to a novel that is a parody of parody, and perhaps that had to fail, at least in this instance. The novel succeeds frequently on the level of rapturous and erotic prose, but these individual prose poems, though there are hundreds of them, and they delight nearly every other time (some are simply puerile), do not come together as a unified structure. Lovemaking in *Ada* is sometimes like two people doing impossible things on parallel bars, or sometimes like fixed scenes in velvet and neon light. The scene in which Van feasts on Ada's nipples and then grasps her "lovely lyre" may be a parody of pornography, but the essential distance of laughter is never established.

What is most striking about the incest in *Ada* is that it has no moral echo at all. John Updike (who is himself gently parodied in the novel) correctly saw that Ada was just a pretext for presenting Van's self-love, though he wanted to believe that it was a way of forming Van's soul. That is affectionate special pleading but does not help to make the novel, either in its characters or in its premises, live. A staff member of *The New Yorker* provided the most succinct statement of the novel's problem that I have heard: Van and Ada, he said, are not people but dolphins. The bringing together of Russia and America in one imaginary country is, simply, not very interestingly done, and the blending of artifacts of two centuries is rather juvenile, while the exceedingly long life-spans of the hero and heroine may be seen as nothing more than a longevity fantasy.

In 1968 Nabokov/Narcissus wandered away from the perfect pool and turned into a garden-variety egotist, one with the powers of a giant, true, but still essentially different from what he had been before. The desire to construct an entirely different world was admirable (this is, by the way, a very Russian thing to do—several poets and writers before Nabokov attempted to re-fashion the world, usually at the end of their careers), but it simply didn't work. Mary McCarthy deserves as much credit for having been one of the first to see clearly the monumental weakness of *Ada* as she does for her early crowning of *Pale Fire*. David Rampton states what has taken place very nicely in his 1984 book on Nabokov when he writes:

> What's the difference between the omnipresence of Nabokov in a novel like *Ada* and the very personal views that take over *The Gift*, for example? I think there is a difference, which can best be summed up by saying that the self-involvement of the younger man has become the self-admiration of the master. This does not make for a very attractive self-portrait, and bespeaks a certain narrowing of vision that has its detrimental effects on the fiction.

Never, in a career characterized by extremes of opinion about his work, did a work produce sharper differences of opinion than did *Ada*. Mathew Hodgart in *The New York Review of Books* said that the novel contained Nabokov's finest writing. Alfred Kazin in *The Saturday Review* found the novel "brilliant, slippery, and enchanting" and placed it on a par with *Lolita* and *Pale Fire*. Alfred Appel, Jr., in the *New York Times Book Review* managed to be a little more cautious but still reviewed the novel with all the warmth and commitment of a true Nabokophile. As against views of this sort, Morris Dickstein, in an essay entitled "Nabokov's Folly" in *The New Republic*, called it the most over-praised novel of the decade, self-indulgent, overblown, and full of stunts. Elizabeth Dalton in *Partisan Review* said that the novel was "intolerably overdecorated." The English reviewers who didn't like the book were even more tart. D. J. Enright in *The Listener* said that the novel was proof that great gifts can be put to small uses, and said that perhaps *Ada* was Nabokov's apotheosis. Gillian Tindall in *The New Statesman* saw the novel as tedious, frivolous, occasionally pornographic, and "beyond a joke." Philip Toynbee in *The Observer* said that the novel was appalling in its unremitting exhibitionism. John Updike's *New Yorker* review was the defensible middle position, relying in the end on the vitality in the figure of Ada herself to justify the novel. Another reasoned response that affectionately gave the benefit of the doubt was Sissela Bok's essay in *Critique* (12, 1971). For Robert Alter *Ada* was a "dazzling, but at times also exasperating, near-master-piece."

The novel, for which Nabokov received considerably more money than he had for *Lolita*, made its splash and then sank, left to the defenses and nervous praise of the faithful Nabokovians. *Lolita* was not going to be repeated. The voice from Lake Leman grew even more aggressive and strident in public pronouncements. John Updike was scolded for having dared to hint that Van and Ada had anything to do with Nabokov and his wife. In an article titled "On Adaptation" in *The New York Review of Books* (December 4, 1969) Robert Lowell was savagely attacked for his imitation of a poem by Mandelstam. In October 1971, Nabokov broke his long-standing rule of not replying to critics of his fiction and attacked an academic book about him that was overly preoccupied with sexual symbolism.

From the late sixties the interview became a major form of expression for Nabokov. The terms of his McGraw-Hill contract eventually allowed him to make a book, *Strong Opinions*, out of them and some occasional reviews in 1973. There is a paradox in these interviews, because, although Nabokov had perfect control over both the questions and the answers (when he didn't like a question, he simply didn't respond to it), that did not translate into control over the effect that the process produced. In 1969 he told interviewer Allene Talmey of *Vogue* that he was striving to reveal a "not altogether displeasing personality." *Strong Opinions* did not, in fact, present his best face.

He wanted his interviews to constitute a kind of intellectual autobiography outside the terms of his proper autobiography. The difficulty was that he struck poses, didn't answer questions, and often wasn't above being gratuitously rude to his interviewer even when he was quite fond of him or her. For his *Paris Review* interview he "suggested" to Herb Gold that it would be a good idea if they were both paid for their efforts, and he was indeed the first writer ever to be paid for a *Paris Review* interview. In his interviews Nabokov shows himself to be what another émigré writer termed the "aseptic-aristocratic" artist, the one who feels a special need to be inaccessible to others. On the other hand, he derived much pleasure in speculating on and gossiping about the sexual tendencies of various writers, interviewers, academics, photographers, and editors who visited him.

Nabokov showed a stubborn tendency to give pedantry a preeminent place in his life. Against all expectations, the row over his *Eugene Onegin* caused the multivolume work to go to a second edition, and Nabokov set about revising his translation so that it was even rougher and less poetic. He treated similarly a selection of his own Russian verse that, together with some chess problems, became *Poems and Problems* in 1970. At the same time, on vacations, he worked on another butterfly book, a never-completed illustrated history of the butterfly in art from ancient Egypt to the Renaissance. He had butterflies in the work of Bosch, Brueghel the Elder, and Dürer, and planned to collect a hundred plates in all, with commentaries, of course. He was interested in questions such as whether or not tiny evolutionary changes could be spotted in a master's depiction of a wing five hundred years ago. Nabokov went through large and small museums throughout Italy in preparation for this work and had plans to do the same in France and Holland.

His Swiss life was very regular. Walks, naps, very occasionally the medicinal eucalyptus injections that were in fashion among older wealthy Europeans. At table the ordering of the wine was almost always a highly polished and amusing occasion for histrionics between the Nabokovs. They would disagree about the wines, and then, when one was finally selected, they would disagree about whether or not it should be sent back. On one occasion with me Vera Evseevna thought she detected sourness in the wine that Nabokov had just elaborately sniffed, sipped, and approved. The always smiling young maître d'hôtel artlessly tried to agree with them both. "You go through all the motions, rolling it about on your tongue, but that's all," Vera told him. A new bottle was brought out, and I wondered whether they were prepared to send it back again if need be. "Yes, yes, oh yes. We have sent the bottle back a second time," said Nabokov. He was a compulsive tipper. There was not a shade of meanness in him in this regard. Italian, Spanish, and Yugoslav waiters would swarm around the Nabokov party, opening doors, bringing menus and wine lists, smiling at his little French pleasantries.

On ordinary days a private cook was employed to come in and do very simple meals for them in their kitchenette. They garnished her plain cooking with jokes. One of her main courses was critically examined and proclaimed to be a cross between a chicken and a turkey. Until Anna Feigan's death in 1973 Vera in particular had the care and concern for her cousin. She flew to New York to get her and bring her back to Switzerland where she was established in a rest home and was visited regularly every other day. Both parents were greatly concerned about Dmitri's health during a period of illness, and, to distract him from his pain during his recovery, he was encouraged to take up race-car driving, which brought still more concern, because he had a serious crash (it was in ordinary driving) in which he might have been killed.

Concerning his Swiss period at least Nabokov was justified when he proclaimed: "My life, I wouldn't call it boring . . . but it has been so . . . it has been centered so much on literature, on writing . . ." One of his walks was to the local shop on the way to the news agent where he bought *fiches Bristol,* index cards, in packs of one or two hundred at a time. He used them for all his writing in the Swiss years. He kept some under his pillow at night. He liked to use a certain mechanical pencil, a gift, for correcting proofs, but he preferred ordinary pencils and bought these in quantity as well. He always boasted that he used up the eraser when there was still long service left in the lead. There was also a kind of ballpoint pen that he liked because it had an eraser and its ink could be rubbed away like graphite.

His index cards accumulated in moderately large varnished

wood boxes. He brought *Ada* out to show me one evening when the cards had nearly filled the two boxes and parodically bounced the boxes on his knees as though they were twin babies. It gave a fine sense of a book as a living thing. He would usually hold his work back until it had reached an advanced state before giving it to his wife to read. Sometimes he would read the material to her himself, with the prior warning: "I am going to read this to you, but I don't want any criticism now." Usually, he told one interviewer, she would make only a few remarks anyway. He was working on the second volume of his autobiography for some years but evidently experiencing some difficulties with it. He spoke with me about the second volume once and expressed fears that it was assuming the appearance of a "mere epic" peopled by anecdotes. He preferred *Speak, Memory,* which he thought of as a lyrical book: "There is an absence of that glow of affection I felt for *Speak, Memory.* It will not be violins but trombones." Nabokov had strong opinions about first drafts for the perusal of scholars and also about the publication of incomplete works posthumously, so the world may have to wait nearly a century for the publication of fragments of *Speak, America,* and also of *Original of Laura,* which his son enthusiastically claimed bid fair to be better than any of his previous novels.

The two novels that Nabokov did publish in the years just before his death, *Transparent Things* (1973) and *Look at the Harlequins!* (1975), were in some ways quite different from any that he had written before. They are self-referential, as are many of his works. Both novels rail against biography. Old literary quarrels are kept alight: Georgy Adamovich appears yet again under a new nom de plume and is once more mocked for his aesthetics and his pederasty. These works amount to an overly cute and teasing retelling of Nabokov's life and literary career (the ante is upped to four marriages in *Look at the Harlequins!,* but reshaped fragments of reality still flash by identifiably, especially in part 2).

What is different in *Look at the Harlequins!* are the motifs of self-reflection (as opposed to self-contemplation) and mortality. The Nabokovian writer Mr. R (a mirror reversal of the Russian first-person pronoun) in *Transparent Things* voices one of the strongest commitments to narcissism to be found in Nabokov's writing, but there is also a strong note of doubt when Person (the name of the printer of Nabokov's first book of verse, by the way) is asked from above: "What had you expected of your pilgrimage, Person?" Novels, words might not have been everything after all. Time may not be something that can be captured and made sacrosanct in art. Life may be ridiculous; art, futile. Though both novels are sucked into their own centripetal passion and fail, *Transparent Things* is a worthwhile marker near the end of the road of Nabokov's life for the notes, if one's ear is attuned to catch them, of weariness and doubt. *Look at the Harlequins!* may be reasonably taken as an assurance to his wife, who is called Reality, that their privacy, though it has sometimes been transformed and used, can never be penetrated. Vadim Vadimych (Vladimir Vladimirovich) looks back on his rich mental life as a kind of barely subdued and concealed madness. More than any other of the "autobiographical" novels, these last two novels constitute personal statements, and any reader who doesn't see that element in them is being quite credulous about Nabokov's remarks designed to prevent such a reading.

In the life of the writer, Nabokov's eighteen-year Swiss period should not be given great prominence, even though it is the best documented time of his life. There is the one early Swiss-period masterpiece, *Pale Fire*, and there are three pseudo-Olympian works. He played the genial *maître* for visiting writers and scholars, polishing a routine of anecdotes endlessly repeated. This Nabokov is enameled and highly polished. It is Nabokov Triumphant . . . or Nabokov from Gogol's destroyed "positive" sequel to *Dead Souls*.

Nabokov began to drink reasonably heavily, though he had to do this somewhat furtively because Vera Evseevna did not approve. When he came down to greet morning visitors, he might stop for a ten o'clock whiskey at the bar. He poured scotch from a teapot during the course of at least two television interviews, one with Robert Hughes on the BBC, the other with Bernard Pivot on *Apostrophes* in France. Nabokov was in the main genial, but sometimes he lost his temper badly, in print and in private, and was quick to express contempt: of an overenthusiastic Nabokovian, "We try to keep his enthusiasm in control, but it's hard," or: of another scholar, "We had no idea until we met him. He's a total pederast!"

An important change came over Nabokov in his relations with

Russians. It was not political, but there were waftings of politics in it. He began to cut old émigré literary friends, and he would, very quietly, receive certain Soviet writers who were on European reading tours. The two warmest of these meetings were with Bella Akhmadulina and Bulat Okudzhava. Nabokov even translated one of Okudzhava's poems into English, though not for publication in order not to embarrass him politically. Ties were established with the Russian intelligentsia in the Soviet Union, which was a great step forward from his scorn for *Doctor Zhivago* and his blanket assertion to Albert Parry that "there is no culture in Russia, even underground." References to Nabokov in his various capacities began to appear (very) occasionally in Russia, and one or two of them were quite positive and objective. An extremely courageous article appeared on "the poetry of Godunov-Cherdyntsev," as though he were a real poet, with no mention of Nabokov.

Nabokov's relations with Alexander Solzhenitsyn were strained. Like Tolstoy and Dostoevsky, Solzhenitsyn and Nabokov never met. When he received his Nobel Prize, Solzhenitsyn wrote to Nabokov assuring him that he was far more deserving of it than he. Nabokov told me haughtily that the sad thing was that the letter was barely grammatical. Several notes were exchanged between them, and Solzhenitsyn actually went so far as to come to Montreux and entered the Palace lobby but then left without meeting Nabokov. One émigré story has it that Solzhenitsyn fled in disgust at the luxury of the Montreux Palace lobby before the meeting, but it is more likely that it was simply a Russian-style nonmeeting, as recounted in the Scammell biography. Nabokov was fond of referring to him as Sol-nezhit-yn, "salty-lack-of-life." The two writers were publicly silent about each other's work. Nor could Nabokov be budged into expressing an opinion about the new emigration's leading writer (from a purely literary point of view), Andrei Sinyavsky, although Vera Nabokov said that it was obvious that Sinyavsky had read *Invitation to a Beheading* and read it well.

A short story by Zinaida Schakowskoi has been a source of controversy and speculation about the last years of Nabokov in Switzerland and the nature of his marriage. Zinaida Schakowskoi has strongly denied that the story is written about Nabokov specifically, and it is true that she has written elsewhere about the generalized phenomenon of the "Russian literary wife" (the wives of Tolstoy and Dostoevsky come first to mind). The story, which appeared when Nabokov was still alive, is titled "The Wasteland."

The hero, Walden, who is very wealthy, has a spoiled actress daughter who plays at having a career. In Russian, Valden could be a Nabokov-style anagram for Vlad. N. Scholars court Walden and quake before him and his blunt ways: "Walden so loved to have sport with readers and the people to whom he talked, to irritate them with provocative declarations such as, 'Mozart is a third-rate rinky-dink pianist in a turn-of-the-century provincial movie house,' or, 'Whatever else you say about Pushkin, he is so clear that any fool can understand him.' " Walden has been widowed, and the way that his wife had looked after him is described in the following way: "Like an emperor who loses one after another all the parts of his empire, Walden had somehow become impoverished bit by bit over the years. Firmly and under the pretext of caring for him and freeing him from all responsibilities, she had removed his participation in life, deprived him of his strength." Walden read his manuscripts to her, allowed her to negotiate the contracts, and it was she who decided whom he would see and whom he shouldn't see. Walden has become totally isolated from all natural human feeling.

An account of the Nabokov marriage is given in a rare interview for CBC radio in March 1973. There Nabokov, unusually, responds to a question about his wife and marvels at the way in which she is able to find a necessary piece of paper in a great pile of materials or come up with old Russian sayings new to him even though they have lived together for nearly half a century. He credits his wife with a domestic telepathy so precise that she can finish a sentence for him with exactly the words he had been thinking. His wife's presence, Nabokov said in another place, can be felt as a warm glow at various places throughout his novels.

It seems quite possible, judging by Lord Snowdon's photographs, that Nabokov suffered from some form of cancer in his last years. His neck grew thin within his collar, his cheeks were stretched taut. When he died, the family withheld information for several days. Nabokov had died of a "mysterious cause" that none of the doctors had been able to identify. It was, in other words, a special, unique, individual death, even though it took place quietly in a hospital and was apparently triggered by a flu acting on his weakened physique. In a memoir written for a memorial volume about Nabokov, his son said that his father caught a flu from him and, later, that he died as a result of a hospital infection contracted while being treated for this flu. This version replaced the "mysterious disease" and also death caused by a window left open by a careless nursing sister as family explanations of the death. It is said that Nabokov's emaciation came after a severe fall while chasing butterflies after which, like Tolstoy's Ivan Ilych bruising himself, the fatal illness commenced. That is mere rumor. There was no final Tolstoyan religious light for Nabokov, however. He held the view that he died every night. The Lausanne Hospital claims that he died only once, on July 2, 1977, at 6:50 P.M.

Conclusion

THERE SHOULD BE NO SINGLE CONCLUSION ABOUT NABOKOV.
He was not a simple man, nor was his art simple. He said about
the émigré years: "No one who hasn't lived through the émigré
experience can possibly understand it. I myself don't know how
to understand it looking back on it.." Nabokov then is a conjec-
ture within a conundrum. From time to time there appears the
semblance of what one would call a normal Eriksonian life stage,
but in the main there is what can only be classified as a Life of a
Great Russian Writer in the peculiar line of Gogol, Tolstoy, and
Dostoevsky. But Nabokov, of course, was a conjuror, and so the
patterns of both his life and his art are frequently characterized by the basic skill of all magicians, misdirection. Some of the
writers and thinkers he most despised—Dostoevsky, Freud,
Lawrence—are his principal competitors. One of his more interesting intolerances, scattered throughout his work and his interviews, is of Einstein, the man of our time who came closest to
finding a "key." Nabokov had a low tolerance for the universally
acknowledged genius who, as Vera learned when she translated
for him once in the thirties, had a weakness for dubious "peace
movements."

Judge Nabokov as you will, there is evidence on all sides. He is
a hero of our time, the time of the culture of narcissism, though
his narcissism is in a class all its own. He championed nobility of
spirit, which sometimes failed him, and believed in himself and in
art with a colossal fanaticism worthy of wonder. He was a Don
Quixote who built his own windmills and waged his own psychic

battles on the perilous staircases within them. He possessed enormous freedom . . . and was a prisoner of his self. He was unique, and a self-caricature. No one was indifferent to him. For some he was the most extraordinary and attractive person they had ever encountered, for others, a somewhat frightening reptilian creature in which the human element was wanting.

He was a Russian, always a Russian, however odd some other Russians judged him to be. He himself told me: "One Russian will know another Russian from I do not know what distance. A hundred miles perhaps." A French critic reconciled this with Nabokov's cosmopolitan fate by terming him the most *American* of all Russian writers, which is quite an elegant and apt way of resolving that problem.

Nabokov's artistic achievements in the 1920s and 1930s are great, but they pale beside what he accomplished in the so-called postmodernist period. Another émigré, from a different Eastern European culture and a slightly younger generation, Eugene Ionesco, has complained of our time: "Since Beckett stopped writing, since Faulkner stopped writing, since Joyce stopped writing, since Proust stopped writing, we are trying to fill a void that cannot be filled. All is repetition. . . . This era is not made for art." Nabokov did not grant aesthetic recognition to his era in this way. He was an individualist on the nineteenth-century scale when individualism seems to have become a trace element in modern literature, and, since art was the one thing that was eternal, he did not have to be bothered if contemporaneity had little time for it. By the sheer force of his art and his opinions Nabokov taught a generation, especially in America, but also in England, France, Holland, Japan, and many other countries, to reconsider the possibilities of art. He brought all of the Russian émigré experience to the notice of a world that for too long hadn't wanted to know about it. The dictatorship of theory and ideology reigned less confidently because he lived and wrote.

Even more important has been the effect that he has already had and will continue to have on Russian literature and culture. One of the minor casualties of the decades of Leninism-Stalinism (a tragedy that has not yet played itself out) was that Russia was virtually deprived of a modernist epoch. Nabokov will in time supply that almost single-handedly, and it is indicative of this growing swell of pride in Nabokov that one hears Soviet intellectuals speak, though not yet write, of "our Nabokov."

Nearly twenty years ago I wrote that Nabokov is as interesting as any poet or writer in this century. That he did not, in the good company of Tolstoy and Joyce, win the Nobel Prize is neither here nor there. There seems no need to alter that first judgment. There is much that is off-putting in Nabokov's art, but one must read him for his innovative conceptions and his intense lyricism and sensuality.

And his life? There are artists for whom a knowledge and sense of the life are not necessary, but Nabokov is not one of them. Nabokov may be taken at the surface level, but he merits more, even though he very much didn't want it. There is a resonance and an interplay between the life and the art that deepens both. A full-length portrait of Vladimir Nabokov then, Russian-American writer of our time and of his own reality. The world will not quickly forget either him or his stories.

Leaves and other people's memories fall softly onto the surface of the perfect pool of a great Russian-American Narcissus.

Notes

A WORD ON SOURCES

THIS BOOK IS BASED IN LARGE PART UPON A PERSONAL AR-
chive. Of particular importance are fourteen twenty-minute tapes
which contain extensive conversations with Nabokov and his
family and friends. These tapes have what are probably the only
free conversations that Nabokov ever allowed himself to hold
while being tape-recorded.

Other important sources besides the tapes include three notebooks (containing 140, 70, and 106 pages) in which I made notes
while talking and shortly after talking with Nabokov and others,
as well as ten index cards and twenty pieces of hotel stationery.
(These loose notes have been paginated and figure in the notes as
Occasional Notes.)

Although they are not quoted for copyright reasons, Nabokov's letters to his mother between 1920 and 1936 (twenty-seven
pages) are an important background source for his first émigré
period, as is Nabokov's personal diary for 1952 for his American
period.

Of considerable importance as background for this book are approximately seventy-five pages of Nabokov family history in
notes and letters from Nabokov's first cousin, Serge Nabokov of
Brussels, to whom I am deeply indebted.

I made photo records of all the archival materials that were
loaned to me by Nabokov as I worked. In all there were 1,870 ex-
posures including: letters from Nabokov's father; correspondence
with *Contemporary Annals*; letters to George Hessen, Mark Al-

danov, Vladislav Khodasevich, Ivan Lukash, and Yuly Aikhenval'd; a letter from Rachmaninov; unpublished letters-to-the-editor; the Nabokov-Wilson correspondence; Wellesley College
material; material relating to VN's first American speaking tour;
early Sirin poems (printed and unprinted); Crimean notebooks
(poems), November 1918–February 1919 as well as further Crimean poems 1917–19; an early poetic play; Cambridge poems,
1923; and ten early obscure or unpublished works (*Chelovek i
veshchi, Zvuki, Solnechyi Son, Sluchainost', Bogie, Govoryat
po-russki, Dvoe, Mest', Venetsianka, Udar kryla*).

It is my intention to give my personal Nabokov archive a home
in a university library.

Particular thanks must be given to the special collections sections and archives of Cambridge University, Columbia University, Cornell University, Stanford University, and Wellesley
College, and also to Thomas P. Whitney and the Julia Whitney
Foundation of Washington, Connecticut, and to Princess Zinaida
Schakowskoi of Paris. Hundreds of people answered my letters,
and I hope that the book in hand will show them that all of their
responses found resonance and use.

The numbers that appear in the left-hand column refer to book
page numbers.

Page vii   Citation from *Look at the Harlequins!* (London: Weiden-
           feld & Nicolson, 1975), p. 226.

INTRODUCTION

1   The best general guides to early twentieth-century Russian
literature and culture are Renato Poggioli's *Poets of Russia*
(Cambridge, Mass.: Harvard, 1960) and—though it is hard to
obtain—D. S. Mirsky's *Contemporary Russian Literature*
(New York: Knopf, 1926). (Avoid the later Whitfield abridge-
ment of Mirsky.)

The outstanding historical overview of the Russian revolutionary period is Lionel Kochan's *Russia in Revolution
1890–1918* (New York: New American Library, 1967). Other
good sources on the political and social sources of the Russian
Revolution are: K. Breshko-Breshkovskaya's *The Hidden
Springs of the Russian Revolution* (Stanford: Stanford University, 1931); P. Miliukov, *Russia and Its Crisis* (New York: Col-
lier, 1962); and an article, "Pobedonostsev and the Rule of
Firmness" by A. E. Adams in *The Slavic and East European
Review*, vol. XXXII, no. 78, 1953.

2   Nabokov's Russian letters to his sister Helene Sikorskaya, 1974, have been published as *Vladimir Nabokov—Perepiska s sestroi* (Ann Arbor, Mich.: Ardis, 1985).

3   H. Grabes, *Fictitious Biographies: Vladimir Nabokov's English Novels*. Trans. from the German by Pamela Gliniars and the author (The Hague: Mouton, 1977). This little book is one of the most worthwhile in the by-now substantial secondary literature on Nabokov.

CHAPTER 1

5   The portion dealing with Nabokov's great-grandmother is in the second part of chapter 3. The Shishkov estate in Samara was called Semenikha. Genealogical information on the Shishkov family may be found in Prince Dolgorukov's *Velvet Book—a State Register*, SPb, vol. 4, pp. 217–23, 1854.

"Goosefoot," which was written between September 1931 and January 14, 1932, appeared in the Paris émigré newspaper *Poslednie novosti* on January 31, 1932. It is one of the Russian short stories which has still not been translated as of 1985.

6   *Bagazh* by Nicolai Nabokov (Boston: Little, Brown, 1975).

7   The information about the romance between Dmitri Nabokov and Nina von Korf comes from several family sources in addition to the memoirs of Nicolai Nabokov. While there are sharply opposing points of view in regard to the question of royal bastardy, there is no disagreement about the reality of this romance. Field archive: Notebook 2 (p. 35), interviews with S. S. Nabokov and Helene Sikorskaya.

There is interesting material on the theme of incest in Nabokov's writing in D. Barton Johnson's *Worlds in Regression: Some Novels of Vladimir Nabokov* (Ann Arbor, Mich.: Ardis, 1985), which is another of the more worthwhile books on Nabokov to have been published in recent years.

8   The essential information on the career of D. N. Nabokov may be found in Jacques Ferrand's *Les Nabokovs* (Paris: Privately printed, 1982), Entry 23/11, pp. 25–26. Further reading may be done in S. Graham's *The Tsar of Freedom* and W. E. Mosse's *Alexander II and the Modernization of Russia*; in Russian, A. F. Koni's *Ottsy i deti sudebnoi reformy* (Moscow: Izd. Sytina, 1914) and B. V. Vilensky's *Sudebnaya reforma i kontrreforma* are recommended sources. "*Le grand-duc Constantin, qui malgré toute sa fièvreuse activité, n'a su se concilier aucune sympathie dans aucune classe de la Russie, exerce en ce moment une influence plus absolue que jamais sur l'esprit excellent, mais inquiet et perplexe de son frère.*" From *Alexandre II et son temps* by Constantin de Grunwald. (Paris: 1963), p. 222.

The comparison of D. N. Nabokov with a ship's captain who must jettison cargo during a storm is taken from the Brockhaus-Efron encyclopedia article on D. N. Nabokov. There is allusion to this article in *Speak, Memory*.

9   The accusation of heavy debt as being a disqualifying factor for ministerial office was leveled by Pobedonostsev.

The Grand Duke Konstantin's Chateau d'Yquem purchase is related in *Gault/Millau* magazine (Paris, December 1984), p. 143.

"The blood of Peter the Great." Nabokov interview, Field archive: Tape, "Quill" notebook.

10 For background material on the Russian Dumas, see Richard Pipes's biography of Pyotr Struve. Vladimir Nabokov's own views on the four Dumas were that the first (his father's) and the second were the best and that the third was the most compliant. The fourth was "rather good." Field archive: Notebook 1, p. 46.

"A ego smert' 'za drugi svoya', ot ruki krajne pravogo, zazhgla v dushe Volodi neprimirimuyu slepuyu nenavist' ko vsei proshloi pravoi tsarskoi Rossii." Field archive: Letter written by member of the Nabokov family.

11 Nabokov's claim that he was directly descended from Genghis Khan was made in an interview with N. Garnham for BBC-TV, September 3, 1968.

Filatka, Avdokima, and Vlasska Nabokov. Full document cited in Ferrand, p. 120.

For further information on the place of Tartars in Russian Society, see *Nabokov—His Life in Part*, pp. 41–45.

12 I am indebted to S. S. Nabokov for extensive material on Nabokov family history. Field archive. Letter from Prince Alexandre Nicolaevitch Galitzine. April 14, 1983. Field archive.

CHAPTER 2

13 One of the historians writing shortly after the 1905 revolution on the role of the modern nobility was distantly related to Nabokov. See S. Korf's *Dvoryanstvo i ego soslovnoe upravlenie za stoletie* (SPb, 1906).

14 There is a somewhat fuller account of the career of D. N. Nabokov in *Nabokov—His Life in Part*. Another useful collection for those who read Russian is *Imperatorskoe Uchilishche Pravovedeniya i Pravovedy v gody mira, voiny, i smuty* (Izd. Pravovedskoi, Kassy: 1967).

The account of D. N. Nabokov at the time of Alexander II's assassination is taken from the memoirs of his aunt, Vera Pykhatchev.

15 Letter from Alexander III, November 4, 1885, Gatchina. Photoreproduction of full text of original letter in Ferrand, pp. 88–90.

15–16   A. F. Koni *op. cit.:* "... *iz za ofitsial'noi obolochki ministra skvozit serdechnyi chelovek, znaiushchii skol' chasto tyazhelo byvaet bremya zhizni,"* p. 170.

16 The description of D. N. Nabokov's St. Petersburg townhouse is taken from the memoirs of Vera Pykhatchev. D. N. Na-

bokov possessed the following government honors: Cavalier of the Order of St. Andrew (1895); the Order of St. Alexander Nevsky (with diamonds); the Order of St. Vladimir (first class); the Order of The White Eagle; the Order of St. Anne (first class); the Order of St. Stanislas (first class); and bronze and gold medals commemorating the Crimean War of 1853–56.

17   Details of the Nabokov marriages and divorces are taken from Ferrand *passim*. There is an English-language book that deals with the Falz-Fein family: *Askania-Nova—Animal Paradise in Russia* by L. Heiss (London: 1970).

18   Konstantin Nabokov's memoirs, first published in Russian in Sweden, appeared in English as *The Ordeal of a Diplomat* (London: 1922).

19   Information about the unsuccessful courtship of Katya Ignatiev. Field archive: Notebook 2, p. 36.

Information on the Rukavishnikov family is to be found in N. V. Shaposhnikov's *Heraldica—istoricheskii sbornik* (SPb, 1900).

20   The portrait of the senile D. N. Nabokov is in chapter 3 of *Speak, Memory*.

V. D. Nabokov's *A Collection of Articles on Criminal Law* (*Sbornik statei po ugolovnomu pravu*, SPb, 1904) is not, as cited in *Speak, Memory*, a unique copy. The book is held by the U.S. Library of Congress.

21   The portrait of V. D. Nabokov is from the memoirs of Ariadna Tyrkova-Williams, *On the Way to Freedom* (*Na putyakh k svobode*) (New York: Izd, im. Chekhova). Further information on V. D. Nabokov may be found in chapter 3 of *Nabokov—His Life in Part*.

24   V. D. Nabokov's two long articles on duelling were published as a monograph, *The Duel and Criminal Law* (*Duel i ugolovnyi zakon* SPb, 1910). It would appear that Nabokov's references to his father's duel in *Speak, Memory* refer, in fact, to the Guchkov-Uvarov duel in which an insubstantial provocation to duel was used in an attempt to eliminate (literally) a political opponent from the Duma. The two articles to which V. D. Nabokov refers as having reference to "his" duel are both in the Kadet newspaper *Russkie vedomosti*—"Politicheskaya duel' " by E. Trubetskoi, no. 267, November 20, 1909, p. 2; and "Treteiskii sud i duel' " by K. Arsen'ev, no. 269, November 24, 1909.

Russkie vedomosti reported this duel extensively but with no mention of V. D. Nabokov. Articles appeared in numbers: 245, 25 October 1909, p. 2; 253, 4 November 1909, p. 2; 254, 5 November 1909, p. 3; 255, 6 November 1909, p. 3; 256, 7 November 1909, p. 4; 258, 10 November 1909, p. 4; 259, 11 November 1909, p. 2; 262, 14 November 1909, p. 3; 265, 18 November 1909, p. 3; (the duel itself); and 266, 19 November 1909, p. 4.

Inasmuch as *Russkie vedomosti* reported not only the Guchkov-Uvarov duel, but also most others, including several "secret" duels, there must be at least doubt as to whether V. D. Nabokov was "involved in" another duel.

I wish to express my gratitude to the staff of the Hoover Institute at Stanford University who made possible this thorough search of *Russkie vedomosti.* All searches for the offending cartoon mentioned in *Speak, Memory* have to date been in vain.

25   The fears about Nabokov as an overpampered child are expressed in Iosif Hessen's *The Years of Exile—a living account* (*Gody izgnaniya—zhiznennyi otchyot*) (Paris: YMCA Press, 1979).

26   Nabokov's account of his childhood. Field archive: Notebooks 1–3 *passim.*

A good survey of Mstislav Dobuzhinsky has recently been published in the Soviet Union, making him one of the few "fully rehabilitated" émigré artists. The study, which has no named editor, is *Mstislav Dobuzhinsky* (Moscow: Izobrazitel'noe iskusstvo, 1982). It has many excellent color plates and gives a reasonably fair account of Dobuzhinsky's artistic career from the prerevolutionary period through emigration.

Helene Sikorskaya on the relationship between Nabokov and his mother. Field archive: taped interview.

27   Nabokov on his sister Olga. Field archive: taped interview.

29   Some basic works on the theory of narcissism: J. Chassegnet-Smirgel. *L'idéal du moi.* (Paris: Tchou, 1975). Also by J. Ch-S: *"Corps recu et corps imaginaire dans le premiers travaux psychoanalytiques."* RFPsa, vol. 27, November 2–3, 1963. S. Freud, "Three essays on the theory of sexuality" (1905); "An Introduction to Narcissism" (1914); "The Devil and Melancholy" (1917). B. Grumberger. *Le narcissisme.* (Paris: Payot, 1971). Also by B. Gr: "Étude sur le narcissisme." *RFPsa*, vol. 29, nos. 5–6, 1965.

30   On *audition colorée* and literary synesthesia: Stephen Ullmann's *The Principles of Semantics* (Oxford: Oxford University, 1957). Also, "Literary Synesthesia" by Glenn O'Malley, *Journal of Aesthetics and Art Criticism*, vol. 15, 1957, pp. 391–411.

30   Spiritualism in Nabokov's art has been catalogued in W. W. Rowe's *Nabokov's Spectral Dimension* (Ann Arbor, Mich.: Ardis, 1981).

Field archive on spiritualism: Notebook 1, pp. 46, 95. Nabokov claimed that a medium predicted his father's death.

31   Nabokov on space, time, electricity. Field archive: taped interview.

CHAPTER 3

32   George Steiner's *Babel* (London: Weidenfeld & Nicolson, 1981).

33 There is an interesting monograph on the problems of exile and multilingual writers by André Karátson and Jean Bessière: *Deracinement et littérature* (Lille: University de Lille, 1982). It has a short chapter on Nabokov.

34 The photograph of Vyra may be found in *Vladimir Nabokov: A Tribute*, ed. by P. Quennell (London: Weidenfeld & Nicolson, 1979).

35 Nabokov's "foible for" Apukhtin. Field archive: Notebook 2, p. 28.

35 The images of St. Petersburg are a mosaic compiled from Nabokov's youthful poetry. In his comments on the ms. of *Nabokov—His Life in Part* Nabokov declared the passage to be a "dreadful macedoine." On romance with Valentina Shulgina. Field archive: Notebooks 1–3, taped interview.

36 "You filled that girl." Field archive: Notebook 1, p. 82.

38 Uncle Ruka's love for Vladimir. Field archive: Notebook 1, p. 63.

38 The Japanese text of the haiku is:
*Cho Wo Ou
Kokoro-Mochitashi
Itsumademo!*
Nabokov claimed that his very first poem was a plagiarism done in order to match a poem that his cousin Iury had written. The poem was too good, and, when the truth came out, he and Iury fought a mock duel over it. Field archive: Occasional notes, p. 30.

39 Hessen's *Gody izgnaniya. op. cit.*
Nabokov's account of his talismanic purple carbon was in a proxy statement written for the acceptance of an American literary award. Text in *The Vladimir Nabokov Newsletter*, Number 13. Fall. 1984.

CHAPTER 4

40 I am indebted for extensive information on the Tenishev School to Vladimir Sozonoff (Antwerp, Belgium, in December 1984); Marc Wolff (London, in August 1972); and Eugene Rabinowitch (Vermont, in August 1972). Letters and manuscripts from all three are in the Field archive.

42 Mandelstam's essay on the Tenishev School is in *The Noise of Time* (*Shum vremeni*) in *Sobranie sochinenii v dvukh tomakh* (New York: Inter-Language Literary Associates, 1966), vol. 2, pp. 112–17.

45 Mandelstam, *op. cit.*

45 Material on Nabokov's teachers at the Tenishev School from interviews with Nabokov. Field archive: Notebook 1, p. 27; Notebook 2, p. 4; Notebook 3, pp. 29–30, 47–49.

46   Nabokov on Sergei's romances as a schoolboy. Field archive: Notebook 1, p. 7. Nabokov said that he took the diary to his tutor, Sakharov, and that the family doctor, Bekhetev, was called in to hypnotize Sergei. (Dr. Bekhetev remained the Nabokov family doctor for some years in emigration.)

47   Andrei Balashov and the fight. Field archive: Notebook 3, p. 72. Balashov's book of poetry is entitled *For the Few (Dlya nemnogikh)* (Brussels: Chuzhbina, 1956). The book went to a second edition, which was very rare for volumes of émigré poetry.

47   Nabokov's letter to Samuil Rozov, six pages handwritten, August 1937. Field archive: in photocopy.

48   Nabokov in Finland. Field archive: Notebook 3, pp. 51–52. Also, Vladimir Sozonoff *op. cit.*

48   The trips that Nabokov would have had to suffer if they had not been cancelled went to Novgorod and the famous monastery of Nil-Sorsky, after which the boys had a hike of about twenty-five kilometers accompanied by two carriages which carried all their knapsacks, and then traveled across Seliger Lake on a paddle steamer so old and precarious that one passenger out of place could dangerously heel the boat. The third excursion lasted fifteen days and went to Moscow, Kiev, and a steel-making town. The highlight of this outing was going down the Dnepr and through the rapids in four large wooden rowing boats.

49   V. D. Nabokov described his February 1916 trip to England, together with Alexei Tolstoy, Kornei Chukovsky, and Nemirovich-Danchenko, in a book titled *From England at War (Iz voyuyushchei Anglii)* (Petrograd: 1916).

CHAPTER 5

51   Nabokov's youthful haughty poem is cited in its entirety in Zinaida Schakowskoi's excellent Russian book on Nabokov, *In Search of Nabokov (V poiskakh Nabokova)* (Paris: La Presse Libre, 1979). It is one of the essential books written on Nabokov.

52   Material in regard to the family in (as well as the trips to and from) the Crimea. Field archive: taped conversations with Helene Sikorskaya.

53   Vladimir Pohl's account of Nabokov in the Crimea is to be found in *Russkii al'manakh—1981* ed. by Z. Schakowskoi, Rene Guerra, and E. Ternovsky (Paris, privately printed), pp. 231–35.

54   On the popularity of Schnitzler among Russians see an article by Georgii Adamovich in *Illustrated Russia (Illustrirovannaya Rossiya)* Paris, no. 48, November 21, 1931).

55   On the poetry of Voloshin, Minsky, and Bely, see Poggioli's *Poets of Russia* (Cambridge, Mass.: Harvard, 1960).

59   *Glory* (London: Weidenfeld & Nicolson, 1972), p. 200.

59   Gorodkovskaya and Novotorshskaya were cited by Nabokov in interview. Field archive: Notebook 2, pp. 18, 53.

CHAPTER 6

61   Nabokov's entrance to Cambridge, unhappiness at: Field archive: Notebook 2, pp. 1, 18. Nabokov's description of his father as Senator Nabokov and his student status furnished on documents supplied by Alan Kucia, the manuscript cataloguer of Trinity College, Cambridge. Thanks should also be given to Mrs. Sheila Clare of the College Office, Trinity, for her assistance in providing the addresses of the several hundred surviving Trinity classmates of VN.

62   I am indebted for information on Paul Leiris to R.STL.P. Deraniyagala, CBE, of Colombo, Sri Lanka.

63   The account of the M&S Visitors' Debate (October term, 1919) is in the society's record book: Rec. 9.10.

64   The record of VN as soccer player at Trinity. Letter from Alan Kucia, March 1, 1985.

64–65   Kalashnikoff. Field archive: Notebook 1, pp. 16, 43.

66   Nabokov's Cambridge love affairs. Field archive: Notebook 1, pp. 6, 80, 81, 83; Notebook 2, p. 14.

67   Nabokov's identification of Rab Butler as "Nesbit." Field archive: Notebook 1, p. 72.

68   Nabokov's tailor debts. Field archive: Notebook 1, p. 20.

CHAPTER 7

71   Nabokov and the German bank. Field archive: Notebook 1, p. 62. See also the Berlin memoirs of E. Cannac, *"Iz vospominaniykh o Sirine"* in the Paris émigré newspaper *Russkaya mysl'*, December 29, 1977.

76–77   Nabokov on the death of his father. Field archive: taped interview.

CHAPTER 8

78   Nabokov on Sasha Chyorny. Field archive: taped interview.

79   Ofrosimov review. *The New Russian Book* (*Novaya russkaya kniga*), Berlin, May–June 1923, p. 23.

81   The unpublished poem "In Memory of V. D. Nabokov" is in the archive of the Julia Whitney Foundation.

CHAPTER 9

89   The letter of Nabokov to Svetlana. Field archive: a copy of this letter was transcribed by a friend to whom Svetlana showed the letter in later years. Anonymous source. The source of the copy of the letter as well as its style and content allow no doubt that it is genuine.

90   Svetlana Zivert' in St. Petersburg. Vladimir Sozonoff *op. cit.*

92   Nabokov on Solomon Krym and the Nice farm. Field archive: taped interview.

CHAPTER 10

94   Information on Vera Nabokov. Field archive: Notebook 1, pp. 7, 8, 26, taped interview. Also, *Eidestattliche Erklarung*, an autobiographical affidavit filed with the West German government (June 24, 1957) seeking compensation for lost employment in Nazi Germany. The Goldenweiser Collection, Butler Library, Columbia University.

95   Vera Nabokov's defense of the style of émigré life. Field archive: Letter from Vera Nabokov to AF, six pages, March 10, 1973.

97   Information about Nabokov's early lovers in Berlin. Inaya and Gzovskaya. Field archive: taped interviews with Nabokov (in which there is one passing reference to Klyachkina). *cf.* Soviet memoirs of Gzovskaya (with no mention of Nabokov).

    Further information on Nabokov and Klyachkina is contained in a signed three-page document "One Romance of Nabokov" (*Odin roman Nabokova*), which is, however, about another affair of Nabokov's (see note to p. 176). This same document contains the information about the "fat woman."

98   Conversation between Nabokov and his wife. Field archive: taped interview. Nabokov on the similarity between the character Mashen'ka and Valentina Shulgina. Field archive: taped interview.

99–100   Conversation between Nabokov and his wife about the maid Adele. Field archive: taped interview.

100–101   Nicolai Nabokov. *Bagazh. op. cit.*

101   Nabokov on his work as a tutor in Berlin. Field archive: taped interview. Also cited in *Nabokov—His Life in Part*.

102   Shura Zak. Field archive: Notebook 1, p. 3.

103   Nabokov on Gorlin and Blokh. Field archive: taped interview.

104   "Oooloo, ooo!!!" Field archive: taped interview. In negotiations over the manuscript of *Nabokov—His Life in Part*, Nabokov vehemently denied he had said this. Field archive: Nabokov's commentary on *Nabokov—His Life in Part*.

Tennis in Berlin. Field archive: Notebook 1, p. 33. The man who taught the young Nabokov to play tennis in St. Petersburg was the trainer of the reigning French tennis champion. Field archive: Notebook 2, p. 25.

Soccer in Berlin. Field archive: Notebook 3, p. 33.

105 Nabokov on the future of Soviet literature. E. Cannac's "From recollections about Sirin" (*"Iz vospominanii o Sirine"*), *Russkaya mysl'*, December 29, 1977. Also in *Russkii al'manakh, op. cit.*

105–106 Nabokov on Bunin, Bely, and Aleksei Tolstoy. Field archive: taped interview.

106 Nabokov on the meeting with Tarasov-Rodionov. Field archive: taped interview.

107 Nabokov's article "An Anniversary" (*"Iubelei"*) is cited more fully (trans. by A. Field) in *Nabokov—His Life in Art*.
Nabokov on émigré prospects in the thirties. Field archive: taped interview.
Vera Nabokov's career in Berlin. See the *Eidestattliche Erklarung* which she filed (June 24, 1957) in order to claim compensation from the West German government for employment lost under the Nazis. The Goldenweiser Collection, Butler Library, Columbia University.

108 The Nabokovs on Berlin. Field archive: Notebook 1, p. 37.

CHAPTER 11

109–110 The dispute over where the Nabokovs were living. Field archive: taped interview.

110 Nabokov's account of the reading of *Mashen'ka* is taken from a letter to his mother, February 1926. Field archive: in photocopy.

111 It was, however, only a *succés d'estime,* because the publisher Slovo gave Nabokov a contract in which he agreed to waive royalties for the first one thousand copies in return for a higher royalty of 20 percent on sales after that. Needless to say, the publisher sold nine hundred copies. Field archive: Occasional Notes, p. 49.

112 Citation from *Mary* (London: McGraw-Hill, 1970), p. 53.

113 Nabokov on Aikhenval'd. Field archive: taped interview.

114 In a short memorial article about Aikhenval'd that he published in *The Rudder* in 1928 Nabokov put forward for the first time his theory that man's immortality consists simply of bits of living memory of him until the last person who actually knew him has died.

115 Sedykh interview. "With V. V. Sirin" (*"U.V.V. Sirina"*) by Andrei Sedykh, *Poslednie novosti*, Paris, November 3, 1932, p.

2. Further excerpts from this review may be found in *Nabokov—His Life in Part*.

116   The discovery of the Frank-Nabokov connection was made by D. B. Johnson in *The Vladimir Nabokov Research Newsletter*, no. 7, Fall 1981, pp. 21–24.

117   *Dada Almanach*. ed. by Richard Huelsenbeck (Berlin: Erich Reiss Verlag, 1920).

CHAPTER 12

118   Nabokov's connection with German film of the thirties has been made the subject of a book by A. Appel, Jr., *Nabokov's Dark Cinema* (New York: Oxford University, 1974). Though it is in some respects a rather silly book, it does have a valid point to make.

120   The entomologist Moltrecht. Field archive: taped interview.

121–122   Nabokov's charm. Field archive: taped interview.
       Émigré film in Berlin. The overwhelming majority of émigré films produced in Berlin perished in the bombings of World War II. However, the Deutsches Institut fur Filmkunde (Frankfurt) possesses copies of: *Danton* and *Der Galiläer* (Dimitri Buchowetzki); *Die freudlose Gasse, Der Mörder Dimitri Karamasoff* and *Raskolnikow* (Gregori Chmara); and *So ist da Leben* and *Geheimnisse einer Seele* (Carl Junghans). (One of the most likely sources, *Der Liebe Pilgerfahrt* [Protosanov, 1922] is not available.) It is excruciatingly slow work searching film texts for extras—I made the fruitless search for Barnes and Joyce in my work on *Djuna—The Formidable Miss Barnes*—but I trust that some German scholar will eventually undertake the search now that the possible sources have been located. I am indebted to my former postgraduate student Bettina Stoll, now of Albert Ludwigs Universität in Freiburg, for this information.

121–122   Nabokov on how he became a film extra. Field archive: taped interview.

122   From the Russian memoirs (privately printed) of Serge Bertensson, who was the co-translator of "The Potato Elf," the first Nabokov work to appear in America.

124   Ivan Lukash. *The Flames of Moscow* (London: Macmillan, 1930).

124–125   Nabokov on Ivan Lukash. Field archive: taped interview.

125   Nabokov on Plevitskaya and *The Assistant Producer*. Field archive: taped interview.

126–127   Discussion of Korostovetz. Field archive: Notebook 3, p. 34.

129   Nabokov on his trip to the Pyrenees. Field archive: taped interview.

129   A brief article about how Nabokov played the part of Evreinov, together with a photograph, appeared in *Russkaya mysl'*, no. 3184, December 29, 1977, p. 10. Unfortunately, all but the newspaper picture itself, not suitable for book reproduction, has been temporarily lost because Evreinov's wife returned his entire archive to the Soviet Union after his death.

130   Nabokov on chess. Field archive: Notebook 1, p. 56; Notebook 2, p. 12. The best article on Nabokov and chess is by Paul Kleinpoppen, "Chess Through the Eyes of a Master Writer" in *Chess Life*, June 1984, p. 11.

Nabokov's neologism *krestoslovitsa* has, unfortunately, not prevailed over the loan word *krosvordy*.

132   Nabokov on abandoned aspects of *The Defense*. Field archive: Notebook 2, p. 11.

135   Nabokov on Adamovich. Field archive: taped interview.

136   Information on Mark Levi is given in *Liberation*. Paris, December 26, 1985, pp. 21–24.

136–137   E. Cannac, "The Berlin Circle of Poets" (*"Berlinskii kruzhok poètov"*) in *Russkaya mysl'*, Paris, no. 2835, March 25, 1971.

CHAPTER 13

139   Further excerpts from Nabokov's anti-Freudian article in *Nabokov—His Life in Art*, pp. 263–64, (trans. by A. Field).

141   Letter to Zinaida Schakowskoi about Kirill. Reference in *V poiskakh Nabokova*. The letters from Nabokov to Schakowskoi are in the U.S. Library of Congress. Several letters from Nabokov to Kirill are appended to *Perepiska s sestroi*.

141   The death of Sergei. Details in a letter from Olya Nabokov, October 1979. Field archive: photocopy. Original in the archives of the Julia Whitney Foundation.

142   Eulogy to V. D. Nabokov by Nikolai Astrov. Panina Collection, Butler Library, Columbia University.

144   Khodasevich's review of *Camera obscura* appeared in *Renaissance* (*Vozrozhdenie*), Paris, January 5, 1932.

145   Khodasevich's review of *Invitation to a Beheading* appeared in *Renaissance*, Paris, July 11, 1935.

146   Bitsilli's remarks on *Invitation* appear in an essay in *Contemporary Annals* (*Sovremennye Zapiski*), Paris, vol. 68, 1939, pp. 474–477.

146   Bitsilli on Saltykov-Shchedrin and Nabokov. "The Rebirth of Allegory" (*"Vozrozhdenie allegorii"*) in *Contemporary Annals* (*Sovremennye zapiski*), Paris, 1936, vol. 61, pp. 191–204. In English (trans. by D. Stephens) in *Nabokov: Criti-*

cism, Reminiscences, Translations, and Tributes, ed. by Appel
and Newman (London: Weidenfeld & Nicolson, 1971).

148   Vladimir Varshavsky. *The Unnoticed Generation (Nezame-
chyonnoe pokolenie)* (New York: Izd. imeni Chekhova, 1956).

148–149   Khodasevich on *Invitation. op. cit.*

149   The importance of Baudelaire in regard to the conception of
Invitation to a Beheading cannot be too heavily stressed. I have
in mind Baudelaire's lines: *"Even death on the scaffold/is but a
dream."* To a much greater degree than Nabokov's tradition can
be traced back to Romanticism (which one might expect owing
to his devotion to the ideal of Pushkin), one sees the furthest—
though not necessarily the main—root of Nabokov's art as located in the post-Symbolist literary line of descent.

151   Gogol on his own ability to unmask *poshlost'*. See essays on
Gogol in my book, *The Complection of Russian Literature*
(New York: Atheneum, 1971), particularly the article on Gogol
and Dostoevsky by Yury Tynyanov in which Gogol's remark is
quoted (p. 79).
        Playboy interview, January 1964. Also in *Playboy Interviews*
(Chicago: Playboy Press, 1964) and *The Twelfth Anniversary
Playboy Reader* (Chicago: Playboy Press, 1965).

CHAPTER 14

153   Material on Anna Feigin. Field archive: Notebook 1, p. 90. In
addition to the information gained from the Nabokovs themselves, there is one further source (anonymous) by an émigré
who knew Anna Feigin in Berlin.

154   The planned immigration to Australia. Field archive: Occasional Notes, p. 31.
        Zimaida Schakowskoi's letters written to her by Vladimir
Nabokov at the U.S. Library of Congress. Detailed reference to
the contents of the letters though not the texts themselves are to
be found in her 1979 book (the Nabokov estate did not cooper-
ate in its publication) *V poiskakh Nabokova* (Paris: La Presse
Libre, 1979).

154   Nabokov on the lakeside land and its use in *Despair*. Field archive: taped interview.

155   Nabokov on his inertia in regard to where he lives. Field archive: taped interview.
        The parody of Sirin in *Pravda* was by the Stalinist court
lackey and rhymster Demyan Bedny. It is interesting that,
whereas such émigré publications as *The Rudder* were totally
unknown to Western European readers, they were being read
carefully in Stalin's court. The Bedny and Sirin poems are given
in "Official and Unofficial Responses to Nabokov in the Soviet
Union" by Slava Paperno and John Hagopian in *The Achievements of Vladimir Nabokov* (see note to p. 273).

156   Andrei Sedykh interview. *The Latest News. op. cit.* N.B. This interview originally appeared in the Riga newspaper *Today* (*Segodnya*), November 4, 1932, but *Today* is a far more difficult to obtain source than its reprinting in *The Latest News.*

158   The story of Bunin's "cleansing" by the Nazis. Field archive: Notebook 1, p. 36. Going into the Jewish shops with Cannac the day after Kristalnacht. Field archive: Notebook 3, p. 2. Nabokov's conversations with Fyodor Stepun. Field archive: Notebook 1, p. 25.

159   Émigré Writers' Fund. The letters of application are on file in the Rare Books Division, Butler Library, Columbia University.

160   Albert Parry on Nabokov in *The American Mercury*, 1935.
        A Russian article about Nabokov for his English tour was written by G. Struve. "About V. Sirin" (*"O V. Sirine"*) in *The Russian in England* (*Russku v Anglii*), London, May 15, 1936.

161   According to Nabokov, Khodasevich read a poem that mentioned a "Zhorzhik Sodomovich." (No such poem appears in the collected poems of Khodasevich, however.) Field archive: Notebook 1, p. 43.

161   Nina Berberova's recollection of this evening is in her autobiography, *The Italics Are Mine*, trans. by P. Radley (London: Longmans, Green, 1969).

162   Galina Kuznetsova. *Grasse Diary* (*Grasskii dnevnik*) Washington, 1967.

163   Vera Nabokov's attitude toward some of Nabokov's fictional women, as related to Nabokov. Field archive: Notebook 2, p. 26.

164   Schakowskoi. *V poiskakh Nabokova. op. cit.*
        In an interview with "Nina," she said rather archly that there is an important love of Nabokov's living in this city, but that she could not tell me who she is.

164   George Hessen interview. New York, 1971. At this same interview Hessen informed me that Nabokov had written to him cautioning him not to tell me too much. In a subsequent letter Hessen informed me that he was forwarding copies of all his letters from Nabokov except one that was not "cleared" by VN.
        As a name Hermann may refer to a famous Pushkin character—the assumption that most scholars have made—but it more likely refers to the German hero Hermann who massacred Romans in the Teutoberg forest in A.D. 9. The figure of Hermann was quite popular in Germany. The same sort of arcane reference for a character's name can, of course, be observed for Cincinnatus in *Invitation.*

167–168   Jean-Paul Sartre. Review of *La meprise* in *Situations I.* (Paris: Gallimard, 1947), pp. 58–60.

168   Review of *Despair* by Vladimir Weidle in *The Circle* (*Krug*). Paris, 1936, no. 1, pp. 185–87.

Khodasevich on *Despair* in "On Sirin" ("*O Sirine*") in *Literary Articles and Recollections* (*Literaturnye stat'i i vospominaniya*) (New York: Izd. imeni Chekhova, 1954).

170   Interview with Nicolas Garnham, "The Strong Opinions of Vladimir Nabokov" in *The Listener*. London, October 10, 1968, pp. 463–64.

172   Nabokov's memorial article on Khodasevich appeared in *Contemporary Annals:* "On Khodasevich" ("*O Khodaseviche*"). Paris, 1939, no. 69, pp. 262–65.

173   Khodasevich's comments on *The Gift* appeared in a review of No. 66 of *Contemporary Annals* in *Renaissance* (*Vozrozhdenie*), June 24, 1938, p. 9.

CHAPTER 15

175   Letter by Vera Nabokov to Alexis Goldenweiser. Bakhmeteff archive, Butler Library, Columbia University.
      The notice seeking claimants to the Graun estate was called to Nabokov's attention by his cousin Olya Nabokov.
      Nabokov's routine as a child-minder is taken from his correspondence with his mother. Field archive: in photocopy.

176   All information on Irina Guadinini is from a signed document which must temporarily remain anonymous. Field archive: in photocopy.

179   Nabokov's complaint about *The Latest News* is taken from a letter to Fondaminsky. Field archive: photo negative.

179   Information on Fondaminsky from conversations with Nabokov. Field archive: taped interviews.

182   Nabokov's account of his stay with Fondaminsky and his wife in the privately printed collection *In Memory of Amaliya Osipovna Fondaminskaya* (*Pamyati Amalii Osipovny Fondaminskoi*), Paris, 1937, pp. 69–72.

182   Nabokov's account of Kerensky in St. Petersburg. Field archive: taped interview.

183   The two plainspoken paragraphs which were deleted from *In Memory of A. O. Fondaminskaya* are in the Fondaminsky Collection, Butler Library, Columbia University. They are an extremely important document in regard to some of VN's theosophical poses.

183–184   Nabokov on Shteiger. Field archive: taped interview.
      Shteiger letter. Letters to Zinaida Schakowskoi March 1934; July and September 1935. Reprinted in *Reflections* (*Otrazheniya*), by Zinaida Schakowskoi (Paris: YMCA Press, 1975).

185   Aldanov/Nabokov letters are in the Field archive: photo negative copies, and also at Butler Library, Columbia University.

186   Nabokov on Khodasevich in his kitchen. Field archive: Note-book 2, p. 20. Nabokov on the lock of Khodasevich's hair which he received from Berberova. Field archive: Notebook 3, p. 30.

187   Nabokov on Georgy Ivanov. Field archive: Notebook 1, p. 10.

188   Nabokov on Remizov. Field archive: Notebook 3, pp. 5-6. Detail on the literary court of honor brought against Nabokov by Zaretsky is contained in a letter from Eugene Rabinowitch, September 30, 1972. Field archive. Rabinowitch felt that Nabokov walked out of the room because he felt that the affair wasn't going his way.

190   Khodasevich on *The Event* in *Contemporary Annals* (*Sovremennye zapiski*). Paris, 1938, vol. 66, pp. 423-27.

191   Nabokov estimated that he had in all approximately eighty-five regular pupils in his European years. Field archive: Notebook 1, p. 23; Notebook 2, p. 10.

192   Nabokov's opinion of *Mademoiselle O* as a second-class piece of work was expressed in a letter to Zinaida Schakowskoi. Cited in *V poiskakh Nabokova op. cit.*

193   Nabokov on Jaloux. Field archive: taped interview.

193   Nabokov's French. Field archive: taped interview.

194   Paris as dingy. Field archive: Notebook 1, p. 34.

196   Rachmaninov letter. Field archive: photo negative.

197   A signed, handwritten letter from a person, who must remain anonymous, having interviewed Nabokov when he was trying to obtain passage from France. Field archive: in photocopy.

198   Nabokov on Gippius. Field archive: taped interview.

199   Don Aminado. "A Trial of the Russian Emigration" (*"Sud nad russkoi èmigratsiei"*) in *Illustrated Russia* (*Illustrirovannaya Rossiya*), nos. 44-47, October–November 1930, Paris.

CHAPTER 16

207   Dorothy Leuthold. Field archive: Notebook 1, p. 18.

209   Nabokov at Stanford. Much of the information on Nabokov as a teacher at Stanford comes from a delightful eight-page letter from a former student, which, unfortunately, was not signed. I should be pleased to hear from this former student for identification in future editions. June 20, 1985. Field archive.
       Another source for Stanford was a manuscript chapter of a forthcoming book by W. Zalewski, *Slavic Collectors and Collections at Stanford University.*

210   Henry Lanz. Basic biographical information may be found in the *Stanford Alumni Review*, December 1945, p. 35, and also in the *Memorial Resolution* passed after his death, Stanford University Archives.

211–212   Nabokov on Lanz. Field archive: taped interview. (Havelock Ellis had been to Australia as a young man, and many of his case histories do indeed concern Australians.)

212   "Vladimir Nabokov at Wellesley" by Barbara Breasted and Noelle Jordan in *The Wellesley Alumnae Magazine*, Summer 1971.

213   Nabokov's first American agent. Field archive: Notebook 3, p. 40.

219   Zenzinov letter. Field archive: photo negative.

CHAPTER 17

220   Wellesley course and salary information courtesy of the Wellesley College archive.

222   Petition on behalf of Nabokov by Wellesley staff members to Dean Ella Keats Whiting. March 12, 1942. Wellesley College archive.

222   Nabokov's method of instruction at Wellesley is drawn from an article about him in the undergraduate magazine *We* (vol. 1, no. 2, 1943).

224   For accounts of Nabokov as their teacher I wish to thank Betty Twamley Hinman (Berlin Heights, Ohio), Rosemary Farkas Meyerson (Essex, Conn.), Marjory Bartlett Sauger, and Lois Stevens Streell (St. Simon's Island, Georgia). In addition, the Wellesley College files contain interviews on the subject of Nabokov with Katherine Reese Peebles, Mrs. Edward G. Proctor, Jr., Hannah French, Wilma Kirby-Miller, Isobel Stephens, Sylvia Berkman, and Elena Levin.

227   Nabokov's preparation of his language students. Letter from W. Jedrzejwicz, May 13, 1984. Field archive.

228   The Wellesley archive contains an interview—statement from the President which is essentially similar to Nabokov's own account.

229   Nabokov letter to President Horton, February 6, 1946. Field archive: in photocopy.

229   Letter from President Horton expressing regret that Wellesley cannot match Cornell's offer, November 10, 1947. Wellesley archive.

230   Nabokov on the powerful women of Wellesley. Field archive: Notebook 1, p. 29, Notebook 2, pp. 65–66. (Nabokov made sexual puns on the names of various administrators who, he thought, didn't like him.)
Nabokov sitting for his bust. Letter from Grace Pologe (Teaneck, N.J.), February 2, 1985. Field archive.

232   Wellesley car pool. Field archive: Notebook 2, p. 64. Also, interviews in the Wellesley College archive.

233   *The Person from Porlock* refers to a tradesman who interrupted Coleridge's work on *Kubla Khan* and caused the poet's recollection of his opium-inspired dream to vanish. First pointed out by D. Barton Johnson in his book *Worlds in Regression: Some Novels of Vladimir Nabokov* (Ann Arbor, Mich.: Ardis, 1985). The theme of interruption, which has its roots in the murder of V. D. Nabokov, was to be developed fully in *Pale Fire.*

234   Nabokov's illness at the MCZ. Field archive: taped interview.

236   Nabokov's citizenship ceremony. Field archive: taped interview.
      Elena Levin on Nabokov's interaction with Harvard staff members. Interview, Wellesley College archives.

238   "Gentlemen, even if one allows . . ." The source of this information was Professor Richard Pipes of Harvard.

CHAPTER 18

242   Nabokov's letters to his wife on the 1942 speaking tour were read by her into the author's recorder, and transcripts were made from these recordings. Field archive. As Vera Nabokov elected to do this rather than have the letters photocopied, it might be assumed that there are deletions in her readings of them.

247   Nabokov's account of how he tried to join the U.S. Army. Field archive: Notebook 1, p. 17; Notebook 2, p. 14.
      Dartmouth lecture. Field archive: Notebook 3, p. 65.

248   Nabokov's health. Field archive: Notebook 1, pp. 84, 88; taped interviews.

255   "Yes, yes, exactly!" Field archive: taped interview.

258   Nabokov and Wilson. Field archive: Notebook 1, pp. 13, 17, 44, 87; Notebook 3, pp. 32, 37–38, 62.

259   Wilson's Russian. In spite of Nabokov's proposal that he and Wilson should collaborate on the *Onegin* translation, Roman Grynberg was indiscreet enough to tell Wilson that Nabokov had said he didn't know Russian. Field archive: Occasional Notes, p. 14.

264   Wilson's attempt to raise money for Nabokov from their mutual friends. Field archive: Notebook 1, p. 85.

CHAPTER 19

268   Letter from May Sarton, November 1, 1970. Field archive: in photocopy.

269   Letter from T. C. Heine, Jr. *Cornell Alumni News,* April 1977. Also, letter from T. C. Heine, Jr., to A.F. January 6, 1985. Field archive.

270   Dispute over the cars. Field archive: taped interview.

273   Much valuable information on Nabokov at Cornell is to be
found in *The Achievements of Vladimir Nabokov*, ed. by G.
Gibian and S. J. Parker. (Ithaca, N.Y.: Center for International
Studies, 1984). This volume is drawn from a conference devoted
to Nabokov that was held in 1983. I am further indebted to Dr.
Nancy Levine, who lent me her notes on many informal hours of
conversation at the conference that did not find a place in the
volume.
        In addition to the material on language instruction in the Gib-
ian–Parker volume, I have used opinions expressed by Stephen
Parker in a much earlier letter to me, November 4, 1971. Field
archive.

275   Material related from Nabokov's diary, 1952. Field archive: in
photocopy.

279   The judgment of how Nabokov was viewed by his colleagues
is by Professor Stephen Parker of the University of Kansas.
        The information that the unseen passage for translation was
taken by Nabokov from *The Gift* comes from Leigh Bienen
(Princeton, N.J.).

281   From Nabokov's side at least there was considerable animosity in his relationship with Cowan. He told me that on one occasion he nearly slapped him. Field archive: Notebook 1, p. 6.

284   Nabokov in the Midwest. Field archive: taped interview.

289   Albert Parry, "In Memory of Vladimir Nabokov" ("*Pamyati
Vladimira Nabokova*") in *The New Russian Word (Novoe
Russkoe Slovo*), July 9, 1978, p. 2.

292   Letter from Kitty Szeftel. March 4, 1985. Field archive.

292   It should be mentioned that the "rhythmically scraping
barges" taken by me from an early poem were forcefully denied
as anything he had actually ever heard by Nabokov. See note to
page 35.

298   Edmund Wilson, *Upstate* (New York: Farrar, Straus &
Giroux, 1971), pp. 156–62.

299   The letters-to-the-editor in the *New York Times Book Review* after the review of *Upstate* were signed Diron Frieders and
Mark Hamburg. The exchange over *Upstate* ran between November and December 1971. (N.B.: It has been suggested that
the names might be made up.)

303   The association of President Malott with the FBI. "Seeing
Reds" by Michael Ullmann in the *Cornell Alumni News*, June
1981, pp. 34–37.

304   Morris Bishop. Articles on Bishop by Charlotte P. Reppert
and David McCord in the *Cornell Alumni News*, November
1980.

306   Marc Szeftel on Nabokov. "Lolita at Cornell" in the *Cornell Alumni News*, November 1980, pp. 27–28.

308   Graham Greene's John Gordon Society is described in "Greene's Jests," an article by John Sutro in *The Spectator*, September 29, 1984, pp. 16–19.
Thanks are due to the CBC and its then director of international relations, Tony Partridge, for locating the tape of the Nabokov/Trilling interview, and for granting of rights to quote from it.

309   On the English publication of *Lolita*. Letter from Nigel Nicolson, October 23, 1970. Field archive.

312   "You can have the movie rights." Field archive: taped interview.

313   A. Parry, "In Memory of Vladimir Nabokov." *op. cit.*

CHAPTER 20

314   Article by V. Weidle, "Nabokov's First *Lolita*" (*"Nabokov—Pervaya Lolita"*) in *Russian Thought* (*Russkaya mysl'*), December 29, 1977, p. 9.

315   This fragment from *The Magician*, trans. by A. Field, is reprinted from *Nabokov—His Life in Art*. (The translation given in that volume is more lengthy.)

317   The confessions of "Victor X," trans. with an intro. by Rayfield, have now been published for the first time in English by Grove Press.

322   V. S. Pritchett in *The New Statesman*. January 10, 1959, p. 38.

CHAPTER 21

333   *A Note on an Old Lewis Carroll Ms.* The Morris Bishop Collection, Cornell University Library.

333   Dedicated Nabokov readers will remember that Atman appears as a (different) minor character in *Transparent Things*.

334   Further information on *"Atman"* is provided in a letter to me from Professor Cowan, June 1966. Field archive.

336   Nabokov and Robert Frost. Field archive: Occasional Notes, p. 30.

345   The derivation of Nabokov's Word Golf from Lewis Carroll was first pointed out in *The Vladimir Nabokov Newsletter* by D. B. Johnson.

CHAPTER 22

350   Interview with Alain Robbe-Grillet. *Arts*, Paris, October 1959.

351   The Philadelphia record of the remains of *Lolita, My Love* is to be found in *Playbill*, vol. 9, issue 2, February 1971.

354   Helene Sikorski. Field archive: taped interview.

354   Nabokov in Switzerland. Field archive: *Notebooks, passim.*

358   Nabokov on Arndt. Field archive: Occasional Notes, p. 21. Nabokov termed Arndt "an old enemy" and regretted that in the beginning he had helped him by correcting some of his translation errors.

358   Nabokov on Lowell. Field archive: Notebook 3, p. 56. Nabokov combined his antipathy to Lowell and Auden in the character Lowden in *Ada*.

362   For additional information on the Nabokov/Field relationship see chapter 1 of *Nabokov—His Life in Part.*
   This interview with the CBC radio, taped in Montreux (and not to be confused with the CBC "Close-Up" program), was done on March 20, 1973. The interview was broadcast twice and subsequently printed in *The Vladimir Nabokov Research Newsletter*, no. 10, Spring 1983, pp. 39–48.
   The speed with which *Ada* was written. Vera Nabokov. Field archive: "Quill" Notebook, p. 13.

363   The gushy review of *Ada* in the *New York Times* was by John Leonard, May 1, 1969. A much more intelligent assessment was provided by Eliot Fremont-Smith, writing, oddly enough, in *The Literary Guild Magazine* (Spring 1969). Fremont-Smith was cautious and termed the novel a "moving saga," but also "this boffo hoax, this ineffable caress, this great, sighing exhale of a book."

364   The *New Yorker* staff member was William Maxwell. Letter to VN. Field archive: in photocopy.

364   *Vladimir Nabokov—a Critical Study of the Novels* by David Rampton (Cambridge: Cambridge University Press, 1984), pp. 122–47.

366   Nabokov at table. Field archive: Notebook 1, p. 48.

369   *"La dernière interview de Vladimir Nabokov"* by Bernard Pivot in *Lire*, Paris, March 1978, pp. 22–32, 37–38, 40–41.

370   "Several Remarks on the Poetry and Poetics of F. K. Gudonov-Cherdyntsev" (*"Nekotorye zamechaniya o poèzii i poètike. F. K. Gudonova-Cherdyntseva"*) by Mikhail Lotman in *Parallel Secondary Systems* (*Vtorichnye modeliruyushchie sistemy*) (Tartu: 1979). This article by the son of a famous Soviet literary scholar constitutes an act of considerable quiet bravery.
   The Solzhenitsyn nonmeeting. See also the Scammell biography of Solzhenitsyn (London: Hutchinson, 1985).

370   *The Wasteland* (*Pustynya*) by Zinaida Schakowskoi in *Stories, Articles, Poems* (*Rasskazy, stat'i, stikhi*) (Paris: Les editeurs réunis, 1978). The story first appeared in *The New Review*, no. 111, 1973.

371   The Snowdon photos appeared, together with one of the bet-
        ter interviews done with VN (by George Feifer), in *The Satur-
        day Review*, November 27, 1976, pp. 20–24, 26.
            The story of Nabokov's fall is from an anonymous source
        close to the Nabokov family. Field archive: in photocopy.

372   *Acte de décès. Extrait du registre des décès de l'arrondisement
        de l'état civil de Lausanne,* Canton de Vaud, vol. 159, no. 924,
        p. 278. A later family account of the death is related in *Libera-
        tion.* (Paris, December 26, 1985, p. 21).

Index